TIME *for* BUSINESS

Junior Cycle Business Studies

Joe Stafford ● Siobhan O'Sullivan
James Cumiskey ● Ultan Henry

The Educational Company of Ireland

First published 2016

The Educational Company of Ireland

Ballymount Road

Walkinstown

Dublin 12

www.edco.ie

A member of the Smurfit Kappa Group plc

ISBN: 978-1-84536-655-1

Proofreader and Indexer: Jane Rogers

Design: Identikit Design Consultants

Layout: QBS

Artwork: David Benham, QBS

Cover: Identikit Design Consultants

The paper used in this book comes from Managed Forests in Northern Europe For every tree felled, at least one new tree is planted

Acknowledgements

The authors and publisher would like to thank the following for permission to reproduce articles, graphs and data:

Page 39, article adapted from 'Elder financial abuse: Demands from family members for money among issues – survey', *Irish Independent* (15 June 2015); page 78, article adapted from 'Most credit users don't know what interest they pay', Charlie Weston, *Irish Independent* (19 August 2015); page 81, Triodos Bank website homepage, https://www.triodos.co.uk/en/personal/; page 98, article adapted from '"It Makes Sense" loans': citizensinformation.ie, Citizens Information; page 99, article adapted from 'Your creditworthiness', Irish Credit Bureau (www.icb.ie); page 101, article adapted from 'Students beware gimmicks and lure of easy credit', Fiona Reddan, *Irish Times* (18 August 2015); page 120, article adapted from 'Premiums for home insurance still competitive – but look set to rise', John Cradden, *Irish Independent* (26 July 2015), with thanks to John Cradden for permission to reproduce this content; Chapter 12, Office of the Revenue Commissioners; page 139, 'How much food do we waste?', Stop Food Waste, www.stopfoodwaste.ie; page 157, article adapted from 'A Product's Life Cycle'; https://sustainabledevelopment.un.org/content/documents/846Why, UN Department of Economic and Social Affairs; page 163, article adapted from 'Debunking Ethical Consumer Myths': www.ethicalconsumer.org, The Ethical Consumer; page 167, 'The Body Shop – About us', http://www.thebodyshop.com/content/services/aboutus.aspx, The Body Shop International plc; page 167, ReCreate Ireland; page 169, article adapted from 'Shop local': www.isme.ie, ISME, with thanks to Mark Fielding, Chief Executive of the Irish Small and Medium Enterprises Association for permission to reproduce this content; page 170, article adapted from 'In all fairness: How to consume with a clear conscience', Conor Pope, *Irish Times* (24 February 2014); page 178, article adapted from 'Tickets for all four U2 Dublin shows sell out in minutes', Claire Healy, *Irish Mirror* (14 September 2015); page 197, article adapted from 'Former BBC Apprentice star gets her innovation to market', Olive Keogh, *Irish Times* (10 August 2015) with thanks to Olive Keogh for permission to reproduce this content; page 223, *The Salmon of Doubt*, Douglas Adams (New York: Random House, 2002); page 239, article adapted from 'What social enterprise can do for you', Barry Flinn, *Irish Times* (13 December 2014); page 253, article adapted from 'Boost as new car sales for January up to 40,000', Eddie Cunningham, *Irish Independent* (1 February 2016); page 372, article adapted from 'Cork–Limerick motorway plan "too expensive" says Transport Minister Paschal Donohoe', Daniel McConnell, *Irish Examiner* (3 January 2016); page 403, article adapted from 'Panama Papers show morals matter little – and only the little people pay their taxes', Shane Phelan, *Irish Independent* (5 April 2016); Chapter 37, Budget 2016, www.budget.gov.ie; page 424, article adapted from 'Ireland remains fastest growing economy in the euro zone': RTÉ News online, 4 February 2016; page 429, article adapted from 'Global examples feed arguments for and against sugar tax', Mark Hilliard, *Irish Times* (18 March 2016); page 432, obesity epidemic, Safefood, http://www.safefood.eu/SafeFood/media/SafeFoodLibrary/Documents/Publications/Research%20Reports/Final-Exec-Summary-The-Economic-Cost-of-Obesity.pdf

Contents

Strand 1: Personal Finance

1	Making the Most of Your Resources	2
2	Household Income	9
3	Household Expenditure	19
4	Financial Planning for Your Future	30
5	Household Budgets	41
6	Recording Income and Expenditure	49
7	Budget Comparison Statements	58
8	Financial Services for Individuals and Households	63
9	Saving and Investing Money	82
10	Borrowing for Households and Individuals	92
11	Insurance for Households and Individuals	107
12	Household and Personal Taxation	124
13	Introducing the Consumer	136
14	Protecting the Consumer	144
15	The Impact of Consumer Choices	157
16	The Bigger Picture	172

Strand 2: Enterprise

17	Enterprise	182
18	Developing Business Ideas	196
19	Types of Employment	205
20	Rights and Responsibilities of Employers and Employees	215
21	Impact of Technology	223
22	Impact of Organisations	235
23	Market Research	245
24	Marketing Mix	255
25	Financial Planning for Business	271
26	Writing a Business Plan	288
27	Business Documents	294
28	Double Entry Bookkeeping	312

29	Income Statements 1 (The Trading Account)	322
30	Income Statements 2 (The Profit and Loss Account)	328
31	The Statement of Financial Position	339
32	Analysing and Assessing Financial Accounts	353

Strand 3: Our Economy

33	Scarcity and Choice	370
34	Distribution of Economic Resources	376
35	Demand and Supply	386
36	The Purpose of Taxation	399
37	Government Revenue and Expenditure	405
38	Economic Indicators	413
39	Government Economic Policy	426
40	Sustainable Development	437
41	International Trade and Globalisation	448
42	The European Union	457
	Index	469

Introduction

For the student

Welcome to secondary school and your new business textbook, *Time for Business*. This textbook comes with a **Student Activity Book** which has a wide range of **activities** for you to work on at home and in school. This book aims to develop your knowledge of business in everyday life – at a local, national and international level.

For the teacher

This book has been written for the new Junior Cycle and aims to foster students' interest in business. It is based on the **statements of learning** from the NCCA specification and develops students' knowledge of business through the three strands of **Personal Finance**, **Enterprise** and **Our Economy**.

Key aspects of *Time for Business*

> **Learning outcomes** are stated at the beginning of each chapter in student-friendly language.
> **Key terms** are listed at the end of each chapter to allow students to revisit terms used in the chapter.
> **Activities** interspersed throughout the text are designed to develop the eight key skills of the Junior Cycle; additional activities in the Student Activity Book will build on and consolidate students' knowledge.
> **Special features** include Definitions; Think, Pair, Share (T-P-S); Chapter links; Key skills; Did you know?; Discussion; Research; Groupwork; In the news; and Enterprise in action.
> The **language** used is clear and simple to suit students of varying reading levels.

Key skills

KSBC	Being Creative
KSBL	Being Literate
KSBN	Being Numerate
KSC	Communicating
KSMIT	Managing Information and Thinking
KSMM	Managing Myself
KSSW	Staying Well
KSWwO	Working with Others

Key features

Enterprise in action	A case study of a business
In the news	Relevant news features
Did you know?	Facts to help foster an interest in the subject
Definition	Definition of key terms
Groupwork	Work with a partner or in a group
Research	Active participation in learning by specific research
TPS	Think–Pair–Share
Discussion	Class or group discussions
Rule	A rule that must be learned for accounting practice
Formula	An accounting formula

About the authors

Joe Stafford teaches both Junior and Leaving Certificate Business in Skerries Community College, Dublin. He has 22 years' teaching experience. He has written a range of Business Studies textbooks and is an active member of the BSTAI.

Siobhan O'Sullivan is currently on secondment from Malahide Community School, Dublin, as a teacher educator. She also lectures on Business Studies Methodologies on the Professional Masters of Education in UCD. As well as 20 years' teaching experience, Siobhan has authored many business articles and resources. She is a former Secretary and Chairperson of the BSTAI Dublin branch and a member of the national executive of the BSTAI since 1999.

James Cumiskey teaches Junior and Leaving Certificate Business in Dunshaughlin Community College, Co. Meath. He has 15 years' teaching experience. James has been a corrector for the State Examinations Commission since 2005. He is a member of the BSTAI and is currently the Treasurer of the North-East region branch.

Ultan Henry has been teaching Junior and Leaving Certificate Business in St Vincent's Secondary School, Dundalk, Co. Louth, for the last 16 years. He is an active member of the BSTAI, is a former Chairperson of the North-East branch and is currently the Honorary National President of the Association.

Strand One ::
Personal Finance

Chapter 1 ::
Making the Most of Your Resources

Learning outcomes

When you have completed this chapter you will be able to:

✔ Explain what resources are
✔ Identify the main resources available to you
✔ Understand and illustrate the difference between needs and wants
✔ Match your resources to your needs and wants
✔ Illustrate how your needs and wants are likely to change over time
✔ Understand the difference between financial cost and opportunity cost
✔ Appreciate the impact of your use of resources on the lives of other people.

What is a resource?

 **Definition**

A **resource** is anything that we can use in order to meet our needs or achieve our goals. Resources include: materials, goods, people, knowledge, money and time.

Resources:

> Help us to achieve things.
> Are useful and valuable.
> Are often limited or scarce.

See Chapters 33 and 34

Types of resources

Households and individuals have a variety of resources available to them, such as:

> Physical/capital resources
> Natural resources
> Financial resources
> Human resources
> Time resources.

Figure 1.1 It doesn't matter how many resources you have – if you don't know how to use them, you will never have enough

Physical/capital resources

These are goods that are made by people and which can be used to provide other goods and services. These resources allow people to meet their day-to-day needs for food, clothing and shelter. They also provide us with the ability to travel, communicate and enjoy our leisure time.

Examples of physical or capital resources are:

> Buildings and property
> Vehicles
> Computers
> Equipment
> Phones
> Books.

Natural resources

A household may have access to resources that are provided by nature, such as:

> Land
> Water.

Financial resources

This category includes all types and sources of money available to households and individuals. These resources allow people to buy goods and services. Managing financial resources is a very important life skill which you will need to develop as you grow older. Studying business should help you develop that skill.

Examples of financial resources include:

> Employment income
> Income from benefits (e.g. child benefit)
> Savings
> Access to borrowings.

Human resources

This refers to your skills, abilities and experience. It also includes all the other people who are available to help you. For example, if your school has a counsellor or a librarian, these are a valuable resource and you may be able to make use of their skills and expertise to assist you.

Examples of human resources are:

> An ability to read and write
> An ability to solve problems
> Skills in music, sport or technology, etc.
> Creativity
> Experience

> Family and friends
> Librarians
> Teachers and coaches
> Industry professionals
> Community leaders.

Discuss these in pairs.

1.1 What personal resources (skills) do you have? List **all** the things that help you in life, e.g. being able to read, being able to calculate, being able to change a bicycle tyre.

1.2 What human resources can you access at the moment – e.g. librarian, doctor – who you can ask for help if you need it?

Time resources

Time is a valuable resource, so it is important to use it wisely. It is also our most limited resource and, unlike many physical and financial resources, you cannot earn, borrow or buy more time.

'My favourite things in life don't cost any money. It's really clear that the most precious resource we all have is TIME.'
Steve Jobs

However, if you make the best use of it, it will allow you to gather other resources, including education and skills that will help you achieve your goals. Time also allows you to work in order to earn the money needed to support your lifestyle.

For all of these reasons it is really important to make the best use of the time available to you!

1.3 Next weekend, keep a note of how long you spend doing things, e.g. homework, chores, playing games, sleeping and so on. Make a list or, if you can, create a pie chart of what you spent your weekend doing. Was there any time you could have spent doing something more useful? Or were you happy with the amount of time you spent on 'work' and 'leisure'?

Access to resources

Access to resources is more important than ownership of them.

See Chapter 4

Once you can make use of a resource, then it is valuable to you. For example, you may not own the computers in your school, or the books in the library, but you have access to these resources and can use them to help with your education. As you grow and develop you will need to learn how to gain access to resources that best meet your needs and wants.

1.4 In pairs, list five resources that you have access to, outside those of your home and family.

Needs vs wants

A **need** is something we simply can't do without; that is, something that is *essential* for our survival or something that plays a very important part in our daily lives, e.g. food.

A **want** is something that we would really like to have. It may improve our quality of life, but it is *not essential*, e.g. a mobile phone.

Some **needs**, such as food, clothing and shelter, are essential at every stage of our lives. Other important needs change as we grow and develop, and our needs as children and as adults are unlikely to be the same.

See Chapter 4

The list of **wants** could really be endless since most of us could think of many desirable things which we would love to go out and buy if only we had the money to pay for them!

We might want an expensive sports car or jeep, but the money available only allows us to buy a small second-hand car. In this example our financial resource (money) is able to satisfy our basic *need* for transport but not our *want* for an expensive sports car.

While our list of wants may be endless, the resources available to us are not. This forces us to make choices. The choices we make and our use of resources has consequences for other people. For example, if we want cheap 'designer' clothing, this will require others to work for low wages and possibly in poor conditions. In addition, as the lowest wages will be in countries far away, this means that goods will be transported long distances.

See Chapter 15

KSMM
KSSW
KSMIT

1.5 Make two lists: (a) five items that you currently **need**, (b) five items that you currently **want**.

1.6 Look at your list of wants.

(a) How will each of these make your life better or more enjoyable?

(b) Do you think in a year's time if you haven't acquired each of these things your life will be the worse for it? Think back to a year or two ago and the things you desperately wanted then. If you haven't got them, has it mattered to your life?

(c) Are there cheaper, perfectly acceptable alternatives to the items on your wants list? Why do you want the more expensive alternative?

1.7 Mary is growing out of her clothes, so she and her friends go shopping. Mary has saved up €150 to spend on new clothes. Mary falls in love with a designer dress that costs €125 and thinks about buying it; Joan says they should go to the department store where Mary could buy a dress for €30. How does this illustrate the difference between a need and a want?

Making use of financial resources

A key part of managing our personal finances is learning how to buy the things we need from the money we have available to us. Knowing how to **prioritise** our spending helps us to make informed and balanced decisions about what goods and services to buy.

'The earth has enough resources for our need, but not for our greed.'
Gandhi

As a general rule, money should be spent on essential items first. When we look at household budgeting you will examine these priorities in greater detail, which will provide you with the skills needed to plan your spending and manage your money more carefully.

Money is just one of many resources which we can use to improve our lives and the lives of those around us.

See Chapter 5

Money is anything of value that is accepted by people in exchange for goods and services.

 Definition

1.8 Have you ever used anything other than coins and notes in exchange for something you wanted? What was it?

 KSWwO KSMIT

Whatever we buy has a cost. In fact, everything we consume actually has two costs. The first of these is a **financial cost**. This is a money cost and is the price of the goods we have chosen to buy. For example, your phone credit has a financial cost of, say, €10.

We often have to make choices about what to buy. This gives rise to an **opportunity cost**. This is measured in terms of the 'next best thing' we could have done with our money. When we decide to use our money for one particular purpose we lose the chance (opportunity) to do something else with that money.

For example, if you have €10 and choose to spend it on a T-shirt you will not be able to use that money to buy phone credit. In this example the *financial cost* of the T-shirt is €10 and the *opportunity cost* is the phone credit you do not now have the money for.

Understanding this idea of an opportunity cost is important for getting the best value out of our money.

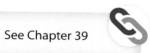

> **1.9** Looking back to question 1.7, where Mary wanted to buy a designer dress instead of a department store dress, what would you say was the financial cost and the opportunity cost of her buying the designer dress?
>
> **1.10** Think of a recent example of where you had only a certain amount of money and you had to make a decision on what to spend it on. What was the financial cost and what was the opportunity cost?

Your parents/guardians, business owners and even the government have to make these kinds of choices too, because just like you, they don't have enough money to do all the things they would like. When we look at economics we will examine the impact of these choices on local, national and global economies.

See Chapter 39

Money doesn't grow on trees!

Think about the last time you needed money to buy something. Where did you get the money from?

> Was it money you had stored away or *saved*?
> Was it money you had to *earn* by doing jobs for friends and family?
> Or was it money you had to *borrow* from parents/guardians or other family members?

If you asked your parents/guardians or family members for the money, think about their response. Did they ask you what you wanted it for? Did they remind you that *money doesn't grow on trees*?

Money plays an important part in our daily lives and as we grow older our need to earn and manage money increases.

We value money because it enables us to access other goods and services. Money is a *resource* because it enables us to buy other things which we *need* or *want*.

> **1.11** List where your personal money comes from.
> **1.12** List where your personal money might come from in the future:
>   **(a)** While you are still at school and college.
>   **(b)** When you have left college.
> **1.13** How would you explain to someone the phrase *money doesn't grow on trees*?

Being money smart

As you grow older your need for money will increase greatly and you may have to provide for the financial needs of others as well as for yourself. While money isn't the most essential thing in life, it is still important to manage the money at your disposal in order to get the maximum value and benefit from it.

See Chapter 4

Financial problems can be very stressful, but a lot of financial problems can be avoided by good planning.

When you have completed this section on **financial literacy** you should have a set of skills that will enable you to manage your money in a planned and realistic way. This is a big part of being money smart, but it also involves:

See Chapter 5

> Thinking about where your money comes from and where it goes.
> Being able to live within your means.
> Being able to plan for future spending needs.
> Being able to save regularly.
> Understanding the consequences of overspending and borrowing.
> Being able to evaluate different sources of finance and make informed decisions about managing personal finances.
> Understanding what a personal financial life cycle is, and being able to prepare one for yourself.
> Using your money wisely.

See Chapter 9

See Chapter 10

See Chapter 4

Key Terms

KSBL
KSC
KSMIT
KSBC

You should be able to *define*, *spell*, give *examples* and *apply* to real life each of the following key terms associated with this topic.

Exercise: Write a sentence using each of the following terms. You may use more than one of the terms in your sentence if appropriate.

financial cost	opportunity cost
financial literacy	prioritise
money	resource
needs	wants

Chapter 2 ::
Household Income

When you have completed this chapter you will be able to:

✔ State the main sources of household income
✔ Distinguish between regular and irregular sources of income
✔ Explain 'benefit in kind' income
✔ Explain why tax must be paid on income
✔ Interpret a payslip
✔ Calculate gross and net income
✔ Differentiate between statutory and voluntary deductions from income
✔ Prepare and evaluate a household income plan.

What is income?

In chapter 1 we looked at the differences between needs and wants and concluded that everyone requires a certain amount of money in order to satisfy them. We now need to consider where exactly that money comes from. Money coming to a person or into a household is called **income**.

Income comes in a variety of different types and from a number of different sources. This means that every household is unique and its income reflects the age and circumstances of the householders.

© Telegraph Media Group Limited 2014

Income refs to all of the money received over a period of time.

Definition

2.1 **(a)** On your own, list all the ways households might receive income.

(b) Compare your list with the person sitting next to you.

T-P-S

KSMIT
KSMM
KSWwO

The following are some of the most common sources of household income:

> **Wages and salaries:** income received as a reward for work. People who are self-employed take money out of their business as **drawings**.

> **Pensions:** income paid to those who have retired from work.

> **Child benefit:** a payment made to parents/guardians of children.

> **Jobseeker's benefit:** a payment to individuals who are unable to find employment.

> **Family income supplement:** a payment made to households with low levels of income. A supplement is a top-up payment.

> **Interest on savings:** financial institutions such as banks, building societies, the post office and credit unions reward those who save money with them by paying interest on their savings.

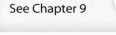

See Chapter 9

> **Dividends on shares:** a dividend is the portion of company profits paid to shareholders. Anyone who buys shares in a company is called a shareholder. Shareholders are the owners of a company and may be rewarded for their investment by receiving a dividend.

> **Windfall:** this is an amount that you don't expect, such as a win on the National Lottery or prize bonds, or an inheritance.

Some household income may also come from rent or the sale of goods. If, for example, a householder rents out part of their property to students, they will earn rental income.

Households might also generate extra income by selling items they no longer need. This might be done through car boot sales, or websites such as eBay and Done Deal, or through local papers etc.

Enterprise in action

Money for old rope ...

In the summer of 1995, shortly after leaving college, Pierre Omidyar set up a website so that collectors of toys could interact with each other online. The site, called Auction Web, also allowed for goods to be exchanged, bought and sold. It proved extremely popular and quickly expanded to include auctions for a range of household goods. Though it has changed a lot since those early days, we now know this website as eBay.

Pierre Omidyar has developed or bought several other businesses in a successful career and has an estimated net worth of $8.1 billion. He has donated over $240 million to a variety of charities and not-for-profit organisations.

 Groupwork

2.2 In your group, think of all the things you and your families might consider selling, e.g. the family car when you want to buy a newer one, school textbooks that you have finished with, birthday cards you have made. Can you think of any others?

KSWwO
KSMIT

Households may also receive income in the form of **benefits in kind** (BIK). This means that the household does not actually receive any cash, but is provided with goods or services that have a money value. For example, an employee may receive the use of a company car or mobile phone, or have their health insurance paid for by their employer. These are also called 'perks', or 'fringe benefits'.

Certain social protection payments such as free travel or medical cards are also examples of benefits in kind as the household will not have to spend part of its own income for these services.

Regular versus irregular income

Some sources of income are received on a regular or ongoing basis whereas other types of income are less predictable and may be received only irregularly. This distinction is very important for household planning.

Income such as wages, salaries, child benefit, pensions and jobseeker's benefit, which are received every week or every month, are all examples of **regular income**.

Any additional income received for working extra hours (overtime), or as a reward for meeting certain targets (a bonus), or even just money received from a lottery win are all examples of **irregular income**. This is because the timing and amount of these income sources are less predictable and cannot be guaranteed.

2.3 Thinking about your own money, what types of regular income (if any) do you receive? On what occasions or from what sources might you receive irregular income? How, do you think, these income sources might change as you get older?

KSMIT
KSMM

Income from employment

Salary

A salary is a fixed annual payment made to an employee as a reward for work, e.g. a job may carry an annual salary of €40,000. It is usually paid in equal monthly instalments and employees who are paid a salary do not normally receive overtime payments for extra hours worked. Managers, for example, are often paid an annual salary for the work that they do.

Did you know?

Sal is Latin for salt and the word salary comes from the Latin *salarium*. This was an allowance given to Roman soldiers so they could buy salt, which at the time was a valuable commodity. This allowance was generally given as an extra payment on top of their wages.

Someone who is 'worth their salt' is deemed to be efficient and deserving of their pay.

Wage

A wage is a payment received for work done. It is normally calculated on the basis of actual work completed or on the amount of time spent working. Unlike a salary, which is a fixed regular payment, wages are more likely to vary from one payment period to the next. Wages may be calculated using a number of different methods, including:

> **Time rate:** This is a wage calculation based on the number of hours worked. Employees insert a card or code into the machine when they come into work and again when they leave so their employer knows how many hours they have worked.

Figure 2.1 A 'clocking-in' machine.

For example, a 40-hour working week for an employee who is paid €15 per hour would generate a wage of €600 per week (40 hours × €15 per hour = €600).

> **Overtime payments:** When an employee works for longer than the standard working week (usually 39 hours) they may be entitled to receive a higher rate of payment for those extra hours. Common overtime rates include 'time and a half' and 'double time'.

For example, Erin is normally paid €10 an hour for a standard 39-hour working week. If she works more hours during the week, for those extra hours she is paid at *time and a half* and so receives €15 for each extra hour (€10 × 1.5); if she works extra hours at the weekend she is paid at *double time* and receives €20 per overtime hour (€10 × 2).

> **Piece rate:** This is a wage calculation based on the amount of work actually completed.

For example, a machinist employed in a clothing factory may receive €3 for each garment made. An employee who successfully completes 200 garments will earn a wage of €600 (200 × €3 = €600).

2.4 If Erin, from the example above, worked 41 hours one week, plus 2 hours at the weekend, how much would she earn before paying tax, etc.?

KSBN

> **Commission:** Some employees, particularly sales staff, receive a payment based on the value of the goods or services they have *sold*. This type of payment system rewards staff only for goods and services they actually sell and motivates them to seek a high price for these goods and services. Some jobs have a low basic salary that is paid no matter how the employee performs but also has a commission element to increase the salary and motivate the employee.

For example, an estate agent might earn 2% commission on each property sold. So, a house sold for €200,000 will earn the agent a commission payment of €4,000 (€200,000 × 2% = €4,000).

> **Bonus payments:** Some employers reward their staff with extra payments if performance targets are achieved or if deadlines are met ahead of schedule.

For example, a job has a completion date of 11 July and if this deadline is met the employee will receive a €100 bonus; if the job runs over time, they forfeit the bonus.

Basic pay is the amount earned before any additional payments.

Definition

2.5 In each of the following cases, in your copy calculate the employee's basic wage and gross wage – be sure to show the different figures. Name the payment method used to calculate the wages in each case.

(a) Calculate the gross wage for Cian, who is paid €15 an hour for a 39-hour working week.

(b) Calculate the gross wage for Niamh, who is employed to pick fruit. She picked 73 kilograms of fruit last week and is paid €3.50 per kilogram.

(c) Calculate the income earned by Hisoka, who sold a €37,000 car and who receives 5% of the value of all car sales made.

(d) Calculate the income earned by Thomas, who packs boxes for €9 an hour for a 39-hour week. Last week he also did overtime of 8 hours at time and a half and earned a bonus of €75 for reaching his packing target.

(e) Calculate the monthly income of Bríd, who earns a monthly salary of €1,750, and commission on monthly sales of 5% of sales of mobile phones. Last month she sold €15,000 worth of phones.

Payment received

Gross pay is the employee's income before anything is deducted from it. Gross pay is the sum of an employee's basic pay plus any extra income earned from overtime or bonuses.

Net pay, also called 'take-home pay', is the amount left for the employee after all deductions are taken from their gross pay.

Gross pay = Basic pay + Overtime + Bonuses

 **Formula**

Net pay = Gross pay − Total deductions

Formula

Deductions

There are two main types of deduction from pay:

> **Statutory deductions:** These are *compulsory deductions*, which every worker is required by law to pay.

> **Voluntary deductions:** These deductions are *not compulsory* but workers may choose to pay them.

Statutory deductions

All household income generates a tax liability and a corresponding responsibility to pay it. Governments use tax revenue to pay for State services such as health services and education, and to redistribute wealth across the economy.

See Chapters 12 and 36

Most employees in Ireland are subject to the **Pay As You Earn (PAYE)** income tax system. Under this system, tax is levied on the income as it is earned (weekly, monthly, etc.). The income tax is deducted at source, which means the employer calculates the tax due and submits it directly to the Office of the Revenue Commissioners, which is the government agency responsible for taxation in Ireland.

Workers in Ireland also contribute to a system of **Pay Related Social Insurance (PRSI)**, which provides them with benefit entitlements should they require them in the future. These benefits include a state pension, jobseeker's benefit, maternity benefit, carer's benefit and some treatment benefits for dental and eye-care needs.

An additional tax called the **Universal Social Charge (USC)** also applies to all workers whose income exceeds a certain limit.

2.6 What is the level of income at which workers have to pay USC?

2.7 Do you think it is fair that people who work should pay PAYE taxes, PRSI and USC? It would be nice to be able to spend all the money we earn, but then how would we pay for things that the whole country needs? Discuss your views within your group.

Voluntary deductions

Some workers may also choose to have extra money deducted from their gross pay in order to provide for pensions, savings, loan repayments, private health insurance or trade union membership. (A trade union is an organisation that represents the views and interests of a group of workers.)

See Chapter 20

After all deductions have been made, the figure left is what the employee takes home, i.e. the amount paid in cash, by cheque or direct into their bank account.

Disposable income

The income that remains when all income taxes and compulsory payments have been made is called **disposable income**. While this money is available for spending and saving, some of it will be required for *essential* spending. Items of essential spending include food, clothing, shelter, childcare, payments for utilities (light, heat, etc.) and cost of travel to work or school. This means that householders may not have an entirely free choice about how to spend their income.

"I've got a large disposable income"

Disposable income = Gross income − Statutory deductions

For example: Paula Dunne earns €2,000 gross income per month but has to pay €450 in statutory deductions (PAYE, PRSI and USC). This leaves Paula with a monthly disposable income of €1,550 (€2,000 − €450 = €1,550).

2.8 In our example, why do you think we haven't included voluntary deductions in the calculation for disposable income?

Discretionary income

The income left over after taxes and essential spending is called **discretionary income**. Householders have much greater freedom and choice when it comes to spending discretionary income. Discretionary spending includes, for example, a family holiday or a trip to the cinema.

Discretionary income = Gross income − Statutory deductions −
Essential payments (bills)

For example: Paula Dunne makes €1,100 essential payments from her income. This leaves Paula with €450 discretionary income from her salary (€2,000 − €450 − €1,100 = €450). Since Paula has paid all her taxes and accounted for all essential payments, she is now free to choose how to spend her discretionary income.

If you receive pocket money it is likely that almost all of it is discretionary income and you have a lot of choice about what to spend it on. Your parents, on the other hand, despite receiving a larger amount of income, may have very little discretionary income remaining after meeting all essential household costs.

Income calculation

Colm Kavanagh is paid €22 per hour for a standard 39-hour week. Overtime is paid at time and a half for the first 5 hours and double time for each additional hour after that.

In week 27 he worked 48 hours and had the following deductions from his gross salary:

PAYE €275; PRSI €48; USC €52; health insurance €50; trade union dues €25; savings €75.

Employees are given a **payslip**, either on paper or electronically, to show how much they have earned and what deductions have been taken. These should be checked and then kept safe in case the employee ever needs to refer to them.

Colm's payslip for Week 27 is as follows:

Name Colm Kavanagh				Week no. 27		
PPS no. 49320170E				Date 27 July 2017		
Payments	No. of hours	Rate	Amount	Deductions	Amount	
Basic	39	€22	€858	PAYE	€275	
Overtime @ ×1.5	5	€33	€165	PRSI	€48	
Overtime @ ×2	4	€44	€176	USC	€52	
				Health insurance	€50	
				Union membership	€25	**Net pay**
				Other – Savings	€75	
Gross pay			€1,199	**Total deductions**	€525	€ 674

Workings

Basic pay: 39 hrs × €22 = €858

Overtime: 5 hrs × €33 = €165 (time and a half pays €33 per hour: €22 + €11)

plus 4 hrs × €44 = €176 (double time pays €44 per hour: €22 × 2)

Total overtime pay   €341

2.9 Assuming a standard working week of 40 hours, for each of the following situations in week 31, calculate the gross pay earned, then complete the blank payslips in the Student Activity Book and calculate the net pay.

(a) Daria Tchoryk worked 48 hours last week. She earns €10 per hour for her standard week and overtime is paid at time and a half. Her deductions were: income tax €36.50, PRSI €20.80, USC €15.00.

(b) Peter Hogan worked 47 hours last week. He earns €12 per hour for his standard week. Overtime is paid at time and a half for the first 5 hours and at double time for any additional hours worked. His deductions were: income tax €41.25, PRSI 24.72, USC €20.40, health insurance €20.

(c) Aoife Regan received €340 for working a standard week. Her payslip also showed that she worked 5 overtime hours, which were paid at double time. Her deductions were: income tax €12.87, PRSI €17.00, USC €9.78, union fee €3.07.

Planning and recording income

Households can use an **analysed cash book** to keep records of actual income received. This might be in a record book or a spreadsheet or other program on the computer. These income records are useful for planning purposes. This is especially true for regular income as the household can see the source and amount of recurring income. **Income plans** of this type will help a household to estimate their future income and ensure that they are living within their means.

See Chapter 6

Here is an income plan for the Wilson household for three months. James and Louise Wilson both work outside the home; they have three children who are all at school.

WILSON HOUSEHOLD INCOME PLAN				
PLANNED INCOME	**JANUARY**	**FEBRUARY**	**MARCH**	**TOTAL**
	€	€	€	€
James Wilson – Salary	1,700	1,700	1,700	
Louise Wilson – Salary	1,900	1,900	1,900	
Child benefit	420	420	420	
TOTAL INCOME				

The columns will be added up at the end of each month, and the rows added at the end of the chosen time period.

2.10 On the copy of the Wilson household income plan in the Student Activity Book, complete the total column and total row. Alternatively, copy the income plan into your record book 1 or on to a spreadsheet.

KSBN
KSMIT

2.11 Create a spreadsheet or write in a notebook or record book an income plan of your own, noting regular income such as pocket money or money for jobs. We'll expand on this in later chapters.

KSBN
KSMM

2.12 Have you heard the phrase 'perk of the job'? Discuss what this means and think of some examples.

2.13 Steven takes a packet of paper from the office stationery cupboard and puts it in his backpack. His colleague Josie sees him, and Steven justifies taking the paper by saying, ' I've run out of printer paper at home. It's just a perk of the job. The company buys enough and won't miss it.' Josie is shocked and considers it stealing. What do you think?

In light of your discussion, define what you consider a 'perk of the job'. Give some examples of perks.

Discussion

KSWwO
KSSW
KSC

Key Terms

KSBL
KSC
KSMIT
KSBC

You should be able to *define*, *spell*, give *examples* and *apply* to real life each of the following key terms associated with this topic.

Exercise: Write a sentence using each of the following terms. You may use more than one of the terms in your sentence if appropriate.

basic pay	overtime
benefit in kind	PAYE
bonus	payslip
commission	pension
deductions	piece rate
discretionary income	PRSI
disposable income	regular income
dividend	salary
gross pay	statutory deductions
income	time rate
income plan	USC
interest	voluntary deductions
irregular income	wage
net pay	

Chapter 3 :: Household Expenditure

What is expenditure?

Expenditure refers to the way people choose to spend their income in order to satisfy various needs and wants.

Definition

Types of expenditure

Fixed expenditure

These are important items of expenditure that involve the same amount of money being spent on a regular basis (weekly, monthly or annually). Since the expenditure is fixed, the payment is not dependent on usage. Examples of fixed expenditure are:

> Mortgage repayments
> Rent
> Car tax

> Local property tax
> TV licence
> Insurance premiums.

Irregular expenditure

These items of expenditure occur on a less regular basis and the amounts involved also tend to vary with usage. Since both the timing and the amount of the payment are *less predictable* it is more difficult to plan for irregular spending. Examples of irregular expenditure are:

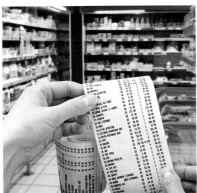

> Groceries
> Clothing
> Motor fuel
> Light and heat

> Waste/recycling charges
> Telephone bills
> Education costs
> Repairs.

Discretionary expenditure

This is spending on non-essential items that we choose to buy. Spending of this type tries to satisfy our wants rather than our needs. For that reason, money should be spent on discretionary items only after all essential items or needs have been paid for. Examples of discretionary expenditure are:

> Entertainment

> Holidays

> Gifts

> Upgrades to expensive items such as cars, furniture and household electronics

> Premium sports channels/movie channels.

Current expenditure versus capital expenditure

Current expenditure

Some expenditure is continuous and regular. This type of ongoing expenditure is called **current expenditure**. Examples of such expenditure are:

> Groceries

> Utility bills, such as gas and electricity

> Rent/mortgage

> Education

> Travel.

Capital expenditure

There is also another type of expenditure which is far less regular and will generally not be repeated for a long time. For example, a household may install a new dishwasher in their home. This is a large item of expenditure but the dishwasher is expected to last for several years. Spending on items that will last a long time or once-off spending of this type is called **capital expenditure**.

Other examples of household capital expenditure are the purchase of:

> A new car

> Furniture

> A laptop

> A TV.

3.1 The purchase of the dishwasher represents capital expenditure, but there is another type of expenditure relating to the running of the dishwasher. What is the name of this type of expenditure, and what items would be included?

Guidelines for effective spending

Households should look at all aspects of their spending to ensure that they live within their means. Here are some tips on how to do that.

A. Prepare a budget

B. Prioritise expenditure

C. Avoid impulse buying

D. Beware of false economies

E. Consider opportunity cost

F. Check bills, invoices and interest rates

A. Prepare a budget

The single most important item for effective spending is to prepare a budget based on expected income and future household spending needs.

See Chapter 5

B. Prioritise expenditure

Examine the household's needs and wants and decide which are the most important and urgent items. Needs should get priority over wants. For example, food, heat and rent/ mortgage payments must take priority over a TV subscription.

C. Avoid impulse buying

Impulse buying occurs when we buy things in an *unplanned* way or just 'on the spur of the moment'. This creates a risk of buying items that are not required and may even turn out to be wasteful or just poor value for money. It can also mean that the household does not have enough money available for more essential or urgent spending.

Making a shopping list, and sticking to it, can help people avoid impulse buying.

3.2 What do supermarkets do to try to get their customers to impulse buy?

3.3 What might magazine publishers do to persuade people to impulse buy their magazines?

3.4 What might small convenience shops do to persuade customers to impulse buy?

3.5 Think of a time recently when you bought something on impulse.

(a) What was the item?

(b) Can you think of what it was that persuaded you to buy that item?

(c) Did you regret spending your money on that item? Could you have put the money towards something you wanted more?

(d) How could you prevent yourself impulse buying? Think of at least two things. Share them with your group, note what others would do and think about whether that would work for you too.

3.6 Think of an occasion when impulse buying might be a good thing. Share your reasoning with the group and see if they agree that this might be an occasion when impulse buying is not so bad.

Groupwork

KSWwO
KSMIT
KSSW
KSMM
KSC

D. Beware of false economies

A false economy is a purchase that initially appears to be good value for money but in the longer term turns out to be more expensive.

Examples of false economies include:

> A decision to postpone a routine car service may result in major engine faults later. The cost of fixing these major faults is likely to be far greater than the routine service that could have prevented them.

> A decision to stop paying for house insurance may save a household a few hundred euro a year, but may cost tens of thousands in the event of a fire, flood or burglary.

'I told you it was false economy to buy them in the sale yesterday!'

3.7 Which of these would you consider to be a false economy and which are sensible?

(a) Margaret buys two rolls of kitchen towel for €2; each roll has 200 sheets of one layer of tissue. She chooses this over one roll costing €1.50, which has 175 sheets of two-ply. When she uses it, she finds that she has to use two sheets instead of one as it doesn't soak up liquids very well.

(b) Roland buys a pack of five cereal bars for €3, when normally each bar costs €1.20, and takes one bar for a morning snack at school each day for a week.

(c) John buys the same pack of bars as Roland, but has no willpower and eats them all on the day he bought them. He has to buy more for his morning snacks for the rest of the week.

(d) Deirdre goes to the supermarket to buy an evening meal. She looks at meat and vegetables to make a stew, which will cost €4.50 and make a huge pot. Then she sees a pre-packaged stew for one meal that costs €2.50 and decides to buy that as it doesn't cost so much money.

(e) Hettie goes to the farmer's market at the end of the day to buy a punnet of tomatoes and finds two huge boxes of tomatoes on offer for just three times what one punnet would cost. Since she has space in her freezer and loves tomato sauce, she buys the lot.

3.8 Which of the above list is an impulse buy? On this occasion, is it worth it?

3.9 Which of the above list could be considered a 'calculated risk'? On this occasion, is it worth it?

E. Consider opportunity cost

Before making a decision on spending, households need to consider the alternative uses they might have for their money. This raises the issue of **opportunity cost** and is especially important when considering spending on wants rather than needs. Remember also that saving is an alternative to spending.

F. Check bills and interest rates invoices

Households and businesses also need to get into the habit of checking all **bills** and **invoices**. An invoice is a type of bill received whenever goods or services are bought, very often on credit. In this context, credit means 'buy now, pay later'. For example, households use electricity and receive a bill (or invoice) requesting payment for the units of electricity consumed during the previous two months.

As well as checking that the bills are accurate this should give the householders a better understanding of how and why they are being charged. Having this understanding will help the household examine ways of cutting back on unnecessary or excessive expenditure.

Interest rates on credit cards and loans vary enormously and switching to a different lender can help save money.

See Chapter 10

3.10 Grace's electricity bill included the following information:

Research
KSBN
KSMIT

Current reading	Previous reading	Unit usage	Unit price	Amount €
10,518 units	8,332 units	2,186	0.1659	362.66
Standing charge	59 days @ €0.4493 / day			26.51
PSO Levy Jul/Aug				10.72
				399.89
VAT @ 13.5%				53.99
Amount due				453.88

(a) What is:

   (i)   A standing charge?

   (ii) A PSO levy?

   Why do we have to pay these charges on our electricity bills?

(b) Grace takes her own readings and phones the electricity company, who makes a note of them and sends a new bill. In your copy, write out what the new bill will look like, using Grace's reading of 8,846 units.

3.11 Kate and Ella go out for a pizza. The menu is on the right.

Kate has a pizza with mushrooms, sweetcorn, onion and olives, and a large orange drink.

Ella has a pizza with ham, pineapple and chorizo, and a small lemonade.

They share a large dessert.

At the end of the meal they receive the following bill.

Luckily Kate and Ella checked the bill. Write out what it should look like, and include a 10% tip (because the pizzas were lovely and the service was great, despite the bill being incorrect).

Menu	Prices
Basic pizza	€4.35
Each topping	75c (chorizo €1)
Large drink	€2.75
Small drink	€2.00
Desserts	€4.50
Shared dessert	€6.00

Bill

Thank you for your order!

pizza + 4 toppings	€7.35
pizza + 3 toppings + chorizo	€7.90
2 large drinks	€5.50
2 desserts	€9.00
Total	€30.00

3.12 Energy bills (gas, electricity, oil, coal and wood, etc.) can be a huge cost for households, but even tiny changes to the way you use energy will help save money. Think of all the ways you could save on energy at home, and create an infographic or poster that will inform others about how they can save energy (and money!) too.

Groupwork

KSWwO
KSBC
KSMIT
KSMM

An **infographic** is a chart or diagram that represents information in a visual way.

See Student Activity Book Introduction

Recording and planning household expenditure

Householders who are in the habit of recording ongoing expenditure and planning for future spending will be better able to keep control of their spending.

See Chapter 5

Both income and expenditure can be recorded in an **analysed cash book** or on a computer in a spreadsheet or accounting program. Income and expenditure records should help the household to plan future spending and household budgets.

See Chapter 6

Planning expenditure

Planning is based on the best information you have available at the time. If something unexpected happens, you may need to review and change your plan.

Here is a three-month expenditure record for the Wilson household.

PLANNED EXPENDITURE	JANUARY €	FEBRUARY €	MARCH €	TOTAL €
Fixed:				
Mortgage	1,100	1,100	1,100	
House insurance		640		
Motor tax	190			
Motor insurance	65	65	65	
Subtotal				
Irregular:				
Household costs	870	870	870	
Light and heat	280		240	
Telephone	60	110	60	
Car running costs	140	140	140	
Subtotal				
Discretionary:				
Entertainment	160	160	160	
Presents	60		145	
Holidays			1,500	
Subtotal				
TOTAL EXPENDITURE				

3.13 On the copy of the Wilson expenditure plan in the Student Activity Book complete the total column and subtotal and total rows. Alternatively, copy the expenditure plan into your record book 1 or on to a spreadsheet.

Charts

You can present the Wilson budget in chart format, as follows.

Fixed expenditure

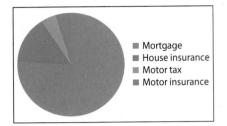

- Mortgage
- House insurance
- Motor tax
- Motor insurance

Irregular expenditure

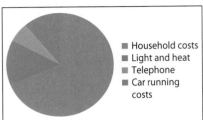

- Household costs
- Light and heat
- Telephone
- Car running costs

Discretionary expenditure

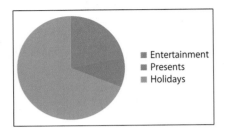

- Entertainment
- Presents
- Holidays

3.14 Make bar charts using the same information.

3.15 Do you think the pie charts or the bar charts are better for analysing spending? Give reasons for your answer.

3.16 Open the personal income plan you created in chapter 2. Add an expenditure plan of your own. You might include spending such as phone credit, magazines you buy regularly, an amount to put aside for buying birthday presents for family and friends. It might change later, but this will get you thinking about what you spend your money on. Present your personal expenditure in chart format.

Solutions to overspending

If you keep detailed and up-to-date records of your actual spending and check them against planned spending, you can put in place measures to prevent overspending.

A. Cut back on spending

B. Postpone non-essential spending

C. Spread large payments over a longer period of time

D. Use savings or surplus money from previous months

E. Generate extra income

F. Borrow money

A. Cut back on spending

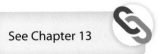

See Chapter 13

1 Since discretionary spending tends to be the least essential, this is where spending cuts should be made first.

2 Some items of irregular spending are based on usage and these should be monitored to make sure the household is getting good value for money. For example, it may be possible to save money on energy bills by ensuring that lights are not left on unnecessarily or turning down radiator thermostats slightly.

3 It is also important to 'shop around' for the best value available. Are there cost savings to be made by switching service providers from time to time? Shopping comparison websites are useful for choosing current best deals.

3.17 (a) In small groups, find five comparison websites and list them in your copies.

(b) Choose one of the sites and create an advert to encourage people to use it. Put all the adverts up on the wall of your classroom.

Groupwork

Research

KSMIT
KSBL
KSC
KSBC
KSWwO

3.18 In what other ways can a household cut back on spending? At first, it might seem as though you can't cut back on anything, but if you look closely there are often some things, even little things, where you could make savings. One example is not buying magazines until you are in a better financial situation. In your group, try to think of other things.

Groupwork

KSWwO
KSSW
KSMM

3.19 Discuss the benefits of making savings, other than purely personal financial benefits.

3.20 On your own, think about ways you personally can help save money:

(a) In your own spending (for example, be more careful with your stationery so that you don't lose it and have to replace it)

(b) In your household (for example, make sure you turn lights out when they are not needed).

B. Postpone non-essential spending

It may be possible to get better value for money by planning your purchase for a different time, e.g. buying plane tickets at a time when airlines have a sale on.

C. Spread large payments over a longer period of time

For example, it may be possible to pay a €570 annual house insurance bill over a 10-month period at a monthly cost of €57. In general it is more affordable to make a number of small payments rather than one large payment in a single month.

In some instances it may cost a bit more to spread the payments out, but it still remains the best option from a **cash flow** point of view. For example, a household has the option to pay its annual car tax with a once-off payment of €400 or can make four quarterly payments of €105. Despite the extra cost involved in spreading the payment across the entire year, it may be easier to manage four smaller payments rather than take 'one big hit' to monthly household income.

KSBN

3.21 Based on the above example, calculate the additional annual cost to a household which chooses to pay its car tax on a quarterly basis. What is the percentage increase involved for those who choose to pay quarterly?

Cash flow This is the day-to-day money coming in and money going out of a household. You may be owed a big sum of money but if it is not going to come to you for another month, in the meantime your cash flow will be affected because you still have payments to go out.

Definition

D. Use savings or surplus money from previous months

If it is not possible to reduce or defer the spending, the extra cost involved might be covered by using money that has been saved in previous months.

E. Generate extra income

While this is not a direct solution to the problem of overspending, the ability to generate extra income helps reduce the negative effects of excessive spending. Extra income can be earned by working overtime, taking on a part-time job, or selling items you no longer need.

3.22 In your group, think of ways you could earn extra money as a teenager. Is it possible for you to earn money by working? You may have to wait until you are older. Consider ways an older student might be able to earn money or how an adult might be able to increase their income.

See Chapter 19

Groupwork

KSWwO
KSSW

F. Borrow money

This 'solution' should only ever be used as a last resort and only for essential and unavoidable expenditure. The problem with borrowing is that it creates debt that must be repaid (normally with interest), and this reduces future disposable income.

See Chapter 10

When borrowing money it's important to avail of the services of legitimate financial institutions such as banks, building societies and credit unions. Avoid moneylenders as their rates of interest can be very high.

3.23 Discuss the people and things that influence our attitudes to money and expenditure (such as parents and family, friends and peers, media and culture, access to money).

Discussion

KSWwO
KSSW

3.24 Although there is no denying that the way we live in our country today requires a certain amount of expenditure, once we have paid out on our needs, it is up to each of us to make decisions on how important our wants are. Look at this quote:

'Wealth consists not in having great possessions, but in having few wants.' Epictetus

Epictetus was a philosopher born nearly two thousand years ago. Discuss whether this quote is still relevant for today. Do you think there is a lot of pressure on us to gather possessions, and have the newest gadget as soon as it comes out?

Discussion

KSWwO
KSSW
KSMIT

3.25 Find other quotes that are relevant to spending and possessions. Choose one you really like, or think is really relevant to today, and create a poster of it – this can be very simple, or as artistic as you like. On a separate piece of paper, write or type why you think the quote is one we should all take note of (what its relevance is, why you like it, how it relates to our lives). Put everyone's quotes up around the walls of your classroom and make sure that you read everyone else's quotes and why they chose them.

Research

KSMIT
KSBC
KSSW
KSMM

3.26 Write in your copy a definition of **consumerism**.

Key Terms

You should be able to *define*, *spell*, give *examples* and *apply* to real life each of the following key terms associated with this topic.

KSBL
KSC
KSMIT
KSBC

Exercise: Write a sentence using each of the following terms. You may use more than one of the terms in your sentence if appropriate.

capital expenditure

cash flow

consumerism

current expenditure

discretionary expenditure

expenditure

false economy

fixed expenditure

impulse buying

invoice

irregular expenditure

Chapter 4 :: Financial Planning for Your Future

What is a personal financial life cycle?

A life cycle describes a series of stages that a person goes through during his or her lifetime. A **personal financial life cycle** reflects these changes and will help the person to adjust their financial needs at each stage of their life. A typical financial life cycle is shown in figure 4.1.

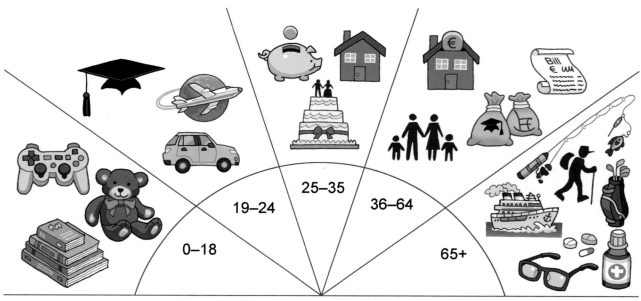

Figure 4.1 The personal financial life cycle

As you grow older your financial needs and priorities will change. Understanding and **planning** for these ongoing changes is an important life skill.

For most of your childhood and teenage years you are financially dependent upon your parents or guardians. You have very few sources of income and most of your needs are met out of general household expenditure. Most of your personal income is disposable and most of your expenditure is discretionary.

4.1 As a brief recap, explain:

  (a) Disposable income.

  (b) Discretionary income.

When you leave school you are likely to become more financially independent and as an adult your financial needs will increase greatly. Your sources of income will also increase and this should make it easier to satisfy your growing list of needs and wants. You may also reach a stage in your life when other people become financially dependent on you, e.g. if you have children, or you care for another family member.

Later in life your needs will be concerned with funding your retirement. You will also have to plan what happens to your estate when you die.

Your **estate** is made up of everything you own. At the moment it might be your bicycle, your books and your iPad. Later it might include a car, property and investments.

Definition

Financial planning is an **ongoing process**. A plan is like a route map, which sets out where you wish to go and how you expect to get there. The benefit of planning is that people are prepared for each life stage well in advance and are not left stumbling from financial crisis to financial crisis as they grow older. It involves being ready for financial challenges and also being in a position to enjoy the opportunities life offers.

Every person has financial needs, which will vary throughout their lifetime. Your financial goals and priorities will depend on your circumstances, values and life choices.

There is no 'perfect' financial plan and it is not possible to adopt a 'one size fits all' approach. Every person is different, every life journey is different and every financial life cycle will be slightly different.

Financial planning

When you were younger, you probably didn't have much of your own money, and planning was unlikely to be in your thoughts. We have looked at income and expenditure plans, so you have already started planning. This might be planning just one week at a time, or it might involve longer-term planning, such as if you are saving for an expensive item you really want. You might even be planning for the future and saving for a really expensive item, such as for a car when you are older.

See Chapters 2 and 3

Key financial planning during the personal financial life cycle

> Income and expenditure planning (*budgeting*)
> Risk management planning (*insurance*)
> Taxation planning
> Savings and investment planning
> Retirement planning (*pension*)
> Estate planning. This is deciding what will happen to your assets after your death. Making a **will** is part of this planning process.

A **will** is a legal document containing instructions for what should be done with personal money and property after death.

Definition

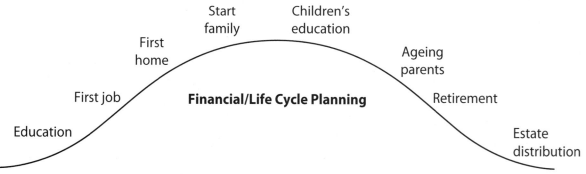

Figure 4.2 Financial life cycle planning

Much of the material you will study in strand 1 will help you with your own financial planning. You will learn how to:

> Prioritise needs over wants
> Plan your spending
> Arrange savings

> Assess the consequences of borrowing
> Examine your insurance needs
> Meet your tax liabilities.

You will learn to be smarter with your money and will be in a position to get the best value out of the money available to you. Starting all this early will prepare you for planning your finances throughout your own personal financial life cycle.

How your stage of life affects your personal financial life cycle

As you get older, your personal circumstances and lifestyle choices will impact on your financial life cycle. For example, a single thirty-year-old with no children who rents an apartment will have different priorities from a married thirty-year-old with two children and a mortgage.

Here are some of the main factors that will impact on your financial planning:

> **Employment status:** employed, unemployed.
> **Age:** related to your earnings potential, your health, your family size and your spending priorities.
> **Number of dependents:** children, spouse, parents, etc.
> **Health status:** medical treatment can be very expensive and developing a serious long-term illness has financial consequences. Medical insurance is also a financial consideration.
> **Economic outlook:** unemployment levels, interest rates, taxation, etc.
> **Marital status:** single, married, divorced, widowed, etc.

Any change in your circumstances will be a cause for re-evaluating your financial position and plans. Some people will revise their plan every year to check it is still suitable for their circumstances; others will revise it as their circumstances change.

Case studies: How different decisions affect financial planning

Emily and Priyal are friends at school. Once they leave their paths take different routes.

Emily

Emily completes her Leaving Certificate and decides to continue in full-time education, She gets a student loan and part-time job so she can pay college fees and day-to-day living expenses. She will continue to live at home during her first year in college, but hopes to move out to rented accommodation in second or third year. Emily will rely on public transport as she cannot afford to buy a car and is not in a position to take out a second loan.

She is no longer covered by her parents' health insurance policy and feels she has no option but to go without private health insurance for a few years. She is hopeful that her college education will enable her to get a good job and she will then be in a position to repay her loan and save money to buy a car and home of her own.

Priyal

Priyal completes her Leaving Certificate and seeks full-time employment. She finds a job in a neighbouring town but will continue to live at home in the short term. Priyal plans to move out of the family home in two or three years' time but is prepared to wait until her job situation is more secure and she has some savings to support her.

Priyal agrees to pay €200 a week to her parents. This is her contribution to household expenditure. She takes out a small credit union loan in order to buy a second-hand car, which she will use to travel to and from work and for socialising. Priyal will pay for her own motor and health insurance and is considering paying money into a pension fund.

4.2 Having read Emily and Priyal's case studies:

(**a**) For each, list the plans they make that affect their finances.

(**b**) List the items they will have to include in their income and expenditure plans for the next three years.

(**c**) Discuss possible events that might cause them to change their plans.

KSWwO
KSBN
KSMIT
KSBL

When to plan and what to plan for

Birth to teens

In your early years you would have had no concept of money or budgeting or saving or planning. None of it would have concerned you, but it definitely would have been of huge concern to your parents! You have been, and still are, very dependent on your parents or guardians for your needs.

4.3 Can you remember when you started getting an appreciation of what money is and what it would mean to you? Share your experiences.

4.4 At what age did you start getting pocket money that you were allowed to spend however you wanted?

4.5 Do you have to work for your pocket money?

4.6 Discuss whether you think it is a good idea to have to do jobs for pocket money. Give reasons for your opinion.

4.7 Some families have rules for children's income, e.g. a certain percentage of income received must be saved. Discuss the benefits and drawbacks of this for the children and the parents.

4.8 Discuss the benefits of budgeting for teenagers.

KSWwO
KSMM
KSC
KSBL

In your teens

In your younger teens you are still likely still to be very dependent on your parents or guardians and birthdays/special days for gifts of money. You may start doing work for money and you will have a greater appreciation of what money means. You may have started saving for more expensive items. Without even realising it, you have started preparing for the all-important financial planning you will need to do later and throughout the rest of your life.

When you are a slightly older teenager, you will need to think about planning and preparation for your career and adult life. Your parents will be involved in this too, but you should take on some of the responsibility – it is, after all, your life!

Key financial concerns will be:

> Full-time education and preparation for career
> Income from part-time employment
> Considering future financial needs and resources.

4.9 Make a list of things that you will need to discuss with your family about planning finances for when you get a little older or leave the school system. For example, you could think about:

> Whether you will get a job, or go on to third-level education. If so, what will you study?
> Will the subjects you study in school affect your course choice?
> Will your course choice affect whether or not you can get a job?
> At what age will you try to get a part-time job if you are in college, and what might that job be?
> What will you do with the money you earn from your job?

Keep this list and revisit it from time to time as your questions and decisions will change. It is fine to make changes, as it means you will have given thought to your future and be prepared for it.

In your twenties

People in their twenties begin to gain financial independence and will try to secure employment. This will provide an opportunity for increased personal and household income and expenditure. Twentysomethings with few family commitments tend to have relatively high levels of disposable income and may enjoy significant discretionary spending.

See Chapter 10

See Chapter 19

People in their twenties will probably be thinking about:

> Finishing education/apprenticeship/career preparation
> Starting employment and building wealth

See Chapter 9

- Establishing financial independence and a personal credit rating
- Repaying student loans
- Beginning regular savings
- Buying a house
- Household budgeting
- Exploring insurance needs
- Considering a pension
- Considering estate plans/making a will.

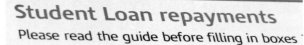

Student Loan repayments

Please read the guide before filling in boxes

1 If you have received notification from
Loans Company that repayment of an

 See Chapter 5

 See Chapter 11

> **Definition**

A **pension** is a fund into which payments are made during a person's employment years, and from which payments are drawn to support the person's retirement from work because of age or ill health.

> **Discussion**

4.10 The State pension is currently paid to people when they reach the age of 66. This will change to age 68 in 2028. Think of two reasons why the government is making this change.

KSWwO
KSMIT

Pensions

Pensions are a specialised area of finance and a lot of people like to get professional help with planning for their pension.

Anyone who has paid sufficient PRSI will be eligible for the **State pension**.

Some employers will have a pension scheme and money is deducted from your wages to pay into it. The employer may make a contribution towards it as well (as a 'perk' of the job). This is called an **occupational pension** and is in addition to the State pension.

People who don't have an occupational pension can pay into a **personal pension** that will pay out on top of the State pension.

There is also a particular type of savings account called a **personal retirement savings account (PRSA)**, which is a long-term, flexible savings account. Payments from a PRSA will also be in addition to the State pension.

All these different methods of saving for retirement have rules and regulations and tax implications. A lot of decisions need to be made, such as:

- Will you want to retire early?
- Will you want a lump sum or a regular payment?
- Can you take out the money early?
- How much can you save regularly?

Professional advice is often the best way to plan your pension needs. Revisiting your plans every few years is a good idea to make sure you are still on the best path for the future.

4.11 People in their twenties are barely out of college and retirement is a long, long way off – they have lots to experience before then! Why is it advisable to start thinking about pensions as soon as you start work? Discuss your thoughts.

Discussion

KSWwO
KSMIT
KSC
KSBN
KSSW

In your thirties

People in their thirties are likely to have greater family and household commitments that will probably require an increase in household income. Many people will get a mortgage at this point. As the level of household risk and responsibility increases it will be necessary to have appropriate and adequate insurance. If they have not already done so, this is a good time to consider retirement goals and pension needs.

People in their thirties will probably be thinking about:

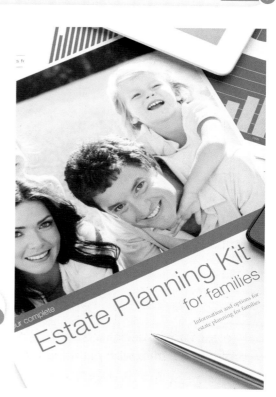

> Increasing income
> Paying mortgage/rent
> Continued personal savings/creating an emergency fund

See Chapter 9

> Children's education costs and savings
> Household expenditure
> Life assurance
> Health insurance needs
> Pension

See Chapter 11

> Considering retirement goals
> Considering estate plans/making a will.

4.12 If you started a pensions plan in your twenties, what advantage will you now have over people in their thirties?

4.13 At what stage in their lives do you think most people purchase life assurance? Why is this?

KSMIT
KSBN
KSSW

In your forties

Fortysomethings who have families are likely to see increased spending on current and future education needs for their children. If income levels allow it may be possible to avail of investment opportunities. Health insurance and pension planning become increasingly important as a person gets older.

People in their forties will probably be thinking about:

> Children's education (second and third level)
> Investments
> Updating retirement plans
> Life assurance
> Considering estate plans/making a will.

4.14 Why do you think people alter their wills at different stages of their lives?

In your fifties

People in their fifties will tend to have older children. Education spending is likely to be for third level. There may also be a need to provide for additional health and life insurance. It may also be timely to make catch-up payments on a pension.

People in their fifties will probably be thinking about:

> Children's education (third level)
> Pension funding
> Life assurance and health insurance
> Meeting the responsibilities of aging parents.

In your sixties

People in their sixties will probably be thinking about:

> Retirement planning
> Paying off a mortgage
> Checking the contents of a will
> Inheritance planning.

At retirement

People of retirement age will be:

> Re-evaluating living conditions – maybe downsizing (buying a smaller home)
> Spending based on retirement income
> Living off saved wealth
> Adjusting insurance for increased risk
> Considering what care needs they might have as they get older
> Finalising will and estate plans.

4.15 Complete question 4 in the Student Activity Book to identify your sources of income and main items of expenditure throughout your life. You should include why you might need to save and suggest what debts you may have at each stage of your life.

In the news

Elder financial abuse: Demands from family members for money among issues – survey

Demands from family members for money are among the issues that arose in new research on elder financial abuse in a survey from Age Action and Ulster Bank.

45pc of the survey's respondents had dealt with suspected elder financial abuse cases.

There were more than 13,000 cases of elder abuse referred to the HSE up to the end of 2013. Financial abuse is the second most common form of elder abuse, accounting for more than one in five cases.

Justin Moran, Head of Advocacy and Communications at Age Action, said: 'Every year, hundreds of older people are facing demands for money from family members, having their income withheld from them or finding their possessions taken.

'To make it worse, in the overwhelming majority of cases of elder abuse, the perpetrators are immediate family members.'

Among the case studies detailed was the story of Sineád, who has been diagnosed with dementia. During a period when she was experiencing reduced mental capacity, her son persuaded her to set up a joint bank account.

Her son then used this account to obtain a credit card and made a number of purchases on the card for which Sineád was charged.

Afterwards, Sineád realised what had happened. With the help of her daughter, she approached her bank which recognised it as fraud and reimbursed her.

Source: Article adapted from the *Irish Independent*, 15 June 2015

4.16 Discuss the following questions.

Discussion

KSWwO
KSC
KSBL
KSSW

   (a) Are you shocked by the number of cases of elder abuse involving money that the bank's staff have come across? Do you think it is a large number?

   (b) Do you think the numbers of elderly people suffering this will get larger or smaller in the future? Why do you think this?

   (c) How does reading this article make you feel? Can you imagine this happening to an elderly person you are fond of? Can you imagine it happening to *you* when you are elderly? How does that make you feel?

   (d) If you thought an elderly person you know was being abused in this way, would you report it? Give reasons for your answer.

   (e) What makes what Sineád's son did to her a case of fraud?

Key Terms

You should be able to *define, spell*, give *examples* and *apply* to real life each of the following key terms associated with this topic.

KSBL
KSC
KSMIT
KSBC

Exercise: Write a sentence using each of the following terms. You may use more than one of the terms in your sentence if appropriate.

estate

pension

personal financial life cycle

will

Chapter 5 ::
Household Budgets

What is a household budget?

A **budget** is a financial plan that sets out expected future income and expenditure.

Definition

A household budget combines the income and expenditure plans in chapters 2 and 3 and enables a household to see if they are living within their means for a given period of time.

Since budgets are just **estimates** of future income and expenditure they are unlikely to be an exact match for *actual* amounts received or spent. The figures used to prepare a budget should ideally be based on actual records of previous income and expenditure. These records are best kept in an analysed cash book (see chapter 6). Since most household income and expenditure follows a similar pattern from month to month, understanding these patterns and using them to guide future plans is an important part of being money smart.

Why prepare a budget?

There are many good reasons to prepare a household or personal budget. The benefits of budgeting are:

> Budgets help people to **live within their means**. For example, if income is expected to be €1,800 for the coming month, then this sets the limit for that month's spending.

> A budget encourages people to **think about their spending**. They will need to consider the type, the timing and the amount of that spending.

> Budgets allow households to **identify months when there are a lot of bills and expenses**. They can then try to take steps to spread these payments out over several months or borrow the necessary funds.

See Chapter 10

> Budgets allow people to **plan for large items** of future expenditure (such as special occasions, holidays, family events, a new car) and also help people to save for these items.

> When completed, a budget will **illustrate the *estimated* monthly net cash position** for the household (i.e. the difference between planned income and planned expenditure).

> A **balanced budget** refers to a situation where income exactly equals expenditure.
>
> A **budget surplus** occurs when income is greater than expenditure.
>
> A **budget deficit** occurs when expenditure is greater than income.

Definitions

The budget allows a household to plan for expected deficits or surpluses.

Dealing with a surplus

When a household predicts that it will have a large surplus, it may consider how to make the best use of that money. For example:

> **Save** or **invest** it until it is needed.

> Use it to **repay a loan**.

See Chapters 9 and 10

Dealing with a deficit

All budget deficits can be resolved using one or more of three possible solutions:

> **Increase income:** This can be difficult to achieve, especially in the short term. Examples include taking on overtime or an additional part-time job.

> **Reduce expenditure:** This is a more immediate solution but it is important to reduce discretionary expenditure first rather than make cuts to more essential fixed and irregular spending. For example, a household may have to postpone a planned holiday or spend less on entertainment or presents in order to ensure they can still afford to pay their mortgage and household running costs.

> **Avail of credit:** Households may choose to take out a loan and borrow the money needed to make up the shortfall. This is most likely to be achieved by seeking a bank overdraft.

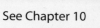

See Chapter 10

These solutions are valid for all budget deficits and are used by individuals, households, businesses and even by governments when planned expenditure exceeds planned income. In most cases the solution is likely to involve a combination of two or more of these strategies.

5.1 When faced with a budget deficit, how might each of the following
(a) increase income, **(b)** reduce expenditure?

    (i) A household   **(ii)** A business   **(iii)** A government

Remember:

Balanced budget:	Income = Expenditure
Budget surplus:	Income > Expenditure
Budget deficit:	Income < Expenditure

Once you have noted your income and expenditure, you need to calculate the difference to see whether your plan shows a surplus or a deficit at the end of the month. This is how you do the calculation:

1 Income *less* Expenditure = Net cash
2 *Add* Opening cash
3 *Equals* Closing cash
4 Closing cash of one month becomes the opening cash for the next month.

Example:

	January	€	February	€	March	€
Income		1,600		2,000		1,400
Expenditure		950		2,100		2,150
Net cash	=	650	=	(100)	=	(750)
Opening cash		3,200		3,850		3,750
Closing cash	=	3,850	=	3,750	=	3,000

Did you know?

Negative amounts can be shown in different ways. These all mean there is a deficit (shortfall) of €159 (you can include the € sign if it is appropriate):

See Chapter 10

−159   159   −159   (159)

As you can see, one of the ways is to show the figure in red ink. That's how we get the term *in the red*, meaning overdrawn at the bank (i.e. having a minus amount in your bank account), or owing to a supplier.

Creating the household budget

We will look again at the Wilson family, whose income and expenditure we examined in chapters 2 and 3. They are preparing a household budget for the first three months of the year. They do this by combining their planned income (chapter 2, page 17) and planned expenditure (chapter 3, page 25) and then calculating the net, opening and closing cash for each month.

WILSON HOUSEHOLD BUDGET				
	JANUARY	FEBRUARY	MARCH	TOTAL
PLANNED INCOME	€	€	€	€
James Wilson – Salary	1,700	1,700	1,700	5,100
Louise Wilson – Salary	1,900	1,900	1,900	5,700
Child benefit	420	420	420	1,260
TOTAL INCOME	**4,020**	**4,020**	**4,020**	**12,060**
PLANNED EXPENDITURE				
Fixed:				
Mortgage	1,100	1,100	1,100	3,300
House insurance		640		640
Motor tax	190			190
Motor insurance	65	65	65	195
Subtotal	*1,355*	*1,805*	*1,165*	*4,325*
Irregular:				
Household costs	870	870	870	2,610
Light and heat	280		240	520
Telephone	60	110	60	230
Car running costs	140	140	140	420
Subtotal	*1,350*	*1,120*	*1,310*	*3,780*
Discretionary:				
Entertainment	160	160	160	480
Presents	60		145	205
Holidays			1,500	1,500
Subtotal	*220*	*160*	*1,805*	*2,185*
TOTAL EXPENDITURE	**2,925**	**3,085**	**4,280**	**10,290**
Net cash	1,095	935	(260)	1,770
Opening cash	150	1,245	2,180	150
Closing cash	1,245	2,180	1,920	1,920

5.2 (a) How did the Wilsons calculate their figures? Write out the calculations to get the following totals.

    (i) Net cash of €1,095 in January.

    (ii) Closing cash of €1,235 in January.

(b) How do they know what the opening cash figure is for February?

(c) Where would the figure of €150 for the opening cash figure for January have come from?

(d) Why is the opening cash figure of €150 for January also written in as the opening cash in the total column?

(e) Why is the closing cash for March the same as the closing cash for the period January–March?

Analysing budgets

There is little point in preparing a household budget if you don't take the time to **analyse** it. This means looking at it closely to understand the **key trends** and **patterns** within the budget. Once you have done the analysis, you may need to revise spending patterns or perhaps even the entire budget. You will also need to deal with any surplus or deficit highlighted by the budget.

Analysis of the Wilson household budget

> The Wilsons expect to have a net cash surplus in both January and February but expect to have a small budget deficit in March.

> This deficit is largely down to the decision to spend €1,500 on a family holiday in March.

> They can afford the small overspend in March because they can cover that deficit by using money left over from previous months. The budget clearly shows that they should begin March with opening cash of €2,180 and this is more than enough to cover that month's deficit of (€260). This will leave them with a healthy closing cash surplus of €1,920 at the end of the three-month period.

> The total income for the three-month period is €12,045 while the total planned expenditure is €10,290. Overall, this is a good budget and will ensure the Wilson household lives within their means.

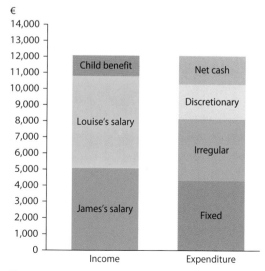

Figure 5.1 Breakdown of income and expenditure for the Wilson household for January–March

5.3 Calculate what percentage of the Wilsons' total expenditure is:

(a) Fixed

(b) Irregular

(c) Discretionary.

The Wilson family's irregular expenditure can be shown in a bar chart.

	January	February	March	Total
Irregular spending	1,350	1,120	1,310	3,780

Bar charts clearly show a household's expenditure over a period of time.

5.4 Create a bar chart showing the Wilson household's fixed expenditure for January–March.

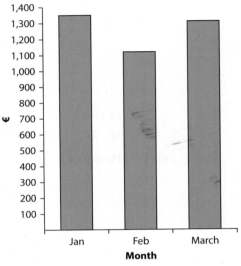

Figure 5.2 Bar chart of irregular expenditure for the Wilson household January–March

Revised budget

After the Wilson household had prepared their original budget for January–March, Louise Wilson's work changed to part time. To help make up for the reduction in her income, James increased his working hours and salary. The Wilsons decided to **revise** their budget in the light of these changed circumstances.

5.5 Use the budget outline for the Wilson household in the Student Activity Book to write up the Wilsons' revised budget using the figures from the budget on page 45 of this book updated with the following figures. Make sure you do all the calculations necessary.

(a) James's salary increases by €600 per month from February.

(b) Louise works part time and will have a reduced salary of €800 from January.

(c) The family now expects to receive €120 interest on their savings in March.

(d) Louise will now use public transport to travel to and from work. She intends to sell her car and expects to receive €3,200 in February.

(e) The Wilsons change their mortgage to a different type, which means their monthly payments are halved for the time being.

(f) Motor tax will be reduced by 50%.

(g) Motor insurance will be reduced because of the sale of Louise's car. James will now pay his annual car insurance with a single payment of €420 in February.

(h) Household costs will increase to €950 per month.

(i) Car running costs will be reduced to €100 per month from January.

(j) Louise will spend €80 per month on public transport.

(k) Entertainment costs increase to €220 per month.

(l) The Wilson household decides to increase spending on their family holiday to €4,000 in March.

(m) The Wilsons plan to redecorate the house in February at a cost of €1,800.

All other income and expenditure remain unchanged.

Analysis of the Wilson household's revised budget

5.6 Discuss the Wilson household's revised budget, using the text below as a prompt. Pick the right word or phrase from the options given.

KSBL
KSMIT
KSBN

The Wilsons' total income in the revised budget is slightly **(a)** higher / lower than it was in the original. This is mainly because of the income received from the sale of the car. In the future their spending plans will need to be adjusted **(b)** upwards / downwards in order to reflect the **(c)** higher / lower level of regular income.

The levels of both fixed and irregular expenditure remain largely unchanged with **(d)** reductions / additions in motor tax and car running costs due to the sale of the vehicle.

There is a modest **(e)** increase / decrease in household costs.

The Wilsons have taken the unusual step of increasing their planned level of discretionary spending despite the **(f)** increased / reduced household income. This will give rise to a large net cash **(g)** surplus / deficit in March.

This revised budget illustrates that for the three months in question the Wilsons **(h)** will / will not be living within their means. Total planned income for the three-month period is **(i)** €13,280 / €14,360, while total planned expenditure is **(j)** €13,280 / €14,360.

They can expect a large net cash **(k)** surplus / deficit in March and an overall closing cash **(l)** surplus / deficit of €930 for the three-month period.

5.7 In chapters 2 and 3 you started a spreadsheet or a notebook for your own income and expenditure planning. Go back to these now and create a budget similar to the ones here but relating to your own personal circumstances. It will of course not contain most of the headings that a household's would, but it will act as an excellent introduction to taking control of your own finances.

5.8 Your friend says to you: 'Everyone else has the latest tablet, but my dad says mine is perfectly all right and we can't afford a new one. My mum says she will buy me one but she will have to borrow the money from the Credit Union. I really want the new tablet, but I don't know what to do.' What advice would you give to your friend?

5.9 Living beyond your means can get out of control and you end up working just to pay the interest on loans. Debt can cause a lot of stress and hardship for individuals and families.

Some people have to really minimise spending on birthday presents, going out or having a holiday and they have to make do with old stuff they'd rather replace to get out of debt.

What could you/your family cut back on if you faced large debts?

What steps could you take to avoid getting into debt in the first place?

Key Terms

You should be able to *define*, *spell*, give *examples* and *apply* to real life each of the following key terms associated with this topic.

Exercise: Write a sentence using each of the following terms. You may use more than one of the terms in your sentence if appropriate.

balanced budget	closing cash
budget	net cash
budget deficit	opening cash
budget surplus	

Chapter 6 ::
Recording Income and Expenditure

Learning outcomes

When you have completed this chapter you will be able to:

✔ Explain why households and businesses keep financial records

✔ Outline and demonstrate the rules that apply to cash book entries

✔ Complete an analysed cash book

✔ Balance and total an analysed cash book

✔ Explain the difference between opening and closing balances in an analysed cash book

✔ Interpret and evaluate an analysed cash book

✔ Account for opening and closing bank overdrafts in an analysed cash book.

Why keep income and expenditure records?

Everyone benefits from keeping accurate records of all money they receive and spend. Not only does this help keep track of *actual* income and expenditure, it also helps with financial planning and budgeting.

See Chapter 5

For businesses, such records are an important part of a larger set of accounts that are used to monitor business activity and calculate its profitability. Since businesses pay taxes on their profits there is a legal requirement for all businesses to keep accurate financial records. While households are not legally required to keep such records it can be a very useful activity and certainly helps householders to be money smart.

See Chapter 28

The analysed cash book

The analysed cash book is used to record **all money actually received and spent**.

6.1 How does the analysed cash book differ from a budget?

It is called an *analysed* cash book because all items of income and expenditure are categorised under suitable headings. This will enable the household or business to look in detail at where its money comes from and what it gets spent on. This is very useful for identifying patterns of spending and, in particular, for highlighting areas of overspending.

The rules

Accounting rules help everyone using accounts to understand them. They provide a structure for ensuring everything is recorded correctly.

The analysed cash book is divided into a **debit (Dr)** side and a **credit (Cr)** side.

A **debit is money received** (income/receipts) and a **credit is money spent** (expenditure/payments).

Here is a very simple two-sided account (sometimes called a **T-account**), which shows the basic accounting rules for all cash book entries. The cash book is used to record **all money** received and paid out.

This is the basic rule for all cash and bank transactions. *Learn it well.* A transaction occurs whenever money is received or spent and each transaction requires a separate entry in the analysed cash book.

Cash Book	
DEBIT: Money received/ money in	CREDIT: Money spent/ money out

What the analysed cash book looks like

The analysed cash book takes the concept of the T-account and expands on it, using columns to record detailed information about each transaction.

Here is a more detailed layout for an analysed cash book. This could be completed on paper, on a spreadsheet or using a specialised computer program. You can use Business Studies Record Book 1 to prepare an analysed cash book.

ANALYSED CASH BOOK														
DEBIT SIDE														**CREDIT SIDE**
Date	Details	Folio	Cash	Bank	Wages	Child benefit	Date	Details	Folio	Chq No.	Cash	Bank	Grocery	Light & heat	Travel
20XX			€	€	€	€	20XX				€	€	€	€	€

The columns of the analysed cash book

Date: The date – day, month and year – of each transaction.

Details: Identifies the business or person from whom the money was received or to whom it was paid.

Folio (F): This is a reference column. We will use it for double entry book keeping in chapter 28.

Cash: The actual amount of cash (notes and coins) received or spent.

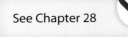

See Chapter 28

Bank: This column records all amounts received or paid through a bank account.

Chq No.: This is used to record the cheque number for all cheque payments made by the household.

Analysis columns: These columns are used for recording exactly where the income came from, e.g. wages, and on what it was spent, e.g. groceries, electricity bill. These column names will vary according to what is most relevant to the household or business.

Example 1: Cash transactions

For our first example, we will assume that all transactions are in cash.

Cash only

On 1 March 2016 the Owen household had €280 **cash on hand**. This is money left over from previous months and represents an **opening balance** in their cash book.

Opening balances are labelled 'Balance b/d' (b/d = brought down) in the account. Since this is money that the household already owns it is treated as income ('money in') and will appear on the debit side of the cash book.

The following is a list of all the cash received or spent by the Owen household for the first week in March 2016.

1 March:	Cash on hand €280	5 March:	Received wages €800
2 March:	Child benefit €270	5 March:	Paid rent €320
2 March:	Grocery shopping €158	6 March:	Bought clothes €75
4 March:	Petrol for family car €40	7 March:	Bought cinema tickets €27
4 March:	Paid for school expenses €30		

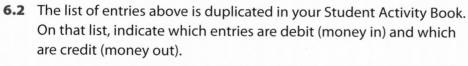

6.2 The list of entries above is duplicated in your Student Activity Book. On that list, indicate which entries are debit (money in) and which are credit (money out).

6.3 On which side of the cash book will the opening balance appear in this case?

Figure 6.1 shows how the above transactions would be recorded in the cash book.

\multicolumn{8}{c}{**ANALYSED CASH BOOK**}														
Dr														**Cr**
Date	Details	F	Cash	Wages	Child benefit	Other	Date	Details	F	Cash	Grocery	Travel	Rent	Other
2016			€	€	€	€	2016			€	€	€	€	€
01/03	Balance	b/d	280				02/03	Groceries		158	158			
02/03	Child benefit		270		270		04/03	Petrol		40		40		
05/03	Wages		800	800			04/03	School expenses		30				30
							05/03	Rent		320			320	
							06/03	Clothes		75				75
							07/03	Cinema		27				27

Figure 6.1 Owen household income and expenditure

Notice that the opening balance appears on the debit side because the Owen family had cash on hand.

Each of the other transactions appears in the cash columns, on either the debit or credit side, *and* in the appropriate analysis column. For example, on 2 March the €158 entry on the credit side records the fact that the household spent €158 in cash. The entry in the analysis column tells us that this money was spent on groceries.

The Owen family have a column for 'Other'. Instead of including the cinema tickets in this column, they could have had a column for 'Entertainment'. They could also have a separate column for 'School expenses'. Remember, the cash book analysis reflects whatever is best for the people using it.

Balancing and totalling accounts

One of the benefits of preparing cash accounts is that it allows us to work out how much money we have at the end of each day, week, month, etc.

When we **balance** our cash account we are really just working out the difference between how much money we received and how much money we spent. This is our **closing balance** on the account. Closing balances are labelled 'Balance c/d' (c/d = to be carried down).

This also tells us the amount of cash we will have available at the start of the next accounting period (week, month, etc). So the balance c/d for one period becomes the balance b/d (i.e. the opening balance) for the next accounting period. If you think back to your work on household budgets you will realise that this is very similar to the way in which the closing cash for one month becomes the opening cash for the next.

The **balance** is the difference between the amounts of money on the debit and credit sides of an account.

Definition

When we balance an account it is very similar to balancing a weighing scales. For the scales (or account) to balance, both sides must total up to the same amount. For example, if you place a 10 kg weight on one side of a pair of scales and 7 kg on the other, you will need to add 3 kg to the lighter side to get the scales to balance. You balance an account in a similar way.

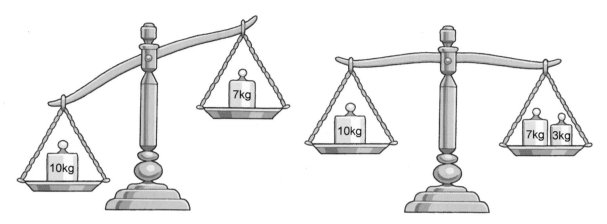

If you received €100 in cash and then spent a total of €80 during the next week, you would have €20 remaining at the end of the week. This €20 is your closing balance at the end of the week and your opening balance at the beginning of the next week. We can show this on a T-account like this:

See Chapter 6, Q. 1 in your Student Activity Book for practice questions

Dr				CASH BOOK				Cr
Date	Details	F	Cash	Date	Details	F	Cash
2016			€	2016			€
03/03	Cash received		100	08/03	Expenditure		80
				09/03	Balance	c/d	20
			100				100
10/03	Balance	b/d	20				

Look at the income and expenditure for the Owen household in figure 6.1. They received €1,350 (debit side) and their total spending (credit side) was €650. From these figures, we calculate the balance of €700 and insert it on the smaller side, then total both sides and carry the balance down. This is shown in figure 6.2.

							ANALYSED CASH BOOK							
Dr														Cr
Date	Details	F	Cash	Wages	Child benefit	Other	Date	Details	F	Cash	Grocery	Travel	Rent	Other
2016			€	€	€	€	2016			€	€	€	€	€
01/03	Balance	b/d	280				02/03	Groceries		158	158			
02/03	Child benefit		270		270		04/03	Petrol		40		40		
05/03	Wages		800	800			04/03	School expenses		30				30
							05/03	Rent		320			320	
							06/03	Clothes		75				75
							07/03	Cinema		27				27
							07/03	Balance	c/d	700				
			1,350	800	270					1,350	158	40	320	132
08/03	Balance	b/d	700											

Figure 6.2 The balanced account of the Owen household

The steps involved in balancing and totalling the cash account are as follows:

1   Add up the amounts on each side and work out which has the biggest total. Write this amount in the total boxes on **both** sides. Underline all totals with a double line. *In our example, the debit side total of €1,350 is the biggest and therefore appears as the total on both sides of the cash account in the ACB.*

2   Calculate how much we need to add to the smallest side in order to bring it up to the total. *In our example, the credit side entries add up to just €650. This means we will need to add €700 to this side in order to match the total of €1,350.*

3   Show the balance c/d on the smaller side. *In our example the Balance c/d of €700 appears on the credit side. Note that it appears above the total box.*

4   Bring this balance across to the other side of the account. It appears as a balance b/d on the opposite side. This represents the amount of money available at the start of the next accounting period. *In our example, a balance b/d of €700 appears on the debit side. Note that it appears below the total box.*

In the ACB it is only the cash and bank columns which require balancing before being totalled. The analysis columns are simply totalled in order to indicate the amount of money received or spent under each heading.

Example 2: Cash and bank transactions

In our second example we will look at an analysed cash book that involves both cash and bank transactions.

Cheque payments, direct debits, standing orders, payments by debit card and withdrawals from an ATM all involve money being taken out of a current account. Lodging money means paying it into an account. We'll look in more detail at current account transactions in chapter 8.

See Chapter 8

Cash and bank transactions

The Walsh household had the following transactions in the week beginning 1 February 2016:

1 February	Cash on hand	€120
1 February	Cash in bank	€370
2 February	Wages lodged	€1,300
2 February	Paid mortgage by direct debit	€900
3 February	Bought groceries, debit card transaction	€180
3 February	Paid for petrol with cash	€40
4 February	Cash lottery win	€25
5 February	Child benefit lodged	€270
6 February	Paid mobile phone bill by direct debit	€45
7 February	Paid school fees (cheque number 103)	€60

6.4 The list of entries above is duplicated in your Student Activity Book. On that list, tick which entries should appear as debit and which should appear as credit.

Figure 6.3 shows how the above transactions would be recorded in the analysed cash book.

ANALYSED CASH BOOK															
Dr															**Cr**
Date	Details	F	Cash	Bank	Wages	Child benefit	Other	Date	Details	F	Chq. no.	Cash	Bank	Grocery	Household	Travel	Other
2016			€	€	€	€	€	2016				€	€	€	€	€	€
01/02	Balance	b/d	120	370				02/02	Mortgage				900		900		
02/02	Wages			1,300	1,300			03/02	Groceries				180	180			
04/02	Lottery win		25				25	03/02	Petrol			40				40	
05/02	Child benefit			270		270		06/02	Mobile Phone				45				45
								07/02	School Fees		103		60				60
								07/02	Balance	c/d		105	755				
			145	1,940	1,300	270	25					145	1,940	180	900	40	105
08/02	Balance	b/d	105	755													

Figure 6.3 The Walsh family's analysed cash book

Note that the cash and bank accounts have been balanced and totalled separately. This means that the cash column on the debit side is balanced against the cash column on the credit side, just as it was in figure 6.2. The same process is then repeated for the bank columns and we do not combine the cash and bank amounts. This shows that they will begin next week with €105 cash and €755 in the bank.

6.5 Why do you think we balance the cash and bank accounts separately?

The benefits of keeping an analysed cash book

To recap what you have already learned in this chapter, the benefits of keeping an analysed cash book, for individuals, households or businesses, are:

> You have a record of all income and expenditure.

> This record can be compared against your budget to (a) make sure you are on track, and (b) find where you might have to amend your budget to make it more realistic.

> You can see where you might be overspending (by looking at the totals) and adjust your habits to make sure you stay within your budgets.

> You can check your bank and credit card statements against what you have recorded to ensure no mistakes have been made and that there are no payments out of the accounts that you have not made.

Bank overdrafts

A bank overdraft is an arrangement with the bank that allows an account holder to withdraw or spend more money from their current account than they actually have in the account.

See Chapter 10

The overdraft must be arranged in advance and the bank will set a limit on the amount that can be overdrawn. It is a useful way of getting a short-term loan if, for example, you have an emergency repair that costs more than you have available. You will be able to spend *up to* this amount: the money is available if you need it, but you don't have to use the full amount.

An overdraft means you will have a minus balance in your current account, representing the amount that you owe the bank. Remember, this is only the amount of the overdraft you have used; it is not necessarily the full amount available to you.

If an account holder is overdrawn at the start of an accounting period we show this as a Balance b/d on the **credit side** of their current account, as shown in figure 6.4.

ANALYSED CASH BOOK										
Dr										**Cr**
Date	Details	F	Cash	Bank	Date	Details	F	Cash	Bank
2016			€	€	2016			€	€
					01/03	Balance	b/d		300

Figure 6.4 How an opening bank overdraft appears in the analysed cash book

Example 3: Bank overdraft

Bank overdraft

The Duggan household had the following weekly transactions:

1 April	Cash on hand	€180
1 April	Bank overdraft	€370
2 April	Wages lodged	€1,100
2 April	Paid mortgage by direct debit	€900
3 April	Bought groceries by debit card	€210
4 April	Bought petrol using cash	€50
5 April	Child benefit lodged	€270
6 April	Paid mobile phone bill by direct debit	€65
7 April	Paid school fees by cheque	€150

Figure 6.5 shows how the above transactions would be recorded in the analysed cash book.

						ANALYSED CASH BOOK									
Dr															**Cr**
Date	Details	F	Cash	Bank	Wages	Child benefit	Date	Details	F	Chq. no.	Cash	Bank	Grocery	Household	Travel	Other
2016			€	€	€	€	2016				€	€	€	€	€	€
01/04	Balance	b/d	180				01/04	Balance	b/d			370				
02/04	Wages			1,100	1,100		02/04	Mortgage				900		900		
05/04	Child benefit			270		270	03/04	Grocery				210	210			
							04/04	Petrol			50				50	
							06/04	Mobile phone				65				65
							07/04	School fees				150				150
07/04	Balance	c/d		325			07/04	Balance	c/d		130					
			180	1,695	1,100	270					180	1,695	210	900	50	215
08/04	Balance	b/d	130				08/04	Balance	b/d			325				

Figure 6.5 The Duggan household's analysed cash book

Key Terms

KSBL
KSC
KSMIT
KSBC

You should be able to *define, spell,* give *examples* and *apply* to real life each of the following key terms associated with this topic.

Exercise: Write a sentence using each of the following terms. You may use more than one of the terms in your sentence if appropriate.

account

analysed cash book

balance b/d

balance c/d

bank overdraft

closing balance

credit side

debit side

opening balance

T-account

Comparing the plan with the actual figures

In previous chapters we saw that a budget is a financial plan and the analysed cash book provides a record of actual cash receipts and payments. To provide meaningful and helpful information, the two need to be compared.

You can make the comparison by writing up a **budget comparison statement**. This lists all household income and expenditure by category (your column headings in the analysed cash book). It shows:

❭ The **budgeted** (planned) income and expenditure – from the household budget
❭ The **actual** income and expenditure – from the analysed cash book
❭ The **differences** between the budgeted and actual figures.

Doing this will help with the preparation of more realistic budgets in the future and avoid making the same financial planning mistakes month after month.

> **7.1** Why is it important to use the same time period for the budget and the analysed cash book for the comparison?

Financial control cycle

The process of making budgets, recording income and expenditure and learning from the results is called the **financial control cycle**. The stages are shown in figure 7.1.

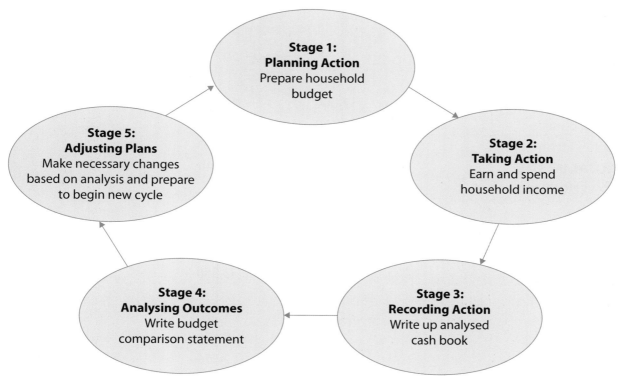

Figure 7.1 The financial control cycle

Example: the Graham household

Look at the budget comparison statement in figure 7.2, which sets out both the budgeted and actual income and expenditure for the Graham household for the whole year 2016.

Where the actual figure is greater than the budgeted amount, the difference column shows a plus (+) sign. This indicates that an item of income or expenditure was over budget.

Where the actual figure is less than the budgeted amount, the difference column shows a minus (−) sign. This indicates that an item of income or expenditure was under budget.

Analysis of key trends

The household received €3,820 more income than they had expected. Most of this extra income came in the form of wages and salaries.

KSMIT

> **7.2** Suggest two possible reasons why the wages and salary figure is €2,800 more than expected.
>
> **7.3** Suggest three possible sources for the €900 that was unexpectedly received as 'Other income'.

Actual fixed expenditure was €910 over budget and this is a little surprising since fixed expenditure tends to be the most predictable category of spending. The biggest difference was with the mortgage where the actual cost was €800 greater than expected.

Graham Household: Budget Comparison Statement (2016)

	BUDGET	ACTUAL	DIFFERENCE
INCOME	€	€	€
Wages and salary	37,000	39, 800	+2,800
Child benefit	3,120	3,240	+120
Other income	—	900	+900
TOTAL INCOME	**40,120**	**43,940**	**+3,820**
EXPENDITURE			
Fixed			
Mortgage	14,000	14,800	+800
House insurance	470	580	+110
Subtotal	*14,470*	*15,380*	*+910*
Irregular			
Groceries	4,600	5,250	+650
Light & heat	3,200	2,800	−400
Car running costs	2,700	2,320	−380
Subtotal	*10,500*	*10,370*	*−130*
Discretionary			
Entertainment	2,400	3,500	+1,100
Holidays	3,500	5,000	+1,500
Subtotal	*5,900*	*8,500*	*+2,600*
TOTAL EXPENDITURE	**30,870**	**34,250**	**+3,380**
Net cash	9,250	9,690	+440
Opening cash	800	800	
Closing cash	10,050	10,490	

Figure 7.2 Budget comparison statement

The Graham household's income and expenditure for the year 2016 are shown graphically in figures 7.3 and 7.4.

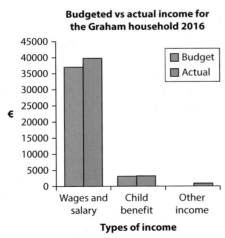

Figure 7.3 Graham household income for 2016

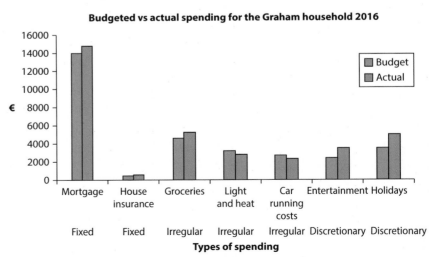

Figure 7.4 Graham household expenditure for 2016

7.4 Suggest a reason for the increase in actual mortgage expenditure.

KSMIT

Actual irregular expenditure was broadly in line with expectations, with this category showing an actual spend that was €130 less than budgeted. Despite an overspend on groceries, the household made savings on light and heat and car running costs.

7.5 Suggest one possible reason for the lower than expected expenditure on:

(a) Light and heat

(b) Car running costs.

KSMIT

Actual discretionary expenditure was much higher than the budget and shows a total overspend of €2,600. This was a result of a €1,100 overspend on entertainment (almost 50% above the budgeted amount) and a €1,500 increase in holiday spending compared to the budget. This is clearly an area where the household struggled to stick to their spending plans.

7.6 What does this comparison result mean for the Graham household as they move on to the next part of the budget comparison cycle?

KSMIT

Despite the unplanned spending increases in some areas, the comparison statement illustrates an improvement in the household's net cash position for the year. This is clearly a result of the increases in actual income and leaves the Graham household with an actual closing cash of €10,490. This is €440 ahead of the budgeted figure.

Discuss the following. Give reasons to support your views.

Discussion

7.7 Do you think the budget was well planned? How could it have been better?

7.8 How might the budget comparison statement be shown graphically other than by bar chart?

KSWwO
KSC

7.9 What are the benefits of showing this information graphically?

7.10 Use the figures from figure 7.2 to create a different type of graph. Explain why you have chosen this particular graph type.

KSBN
KSC
KSBL

7.11 You have created a budget for yourself and have completed an analysed cash book for yourself. Now complete a comparison budget plan for yourself. Do you need to make amendments to your budget?

7.12 Create a graph of your own budget comparison.

7.13 At what point should a person or household amend their budget? Should the financial control cycle be continuous, or just once a year?

Key Terms

You should be able to *define*, *spell*, give *examples* and *apply* to real life each of the following key terms associated with this topic.

Exercise: Write a sentence using each of the following terms. You may use more than one of the terms in your sentence if appropriate.

budget comparison statement   financial control cycle

Chapter 8 ::
Financial Services for Individuals and Households

Learning outcomes

When you have completed this chapter you will be able to:

✔ Describe the services offered by Ireland's major financial institutions
✔ Distinguish between a current and a deposit account
✔ Explain the various methods of making payments from a current account
✔ Analyse a current account statement
✔ Outline the benefits of internet and telephone banking
✔ Recognise the security issues of internet and telephone banking
✔ Compare the use of credit and charge cards
✔ Look up and calculate foreign exchange rates.

What is a financial institution?

A **financial institution** provides financial services for its customers, including storing their money, managing payments and providing loans.

Definition

A number of different types of financial institution operate in Ireland, including:

> Commercial banks
> Credit unions
> Building societies
> The post office (An Post).

A **commercial bank** is a bank that offers financial services to the general public and to businesses.

Definition

Financial institutions offer the following services to customers to help them manage their financial resources:

> Current accounts
> Deposit accounts
> Bill payment and money transmission services
> Internet and telephone banking
> Credit cards
> Foreign exchange services
> Loans.

See Chapter 1

See Chapters 9 and 10

'But if money doesn't grow on trees, why do banks have branches?'

Each institution tries to attract more customers by offering competitive rates on savings and loans.

Types of bank account

Most of the financial institutions in Ireland provide two main types of bank account:

1 **Current accounts** are offered by the commercial banks and building societies. They are used for day-to-day banking needs.

2 **Deposit/savings accounts** are offered by the commercial banks, building societies, An Post and the credit unions. They are used to save money.

Many households or individuals will have both types, as they serve different needs.

What is a current account?

A current account is used for day-to-day banking needs. It is a convenient way for you to:

> Receive your income
> Store money safely
> Pay for goods and services
> Pay bills and transfer money to other people.

How current accounts are used

Current account holders receive regular **statements** detailing all transactions. Amounts paid into the account are known as **lodgements**. Amounts paid out of the account are called **withdrawals**.

Did you know?

The term **lodge** means to leave money or a valuable item in a safe place.

An account holder should keep their own records of all transactions in an analysed cash book and check these against their statements.

See Chapter 6

8.1 Discuss the advantages of using a current account rather than using notes and coins for all our transactions.

Discussion

KSC

Example: Michael

Michael works for an agricultural merchant. His wages are paid directly into his bank account and each week he withdraws cash for spending.

Most of his bills are paid by direct debit, which means they are taken straight from his bank account by the companies he owes money to, such as the electricity company.

He buys his groceries, petrol, etc. using a debit card so the money goes straight from his account to the shop without Michael having to use cash. He has set up a regular bank transfer to his landlord for his apartment and he makes manual transfers from his account to other people's for less regular payments, such as sending his niece some birthday money.

Example: Holly

Holly is a self-employed translator. Her clients usually pay by electronic transfer so that the funds move from their bank account to hers. Occasionally a client will pay her in cash, and she lodges this in her account to keep it with her other earnings.

She pays some bills, such as advertising her business, by direct debit, and she manually transfers money every month to her personal current account as private money.

KSC

8.2 Ask your parents/guardians or other adults how they use their current account. You don't need to know about actual amounts, just whether they pay bills by direct debit, cheque, electronic transfer and so on, and what other services they use via their current account.

Opening a current account

There are several different banks you could open a current account with. A lot of young people will choose the same bank their parents use, or parents may have already set up an account for their child. There are often incentives (rewards) for a young person to open an account with a particular bank (such as free banking while they are a student), so it is worth shopping around and looking at what the different banks have to offer when you want to open an account. You can change to a different bank at a later date, if you wish.

8.3 Discuss at what age or stage of your life you think it is a good idea to open a current account.

8.4 Discuss why banks provide incentives to young people to open an account with them. After all, a young person doesn't normally have enough money to make it worthwhile for a bank to look after it.

Once you have chosen a financial institution you will have to fill out an application form and supply documents to prove your identity and address. The following are required to open a current or deposit account:

1   Photographic proof of identity – passport, driving licence or EU National Identity Card.

2   Proof of address – a (recent) utility bill such as an electricity, gas or telephone bill, or correspondence from a financial institution or government agency, addressed to the person who is opening the account.

3   A PPSN (personal public service number) – this is provided to all citizens by the government.

8.5 Why do you think a person has to provide photographic evidence and proof of address?

8.6 If two (or more) people are opening an account together, do you think both/all of them will have to supply the proofs necessary? Why?

The application form will ask for further information about you and your circumstances. If you are under 16 you will need a parent's or guardian's signature on the application form.

8.7 Download and complete an application form for a current account from the website of a bank of your choice.

Write across it in red ink and big letters 'SPECIMEN', and keep it in your file as an example of what an application form looks like and how it should be completed.

When the customer's application has been approved by the bank, he or she will be given an account number.

8.8 Some people have more than one personal current account. Discuss:

(a) Reasons why this might be useful.

(b) What disadvantages there might be to having more than one current account.

8.9 Jonathan has a small business called Jon's Jewellery. Jon has a personal current account and a business current account, even though all the money in both accounts belongs to him. Discuss why he has two current accounts instead of just one.

Lodging money into an account

Money is **lodged** to an account in various ways, i.e.:

> By the account holder lodging money (cash or cheques) over the counter or using a self-service machine in the bank branch. A lodgement slip (see figure 8.1) may be used.

> By an employer transferring wages or salary directly into the account (via a system called Paypath)

> Pensions or benefits paid directly into a current account

> By a third party transferring money electronically from their account to the account holder's.

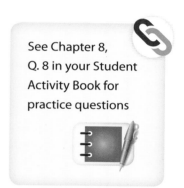

See Chapter 8, Q. 8 in your Student Activity Book for practice questions

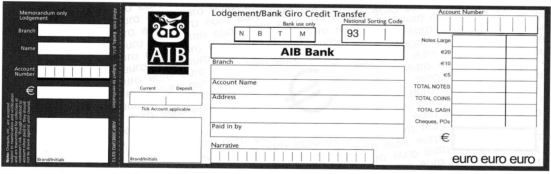

Figure 8.1 Example of a lodgement slip; sample only

Withdrawing money from an account

Money can be withdrawn from your account in a number of ways:

> Using an ATM (see page 68) to withdraw cash with an ATM card or a debit card

> Paying for items using a debit card (see page 69)

> Withdrawing cash at a bank using a withdrawal slip (see figure 8.2); you will sometimes need photo ID for this

> Direct debit (see page 70)

> Standing order (see page 70)

> Credit transfer (see page 70)

> Cheque (a personal cheque or a bank cheque, known as a bank draft)

> Fees and charges.

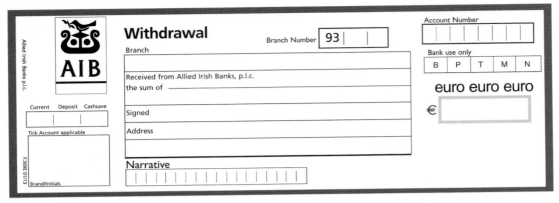

Figure 8.2 Example of a withdrawal slip; sample only

ATMs

ATM stands for **automated teller machine**. Current account holders are given an ATM card with a PIN (see below) and they can use this for withdrawing cash and for other banking services.

Did you know?

Bank counter clerks are called **tellers**. This comes from an Old English word, 'tellan', which means 'person who counts'.

8.10 Use a bank's website to find out the services available via ATMs. In pairs or small groups prepare a poster or leaflet to let others know how they can make use of an ATM. Include on it information on security when using an ATM and instructions on how to actually use the machine.

Display all the posters around the classroom.

Research

Groupwork

KSWwO
KSBC
KSBL
KSMIT

PINs

Most over-the-counter or machine bank transactions require a **personal identification number**, known as a PIN. This is a four-digit number associated with your ATM card, debit card or credit card that you will need to type into the ATM to prove that the card is yours.

When you order a card it is sent to you in the post and then a few days later you will receive a note of the PIN linked to that card.

KSWwO
KSBC
KSMIT

Debit cards

Debit cards allow consumers to pay for goods and services without using cash. They provide electronic access to the money in your bank account, so if there isn't enough money in the account to pay the requested amount, the shop keeper will be told the payment is 'declined'.

Most debit cards contain a small electronic chip in the card and you enter your four-digit PIN into the card machine to authorise its use. This is known as a 'chip and PIN' system (see figure 8.3). Once the payment is approved the money is electronically transferred from the cardholder's current account to the retailer's account.

Contactless payments are an even faster way to use debit cards to pay for items that cost €30 or less without having to key in your PIN.

Look for the logo (see figure 8.4) that shows where you can make contactless payments.

Figure 8.3 A chip and PIN debit card

Figure 8.4 Contactless payment logo

8.12 Why do you think this type of card is called a 'debit card'?

KSMIT
KSBL

8.13 (a) What are the benefits of using contactless payment?

(b) What are the possible risks associated with the contactless payment system?

8.14 Give an example of the type of business you might use that would find contactless payment particularly beneficial.

KSMIT

Direct debit (DD)

A current account holder gives permission to another person or business to request the withdrawal of *variable amounts* from a current account. It is used in situations where the amount to be paid and/or the payment date are likely to change.

> **8.15** Think about which payments are suitable for paying by direct debit and discuss this with your partner.
>
> T-P-S
>
> KSMIT KSC

The supplier sends an invoice to the customer giving the amount due and the date on which the direct debit will be requested from the bank. The bill will automatically be paid on the date stated (providing there is enough money available in the account).

To set up a direct debit, the supplier sends a form (a **direct debit mandate**) to the customer, who fills out their bank details, signs the form and sends it back to the supplier. The supplier then sends it to their bank to make the necessary electronic requests to the customer's bank.

Standing order (SO)

A standing order is an instruction to a financial institution to pay a fixed amount to a person or organisation on a regular date.

> **8.16** List five examples of when a standing order would be used rather than a direct debit.
>
>
> KSMIT

Credit transfer

A credit transfer is a *once-off* instruction from a current account holder to their bank to transfer an amount of money to another account. A credit transfer can be made by phone, on paper, or over the internet.

> **8.17** Think about when a credit transfer might be used and discuss this with your partner.
>
> T-P-S
>
>
> KSMIT KSC

Cheques

Current account holders may request a chequebook. A **cheque** is a written instruction from an account holder to their bank to pay a specific amount of money to a named person or business. For hundreds of years cheques were the main way of paying via a bank account, but cheques have rapidly been taken over by electronic payment and in many countries are now not used at all, although businesses might still use them.

Figure 8.5 shows a cheque and what the various elements mean.

Figure 8.5 A completed cheque

Bank draft

This is like a cheque but it is written on a bank's own account rather than a customer's account. The customer must have sufficient funds in their bank account that the bank can make an immediate transfer into its own account and write a draft made payable to whoever the customer specifies.

Since the money has already been paid to the bank the person receiving the draft can be certain that they will receive payment when they present the draft at their bank. This security of payment means that drafts tend to be used for big-value items, such as a car or a house.

Bank fees and charges

Having a current account comes with associated costs. There are some annual fees and often charges per transaction. The amount charged will depend on what that transaction is.

8.18 **(a)** Use the internet to find the current charges/fees for one particular bank (make a note of which one) for the following transactions:

Research

KSMIT
KSBN
KSWwO

   (i) A debit card purchase.

   (ii) A direct debit.

   (iii) An ATM withdrawal.

   (iv) A lodgement over the counter.

   (v) A lodgement using a lodgement machine.

   (vi) The maintenance fee for the account for one quarter (three months).

(b) Why do you think the charge for making a lodgement using a lodgement machine is lower than the charge for making a lodgement over the counter?

8.19 Terry used his account in the following ways in January–March. Assume he is with the bank you looked at in question 8.18:

(a) Calculate Terry's fees at the end of the quarter.

   (i) He used his debit card 35 times.

   (ii) He has two direct debits every week, and another one once a month.

   (iii) He withdraws cash from an ATM once a week.

   (iv) He lodged money into his account twice over the counter.

   (v) He lodged money using the lodgement machine three times.

   (vi) He had to pay a maintenance fee for the quarter.

(b) If Terry continues to use his current account in the same way for the rest of the year, what will his bank charges be for the whole year?

8.20 Compare the fees and charges from the bank you chose with those of a student who chose a different bank.

T-P-S

Bank statements

A current account holder will receive a bank statement from their bank on a regular (monthly or quarterly) basis. This might be on paper through the post, or electronically, i.e. shown on their internet banking when they log on.

The statement shows *all transactions* (i.e. the money going into and out of an account). The bank column of the statement shows a running balance. It decreases when payments are made (debit) and increases when there are lodgements (credit). The entries are on the exact opposite side to the bank records prepared by the account holder in their analysed cash book as the statement is written from the bank's point of view.

See Chapter 6

Figure 8.6 shows a typical bank statement. Gerry Duffy has an account with AIB, Carrickmacross, Co. Monaghan. He received his bank statement on 4 June 2016.

CURRENT ACCOUNT

AIB

Branch Main Street,
Carrickmacross, Co. Monaghan
Tel: 042 – 123 456

National Sort Code: 93-12-34

Statement of Account

Mr Gerry Duffy

Farney Street

Carrickmacross

Account Name: Gerry Duffy

Account Number: 123456789

Date of Statement: 31 May 2016

Page Number: 321

IBAN: IE25 AIBK 9312 3412 3456 78 (BIC: AIBKIE2D)

Authorised Limit at Date Of Statement €550

Date	Details	Debit €	Credit €	Balance €
01 May 2016	Balance Forward			260.00
04 May 2016	SO Mortgage	590.00		330.00 DR
07 May 2016	DD Electricity	178.00		508.00 DR
12 May 2016	Hendy & Co Paypath		1200.00	692.00
14 May 2016	ATM Francis Street	100.00		592.00
15 May 2016	INET-AIB Visa	340.00		252.00
17 May 2016	Cheque 113456	122.00		130.00
21 May 2016	Credit Transfer – Deposit Account		175.00	305.00
24 May 2016	ATM Francis Street	100.00		205.00
27 May 2016	Bernie Duffy	30.00		175.00
29 May 2016	Bank Charges	14.50		160.50
29 May 2016	Bank Interest	3.50		157.00
31 May 2016	POS McGrath's Garage	50.00		107.00

Figure 8.6 An example of a bank statement

You should check your bank statement against your analysed cash book. Make sure you file your statements and keep them safe – it is an important record of payments and may be useful at some point to prove you have paid for something. The usual advice is to keep bank statements for six years, but if you have the space it would be wise to keep them for even longer.

8.21 Why is it so important to check your bank statement against your analysed cash book?

8.22 Unless you log on to your bank account on the internet regularly, what (unpleasant!) surprises might you find when you receive your bank statement?

8.23 Discuss and answer these questions relating to the bank statement in figure 8.6. Some answers you can get from looking at the bank statement, others you will have to research.

Research

Groupwork

KSWwO
KSMIT
KSC
KSBN
KSBL

(a) What do the following abbreviations stand for (all but the last one are on the statement) and what do they mean in banking terms (that is, what is their function)?

(i) BIC	**(iv)** SO	**(vii)** ATM
(ii) IBAN	**(v)** POS	**(viii)** DR
(iii) DD	**(vi)** INET	**(ix)** SEPA

(b) What is a sort code, and what is the sort code of Gerry's bank?

(c) What is Gerry's account number?

(d) What method of payment does Gerry use for his electricity bill?

(e) What date does Gerry's mortgage get paid, and what method of payment is used?

(f) What date does Gerry get paid, and what is his employer's name?

(g) What method of payment did Gerry use to buy his petrol?

(h) How many times did Gerry withdraw cash during this month, and which cash machine location did he use?

(i) Explain why 'bank interest' appears on the statement on 29 May.

(j) Does Gerry have any other bank accounts? How do you know?

(k) Does Gerry have a credit card? How do you know?

(l) Does Gerry ever use a cheque book? How do you know?

(m) How big is Gerry's overdraft facility?

(n) Gerry's sister lives in Cork. It was her birthday this month and Gerry sent her some money. How did he do this and how much did he give her?

8.24 How do you think your banking needs will change as you get older?

Discussion

KSC

Internet and telephone banking

Internet and telephone banking are useful and convenient ways for customers to pay bills, check their account balance, order statements and transfer money to other accounts.

These services allow account holders to access their accounts twenty-four hours a day, seven days a week and every day in the year. The bank issues customers with a registration number and personal access code (PAC) for accessing their accounts online and over the telephone.

Some banks now provide telephone and internet access in their branch network and customers can use these facilities to check their accounts rather than queueing up to speak to a counter clerk.

Advantages and disadvantages of internet and telephone banking

The **advantages** are:

> Convenience – banking when it suits the customer, 24 hours a day and 365 days a year.

> Higher interest rates – because online banks have fewer expenses, such as wage bills and costs associated with premises, they can afford to offer higher interest rates to people saving money.

The **disadvantages** are:

> The closure of small branches, particularly in rural areas.
> Reductions in the number of people employed by financial institutions.
> The security risks of online banking.

Be secure when using online banking

When you log in to your bank account, check that you see the little padlock to the side of the web address, as shown in figure 8.7. The address will change to start with **https://** – the 's' stands for 'secure'. You will see these security alerts on payment sites for retail websites, too.

Figure 8.7 Make sure you can see the little padlock and https:// in the address when you log in to your bank account

Criminals use fake emails and fake websites as a way of tricking people into giving away passwords and bank details. This is known as **phishing**. Examples of phishing emails are shown in figure 8.8.

Figure 8.8 Examples of phishing emails

You may receive an email that looks as if it comes from your bank. Look out for emails that:

> Just don't look right – they might have an odd email address or include an odd web address.

> Are poorly designed and have bad spelling, grammar or typos.

> Ask you to log in to your bank account or send back personal information – your bank will never ask you to do this.

Always ignore and delete these emails.

If you receive a call from someone claiming to be from your bank, *never* give the caller your log-in details.

Work in pairs for these questions.

T-P-S

KSWwO
KSSW
KSMM

8.25 Although online banking is very safe and secure, there are always people who will try to find ways into your account. Discuss ways of keeping your online account secure.

8.26 Are there additional security measures you can take if you use a smartphone for your banking rather than, say, a laptop?

8.27 An elderly relative has been nervous about doing online banking, but has now decided to try it. Write down some security tips for them, which they can keep by their laptop to remind them how to be safe.

Did you know?

RaboDirect

Rabobank *The straight talking savings bank*

Some banks are exclusively online with no physical branches, such as RaboDirect.

Deposit accounts

Deposit accounts offer a way of saving. Money in deposit accounts is safe and secure and will also earn interest. You can choose from a range of deposit accounts, depending on how much money you want to save and what access you want to your money. Many accounts can be opened with as little as €10 and you can save either regular amounts or lump sums.

See Chapter 9

There are usually no transaction fees or maintenance charges with these accounts, which are available from banks, building societies, An Post and credit unions.

Opening a deposit account is similar to opening a current account.

8.28 Some deposit accounts are called regular saver accounts. They offer a slightly higher interest rates than ordinary deposit accounts.

What would be the benefits to you personally if you could save €10 a month in one of these accounts, even if you don't need to save for anything in particular at the moment?

Credit cards

Buying on credit means 'buy now, pay later' and credit cards are designed to be used in this way, e.g. Visa and Mastercard.

The benefit to the cardholder is that they do not need money available to pay for goods and services at the time of purchase. Credit cards are particularly useful for making online purchases.

Each credit card has a spending limit which is set by the bank and is based on the customer's income and ability to repay. The cardholder enters their PIN at the point of sale, just like with a debit card.

The credit card company issues a bill (or statement) to the customer at the end of each month, which you should check against your analysed cash book.

If you buy online using a credit card, you will be asked for the card's security number (also known as a **CVC** – Card Verification Code, or a **CVV** – Card Verification Value). This is three numbers on the back of the card, above the signature strip. This is to prove that you actually have the card and haven't copied the card number from somewhere.

The credit card statement

The statement sets out all the items purchased during the month, as well as any balance due from previous months.

If the bill is paid *in full* by its due date no interest is charged. However, if the amount due is not paid in full the bank will charge the cardholder interest on the outstanding amount. Interest rates on credit card debt are much higher than on bank overdrafts or loans, which makes this an expensive source of short-term finance.

Credit card interest

The credit card companies give a figure on the statement for the minimum amount due, which is the amount that covers that month's interest plus a small fraction of the amount owing. It can be tempting to pay just this amount but if you do you will end up paying an enormous amount in interest.

Did you know?

You have debt of €3,000 on a credit card that charges 18% interest. If you pay the minimum each month (about €46) and the interest rate stays the same, it will take you over **21 years** to repay and thousands of euro in interest payments!

The golden rule with credit cards is **do not spend more than you can afford to repay at the end of each month**.

The best thing to do is set up a direct debit to pay off your card in full each month, so you don't have to make the payment yourself and be tempted to pay just part of it.

Did you know?

The findings contained in the first Central Statistics Office (CSO) Household Finance and Consumption Survey showed the financial state of Irish people in 2013. The survey found that many Irish people are relying on credit cards to make ends meet. The average amount of debt on a credit card in 2013 was €1,400.

8.29 Years ago people didn't have the option of 'buy now, pay later'. Discuss whether credit cards are a good thing or a bad thing, or a mixture. What are the pros and cons of having a credit card?

 **Discussion**

KSWwO
KSMM
KSSW
KSC

In the news

Most credit card users don't know what interest they pay

By Charlie Weston

The majority of people who have a credit card have no idea what interest they pay for using it and younger women are more likely to use cards for unplanned buys, new research shows.

Men are more inclined to use the plastic card for day-to-day spending than their female counterparts.

Around seven out of 10 people own a credit card. Most people use it for major purchases and unexpected expenses.

But one of the more shocking findings is that 71% of people in the 25 to 40 age bracket admitted they have no idea what interest they are being charged for using the card.

This falls for the over-40s, with almost half knowing the current rate being charged for purchases on their card.

Credit cards' interest rates can be as high as 23% for purchases, with interest rates of up to 21% for cash withdrawals on a card.

Many people said they used their card when they were abroad on their holidays, with women more inclined to use the plastic payment method when outside the country on a break.

The research found that 60% of card users pay off the balance on the card account each month, while 8% pay only the minimum amount.

Source: Article adapted from the *Irish Independent*, 19 August 2015

8.30 **(a)** Are you shocked by the finding that most people don't know how much interest they pay on their credit card?

(b) Which age group is the worst for knowing what their interest rate is? Why do you think people in this age bracket are the least aware?

(c) Why do you think it is important always to know how much interest you are paying?

Charge cards

A charge card is similar to a credit card since it involves buying goods now but paying later. However, *unlike a credit card, the account must be settled when the statement arrives*. Since the bill must be cleared each month, no interest is charged to the customer. Instead the customer pays an annual fee to the card provider for use of the charge card. Examples include American Express and Diners Club.

8.31 What is the difference between a debit card and a charge card?

8.32 What are the benefits and drawbacks of a charge card over a credit card?

Foreign exchange

When you visit countries outside the euro area you need to get the currency that is legal tender for that country, e.g. for a trip to the USA, you would need to get US dollars. You can buy foreign currency from the commercial banks, building societies, An Post and credit unions. In order to purchase the foreign currency you must pay the current price or 'rate of exchange'.

An **exchange rate** is the price at which a currency can be exchanged for another.

When converting euro to foreign currency, multiply € by the 'sell' bank rate.

When converting foreign currency into euro, divide by the 'buy' bank rate.

Below are the bank sells and bank buys rate for four currencies.

Bureau de change			
Country	Currency	Bank sells	Bank buys
UK	Pound sterling (£)	0.68	0.71
USA	Dollar ($)	1.06	1.11
Australia	Australian dollar (A$)	1.44	1.55
Japan	Yen (¥)	134	137

That is, for each €1 we would receive £0.68, or $1.06, or A$1.44, or ¥134.

Using the information from the table, to convert €400 to sterling, multiply 400 by bank sells sterling rate, i.e.

$$400 \times 0.68 = £272$$

If we wanted to convert 1,552 yen to euro, divide 1,552 by bank buy yen rate, i.e.

$$1{,}552 \div 137 = €11.33$$

8.33 Using the table above, how much in Australian dollars would you receive if you changed €650?

8.34 Using the table above, how much in euros would you receive if you changed £345?

Loans

Individuals and households may also receive loans from financial institutions. A number of different types of loan are available to individuals and households, including:

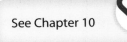
See Chapter 10

> Short-term loans, which will be repaid within one year (e.g. bank overdraft).

> Medium-term loans, which can have a repayment term of one to five years.

> Long-term loans, which will not be repaid for more than five years (e.g. mortgage).

The amount of interest you pay on loans can vary enormously and it is worth shopping around the different institutions for the best rates and terms.

Wherever possible, try to save up for things and pay for them when you have enough money, rather than taking out a loan. Sometimes this isn't possible, of course, such as if you are buying a house, or if you need a car to enable you to work, but a loan shouldn't be seen as an automatic way of getting what you want now. There are financial penalties for having loans, and if you have too many loans you may find it difficult to get a mortgage. Remember, borrowing money has a financial and an opportunity cost.

See Chapter 1

Discussion

KSWwO
KSC

8.35 Banks invest the money that people have in their accounts, in order to make money that they can lend to other people. Sometimes the investments or the lending may be to an organisation that you might not find acceptable; for example, the company might make weapons, use animal testing, or use cheap labour in poor countries. Usually customers of the bank don't know where their money is being invested.

There is a bank called Triodos, which operates in the Netherlands, Belgium, the UK, Spain and Germany. Their website says:

> Do you know what your bank does with your money? We believe banks should be open, which is why we publish details of every organisation we lend to on our website. By lending exclusively to organisations that put people and the planet before profits, our savers' money works to create a positive impact and real returns.

Discuss these questions: **(a)** Do you think all banks should operate ethically like Triodos does? **(b)** Does it bother you if banks invest in organisations that some people might find unethical, or do you think that the bank's purpose is to make as much money as possible?

Key Terms

KSBL
KSC
KSMIT
KSBC

You should be able to *define*, *spell*, give *examples* and *apply* to real life each of the following key terms associated with this topic.

Exercise: Write a sentence using each of the following terms. You may use more than one of the terms in your sentence if appropriate.

automated teller machine (ATM)	direct debit
bureau de change	direct debit mandate
charge card	exchange rate
cheque	internet banking
contactless payments	lodgement
credit card	phishing
credit transfer	standing order
current account	statement
CVC/CVV	telephone banking
debit card	withdrawal
deposit account	

Chapter 9 ::
Saving and Investing Money

What is saving?

When we refer to our **savings** we mean that part of our **income that we choose not to spend**. Savings could also be seen as **deferred spending** because we are making a decision to put this money aside with the intention of spending it at some point in the future.

9.1 Discuss why people save.

9.2 Do you think the reasons you save now will be the same reasons you save in the future? Discuss how your saving patterns might change as you reach different stages of your life.

Discussion

See Chapter 4

KSWwO
KSC

9.3 Have you ever saved for anything? How did you feel when you reached your goal?

KSMM

9.4 Do you have any tips for saving? For example, you might have a jar that you put any loose coins in at the end of the week. You might save all your 50c coins, or put the price of a chocolate bar in a savings jar every time you resist one.

In your groups, make a list of how people can save. One person from each group can give one tip to the whole class to be written on the whiteboard, until all the groups have given all their tips.

Make a note for yourself of any tips you hadn't thought of but sound as if they might work for you!

Investing is often seen as putting money aside in order to get a better return on it in the future. This is very similar to saving, but with the expectation of getting some sort of reward for investing our money.

The simplest way to look at the difference between saving and investing is to consider the risks and liquidity involved.

Liquidity means how quickly we can get our money back when we want it.

Definition

Savings are generally low-risk, low-reward schemes that provide easy access to our money when required.

This explanation clearly covers savings in both piggy banks and commercial banks.

Investing often involves greater risk to the money invested (also known as the **principal**) and it may not be possible to get it back immediately. Investments may, however, offer greater potential for rewards.

Examples of investments include buying property, art or company shares.

See Chapter 4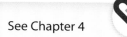

In everyday use, there is little difference between saving and investing, but the distinction becomes more important when it comes to longer-term financial planning. For example, when putting together a personal financial life cycle, we will have some short-term and some longer-term financial needs. In this situation it might be more relevant to look at when exactly we need our money and also what type of return we are expecting.

Figure 9.1 The difference between saving and investing

Reasons for saving money

Here are some reasons for saving money.

(a) For future planned expenditure

(b) For emergencies

(c) For major family events

(d) For retirement

(e) To improve our credit rating.

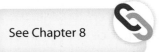

See Chapter 8

9.5 For (a) to (d) in the list above give some examples of what you might be saving for. In each case, explain why you might choose to save for them.

Groupwork

KSMM

Factors to consider when saving or investing

There are various options for where you save your money. The factors you should consider before deciding where to save your money are:

> Risk
> Reward
> Liquidity
> Taxation

> Convenience
> Benefits
> Terms and conditions.

Risk

Will your savings be **safe and secure**? Money saved in a licensed financial institution (e.g. bank, building society, post office, credit union) is far safer than money kept in a drawer or even a safe at home.

Savings with An Post are 'State guaranteed', which means they are 100% secure and will definitely be repaid by the government.

Reward

Will the savings **earn interest**?

Interest is a reward for saving your money with a financial institution. It is extra money you will receive on top of the money you have saved.

Definition

All financial institutions offer slightly different rates of interest. Savers may have to shop around to get the best deal.

The rate quoted by the financial institutions is the **annual equivalent rate (AER)**. This tells the saver the full rate of interest if all of the money is left in a savings account for a full year.

Liquidity

Is it easy to withdraw or access your savings should you need to? That is, how quickly can it be turned back into cash?

Some savings accounts require you to give the financial institution written notice, and penalties may apply if you withdraw earlier than the terms agreed. For example, a twenty-one-day notice deposit account requires the saver to give the bank twenty-one days' notice of their intention to withdraw money. An Post Savings Bonds offer a higher rate of interest than most savings schemes, but this is greatly reduced if the money is withdrawn within three years.

Taxation

Will you have to pay tax on your interest? **Deposit Interest Retention Tax (DIRT)** is a tax on interest earned on savings. Some savings products offered by An Post are not subject to DIRT, e.g. Savings Certificates and Savings Bonds.

Convenience

Is the account convenient for making regular lodgements and withdrawals? For example, is the financial institution located conveniently? What are its opening hours?

Many banks provide online savings accounts for customers, which makes it easy to transfer money into them. Once the savings account is set up, it might be most convenient to transfer money into it regularly by setting up a standing order.

See Chapter 8

Future benefits

Will you qualify for future benefits, including loans or bonus interest payments?

If you save in a financial institution that you may want to borrow from in the future you will have a history of saving with them. This might make it easier for you to get a loan.

Terms and conditions

Are there fees and banking charges involved in operating a deposit account? Is there a minimum/maximum deposit required? Will you be penalised for withdrawing money early?

> **9.6** In pairs, one of you be an interviewer and one of you be a 'financial expert'. Create a podcast or video of questions and answers for the factors you need to think about when deciding where to save your money. Alternatively, you can create a poster or infographic.

T-P-S

KSWwO
KSC
KSBC

Where to save

Money can be saved in the following financial institutions in Ireland:

> Commercial banks
> An Post
> Credit unions
> Building societies.

Commercial banks

A commercial bank offers a range of financial services to its customers. They all offer deposit accounts.

 See Chapter 8

Opening a savings account

You looked at how to open a current account in chapter 8. Opening a savings account is very similar, and you will need to provide proof of identity and address.

 KSMIT

> **9.7** What proof do you need to provide to open an account with a financial institution?

Types of deposit account offered by commercial banks

You can choose from a wide range of savings accounts, depending on how much you want to save and how soon you want to access your money. The interest earned on all deposit accounts is subject to DIRT.

> **Demand deposits** allow you to withdraw (or demand) your money when you choose to. You do not have to give the bank any notice of a withdrawal. Demand deposit accounts typically pay a very low rate of interest.

> **Term deposits** require you to leave your money in the account for a certain length of time. The agreed timeframe (or term) could be anything from seven days to five years. Term deposits will carry a higher rate of interest than demand deposits. It may be possible to withdraw money early, but there will be a penalty for doing so – a lower rate of interest will be applied.

> **Notice deposits** require that you give the bank advance notice of your intention to withdraw money. For example a twenty-one-day-notice deposit account means that the saver must notify the bank twenty-one (banking) days in advance of a withdrawal.

As a general rule, **the greater the liquidity, the lower the rate of interest paid**. Therefore those savers who are in a position to leave their money in the bank for long periods of time will be able to get the highest rates of interest.

 KSMIT

> **9.8** Why do you think financial institutions are willing to pay higher rates of interest to those who agree to leave their savings in a deposit account for longer?

An Post

An Post offers a range of state savings products on behalf of the National Treasury Management Agency (NTMA). These offer competitive rates of interest and are State-guaranteed. In some cases, the interest earned is not subject to DIRT.

As well as a range of deposit accounts, An Post offers **Prize Bonds**. These offer thousands of weekly prizes, and a €1 million tax-free prize in the last draw of every quarter. Prize Bonds do not earn interest but are eligible to win prizes every week.

Credit unions

Credit unions are located all over the country and there is probably one in your local area. A credit union is owned by the members, a group of people in an area, association or workplace who save together (by 'buying' shares in the organisation) and lend to each other at a competitive rate of interest.

Credit unions offer savings accounts and some branches also offer deposit accounts. Your savings are your shares, so the more savings you have, the more shares in the organisation you own.

Savings accounts: Saving in this type of account may give you a **dividend** at the end of the year. Money can be lodged at any time to this account.

> A **dividend** is a payment to shareholders that is proportional to the number of shares owned. It will not be the same amount every payout, as the amount will depend on the available money and the number of people it has to be shared between.

Definition

Deposit accounts: You will receive a competitive rate of interest from a deposit account, but interest on deposits in credit unions is subject to DIRT.

As credit unions are community-based, you will be helping your community by being a member.

If you save with a credit union you can apply for a personal loan for many things, including to buy a car, improve your home or go on a holiday.

Building societies

A building society pays interest on savings and lends money for buying or upgrading property. A building society offers a wide range of services, similar to a bank.

They offer a competitive rate of interest on their savings and they have branches located all over the country. The main reason to save in a building society is to get a mortgage. An example of a building society in Ireland is the Educational Building Society (EBS).

9.9 Using the template in the Student Activity Book to guide you, in small groups compare savings options in each type of financial institution, e.g. credit union, building society, commercial bank, An Post. In your group, choose one type of financial institution and create a group poster to display your findings.

Groupwork

Research

KSMIT
KSWwO
KSC
KSBC

Calculating interest on savings

Interest is a reward for saving money with a financial institution. There are two ways to calculate interest you receive on your savings:

> Simple interest
> Compound interest.

Simple interest

Simple interest (also known as **flat rate of interest**) is money you can earn by investing money (the principal). A percentage (the interest) of the principal is added to the principal, making your money grow.

The simple interest formula is:

Interest = Principal × Rate × Time

Formula

Example

Megan saves €1,000 at a rate of 2% for two years:

Interest = 1,000 × 2% × 2 = €40

KSBN

9.10 Calculate the simple interest for each of the following:

(a) Paul saves €500 for three years at an interest rate of 2%.

(b) John saves €5,000 for five years at an interest rate of 3.5%.

(c) Katherine saves €2,250 for four and a half years at an interest rate of 2.75%.

Compound interest

Compound interest is when interest is added to the savings and that added interest also earns interest from then on. This means that as well as getting interest on their principal, the saver is earning interest on their interest. For this reason compound interest will reward savers with more interest than simple interest savings schemes.

KSBN

9.11 Calculate the compound interest on each of the following.

(a) €1,000 saved for two years at an annual 4% compound interest.

(b) €6,000 saved for three years at an annual 3% compound interest.

(c) €3,750 saved for five years at an annual 4.25% compound interest.

Example showing the difference between simple interest and compound interest

Mary Daly has €2,000 saved in her deposit account. Interest is calculated at 5% per annum. How much will she receive in her account after (a) one year (b) two years and (c) three years with (i) simple interest and (ii) compound interest?

Solution

Interest earned at simple interest rate (5%)			Interest earned at compound interest rate (5%)		
	Amount	**Interest**		**Amount**	**Interest**
Year 1	€2,000	€100.00	Year 1	€2,000	€100.00
Year 2	€2,000	€100.00	Year 2	€2,100	€105.00
Year 3	€2,000	€100.00	Year 3	€2,205	€110.25
Total interest		**€300.00**	**Total interest**		**€315.25**
Note: Interest earned is based on the original amount deposited; therefore, the annual interest payment will not change.			**Note:** The interest from the previous year is added to the principal before the current year's interest is calculated and so interest is paid on a higher amount each year, increasing the amount of interest paid.		

Annual equivalent rate (AER)

AER shows you the real interest you will have gained on savings at the end of a year. It is standard practice in Ireland for financial institutions to show these rates and they provide a good way for savers to compare different financial institutions.

AER is the rate of interest you could earn on your savings in a year with a compound interest rate. That doesn't mean you have to keep your money in the account for a year, but this is what you would earn if you did. It is useful for comparing the return on savings accounts because it shows how much would be earned no matter how often interest is credited to the account. AER is usually given without taking DIRT into account.

If we look at our Mary Daly example again, but this time compare the annual rate of 5% with 5% a year compounded every six months, our table looks like this:

Interest earned at compound interest rate (5%)			Interest earned at compound interest rate (5%) compounded every six months		
	Amount	**Interest**		**Amount**	**Interest**
			After 6 months	€2,000	@ 2.5% = €50.00
After 1 year	€2,000	€100	After 1 year	€2,050	@ 2.5% = €51.25
Total interest		**€100**	**Total interest**		€101.25
Note: Interest rate (AER) = (100 ÷ 2,000) × 100 = 5%			**Note:** Interest rate (AER) = (101.25 ÷ 2,000) × 100 = 5.06%		

9.12 (a) Which is a better investment over a year, assuming DIRT does not have to be paid? Show your calculations.

    (i) €5,000 in a savings account with simple interest at 4.5%.

    (ii) €6,000 in a savings account with compound interest at 4%, compounded every three months.

  (b) What is the AER for both the above?

Deposit Interest Retention Tax (DIRT)

DIRT is a **tax on the interest earned** on deposit accounts. It is deducted by the bank at source and transferred to the Office of the Revenue Commissioners, which collects all tax in Ireland. The account holder is credited with the net interest, i.e. interest minus DIRT.

Example

Louise Hughes has €2,000 saved in a bank. Simple interest is 5% per annum and Louise must pay 41% DIRT on interest earned. How much DIRT does she pay and how much does she have in her account after one year?

Solution

Calculate interest   €2,000 @ 5% = €100 interest

Calculate DIRT   €100 @ 41% = €41 DIRT

Interest received   = €59 net

Louise now has €2,000 + €59 = €2,059 in her account.

9.13 Assume you have €2,000 that you want to save for two years. Where would you place your money and why?

9.14 You work out that you can afford to save €20 a month, every month. What type of account would you open? Give reasons for your answer.

9.15 (a) From the budgets and cash analyses you have completed in previous chapters, how much could you afford to save every week or month? Decide on a figure that you could easily save and decide on a figure that you could manage if you were strict with your other spending.

  (b) Where would you save, and what type of account would you choose? Explain your choices.

9.16 Discuss at what age or time of life you think people should start to save.

9.17 You learned in chapter 8 that when you put money into a savings account, the financial institution invests that money in order to make profits. Would you prefer that those investments are ethical or should the financial institution go for the best monetary return?

Discussion

KSWwO
KSC
KSMIT
KSSW

Key Terms

KSBL
KSC
KSMIT
KSBC

You should be able to *define*, *spell*, give *examples* and *apply* to real life each of the following key terms associated with this topic.

Exercise: Write a sentence using each of the following terms. You may use more than one of the terms in your sentence if appropriate.

An Post	investing
annual equivalent rate (AER)	liquidity
building society	notice deposit
commercial bank	principal
compound interest	rate
credit union	risk
demand deposit	savings
Deposit Interest Retention Tax (DIRT)	simple interest
interest	term deposit

Chapter 10 ::
Borrowing for Households and Individuals

Should we borrow money?

Neither a borrower nor a lender be,

For loan oft loses both itself and friend.

Hamlet, William Shakespeare

10.1 What does the saying from *Hamlet* mean? Do you think it is good advice? Give one reason to support your point of view.

KSBL
KSC
KSMIT

It may not always be possible to purchase everything we need (or want) out of the money available to us. In chapter 5 we saw that households sometimes have budget deficits because their planned expenditure is greater than the money they can earn and save.

See Chapter 5

One solution to this cash shortfall is to borrow the money we need.

Borrowing means receiving money from a person or financial institution, in exchange for an obligation to pay back the money, with interest, at an agreed time in the future.

Definition

Interest is therefore the **financial cost** of borrowing money.

Since borrowing money has costs, it needs to be considered very carefully. The borrower must understand all the costs and consequences involved. Sensible questions to ask before borrowing are:

> **10.2** Borrowing also has an *opportunity cost*. What could that be?

> › **Do I really need the item?** If the item is not essential, it would be better to do without it or to save for it. Perhaps there is a cheaper alternative.

> › **Can I get the money any other way, without resorting to borrowing?** If it is possible to delay the purchase you could save some or all of the money needed. The more you save, the less you will have to borrow and repay.

> › **How much will it cost?** If you have to borrow money to buy an item, it will add to the price because you will be charged interest on the loan. For example, if you have to borrow the money to buy a car costing €20,000, the real cost to you may be €23,000 when you take interest into account.

> › **Can I afford the repayments?** Your income must be sufficient to repay the instalments. How would you cope if you lost your job or the rate of interest increased?

An **instalment** is a fixed sum of money due as one of a number of payments spread over an agreed period of time

Definition

10.3 If there was something you really wanted to buy that cost €150, which you don't have, would you:

(a) Save up for it by not spending any money you didn't need to (e.g. *no treats*) to save the money in the shortest possible time?

(b) Save up for it but still allow yourself to spend a little money on treats, even though it would take a little longer to save the full amount?

(c) Borrow the money so you could have the item now, but you will be paying back the loan for two years and end up paying €225 because of the interest?

Give reasons for your answer.

T-P-S

KSC
KSMIT
KSMM
KSSW

Reasons for (household) borrowing

Although it is nearly always best if you don't have to borrow, sometimes it is necessary, such as in the following circumstances.

> › **To pay for very expensive items:** It is very difficult for most people to buy outright a high-cost item such as a car or house. A loan or mortgage may be your only realistic option to raise the finance needed. You will have to repay the money over a number of years but you will eventually own a valuable asset.

An **asset** is anything owned by a person or business that has a monetary value.

Definition

> **To deal with short-term deficits:** If a household is facing a budget deficit and doesn't have sufficient savings to make up the difference, they may have no option but to look for short-term finance.

> **For emergencies:** From time to time things will go wrong or break down and households may need to borrow money to pay for repairs or unexpected costs. Although good financial planning will allow the household to use savings to cover

See Chapter 9

See Chapter 11

the cost of the emergency without the need to borrow money, sometimes this type of borrowing is important and necessary at the time. Insurance cover can also be useful to deal with some of these unexpected problems.

10.4 Discuss which, if any, of the following you think are good reasons to borrow money.

Discussion

KSWwO
KSC
KSMIT
KSMM
KSSW

(a) To buy a house.

(b) To buy a second home.

(c) To go on holiday.

(d) To pay for special occasions (Christmas, birthdays, etc.).

(e) To pay for college fees.

(f) To pay household / utility bills.

(g) To buy a new TV.

(h) To pay for your wedding.

(i) To pay for an emergency operation.

(j) To provide money until next pay day.

(k) To pay a tax bill.

Borrowing money

Borrowers need to match the type of loan with the type of need. The **matching principle** ensures that short-, medium- and long-term needs are matched with appropriate short-, medium- and long-term sources of finance. These are explained in table 10.1.

Table 10.1 The matching principle

Need	Example	Repayment duration	Source of finance
Short term	Budget deficit	Within one year	Bank overdraft, credit card
Medium term	Purchase of a new car	One to five years	Medium-term loan, hire purchase, leasing
Long term	Purchase of a house	More than five years	Mortgage

Types of borrowing for households and individuals

Short term

Bank overdrafts

A current account holder is given permission to withdraw more money from their account than they actually have in it. Borrowing is allowed up to a specific limit. Overdrafts are available from banks, building societies and credit unions.

See Chapter 8

Did you know?

According to the Central Statistics Office (CSO) Household Finance and Consumption Survey, which offered an insight into the financial state of Irish homes in 2013, the average amount of debt on an overdraft in 2013 was €1,000. Around 10% of households had an overdraft, but this rose to 18% for self-employed people.

The average overdraft for a self-employed person was €4,000, compared to €700 for an unemployed person.

10.5 Why, do you think, are self-employed people more likely to need an overdraft than people in regular employment?

KSMIT

Bank overdrafts are expected to be reduced over the allowed term, with interest charged periodically. By gradually reducing the overdraft it should get paid off over time.

10.6 What will be the consequence of not reducing the amount of the overdraft, or of reducing it only slightly, by the time its end date is reached?

KSMIT
KSBN
KSMM
KSSW

Credit card

Cardholders can buy items now and pay for them at a later date. Interest rates on credit card debt can be very high, which makes this an expensive source of short-term finance.

See Chapter 8

10.7 Credit cards are very useful to have, but they also need to be used with caution. What are the benefits and potential drawbacks of using credit cards?

KSMIT
KSMM
KSSW

Medium term

Medium-term loan

This source of finance can be accessed from a range of financial institutions including banks, building societies and credit unions. Borrowers generally make fixed repayments on a monthly basis over an agreed time period. These monthly payments cover repayment of the loan plus interest.

Hire purchase (HP)

Hire purchase is a medium-term source of finance in which the purchaser pays a deposit followed by an agreed number of fixed regular instalments. **Ownership of the asset will eventually pass to the hirer, but not until payment of the last instalment**. There is no security required but the rate will be very high (possibly well in excess of 20%). For that reason HP is often used as a last resort by those who cannot get a medium-term loan.

Hire purchase example

The Hanlons wish to buy a washing machine from Kitchen Electrics Ltd under a hire purchase arrangement. A finance company will pay Kitchen Electrics Ltd the full price of the washing machine and the Hanlons will then repay the finance company in regular instalments over a fixed period of time.

The washing machine belongs to the finance company until the Hanlons pay the last instalment.

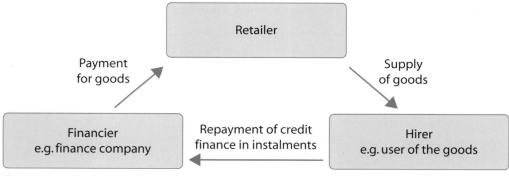

Figure 10.1 How hire purchase works

The hirer has the right to withdraw from the agreement within ten days of receiving a copy of the agreement. This is known as a **cooling-off period**.

Leasing

Leasing involves the renting of an asset (e.g. vehicles).

The lease agreement allows a household or individual to have immediate possession and use of the asset provided they make fixed, regular payments to the leasing company.

The household/individual will never own the asset, which always remains the property of the leasing company.

KSBN

10.8 Mary wants to buy a new television that will cost her €2,000. She does not have the money saved, so she has two options to get the television.

Option 1: Hire purchase – Pay a deposit of €400 plus €150 per month for one year.

Option 2: Rent the TV for €50 per week.

(a) What is the total cost of hire purchase?

(b) What is the total rent for a year?

(c) Which option would you choose? Explain your choice.

Long-term

Long-term loan/mortgage

Households and individuals generally use a special long-term loan called a **mortgage** for buying property. Mortgages are available from commercial banks and building societies.

Did you know?

The word mortgage comes from two old French words meaning 'dead' and 'pledge', so a mortgage is a *dead pledge*. There are two reasons why the word 'mortgage' is used for a secured loan: the first is that the debt becomes void or 'dead' when the pledge (promise to pay) has been fulfilled; the second is that if the person doing the pledging (the mortgagor) fails to repay the loan, the property pledged as security becomes 'dead' to him or her (i.e. it now belongs to the person doing the lending).

When a borrower takes out a mortgage they are entering into a contract with a lender to repay the loan plus interest. They are also agreeing to use their home as collateral for the loan. If they don't repay the debt, the lender can sell the property to recover the outstanding debt.

Mortgages typically have repayment periods of between fifteen and thirty years. Loan rates on mortgages are lower than on medium-term loans but the total cost of the mortgage will be much higher because the repayment period is so long.

Borrowing from moneylenders

Moneylenders are individuals or companies (excluding banks, building societies and credit unions) whose main business is to lend money. In Ireland, moneylenders must have a licence to lend money. Those moneylenders who do not have a licence are breaking the law and are called 'unlicensed moneylenders'.

Licensed moneylenders are subject to strict rules and regulations. Unlicensed moneylenders are not regulated and may charge very high rates of interest (up to 188% APR) and place borrowers under a lot of pressure to repay debts quickly. **For these reasons it is advisable to avoid unlicensed lenders.**

The Central Bank of Ireland issues moneylending licences in Ireland and is responsible for regulating the industry.

Moneylenders must provide the following to the borrower:

› A moneylending agreement giving detailed information about the loan.

› An explanation that the loan has a high cost.

› A ten-day cooling-off period. During this time the borrower can change their mind and may decide not to go ahead with the loan, in which case the borrower should inform the lender in writing that they have decided not to proceed with the loan.

› A repayment book, which states the total amount of the loan and the total number of repayments due. Each time a payment is made, the amount and date must be written into the book.

› A record of each lending agreement, kept by the moneylender.

In the news

'It Makes Sense' loans

In 2015 a microcredit scheme was launched in over thirty credit unions to reduce dependence on moneylenders. This proved so successful that the scheme is being extended (from August 2016) to all credit unions that sign up for it.

It Makes Sense loans are available to people receiving social welfare payments who may not be able to get credit from other sources. Loan values are between €100 and €2,000 and the maximum interest rate is 1% per month, or 12% per year (12.68% APR).

Source: Information from citizensinformation.ie

Applying for a loan from a financial institution

Money can be borrowed from the following financial institutions in Ireland:

› Commercial banks   › Credit unions   › Building societies.

It is important not to borrow on impulse. Take time to consider answers to the following important questions:

› How much money do I need to borrow?

› What can I afford to pay back each week or month?

› How long do I need to repay the money?

› Where can I get the best rates of interest?

You will need to contact the financial institution that you are hoping to get a loan from, either by making a personal appointment or by seeking pre-approval online.

You will need to fill out a loan application form and provide the following information:

> **Personal details:** name, address, date of birth, etc. A person must be over 18 before they can borrow money from a financial institution.

> **Residential details:** your address; whether you rent or have a mortgage.

> **Employment details:** you will be asked for your most recent payslips to see how much you earn. You might also need to supply your most recent P60 (this is an end-of-year tax statement issued by your employer that shows your annual earnings).

> **Savings record:** lenders like to see a history of saving.

See Chapter 12

> **Borrowing history:** lenders like to see evidence that you have repaid previous loans on time and in full.

> **Purpose of the loan:** you may have to provide details and costings, for example if you are building a house, carrying out home improvements or buying a car.

If a loan is taken out by more than one person, each person will have to provide the above information.

Creditworthiness

Before granting a loan, the financial institution will check your creditworthiness.

> **Creditworthiness** is an estimate of the ability of a person to pay off a loan, based on their saving and borrowing history with financial institutions.

Your creditworthiness will also be examined if you apply for a credit card or a hire purchase agreement.

Your creditworthiness can be proved from your bank statements and also by a report from the **Irish Credit Bureau (ICB)**.

Your creditworthiness: information from the ICB

1 What affects my getting a loan?

Most lenders look for information about your income, employment, living costs and existing loan repayments to help them decide whether you can afford to repay a loan. Most lenders also want to look at your creditworthiness. It can be a good indication of how likely

IRISH CREDIT BUREAU

you are to pay back the money. You are likely to have a positive creditworthiness if you have a good history of repayment on previous loans. Your credit record may be poor if you missed repayments on a regular basis or failed to pay off a loan in the past.

2 How do lenders know about my previous loans?

Most lenders in Ireland send information about borrowers and their repayments to a central agency, the Irish Credit Bureau (ICB). The ICB holds information about borrowers and their loans for five years after the loan is concluded. This information is held in an individual credit 'report' that is kept by the ICB about each borrower.

Your credit report includes:

> Your name, date of birth, address(es) used by you in relation to financial transactions
> The names of lenders and account numbers of loans you currently hold, or that were active within the last five years
> Repayments made or missed for each month on each loan
> The failure to clear off any loan
> Loans that were settled for less than you owed
> Legal actions your lender took against you.

So the ICB's information reflects a full picture of your credit history, **good** and/or **bad**.

3 Is my lender allowed to check my credit history?

When you sign a mortgage or loan application you also give your lender permission (consent) to send information about your repayments to a credit reference agency such as ICB, and to seek information about your credit history. If your credit history is poor, a lender is unlikely to give you a loan even if you have the income to repay it. However, even if your credit history is excellent, you still may not be given a loan if, in the view of the lender, you have reached your repayment limit.

Source: Adapted from www.icb.ie

10.9 There is a house for sale for €200,000. Three parties are interested in it, but they all need a loan. All of them are first-time buyers, which means they need at least a 20% deposit to buy the house.

   (a) Pat has a good job and can easily afford the mortgage repayments each month. At the moment he is living rent-free with his parents and has no savings, but his parents have offered to give him €40,000 of the house value as a deposit.

   (b) Enda and Siobhan have savings of €45,000 for a deposit. Only Siobhan is bringing home a salary at the moment, a third of which goes on paying rent on the couple's apartment. Enda has not yet paid off a loan that should have finished five years ago and he has credit card debt of €16,500. Siobhan has two credit cards with a total debt of €8,950; for three months earlier this year she was late with repayments.

(c) Julie and Rachel have savings of €40,000. Julie had a loan in the past that was paid regularly every month and completely paid off a year ago. Rachel has a credit card with €600 owing on it, but no charges for late payments. Rachel is renting an apartment and Julie is currently living with her parents, paying them €300 a month rent.

How do you think lenders would look upon the three loan applications based on the above information? Give reasons for your answer in each case.

If the lender is unhappy with your credit history or your ability to repay, you may be asked to get a guarantor.

A **guarantor** is a person of good financial standing who agrees to repay a loan for you should you be unable or unwilling to do so.

Definition

For example if you need to get a loan for college but do not have a regular source of income, the bank may allow your parents to sign as guarantors for the loan. This means your parents are now liable for your debt if you default on repayments. To become guarantors, your parents would have to prove their creditworthiness.

In the news

Students beware gimmicks and lure of easy credit

By Fiona Reddan

Many get out loans to cover fees and living costs, but sooner or later it's payback time.

Banks are often far more generous in their lending practices with students than they are with people who actually have an income. But if you're a student looking for access to credit, remember that while it may be easy to come by, it can be a lot more difficult to repay. If you fall behind on repayments during your student years, this may affect your credit rating in later years and your ability to get a mortgage or car loan.

Consider the example of a student who applies for the loan for each year of their undergraduate degree. While monthly payments will come to just under €150 a month over eight years, the cost of credit will come to a significant €2,271.32. So, those €12,000 contribution charges have now turned into a €14,271 charge.

Source: Article adapted from the Irish Times, 18 August 2015

The financial institution may also ask for **collateral** if you are getting a loan.

> **Collateral** is something used as security for repayment of a loan. If you cannot pay back the loan, the financial institution can take the asset, e.g. the title deeds to property, and sell it to recover the money owed by you.
>
> **Definition**

Financial institutions are more likely to lend to households if the **risk is shared**. This usually requires the borrower to part-finance the project with some of their own money. For example, the O'Donoghues want to build an extension on their house that costs €22,000; the bank agrees to lend them €18,000 if the O'Donoghues use €4,000 of their own money for the balance of the cost.

Lenders often **stress test** each client's ability to repay the proposed loan. Stress testing a loan application looks at the change to monthly repayments if interest rates were to increase. If a very high proportion of disposable income is committed to loan repayments the lender may conclude that a smaller loan or longer time period is more appropriate.

Money Advice and Budgeting Service (MABS)

MABS is the state's money advice service. It guides people through dealing with problems in paying money they owe and helps them manage their money. MABS provides a free and confidential service. Money advisers for the organisation provide practical help to people in debt. The MABS website contains a useful budgeting tool to help manage your finances and avoid getting into debt.

The Insolvency Service of Ireland (ISI)

The ISI is an independent statutory body that was set up by the Personal Insolvency Act (2012). It is responsible for all matters concerning personal insolvency.

> Being **insolvent** means being unable to pay your debts as they fall due.
>
> **Definition**

Instalment costs

When you take out a loan with a financial institution you will agree a time limit before the loan is approved. You will need to determine **how much you can afford to pay back each month**.

The **longer the repayment period, the more it will cost** since interest will continue to be charged until the loan is repaid. What may appear to be a good reason for a loan at the beginning may eventually become a burden later.

If, on the other hand, **the repayment period is short, the monthly repayments will be high**, which may have a major impact on household cash flow. For example, a €20,000 car loan will have monthly repayments of around €410 if repaid in five years, but may be about €630 per month if repaid in just three years. The interest and therefore the overall cost will be less, but the strain on the household in the meantime may not make it worthwhile.

Make sure you will be able to keep up the monthly amounts for the duration of the loan before agreeing to it. This is **responsible borrowing.**

Responsible borrowing means that you do not borrow more than you are able to pay back.

10.10 The Murphy family wanted to go on a sun holiday for two weeks. The only way they could afford it was to take out a loan that would take three years to pay off.

(a) Discuss how you think they would feel, still paying off the loan long after the suntan and the holiday memories have faded.

(b) What do you think would be a better timeframe for paying off a loan for a holiday?

(c) Discuss whether a holiday is a good reason for taking out a loan.

KSWwO
KSSW
KSMM
KSC

10.11 How can you ensure that you can afford to repay the loan?

KSMIT
KSBN

10.12 Ben wants to renovate his kitchen. He has had a quote from a kitchen company for €7,800. Ben has worked out that his disposable income will enable him to repay a loan for this amount in one year as long as he goes out less, doesn't take a holiday and spends the minimum on household bills for the year.

Discuss the danger of Ben using up all his spare income on loan repayments.

KSWwO
KSSW
KSMM

How to calculate interest

Interest on loans is shown as an annual percentage rate (APR).

> The **annual percentage rate** is a calculation of the overall cost of a loan and represents the actual yearly cost of the amount borrowed. It takes into account all the costs during the term of the loan including any set-up charges and the interest rate. Fees and charges are added to the loan amount before interest is calculated.

 **Definition**

The higher the APR, the more it will cost you to borrow money. APR is calculated each year on the declining principal of a loan.

> The **declining principal** is the amount you still owe at any point during the loan. It is getting lower every month because of repayments.

 **Definition**

You can use the APR to compare loans that are for the **same amount and the same term**. For example, a loan of €20,000 over 15 years with an APR of 17% will cost more than a loan of €20,000 over 15 years with an APR of 12%. APR is not suitable for comparing loans of different terms – if the terms are different you should look at the cost of credit.

> The **cost of credit** is the real cost of borrowing, i.e. the difference between the amount you borrow and the total you repay.

Definition

Calculating APR

Example 1

Credit Union Education Loan: €600 at 8.5% APR over four years, with the loan amount to reduce by €150 each year (i.e. the repayments must reduce the loan by this much as well as pay the interest). Calculate the total cost of the loan.

Solution

		Interest
Year 1	€600 × 8.5%	€51.00
Year 2	€600 − €150 = €450 × 8.5%	€38.25
Year 3	€450 − €150 = €300 × 8.5%	€25.50
Year 4	€300 − €150 = €150 × 8.5%	€12.75
Total paid = €600 + €51 + €38.25 + €25.50 + €12.75 = €727.50		
Cost of credit = €127.50 (€727.50 − €600)		

Example 2

Mary decides to buy a car for €6,000. She has the following options:

Option 1: Hire purchase: €400 deposit and thirty-five instalments of €240 each.

Option 2: Loan: €6,000 at 10.5% APR over four years, with the loan amount to reduce by €1,500 each year.

(i) Calculate the total cost of each option.

(ii) Which option is better?

Solution

Option 1 – hire purchase (€6,000)		Option 2 – loan (€6,000)		
Deposit	€400.00	Year 1	€6,000 × 10.5%	€630.00
35 instalments × €240	€8,400.00	Year 2	€4,500 × 10.5%	€472.50
Total paid	€8,800.00	Year 3	€3,000 × 10.5%	€315.00
		Year 4	€1,500 × 10.5%	€157.50
		Total interest		€1,575.00
		Payments per year	4 × €1,500	€6,000.00
		Total paid		€7,575.00
Cost of credit = €2,800		**Cost of credit = €1,575**		

Option 2 is the better option as the interest payments are cheaper/lower.

10.13 Donal needs to borrow €16,000 to buy a new car. He is looking at two options and wants to calculate how much each would cost him before choosing which to apply for. The options are:

    (i) 9.75% APR over four years.

    (ii) 8.5% APR over five years.

(a) What is the cost of credit in each case?

(b) If repayments were evenly distributed over the loan term, in each case how much would Donal pay each month (to the nearest cent)?

(c) If Donal could afford no more than €360 each month, which option will he have to apply for?

(d) How much extra is it going to cost him to apply for this loan rather than the other?

Rights of a borrower

A borrower has the right to:

> Written details of the agreement.

> A cooling-off period of ten days.

> Be informed of the APR.

> Know what the cash price and total credit price are for the product, e.g. a car.

> Know the number of instalments and the amount of each one.

> Be made aware of any fees or penalties for paying off the loan early.

Discussion

10.14 Mark's friend Nysa runs a payroll service. Mark asks Nysa if she will print out some false payslips that he can show the bank when he is applying for a long-term loan, as the bank will consider that he doesn't earn enough to lend him the money on his real salary.

Discuss whether or not Mark is right to do this. How do you think Nysa might feel about being asked?

KSWwO
KSSW
KSMIT
KSC

Risks of borrowing

You may not be able to repay the amount borrowed (plus interest) due to a change in circumstances. If this occurs:

> You may lose the item you used as collateral.

> You may be taken to court and risk a fine or prison sentence.

> Your creditworthiness will be affected, which will reduce your ability to get future loans.

Key Terms

KSBL
KSC
KSMIT
KSBC

You should be able to *define*, *spell*, give *examples* and *apply* to real life each of the following key terms associated with this topic.

Exercise: Write a sentence using each of the following terms. You may use more than one of the terms in your sentence if appropriate.

annual percentage rate (APR)

asset

bank overdraft

borrowing

collateral

cooling-off period

credit card

creditworthiness

declining principal

guarantor

hire purchase

Insolvency Service of Ireland

instalment

Irish Credit Bureau (ICB)

leasing

matching principle

medium-term loan

Money Advice and Budgeting Service (MABS)

moneylender

mortgage

personal loan

responsible borrowing

security

stress test

Chapter 11 ::
Insurance for Households and Individuals

Learning outcomes

When you have completed this chapter you will be able to:

✔ Explain what insurance is
✔ Outline the principles of insurance
✔ Determine the types of household/personal insurance that you may need at different times
✔ Identify jobs in the insurance industry
✔ Complete insurance documentation
✔ Calculate a premium.

What is insurance?

> **Definition**
>
> **Insurance** offers **financial protection against possible loss** and is designed to place the insured person back in the same financial position they were in before the loss occurred.

It is important to understand that insurance can only ever provide *financial* compensation for losses, and it may not always be possible to restore people's lives to the way they had been before an accident or loss.

Insurance is based on the sharing of risk and requires many people to pay a small amount called a **premium** into a fund to cover a particular risk. This fund is managed by an insurance company and is used to pay **compensation** to claimants and to cover insurance company expenses. Any remaining money represents a profit for the insurance company.

Figure 11.1 How insurance works

A **premium** is the amount charged by an insurer in return for providing insurance cover for a particular risk.

Compensation is a financial payment made to an insured person if they suffer an insured loss.

Definitions

11.1 The concept of pooling of risk is very important. If people were to falsely claim on an insurance policy, what effect would this have on all the other people who are insured?

KSMIT

Figure 11.2 Some of the companies and brokers providing insurance in Ireland

Principles of insurance

All insurance is based on five basic rules or principles. They are:

> Insurable interest
> Utmost good faith
> Indemnity
> Subrogation
> Contribution.

1 Insurable interest

To insure something, you must benefit by its existence and suffer (financially) from its loss.

For example, a householder can insure their own property and possessions because they have an insurable interest in those items. They will suffer a financial loss if these items are stolen or damaged. The householder does not, however, have the same insurable interest in their neighbour's property and will not be able to insure that against loss or damage.

2 Utmost good faith

When applying for insurance, all material facts relating to the policy must be disclosed to the insurance company.

> A **material fact** is anything that is likely to alter the decision to grant insurance or to affect the level of premium charged.

Definition

You *must answer all questions truthfully* when completing the proposal forms and disclose all relevant information. For example, if you are asked about penalty points when you are applying for motor insurance and you declare that you have none, but in fact have eight, the insurance company may not pay out on an insurance claim as you have not been truthful about all relevant information.

3 Indemnity

A profit cannot be made from insurance. This is the most important rule of insurance and recognises that insurance exists to put the insured person back in the same financial position as they were in before suffering the loss, but not in a better financial position.

For example, if a car valued at €10,000 is stolen, the maximum amount of compensation that will be paid is €10,000.

4 Subrogation

Once an insurance company has paid compensation for any insured item, the right of ownership of that item passes to the insurance company. As a result they are entitled to any scrap or salvage value that remains.

For example, if the insurance company pays €10,000 compensation for a vehicle that is a 'write-off', the insurance company takes ownership of the damaged vehicle. The insured person is now in the same financial position as before the accident and can use the compensation payment to replace the damaged vehicle. The insurance company now owns the damaged vehicle and may be able to sell it for its scrap value, say €800, thereby reducing the cost of the claim.

Note that if the original owner of the vehicle got this €800 in addition to the €10,000 compensation, they would have received a total of €10,800 for a vehicle which was only worth €10,000. This would represent a profit on the claim and would breach the principle of indemnity.

> An insurance **write-off** means that the cost of repairing the damaged item is greater than the item's replacement value.

Definition

The insurance company is also entitled to sue any third party responsible for the loss in order to recover any compensation paid.

For example, an electrician rewires a house that burns down a short time later. An investigation finds that the wiring was faulty and that the electrician is to blame for the fire. The householder's insurance company will settle the compensation claim with the home owner but will take a legal action against the electrician to recover the money paid out.

5 Contribution

Where the same risk is insured with more than one insurer they will divide the cost of the claim between them.

The total compensation paid will not exceed the value of the item (the principle of indemnity). The amount paid by each insurance company will be proportionate to the risk insured by each of them.

For example, a homeowner insures their house for €350,000 with two different insurance companies. In the event that the house is completely destroyed by fire, the homeowner may claim the entire €350,000 compensation from one insurer, or may claim half the money (€175,000) from each insurance company.

11.2 In each case below, identify in your copy which principle has been broken.

(a) Derek's car is written off in a car park accident. He expects to receive the full amount of its worth of €4,500, but he removes some parts and makes another €1,000 by selling them before the insurance company sends someone to collect the vehicle.

(b) Kylie's antique vase was valued at €5,750. On the insurance form she says it is worth €9,000. When it is stolen she expects to receive €9,000 from her insurance company.

(c) Paddy's friend Jack parks his car in front of Paddy's house every day. As this is very close to a junction, Paddy is sure the car will be hit by another vehicle one day and sees an opportunity to try to make a few euro, so he insures Jack's car.

(d) Gwen has insured her engagement ring, which is worth €8,000. When it is stolen from her fiancé's house she makes a claim with her insurance company for €8,000. Her boyfriend also makes a claim for the ring on his household insurance.

(e) Collette takes her dog Bobby for his annual booster and after examining him the vet says that it is likely that in a few months' time Bobby will need to go on heart tablets. Collette thinks this could get expensive so she takes out pet insurance but doesn't say on the form that Bobby has been diagnosed with a heart complaint.

KSBL
KSMIT

Types of household and personal insurance

It would be too expensive for a household or individual to take out *all* types of insurance available. Each person has to decide which types of policies meet their needs and financial resources. Here we look at the most common types of insurance for households and individuals.

Life assurance

Assurance is protection against a *certain* future loss; in the case of life assurance, this means death. A life assurance policy pays out *when* the insured person dies, not *if* they die.

There are three main types of life assurance cover:

> **Term policy:** This is for a fixed time period and usually covers the duration of a loan or mortgage, so that if the insured person dies during the term of the loan or mortgage, any outstanding amount is paid off. The premiums, and therefore the cover, finish at a stated time that corresponds with the natural end of the mortgage term.

> **Whole-life policy:** This pays compensation on the death of the insured person.

> **Endowment policy:** This pays a guaranteed amount on a specified date or, if it occurs sooner, on the death of the insured person.

11.3 Why might someone take out a life assurance policy?

11.4 At which stage of life do you think it makes most sense to take out a whole-life assurance policy?

KSMIT
KSMM
KSSW

Motor insurance

Motor insurance is compulsory in Ireland. This means that it is required by law and this makes it a criminal offence to drive without motor insurance.

There are three types of motor insurance, as shown in table 11.1.

Table 11.1 Types of motor insurance (from the least expensive to the most expensive)

Type of motor insurance	What it covers
Third party *The minimum legal requirement for driving any motorised vehicle on a public road*	Injury to another person or damage to another person's car or property caused by the insured driver. It does **not** cover the policyholder or their vehicle
Third party, fire and theft	As for third party, plus the insured person for their car catching fire or being stolen
Comprehensive	All parties and vehicles that suffer loss in an incident, including the insured person and their car

Policies, benefits and costs can vary widely, so it is worth shopping around for the right policy for you.

In insurance terms:

The **first party** is the person who takes out the insurance.

The **second party** is the insurance company the first party is insured with.

The **third party** is any person or item (vehicle, property, etc.) that suffers a loss caused by the first party.

It is the insurance company of the person who caused an incident that pays compensation.

11.5 In each of the following situations, who would receive compensation and whose insurance company would pay it? Write the answers in your copy.

	First party	Type of insurance	Third party	Incident
(a)	Máire	Third party, fire and theft	Jakob	Máire reversed into Jakob's van in a car park; both vehicles were damaged
(b)	Steven	Third party	Unknown	Steven's car was stolen from its parking place
(c)	Bernard	Third party	Renée	Bernard scraped Renée's driver's door as he passed her on the road; both vehicles were damaged
(d)	John	Comprehensive	Margaret	John drove into the back of Margaret's jeep as she waited at a red traffic light; both vehicles were damaged
(e)	Conor	Comprehensive	None	Conor drove into a tree and damaged the front of his pick-up

If the insured driver does not make a claim on their insurance during the year they will receive a no-claims bonus, which will generally make the next year's premium cheaper.

A **no-claims bonus** is a discount on an insurance premium. It rewards the insured party for not making any claims on the policy.

Sometimes a person may have to pay a **loading** on their premium. For example, motor insurance may be more expensive if a person does not have a full driving licence or has penalty points on their licence.

Loading is an extra amount added to the basic premium to cover increased risk.

11.6 When you start driving, you will to have to pay quite a high premium to insure your car. Discuss why you think this is and whether you think it is fair.

KSWwO
KSMIT

11.7 Young drivers represent a high risk for insurers because statistics show that they cost the insurance companies more than other categories of drivers. There are things you can do, though, to reduce the cost of your motor insurance as a young person. Find out what these things are, and create a newspaper advert from an insurance company saying that your company will provide cheaper insurance for young people that do these things, and list them.

KSBC
KSSW
KSMM
KSMIT

Home insurance (buildings cover)

This covers the building in the event of fire, flood or storm damage. It provides compensation if the structure of the building is damaged.

Home contents insurance

This covers all the contents of the house from damage such as fire, flood, burst pipes, etc. It also covers against burglary.

Most home insurance policies cover both buildings and contents.

11.8 In pairs or small groups, research what you can do around your house to help reduce the risk of loss due to fire, flooding from burst pipes and theft. These precautions are also likely to reduce your insurance premiums as you can show that your risk is reduced because of them. Create a poster, leaflet or podcast informing householders of the precautions they can take and why they should take them.

KSWwO
KSBC
KSMIT

KSMIT

11.9 How do you think your insurance needs will be different if you rent a property rather than live in a property you own?

Personal accident insurance

This covers the insured person in the event of an accident. Every year, students in many Irish schools are given the option of taking out personal accident insurance.

Health insurance

This covers the cost of hospital care and some medical bills in the event of serious illness or accident. It can provide cover for a hospital stay and operations.

Figure 11.3 Main providers of health insurance in Ireland

Critical illness cover

This is cover in the event of a serious illness. It pays out a tax-free lump sum if you are medically diagnosed with one of the serious illnesses or disabilities that your policy covers. Examples include heart attack, stroke, cancer and loss of limbs.

Holiday/travel insurance

This covers the insured person while they are on holiday or travelling, e.g. in case their belongings are stolen or they have an accident, cancelled flights, delayed or missed departure, loss or theft of passport or money and illness or injury.

Mortgage protection insurance

This is a type of life insurance policy that repays your mortgage if you die during the repayment term. The cover lasts until your mortgage is paid off.

Payment Protection Insurance (PPI)

This covers your repayments on a loan for a certain period of time (usually one year) if you suffer from an accident, illness, death or compulsory redundancy.

Income/salary protection insurance

This protects the policyholder in case they get sick and have to take time off work. This insurance will pay a part of their income if they lose their employment income due to a disability, illness or injury. The benefit is paid out for a certain period of time, usually until the policyholder gets better or reaches retirement age.

Mobile phone insurance

This is an insurance a person can take out in case their mobile phone is lost or stolen. Other devices, such as laptops and tablet computers, can also be insured.

Pay Related Social Insurance (PRSI)

By law, all employees must pay this insurance. It entitles the worker to illness, disability, maternity or jobseeker's benefit, should they require them. This payment is deducted at source by employers. Self-employed people pay their contribution when they pay their annual tax bill. Unlike other forms of insurance, this is paid to the government instead of an insurance company.

Jobs in the insurance industry

Insurance broker

A broker helps households and individuals to get the insurance that best fits their needs and their budget. Insurance brokers search the market to find the best policy and price for their client.

Most insurance brokers represent several insurance companies and are able to offer their household clients a wide range of policies. They are paid commission by the insurance company for each policy sold.

Agent

An agent sells policies on behalf of only one insurance company.

Actuary

An actuary decides on the premium that should be charged, based on the risk of a loss occurring and a claim being made. They use statistics and probability to assess risk. The greater the risk, the higher the premium will be.

> **Risk** means how likely a person is to make a claim and how costly any claim is likely to be.

Definition

Loss adjuster

A loss adjuster will investigate a claim for compensation and decide if the claim is covered by the insurance company. They recommend the amount of compensation to be paid.

Taking out insurance

Before you can take out insurance, you have to complete a **proposal form**. This is like an application form and should be filled out by the person seeking insurance cover. It must be completed truthfully and all relevant information must be disclosed. This will enable the insurance company to make a realistic assessment of the risk involved and calculate the premium to charge.

If you are not truthful on your form, the insurance company could use this as a reason to refuse to pay out if you make a claim.

An example of a completed proposal form is shown in figure 11.4.

Car insurance proposal form

Proposer	
Name	Callum Cunningham
Date of birth	01/04/1986
Type of licence	Full Irish licence
Email address	cjhcunningham@xmail.com
Postal address	22 St Joseph's Avenue, Donegal Town, Co. Donegal
Occupation	Architect
Cover to commence from	22/06/2017

The vehicle	
Make and exact model	Toyota Avensis
CC	1600cc
Fuel	Petrol
Registration number	151DL1595
Year of make	2015
Present value	€27,000
Where is the vehicle kept overnight (tick as required)	Garage ☐ Private property ☑ Public road ☐

Cover and use	
Vehicle cover required (tick as required)	Comprehensive ☑ Third party, fire and theft ☐ Third party only ☐
Estimated annual mileage	17,000 km

No Claims Discount	
Do you hold insurance in your own name?	Yes ☑ No ☐
If yes, please specify start date	22/06/2011
Name of insurer	AXA Insurance
Expiry date	21/06/2017
Number of years No Claims Discount	6

Driving history		
Have you had any accidents, losses or claims during the past five years?		No
Have you ever been convicted of any offence in connection with any motor vehicle?		No

Declaration	
I declare that the information given on this form is true.	
Signed	Callum Cunningham
Date	15/06/2017

Figure 11.4 An example of a completed proposal form for car insurance

Details of the types of losses covered and the amount of compensation to be paid are set out in the insurance contract, which is called a **policy**.

An insurance policy sets out:

> What is insured
> The insurable value of the item insured
> The types of loss covered

> The policy excess
> Exclusions
> The maximum amount of compensation that will be paid.

The **policy excess** is the amount the insured person must pay for any loss or damage to the insured item. The insurance company pays the balance.

Definition

Policy excess example

Tracy is awarded €5,000 compensation for damage to her car following an accident. Tracy's policy carries an excess of €250, so the insurance company will actually pay €5,000 − €250 = €4,750 in compensation, as Tracy must pay for the first €250 of any claim.

Exclusions are specific items or risks that are not insured.

Definition

By excluding certain high-risk activities it may be possible for insurance companies to lower the average level of premiums, e.g. injury caused by skiing may be excluded from the terms of standard travel insurance policies. People who wish to insure themselves for these activities may need to pay an extra premium called a loading to reflect the higher level of risk.

How to calculate a house insurance premium

Example

Margaret Finley's house insurance is due for renewal. Her insurance company has given her a quote of €12 per €10,000 value for the house and €20 per €5,000 value for the contents. She estimates that she should insure her house for €180,000 and her contents for €90,000. Calculate the insurance premium that Margaret will have to pay.

Solution

House	$\dfrac{180,000}{10,000} \times 12 = \dfrac{180}{10} \times 12 = 18 \times 12$	€216
Contents	$\dfrac{90,000}{5,000} \times 20 = \dfrac{90}{5} \times 20 = 18 \times 20$	€360
Total premium		€576

11.10 Reza is looking for new house insurance. He has some expensive sports equipment that will need to be insured separately because of its specialist nature.

He calculates that he needs to make the following insurance provisions:

> Buildings: €450,000
> General contents: €110,000
> Sports equipment: €3,000

He receives the following quotations.

Insure All Ltd charges €1.50 per €1,000 for the buildings, €5 per €1,000 for the contents and €20 per €1,000 for the sports equipment.

Cover4U Ltd charges €1.35 per €1,000 for the buildings, €4.50 per €1,000 for the contents and a flat rate of €120 for sports equipment up to a value of €5,000.

Which insurance company offers the best value for money?

Making a claim

In the event of an accident, loss or damage occurring, the first step in making a claim is to talk to the insurance company. They will ask you to complete a **claim form**. This is a standard form from the insurance company that the insured must complete when seeking compensation for a loss that has occurred. The claim form requires details of how the loss occurred and the amount being claimed.

For items that have been stolen, you will usually need a reference number from a garda station, so you will have to report the theft.

Figure 11.5 shows an example of a completed claim form.

11.11 Jones Insurance Ltd will probably ask Michael for a receipt for the iPad. Why will they do this?

11.12 If Michael has an excess policy of €300, how much can he hope to get in compensation from his insurance company?

11.13 Some insurance companies offer you the option to voluntarily increase the policy excess. How does this make a difference to:

(a) The premium when getting a quote for an insurance policy?

(b) The amount received as compensation when making a claim?

Jones Insurance Ltd

Name	Michael Martin
Address	Main street, Enniscrone, Co. Sligo
Policy Number	786543224F
Occupation	Teacher
Details of loss/damage	
Date	14 July 2016
Location	Enniscrone, Co. Sligo
Description of item lost/stolen	iPad
Value	€800
Date of purchase	12 November 2015
Was item lost/stolen reported to the Gardaí? (Tick Yes or No)	☑ Yes ☐ No
If 'Yes' please state:	
Date of reporting	14 July 2016
Garda station	Enniscrone
Name of garda who took the details	Gavin Daly
Garda reference number	SL63532F
Signed	Michael Martin
Date	15 July 2016

Figure 11.5 An example of a completed claim form

Average clause

The average clause applies in the case of **underinsurance and partial loss** and is based on the principle of indemnity.

Underinsurance occurs when the insured person fails to insure their assets for their full replacement value. This might be because the insured person does not know the value, or because they are trying to save money on their premium. As a result the amount of compensation paid will not be sufficient to cover the loss. The insurance company will apply the average clause rule and will pay compensation in direct proportion to the value of the property actually insured.

Example

A house was flooded and partially damaged. The actual value of the house is €250,000 but it is insured for only €200,000. The owners are claiming €20,000 compensation for the damage.

How much compensation will be paid out to the owners in this case?

Solution

$$\text{Compensation} = \frac{\text{Insured value}}{\text{Actual value}} \times \text{Amount claimed}$$

$$= \frac{€200{,}000}{€250{,}000} \times €20{,}000 = €16{,}000$$

Since the homeowner has insured their property for only four-fifths of its replacement value, they are entitled only to four-fifths of any loss.

11.14 What is the term we use when you do something to try to save money but in the long run it costs you money?

Renewing an insurance policy

Insurers will send a **renewal notice** when your policy is due for renewal. At this time it is always worth shopping around for a new deal, as you may be able to get the insurance more cheaply from another company. Check every policy for its conditions, as they will differ from policy to policy and there may be something in the terms and conditions that doesn't suit your needs.

In the news

Premiums for home insurance still competitive – but look set to rise

By John Cradden

Central Statistics Office (CSO) figures show that home insurance premiums have already risen by 3pc since January. It also follows the release of a report last week from the Society of Chartered Surveyors Ireland showing that the national average costs of rebuilding a house has risen by 4pc so far this year, which may push up the costs of some premiums.

The widest disparity in prices was for a three-bedroomed bungalow in Midleton, Co Cork with rebuilding costs of €200,000 and contents of €50,000, which got quotes ranging from €254 to €700 – a difference of €446.

Quotes for a four-bed semi-detached house in Newbridge, Co Kildare with rebuilding costs of €145,000 and €20,000 contents varied from €208 to €622 – a €414 difference.

Source: Article adapted from the *Irish Independent*, 26 July 2015

11.15 Think about your own household. What types of insurance do you think you need?

11.16 Now ask what types of insurance cover your household has. Does your household have insurance you didn't think of? Are there types of insurance that your family doesn't think it necessary to have, or finds too expensive to have?

Research

KSMIT

11.17 Peter and Angela decided to redecorate their living room. Once they had chosen the colours they realised the carpet would no longer match. They didn't want to have the expense of a new carpet, so they decided they would 'accidentally' spill a bottle of varnish in the middle of it so they could claim for a new carpet.

What do you think about Peter and Angela's actions? Were they justified because, as they said, they 'pay enough insurance so why not get something back'? Is this morally wrong and does it cause problems for other people with insurance?

Do you hope they get away with it, or do you hope the loss adjuster will see through their ploy?

Discussion

KSMIT
KSBL
KSC

Is insurance really necessary?

Insurance cannot prevent accidents from happening, but it can enable households and individuals to recover from the financial impact of a loss.

Most people who take out insurance hope that they will never suffer an insurable loss.

While insurance has an obvious financial cost, many are willing to pay it because it protects them from the financial uncertainty of loss and buys them some peace of mind.

If you drive a motor vehicle, you are required by law to have insurance.

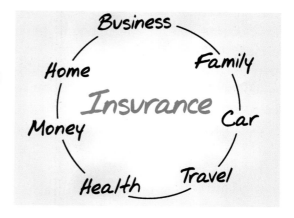

How much insurance is necessary for households and individuals?

There is no exact answer to this question and each household or individual should take into account their own needs and available resources. There are, however, a number of key issues to consider.

Insurance is not always necessary and is just one aspect of household risk management. The steps involved in risk management are:

1   **Identify** the major sources of household or personal risk, e.g. the risk of fire damage to the home.

2   Take appropriate steps to **eliminate or reduce** the level of risk, e.g. install smoke alarms. These measures will also help to reduce premiums if insurance is required.

3   If necessary, **insure** against those risks which cannot be eliminated.

You need insurance with enough cover for potential losses. There are costs associated with having too much insurance cover and also with too little insurance cover.

Discussion

11.18 Discuss what you think the costs and risks are for having:

(a) Too much cover

(b) Too little cover.

KSWwO
KSMIT
KSC

See Chapter 4

Decisions about insurance should be taken as part of your personal financial lifecycle. Insurance needs should be reviewed and updated annually. Whether or not a person takes out insurance is largely a personal decision, but if you have a mortgage a condition of the lender will be that you have adequate insurance on your property, and life assurance on the person(s) paying the mortgage to make sure the debt is paid in the event of their death.

Can all risks be insured?

The answer is no; some risks are **uninsurable**. In general it is not possible to insure a risk where the insurer cannot work out the chances of a loss occurring, e.g. it is not possible to insure against failing an exam or making a business loss.

Other types of uninsurable risk include losses that are certain to occur.

Did you know?

Some celebrities insure parts of their body, such as their legs, their voice or their smile, if they see it as important for the way they earn their living.

11.19 When you buy insurance, the insurance company invests that money in order to make a profit. Is it important to you that those investments are ethical or should the insurance company go for the best monetary return?

KSWwO
KSC
KSMIT

Key Terms

KSBL
KSC
KSMIT
KSBC

You should be able to *define*, *spell*, give *examples* and *apply* to real life each of the following key terms associated with this topic.

Exercise: Write a sentence using each of the following terms. You may use more than one of the terms in your sentence if appropriate.

actuary	insurance policy
agent	life assurance
average clause	loading
buildings and contents insurance	loss adjuster
claim form	material fact
compensation	mortgage protection insurance
comprehensive insurance	motor insurance
contribution	no-claims bonus
critical illness insurance	payment protection insurance
employee's PRSI	policy
endowment policy	premium
excess	proposal form
exclusions	renewal notice
health insurance	subrogation
income protection insurance	term assurance
indemnity	third party, fire and theft
insurable interest	utmost good faith
insurance	warranty
insurance broker	write-off

Chapter 12 ::
Household and Personal Taxation

'... in this world nothing can be said to be certain, except death and taxes.'
Benjamin Franklin, 1789

What are taxes?

Governments, just like households and businesses, need to generate income in order to pay their expenses. Most government income comes from taxation, a compulsory payment in various forms. In Ireland, the State agency responsible for tax collection is the **Office of the Revenue Commissioners** (Revenue for short).

See Chapter 37

Tax is a compulsory payment to the government, charged on income, business profits or added to the cost of goods and services.

Definition

Why pay taxes?

Taxpayers receive certain benefits and financial protection from the State:

❯ Governments use tax revenue (income) to fund essential public services, which benefit the community. Examples include security, health, education and public transport systems as well as a range of recreational amenities such as parks, playgrounds and swimming pools.

❯ The government uses taxes to help make sure there is a more equal distribution of wealth within the economy. People who earn more should pay more tax.

> The government may use taxes to promote or discourage certain activities. For example, lower taxation levels can help to increase consumer spending and job creation, whereas increased tax on cigarettes and plastic bags may reduce their consumption.

See Chapter 39

12.1 There is a recommendation that there should be a tax of 10–20% on soft drinks to help prevent diseases associated with high sugar consumption. Discuss whether you think this tax would mean that fewer soft drinks would be sold and consumed. Why do you think this?

If the government wishes to increase the level or range of public services it will need to introduce new taxes or increase the rate of existing ones. Since taxes have the effect of reducing taxpayers' income, people will have less money available for personal spending on goods and services.

The level and types of taxation paid in each country will depend on the priorities of each government and the willingness of its citizens to support those priorities. For example:

opportunity cost

> The USA has low rates of taxation and low spending on public services. While this leaves households with higher levels of personal income, they have to pay for a greater range of goods and services.

See Chapters 34 and 36

> Sweden has much higher levels of taxation but in return citizens are provided with much greater levels of public services.

12.2 Discuss whether you would prefer to have low tax and few public services, or high tax and less personal spend on services.

Having an income generally creates a **tax liability**. This means that a certain amount of that income must be paid over to the State. It is the responsibility of each person to pay the correct amount of taxation. Without this income the government will not be able to fund public services. This will impact on most citizens but particularly those on low incomes who cannot afford to pay for these services privately.

You may think that tax is just for employed people, but everyone, of any age, who spends money is paying value added tax (VAT) on many of the goods and services they buy. As you get older, your level of income and expenditure will rise, and you will be liable for a greater range of taxes.

Understanding the taxation system, knowing your entitlements and being able to accurately calculate your tax liability are important steps in meeting your responsibilities and planning your financial future. You may be able to reduce your tax liability by knowing how to claim more tax reliefs or by spending your money in particular ways.

Reducing the amount of tax you have to pay in this way is called **tax avoidance** and it is perfectly legal. For example, Revenue allows eligible taxpayers to claim certain tax credits which will reduce the amount of tax they have to pay.

Tax evasion, on the other hand, is illegal and usually happens when people fail to declare some or all of their income. Those found guilty of tax evasion are liable to pay the overdue tax and will also be subject to interest and penalties.

Common household and personal taxes

There are many different taxes. We'll look at the ones most likely to affect you and your family here.

Pay As You Earn income tax (PAYE)

Workers pay tax on all types of earnings arising from employment including wages, salaries, bonuses, overtime, benefits in kind, etc. The income tax is deducted at source by employers and sent to Revenue. From the employee's point of view, this is a very simple system, as the tax has already been deducted from wages when they are received.

Workers on very low incomes may be exempt from income tax.

12.3 What are the current rates of income tax? At what levels of income are they paid?

Research

KSMIT
KSBN

Self-assessed income tax

This is paid by those who are self-employed or on income that is not taxable under the PAYE system. Under self-assessment the taxpayer calculates and makes the relevant tax payment themselves. In order to reduce the risk of tax evasion, these returns are subject to regular checks by Revenue, which are called **tax audits**.

Universal Social Charge (USC)

Incomes over a certain amount are subject to USC, at different rates for different levels of income. USC is in addition to income tax.

12.4 (a) What are the current rates of USC and at what levels of income are they applicable?

(b) How much USC per month would someone earning €30,000 a year pay?

Research

KSMIT
KSBN

Value added tax (VAT)

VAT is a tax on goods and services. This means that it is paid by everyone who buys goods and services. VAT is included in the price of many everyday purchases, so you may not always be aware that you are paying it.

There are a range of different VAT rates for goods and services in Ireland. Some essential goods, including certain foods, medicines and children's clothing, are free of VAT, while many luxury goods and professional services currently carry 23% VAT.

12.5 What are the different rates of VAT in Ireland at the moment?

12.6 Find out the rate of VAT applicable on these items:

Research

KSMIT
KSBN

(a) Milk

(b) Solicitors' fees

(c) DVDs

(d) Newspapers

(e) Crisps

(f) Books

(g) A meal in a restaurant

(h) A take-away meal

(i) Children's clothing

(j) Biscuits without chocolate

(k) Chocolate biscuits

(l) Bin collections

Customs duties

Customs duty is a tax on goods imported into Ireland from outside the EU.

Excise duties

Excise duty is a tax levied on certain goods and materials, including:

> Motor fuel (petrol and diesel)
> Heating oil
> Natural gas
> Solid fuel (e.g. coal)
> Alcohol
> Tobacco.

12.7 The name given to some excise levies is **carbon tax**. It is applied to products that emit carbon into the atmosphere, such as heating oil, solid fuels (e.g. coal and briquettes), natural gas and transport fuels. It was brought in for two reasons: to encourage people to use less fuel, and to pay for ways of combating climate change. Discuss whether this is a good way of reducing our use of fuels that contribute to climate change.

Discussion

KSWwO
KSC
KSBL
KSMIT

Local property tax (LPT)

Owners of residential properties in Ireland are liable to pay this tax. The tax payable is based on the market value of a house/apartment and there are different levels of value (called **bands**).

The LPT is a **self-assessment tax** so the homeowner calculates the tax due based on their own assessment of the market value of the property.

12.8 What are the first five bands for LPT, and what amount has to be paid for each of them?

Research

KSBN
KSMM
KSMIT

Stamp duty

Stamp duty is charged on certain written documents. It is most commonly associated with the purchase of property but it is also charged on cheques and financial cards (debit, credit and ATM cards). On your statement you will see 'Government stamp duty' as a debit item.

12.9 Stamp duty on properties costing less than €1,000,000 is 1%. On properties costing more than this it is 1% up to €1,000,000 and 2% on the remainder. How much stamp duty would be paid by the purchasers of properties costing:

(a) €247,000? (b) €565,000? (c) €1.6 million?

12.10 What is the current stamp duty on:

(a) A debit card? (b) A credit card?

Research

KSBN
KSMM

Motor tax

This is a compulsory tax for all owners of motor vehicles. It is calculated on an annual basis and paid to the local authority (city or county council), which is responsible for the upkeep of local roads. Ireland currently has two systems under which road tax is calculated for passenger cars.

All cars made before 2008 have their road tax calculated based on the car's engine size. All cars made in 2008 or after have their road tax calculated based on the car's carbon dioxide emissions.

12.11 Find a website address that you could use for calculating motor tax in Ireland. How can you be sure this is a trusted website for this information?

Research

KSMIT
KSMM

Vehicle registration tax (VRT)

This is a separate tax levied on those who purchase and register a new car or motorcycle in the State.

12.12 Find a website address that you could use for calculating the VRT on a vehicle you are importing into Ireland. How can you be sure this is a trusted website for this information?

Research

KSMIT
KSMM

Deposit Interest Retention Tax (DIRT)

This is a tax on interest earned on savings. The tax is deducted at source by the financial institution.

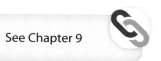

See Chapter 9

12.13 What is the current rate of DIRT?

Research

KSMIT
KSMM

Capital gains tax (CGT)

This is a tax on profits earned from the sale of assets such as property (other than a main residence) and investments.

Profits (capital gains) arise when the value of an asset increases above its original purchase price. For example, an investor buys company shares for €5,000 and later sells them for €7,000. In this instance the capital gain of €2,000 is liable for CGT.

Capital is wealth in the form of money or any item that can be given a monetary value, e.g. property, shares, machinery.

Definition

12.14 What is the current rate of capital gains tax?

Research

KSMIT
KSMM

Capital acquisitions tax (CAT)

This tax is paid on gifts and inheritances. An inheritance refers to wealth (money, property, etc.) left to one person following the death of another. The gift or inheritance is liable for tax if its value is above a certain limit.

Types of tax

Direct taxes

A direct tax is one imposed (*levied*) on income as it is *earned*. Some direct taxes are **deducted at source**. This means that the tax is calculated and submitted to Revenue by the person paying the income, rather than by the person who earns it. Examples include:

> **DIRT** (Deposit Interest Retention Tax), which must be paid by deposit account holders who earn interest on savings. The tax on this interest is deducted by the financial institution and sent directly to Revenue.

See Chapter 9

> Income earned under the PAYE system. The employer deducts and submits the tax before paying the net income to employees.

Indirect taxes

Indirect taxes are levied on money as it is *spent* on goods or services. Examples of indirect taxes are value added tax (VAT), excise duty and customs duty.

These taxes are paid indirectly to Revenue. For example, a customer buys an item in a shop and is charged VAT, which he pays to the shopkeeper. The shopkeeper then pays the VAT to Revenue.

One of the major criticisms with indirect taxes such as VAT is that the rate of tax is the same for all consumers. As a result the burden of tax falls most heavily on those with low incomes because the amount paid in tax represents a far greater proportion of their income. Taxes levied in this way are said to be **regressive**.

The burden of tax

A sofa costs €1,230, which includes €230 in VAT, levied at 23%. Billy and his friend Alex are each planning to buy the same sofa.

Billy earns €1,000 per week, so the €230 VAT payment represents 23% of his weekly income.

Alex, however, earns €500 a week and so the €230 VAT payment will consume 46% of his weekly income.

A system of taxation where those earning higher incomes pay higher taxes would seem to be fairer or more equitable. A **progressive tax** is one where the tax rate increases as income increases. Income tax is an example of a progressive tax.

12.15 Some people say taxation by VAT is better than a high rate of income tax because people can choose whether or not to spend money on items that contain a VAT levy. Alex in the example above could choose to buy a cheaper sofa and so be taxed less. For this reason, VAT is sometimes called a *luxury tax*. Do you agree with this?

KSWwO
KSC
KSBL
KSMIT

Impact of tax on households and individuals

The introduction of new taxes, or an increase in existing tax rates, has consequences for households and individuals.

12.16 Discuss the effect of an introduction of a new tax or a change in tax on each of the following for households/individuals. Following the discussion, make notes in your copy of the effects.

Consequence of new taxes or an increase in existing taxes on:

(a) Cost of living

(b) Disposable income

(c) Savings and investments

(d) Cash flow

Consequence of a decrease in taxes on:

(e) Public services

KSWwO
KSC
KSMIT

12.17 What will be the effect on households and individuals if taxes are abolished or the tax rate is lowered?

Getting started with income tax

Danielle Whelan has just been offered her first job and is excited at the prospect of earning some income of her own. Her new employer tells Danielle that she will have to pay income tax under the PAYE system.

The employer asks Danielle for her PPSN and sends it to Revenue to inform them that Danielle has started working.

Definition

A **Personal Public Service Number (PPSN)** is an individual's unique reference number that is used in all dealings with public service agencies, including Revenue. A PPSN would have been allocated to you by the Department of Social Protection when you were born if your birth was in Ireland; if you weren't born in Ireland you might have been given a number when you moved here, or you might have to apply for one.

Once Danielle has a PPS number she will need to register for tax. First-time employees should register online via myAccount at www.revenue.ie.

When her registration is completed Revenue will issue Danielle (and her employer) with a **certificate of tax credits and her standard rate cut-off point**. This document will tell her employer how much tax to deduct from her wages.

Emergency tax

If you are on emergency tax you will pay more tax than you need to for a while and will have very little take-home pay. Once the tax is sorted out, you will get back any tax you have overpaid.

If Danielle fails to register for a certificate of tax credits, her employer will have to apply emergency tax to her income.

The tax credits reflect her personal circumstances and include a PAYE tax credit and a single person's tax credit. This information determines the deductions from her **gross pay** and therefore what her **net pay** will be.

Definitions

The **tax rate** is the percentage of tax that is levied on a person's income. There are different rates: the standard rate (currently 20%) and the higher rate (currently 40%).

The **standard rate cut-off point (SRCOP)** is the amount of income that will be taxed at the standard rate of tax. Once a person's income exceeds this level, that portion of income above the cut-off point will be taxed at the higher rate of tax.

Tax credit is the amount by which a person's annual tax bill may be reduced. This varies from person to person depending on their circumstances.

Gross pay is pay before all deductions.

Net pay is gross pay minus all deductions. It is also called **take-home pay**.

Deductions are all the payments that must be taken away from gross pay by the employer to calculate net pay. It includes things such as tax, USC, pensions, trades union dues, and so on. This will vary from person to person.

See Chapter 2

Danielle Whelan

Tax credits

Single person's tax credit	€1,650
Employee (PAYE) tax credit	€1,650
= Total tax credits	€3,300 per year (or €63.46 per week)

Standard rate cut-off point

€33,800 per year (€650 per week)

12.18 If Danielle earned €44,000 this year, how much of it would be taxed at 20% and how much at 40%?

12.19 If Danielle is paid monthly, what would her monthly figures be:

(a) For tax credits?

(b) For SRCOP?

12.20 Greg has been given annual tax credits of €2,960 and a standard rate cut-off point of €28,900. He is paid monthly, so what are the:

(a) Monthly tax credits?

(b) Monthly SRCOP?

Income tax calculation

Example 1: Single person weekly tax calculation

Assuming Danielle begins her job at the start of the tax year (1 January) and earns a gross wage of €800, here is her tax calculation for her first *week* of employment.

Taxable income €800

Step	Action	Tax	
1	Tax €650 @ 20%	€130.00	Apply standard rate 20% up to a maximum of the weekly rate cut-off point (€650.00) as per tax credit certificate
2	Tax €150 @ 40%	€60.00	Apply higher rate to pay in excess of the weekly standard rate cut-off point (€800 − €650 = €150)
3	Gross tax	€190.00	Add the standard rate tax figure to the higher rate tax figure
4	Less tax credit	€63.46	Tax credit as per tax credit certificate
5	Net tax	€126.54	Subtract tax credits from gross tax

Danielle also pays PRSI of 4% and USC of €30 on her gross wages.

6	PRSI €800 @ 4%	€32	4% PRSI paid on gross income
7	USC on €800	€30	USC calculation based on gross income

This means that Danielle will have total statutory deductions of €170.54 (€126.54 + €32 + €12).

Her net (take-home) pay for her first week of employment will be €629.46 (€800 − €170.54).

This example shows that tax calculation is another area of personal financial management which varies from person to person and from household to household.

Since household circumstances and the rules governing taxation are likely to change over time it is necessary to keep up to date with current tax policies. This helps ensure that you and your household are paying the correct amount of tax and are benefiting from all tax credits to which you are entitled. Information on up-to-date tax rates, credits and allowances is available on www.revenue.ie.

Most changes to taxation are announced by the minister for finance when presenting the government's annual budget.

12.21 Find out what the current rates are for PRSI.

KSBN

KSBN

12.22 Grace has a part-time job while she is at college. Her hourly rate is €9.15; standard rate cut-off point €33,800 per year; tax credits €3,300 per year; income tax rate is 20%, USC is 1% and PRSI is 4%. In her first week she worked 25 hours. How much will she take home?

12.23 (a) What is the current national minimum wage?

(b) What does this mean?

(c) Where did you find this information? What was it about this source that made you happy the information was correct?

KSMIT
KSMM

12.24 Some big companies have very clever accountants who find all sorts of ways to help the company avoid tax. Tax avoidance, as we saw in the text, is a legal way of not paying some tax. Although legal, do you think it is fair and ethical that some big companies can avoid tax in this way? How does this impact on other taxpayers?

KSWwO
KSC

KSMIT
KSBL

12.25 'When it comes to taxation, the government is a bit like Robin Hood, because it takes from the rich and gives to the poor!' In your copy, write a short speech setting out your reasons for agreeing or disagreeing with this statement.

Key Terms

You should be able to *define, spell*, give *examples* and *apply* to real life each of the following key terms associated with this topic.

KSBL
KSC
KSMIT
KSBC

Exercise: Write a sentence using each of the following terms. You may use more than one of the terms in your sentence if appropriate.

capital acquisitions tax (CAT)	Personal Public Service Number (PPSN)
capital gains tax (CGT)	preliminary tax
certificate of tax credits	progressive taxation
customs duty	regressive taxation
direct tax	self-assessed tax
emergency tax	stamp duty
excise duty	standard rate cut-off point (SRCOP)
gross pay	tax audit
income tax	tax avoidance
indirect tax	tax credit
local property tax (LPT)	tax evasion
motor tax	taxation
net pay	Universal Social Charge (USC)
Office of the Revenue Commissioners	value added tax (VAT)
Pay As You Earn	vehicle registration tax (VRT)

Chapter 13 :: Introducing the Consumer

What is a consumer?

Every time you buy a bar of chocolate, go to the hairdresser or barber to get a haircut, purchase a magazine or pay to download a song from the internet, you are a consumer.

> A **consumer** is a person who buys goods or services for their own use.
>
> **Definition**

> A **good** is something you buy that you can touch or see, e.g. phone, book, shirt.
> A **service** is something that is done for you, e.g. bus ride, haircut, car wash.
>
> **Definition**

Figure 13.1 Examples of goods and services

> **13.1** Name four goods and one service that you or your family has purchased over the last month.

Needs and wants

Consumers have different needs and wants.

Most consumers' requirements when buying products are:

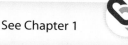

See Chapter 1

> Value for money
> High-quality products
> Finding out information about the product before they buy it
> Getting a good after-sales service if there is a fault or problem with the product.

> **13.2** We know that food is a need, as we can't survive without it. Discuss in your group when food becomes a want rather than a need.

Groupwork

KSWwO
KSC
KSSW
KSMIT

The wise consumer

As we discovered in chapter 1, money is a scarce resource. When consumers want to buy something they have to ask themselves some important questions, such as:

See Chapter 1

> Do I really need it?
> Can I afford it?
> Will there be further costs once I have bought the item?
> Can I buy this product cheaper elsewhere?
> Do I have space for it in my home?
> Is it a safe product? Could it cause harm to me or to others when I use it?
> Are there any hidden extra charges?
> Is there an ethical cost in the way it was produced? Was it produced where slave labour may have been used? Did an animal suffer for this product? Has the environment been harmed because of it?
> Will I be helping to create jobs in Ireland by buying this product? If the product is imported, it will not help to create jobs in Ireland.

> **13.3** The latest smartphone is just in the shops and as you are thinking of getting a new phone you are trying to decide which model to go for. What questions would you ask yourself? In your group list the questions, e.g. if there might be hidden costs, what are they?

Groupwork

KSWwO
KSC
KSBL
KSSW
KSMIT

Information about products

Many products have labels on them, which list contents of the package, technology requirements or safety details. In particular, most packaged food products contain a label. These labels give important information and shouldn't be ignored.

Figure 13.2 Examples of food labels and wrapping

The following information might be included on a food label:

> Name of product – the brand and the item.
> Name and address of producer/seller.
> The weight of the product.
> Price – the cost of the product.
> Best before/sell by/use by dates.
> Ingredients – these are always listed in descending weight order, i.e. the heaviest items are listed first.
> Country of origin.
> Nutritional information.
> Cooking/storage instructions.
> Barcode – this is a series of lines and numbers which identify where the product was made, by which company and the cost of the product.

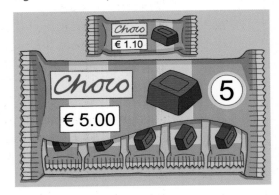

0 10421 25071 3

Figure 13.3 Example of a barcode

13.4 (a) What does 'Best before' date mean?

(b) What does 'Sell by' date mean?

(c) What does 'Use by' date mean?

(d) Is it legal for shops to have items on the shelf that have passed (i) the 'Best before' date? (ii) the 'Sell by' date?

(e) If the dates on the products are getting close, what might the shopkeeper do to make sure the items sell before they have to be taken off the shelf?

(f) Create a poster aimed at shoppers explaining 'Best before', 'Use by' and 'Sell by' dates. Include information on how the consumer should make use of these dates. Make sure to include pictures.

Research

KSMIT
KSSW

13.5 'In Ireland there is over one million tonnes of food waste disposed of each year. Around one-third of this comes from households and this means that, at home, each person is throwing out about 80kg of food waste each year.' From www.stopfoodwaste.ie

Discussion

KSWwO
KSMM
KSMIT
KSC

(a) Discuss how food waste is a burden on the householder, the farmer, the population as a whole and the environment. How can households reduce their food waste?

(b) Supermarkets often throw out perfectly good food because it is past its sell-by date. Do you think they are right to do this, or could the food be put to good use and not wasted?

13.6 Bring a food packaging label to class (without the food in it!). The label may be a biscuit wrapper, ready-meal box, label from tinned goods or any other kind of label that has details about the product. Stick the packaging to a piece of paper and label each element of the packaging. Check the list on the previous page to make sure you don't miss anything, and include anything else that is not on this list. Compare your packaging label with those from the rest of your group. Between you decide:

Groupwork

KSWwO
KSC
KSBL
KSMM
KSSW
KSBC

(a) Why the label contains that information. Hint: Is it a legal requirement? Might the consumer want to know it to compare with other similar products? Is it advertising good value? Does the shopkeeper need to know it?

(b) Are the ingredients what you expect to be included and are they listed in the order you would expect?

(c) Is this a basic food item (i.e. a need) or a treat (i.e. a want)?

13.7 In your groups, research and discuss why each of the above elements are included on packaging labels. Create a presentation with a slide for each element of information explaining what it means, why it might be on packaging, whether it legally has to be there, and some scans of examples from the labels you looked at in question 13.6.

Present the slideshow to your class.

Research

KSMIT
KSWwO
KSBC
KSC
KSSW
KSMM

Value for money

Unit pricing

Question: Which is better value for money?

(a) 9-pack of Brand A toilet rolls, which costs €5.00

(b) 16-pack of Brand B toilet rolls, which costs €8.00

Answer:

(a) $\dfrac{\text{Price}}{\text{Quantity}} = \dfrac{5.00}{9} = 56c$ per roll

(b) $\dfrac{\text{Price}}{\text{Quantity}} = \dfrac{8.00}{16} = 50c$ per roll

In this case, Brand B is better value for money.

KSBN
KSMIT

13.8 Calculate the cost per unit for each of the following. Which is the best value item in each case?

   (a)   **(i)** A 12-pack of Brand A pens at €9.12

        (ii) A 7-pack of Brand B pens at €5.25

   (b)   **(i)** A 125ml bottle of Brand A shampoo at €2.65

        (ii) A 375ml bottle of Brand B shampoo at €7.50

   (c)   **(i)** A 500g box of Brand A breakfast cereal at €3.95

        (ii) A 650g box of Brand B breakfast cereal at €4.29

      (iii) A 700g box of Brand C breakfast cereal at €4.85

While a larger size is often better value for money, you may need to consider that you won't always use all of the product and it could therefore be a **false economy**. Before you buy a larger size of a product, even if it is better value for money, ask yourself if you need all of it, or (if it is a food item) whether you will use it before it goes out of date.

See Chapter 3

A large container of milk often has a smaller unit price than a smaller container. However, you may not drink enough milk every day, so the large container may go off before you can finish it. Even though the larger size is better value for money, it is a false economy if you don't use all of it!

Large (2 litre) = €1.85 (46c per 500 ml)

Medium (1 litre) = €1.20 (60c per 500 ml)

Small (500ml) = €0.62

2 litres

1 litre

500 ml

Cinema tickets	
Adult	€12.75
Young adult (aged 17)	€9.50
Child (up to 16)	€8.50
A couple (18 and over)	€24.00
Family (2 adults and 2 children OR 1 adult and 3 children)	€38.00

13.9 Bernard and Mary have three children: Nick, aged 8; James, aged 12; and Daisy, aged 16. They are going to go to the cinema together on Thursday. What combination of tickets should they buy to give them the cheapest option?

13.10 Daisy is 17 next week. If they go to the cinema again next week, what will be the cheapest combination of tickets for the five of them?

13.11 In the second week, at the last minute, James is invited to go on holiday with his friend, and so decides not to go to the cinema. What is the best combination of tickets now?

Own-label branded products, which are the supermarket's own products, are usually better value than branded goods, e.g. a supermarket's own baked beans are usually cheaper than well-known brands. Most of the frequently bought foods have an own-brand version in the bigger supermarkets.

See Chapter 24

13.12 Look through your cupboards at home and make a note of the brands your family buys regularly. Look at a till receipt or go to the supermarket and make a note of the cost of each of these brands, then look for the own-brand similar products to see how much they cost. Compare the two costs. How much could your family save by switching to own-label brands?

See Chapters 3 and 4

Consumer rights

The Consumers' Association of Ireland (CAI)

The CAI is an independent organisation, founded in 1966, which represents Irish consumers and seeks to protect their rights. Their website, http://thecai.ie/, contains podcasts of common consumer questions and answers, as well as information on your rights as a consumer.

Consumers' Association of Ireland

There is a detailed discussion of consumer rights in chapter 14.

See Chapter 14

13.13 Work in groups. The questions below need to be researched – decide how you will do this, e.g. will you all look up the same questions, or will you divide the questions between you?

KSWwO
KSMIT
KSBC
KSC
KSBL
KSMM

(a) Find answers to the following questions:

(i) What is a deposit?

(ii) Can you get your deposit back if you change your mind about buying the good?

(iii) Does a shopkeeper have to give you a receipt?

(iv) Why would you need a till receipt?

(v) What information will you find on a receipt?

(vi) If you lose your receipt and want to return a good to the shop, how might you prove you actually bought the item there?

(vii) If you buy something and then change your mind about wanting it, can you insist on a refund?

(viii) In what circumstances can you insist on a refund?

(ix) What is a credit note, and when might you be given one?

(x) What are your consumer rights if you buy goods online from a business within the EU?

(xi) What are your rights if you buy goods online from an individual, e.g. on eBay?

(xii) What are your rights if you buy goods online from a business that is not in the EU?

(xiii) What taxes might you have to pay if you buy goods from a business outside the EU?

(b) What sources of information did you use? What made you confident that these were reliable sources?

(c) When you have found answers to the questions, prepare a presentation or make a poster, infographic or booklet to give to the rest of the class to explain consumer concerns. You will need to decide between you how you are going to do this and make a plan of who is going to do what.

Consumer responsibilities

If something seems too good to be true, it probably is! *Caveat emptor* is a Latin phrase that means 'Let the buyer beware'. This means that consumers need to use common sense when buying goods and services.

Consumers have the following responsibilities:

> To behave wisely when buying goods and services.

> To avoid impulse buying and false economies.

> To shop around for the best value for money.
> To use products carefully and in accordance with the manufacturer's instructions to avoid damaging them.

See Chapter 15

> To dispose of packaging responsibly, recycling when possible.
> To know their legal rights.

See Chapter 14

Discussion

KSMIT
KSBL
KSC
KSMM

13.14 Although you can't insist on a refund if you change your mind about buying a product, many shops will give a refund or a credit note out of **goodwill**, i.e. they trust their customer and want to help them.

Sarah has found a dress she really wants to wear to a party, but it costs more than she can afford. Martina says, 'Buy it, wear it for the evening, then take it back to the shop the next day and get a refund.'

(a) Discuss what you think about this idea. Is it ethical?

(b) How does this behaviour impact on other consumers?

13.15 John and Daniel are shopping for T-shirts. This is the conversation they had:

John: Let's go to Kirby's. You can get three T-shirts for €7.50.

Daniel: I'm not going there. I saw this programme that said their clothes are cheap because they are made by children in developing countries who have to work ten hours a day for hardly any money.

John: Not my problem. I only have €20 and I have to make the most of it.

Daniel: No. That's plenty of money to get a decent T-shirt. Get one instead of three and know it has been made by someone getting a proper wage. It'll probably last longer too.

Discuss the attitudes of John and Daniel. Who do you agree with?

Key Terms

KSBL
KSC
KSMIT
KSBC

You should be able to *define*, *spell*, give *examples* and *apply* to real life each of the following key terms associated with this topic.

Exercise: Write a sentence using each of the following terms. You may use more than one of the terms in your sentence if appropriate.

caveat emptor	goods
consumer	goodwill
Consumers' Association of Ireland (CAI)	need
cost per unit	services
deposit	want
false economy	

Chapter 14 :: Protecting the Consumer

Learning outcomes

When you have completed this chapter you will be able to:

✔ Outline the main components of the Sale of Goods and Supply of Services Act 1980 and the Consumer Protection Act 2007 and describe how they protect the consumer

✔ Describe the redress available if a good is faulty or a service is not up to standard

✔ Make a complaint orally or in writing, backed up by your knowledge of consumer legislation

✔ List and explain how relevant agencies can assist in resolving consumer complaints.

Consumer protection

In chapter 13, you learned that a consumer is a person who buys goods and services for their own use. You also learned that wise consumers need to plan their buying carefully and that they have certain rights and responsibilities.

See Chapter 13

While a consumer is not entitled to a refund if they simply change their mind about a product, they do have rights if a product is faulty or if a service has not been provided with proper care.

In addition, consumers are protected from dishonest salespeople and retailers (shops) that make false claims about goods or services.

In this chapter you will learn more about how consumers are protected by two laws:

> Sale of Goods and Supply of Services Act 1980
> Consumer Protection Act 2007.

You will also learn about various organisations that assist consumers who have been unfairly treated.

Sale of Goods and Supply of Services Act 1980

This law protects you when you buy goods from a **trader** and the goods are intended for your own consumption. You are not protected if you buy goods from another **consumer** or **private individual**.

Goods

According to the Sale of Goods and Supply of Services Act 1980, goods must conform to these principles:

> **Be of merchantable quality:** The good must be undamaged, usable and of reasonable quality considering the price paid, e.g. food must be edible up to the best before/use by date.

> **Be fit for the purpose intended:** The good must do what you expect it to do, e.g. a kettle must boil water, a phone must be able to make and receive calls.

> **Be as described:** The good must match the description given by the salesperson, packaging, brochure or advert, e.g. a jacket described as waterproof must not let rain in.

> **Conform to the sample shown:** For certain items bought from a showroom, just a sample will be available, e.g. tiles, wallpaper, sofa, carpet. When the item is purchased, it must be the same as the item shown to you in the shop and you must have an opportunity to check this. The goods purchased must also be free from defects, which would not be obvious on examination of the sample.

14.1 Jack bought an oven from a man on an online advertising board. He went to his house to collect it. When he fitted it into his kitchen, he found that it did not work. Does he have any rights under the Sale of Goods and Supply of Services Act 1980? Give a reason for your answer.

Services

As well as protecting consumers who have purchased goods, this law also protects consumers who have paid for a service. Under this law, services must be:

> Provided by someone who has the necessary skills and qualifications
> Provided with appropriate care and attention
> Carried out using goods or materials of merchantable quality.

Redress

Under the Sale of Goods and Supply of Services Act 1980, if you purchase an item from a **retailer** that is damaged or faulty, you are entitled to some form of redress (remedy or compensation). There are three kinds of redress, known as the **3Rs**:

> **Refund:** You can receive the cost of the item back, either in cash or as money paid back on to your credit card.

> **Replacement:** You can have the same or an alternative product that is free from damage or faults.

> **Repair:** The item may be fixed free of charge. The repair must be permanent.

If the shop offers you a **credit note**, you have the right to refuse this and ask for a refund. This is because a credit note limits you to buying something else from the same shop, which may not suit you.

The longer you wait to make the complaint or the longer the fault occurs after you have bought the item, the less likely it is that you will receive a full refund; you may instead be offered a replacement or repair.

Consumers are *not entitled* to refunds or exchanges if they simply change their minds or if they caused the fault through careless use of the good.

See Chapter 13

Groupwork

KSWwO
KSC
KSBL
KSMIT
KSSW
KSMM

14.2 Have you or your family ever had reason to take something back to a shop or return something by post? What were the circumstances, and how was the situation resolved? Share with your group.

14.3 Karen bought a new phone. She looked at the one in the shop but was given a new one in a sealed box to take home. When she got home she showed her brother the box and he said, 'That's rubbish. You should have got the Xi57, it's way cooler.' Karen now didn't like the phone she had bought. She undid the seal, took out the phone and made a scratch over the screen. Then she went back to the shop, complained loudly that the phone was damaged, demanded her money back and went to a different shop to get the Xi57.

(**a**) How could Karen have handled this situation better?

(**b**) Did Karen have any legal rights in this situation?

(**c**) How could this situation impact on:

  (**i**)   Herself?

  (**ii**) The shop staff?

  (**iii**) The reputation of the shop and the manufacturer?

  (**iv**) The staff at the factory that made and packaged the phone?

(**d**) How could Karen ensure she buys a phone with a good reputation in future?

Responsibilities of sellers

The Sale of Goods and Supply of Services Act 1980 states that:

> Consumer complaints must be dealt with by the seller. You do not have to contact the manufacturer if an item is faulty, as you bought the item from a shop, not directly from the manufacturer of the product.

> Retailers must respect consumers' rights when selling goods and services.

> Retailers cannot display signs that limit their responsibility, such as 'No refunds', 'No exchanges', 'Credit notes only'.

> Guarantees and warranties are an addition to consumers' rights, but they do not replace them.

Guarantees and warranties

Some manufacturers offer a guarantee. This is a written statement provided by the manufacturer promising to replace or repair an item that develops a fault within a certain time frame, e.g. one year. Extended warranties are sometimes offered by shops to consumers at an additional cost. They cover repairs to items after the manufacturer's guarantee has run out. Consumers are under no obligation to buy an extended warranty.

A **guarantee** is a promise by the manufacturer or company that it will sort out any problems with a product or service within a specific, fixed period of time. It is usually free and it is legally binding.

A **warranty** is like an insurance policy for which you must pay a premium. It is legally binding.

Definitions

Guarantees and warranties are additional to your statutory (legal) rights under the Sale of Goods and Supply of Services Act 1980. They do not replace them and you can therefore still make a valid complaint to the retailer.

Consumer Protection Act 2007

This law provides protection to consumers regarding misleading claims about goods, services and prices.

Misleading claims

Businesses cannot make misleading claims about themselves (e.g. 'Ireland's oldest bakery', unless it really *is* Ireland's oldest bakery), goods, services or prices.

For **goods**, claims about the performance of a product, the ingredients contained within it and the weight of the item must be truthful. Examples of misleading claims are:

> A claim that a product will remove acne when there is no scientific proof that it can.

> A claim that a product is made in Ireland when in fact it is made elsewhere.

For **services**, claims about the time, place and effect of a service must be truthful. Examples of misleading claims are:

> A claim that a service is available throughout the country when it is available only in Cork and Galway.

> A claim that a service will be provided within one hour (e.g. photo printing, dry cleaning) if it will take longer.

> A claim that broadband service is unlimited when extra charges occur if the consumer downloads more than 15GB of data.

For **prices**, the recommended retail price, previous prices and actual prices must be truthful. When a retailer advertises a previous price, the item must have been on sale at that price in the same location for twenty-eight consecutive days within the previous three months.

Misleading practices

The Consumer Protection Act protects consumers against unfair practices whether they buy from a local shop or a business within the EU.

There are three main unfair commercial practices:

> **Misleading:** This occurs when false or untrue information is used to deceive the consumer, e.g. a butcher displaying a sign indicating it is an award-winning business when it has not won any awards.

> **Aggressive:** This occurs when harassment, physical force or influence are used to force a consumer into buying a product, e.g. a mechanic carrying out more work on a car than was agreed in advance and refusing to return the car until the work has been paid for.

> **Prohibited:** The law lists thirty-two specific practices that are banned, for example:

>> Telling a consumer that they have won a prize and then demanding payment to claim the prize

>> Claiming a business is closing down when it is not.

Making a complaint

If you discover a fault with a product you have purchased, you will need to make a complaint to the retailer. There are a few simple steps you should follow:

> **Step 1:** Stop using the item immediately.

> **Step 2:** Bring the item back to the shop and ask to speak to the manager. If you still have the receipt or other proof of purchase, bring this with you. If the manager is unavailable, ask to speak to the person who has been left in charge in his/her absence.

> **Step 3:** Explain the problem clearly, including details of purchase and when you noticed a problem with the item. Remain polite but firm. Know your rights under the Sale of Goods and Supply of Services Act 1980.

> **Step 4:** Decide which form of redress you would prefer: a refund, a replacement or a repair.

> **Step 5:** If the retailer does not offer a satisfactory result, you may need to send a written complaint providing details of the problem. Keep a copy of all correspondence.

> **Step 6:** If the complaint is still not resolved, you may have to seek the advice of a third party, e.g. Competition and Consumer Protection Commission, Consumers' Association of Ireland.

> **Step 7:** If the complaint is still not resolved, make a claim through the Small Claims Procedure, if applicable. (See page 155.)

> **Step 8:** Go to court.

14.4 Either:

    (a) Illustrate the steps outlined above for making a complaint, by summarising them on a poster or a presentation. Include suitable images.

    or

    (b) Create a podcast or video in which you advise people of the steps they need to take to make a complaint.

KSBC
KSMIT
KSBL
KSC

When is a consumer complaint not valid?

As a consumer, you do not have any rights:

> If you change your mind about the purchase
> If a fault arises due to your misuse of a product
> If you were told about the fault when you bought the good.

Writing a letter of complaint

Although it is best to complain politely and in person, you may occasionally have to make a complaint in writing.

Letters usually follow a certain format, as shown in figure 14.1.

You should include three separate paragraphs:

1 Describe the details of the purchase.
2 Give the details of the complaint and show how the situation breaches consumer law.
3 Explain what remedy you want.

Keep a copy of the letter to refer to in the future in case you need to take the matter to a consumer agency. This will provide proof that you have already tried to resolve the complaint yourself.

An example of a letter of complaint

Shannon Meehan bought a new Samsung phone costing €199 in LMM Electrics.

After three days she noticed that the battery wasn't charging properly and the phone kept switching itself off. By the end of the week, she noticed that the phone was not receiving any incoming calls, which were instead going straight to voicemail.

Shannon rang LMM Electrical and asked for the name of the manager and the shop's address. She then wrote to the manager. Her letter is shown in figure 14.1.

14.5 Why do you think Shannon rang the shop to get the name of the manager, rather than addressing the letter to 'The Manager'?

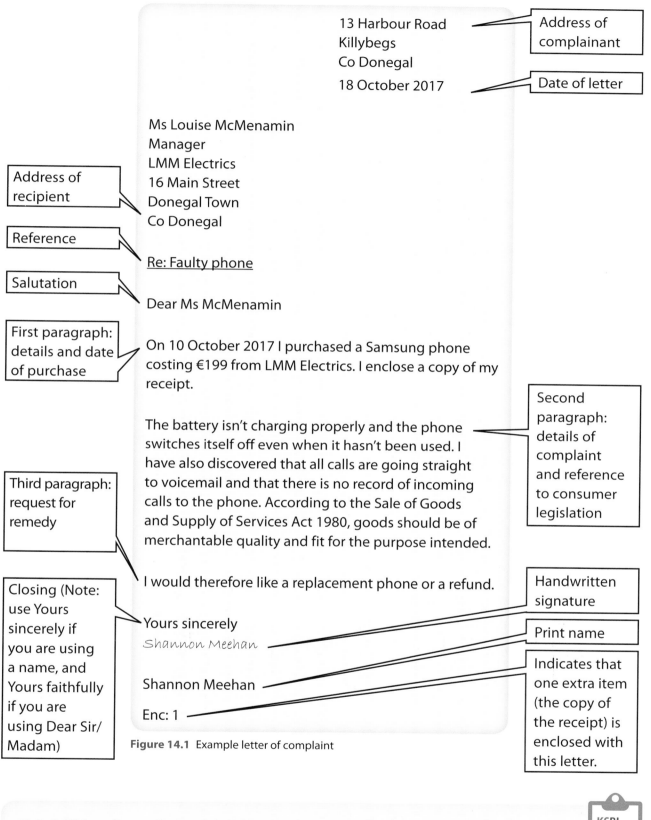

Address of complainant

13 Harbour Road
Killybegs
Co Donegal

Date of letter

18 October 2017

Address of recipient

Ms Louise McMenamin
Manager
LMM Electrics
16 Main Street
Donegal Town
Co Donegal

Reference

Re: Faulty phone

Salutation

Dear Ms McMenamin

First paragraph: details and date of purchase

On 10 October 2017 I purchased a Samsung phone costing €199 from LMM Electrics. I enclose a copy of my receipt.

Second paragraph: details of complaint and reference to consumer legislation

The battery isn't charging properly and the phone switches itself off even when it hasn't been used. I have also discovered that all calls are going straight to voicemail and that there is no record of incoming calls to the phone. According to the Sale of Goods and Supply of Services Act 1980, goods should be of merchantable quality and fit for the purpose intended.

Third paragraph: request for remedy

I would therefore like a replacement phone or a refund.

Closing (Note: use Yours sincerely if you are using a name, and Yours faithfully if you are using Dear Sir/ Madam)

Yours sincerely

Shannon Meehan

Handwritten signature

Print name

Shannon Meehan

Enc: 1

Indicates that one extra item (the copy of the receipt) is enclosed with this letter.

Figure 14.1 Example letter of complaint

14.6 Write a letter of complaint about a waterproof jacket that leaked the first time you wore it in the rain. The shop you bought it from is Gleeson Ltd on the main street of your town. You have phoned the shop to get the name of the manager, who is Desmond O'Rourke.

KSBL
KSC
KSMIT

Who can help you if you have a consumer complaint?

First you should approach the shop or service company and give them an opportunity to redress the problem by providing you with a refund, replacement product or repair. If there is no satisfactory resolution, you can take your complaint to a consumer agency.

In chapter 13 you learned about the Consumers' Association of Ireland, which provides advice to consumers. There are other agencies that you can contact if you have a complaint.

See Chapter 13

Competition and Consumer Protection Commission (CCPC)

Coimisiún um Iomaíocht agus Cosaint Tomhaltóirí | Competition and Consumer Protection Commission

The CCPC was established in 2014. Its role is to:

> Provide information and education to consumers about their rights and personal finance

> Conduct research into consumer matters

> Represent consumers' interests by advising policy makers

> Ensure there is sufficient choice for consumers in Ireland.

The CCPC has a website, www.ccpc.ie, which gives information about the organisation and your rights as a consumer.

14.7 Work in groups of three or four. Go to the CCPC website and research the rights of consumers in one of the following areas:

> Buying goods online

> Buying gift vouchers

> Paying a deposit when buying goods / services

> Mobile phone services and contracts

> Cancelled flights.

In your group, create a presentation / poster / infographic on the rights of consumers in the area you researched and then make a presentation about these rights to the rest of the class.

Groupwork

Research

KSWwO
KSBC
KSC
KSBL
KSMIT

Commission for Energy Regulation (CER)

The CER protects consumers by resolving complaints about energy companies which supply electricity, gas and water (including Airtricity, Bord Gáis, Energia, Electric Ireland and Flogas).

Common types of complaints include:

> Delays in getting connected

> Faulty meters

> Connection costs.

Consumers must first make the complaint to the relevant company themselves, either by phone or in writing. If the complaint is not resolved, the consumer can complain to CER by email, letter or phone. The website www.cer.ie contains helpful information on how to complain initially to the gas, electricity or water supplier.

14.8 On the www.cer.ie website, find the page for Customer Care and then the page for Helpful Hints. On that page, scroll down to the section 'If you have a complaint'. Summarise this information on a leaflet that you could hand to people to help them if they need to use the service. Use pictures to make it interesting.

Compare the leaflet you create with those of your classmates. Use the template in the Student Activity Book to self-assess and peer-assess these leaflets.

Groupwork

Research

KSWwO
KSBC
KSBL
KSC
KSMIT

Commission for Communications Regulation (ComReg)

Commission for **Communications Regulation**

ComReg protects consumers of communications businesses, e.g.

> An Post
> Home phone provider
> Mobile phone provider
> Broadband provider.

Consumers must make a complaint to their provider initially. If this complaint fails, ComReg will contact the provider and seek an official response.

ComReg also examines trends in consumer complaints and highlights any persistent problems with the relevant provider.

The website www.comreg.ie provides advice for communications consumers on how to make a complaint to their provider, and also contains a useful interactive guide to phone and broadband pricing, statistics on consumer queries and complaints.

14.9 On the www.comreg.ie website, find the answers to the following questions. Look at the frequently asked questions (FAQs). Rewrite the answer in one or two sentences so that when your classmate or your teacher asks you the question, you can give a simple answer.

(a) I have been called by someone supposedly from an Irish bank, looking for my personal details in order to 'give me a refund'. What should I do?

(b) I have been contacted by someone claiming to be from my mobile operator asking if they can test my phone. What should I do?

Groupwork

Research

KSWwO
KSBC
KSBL
KSC
KSMIT

Financial Services Ombudsman (FSO)

Financial Services Ombudsman

The Financial Services Ombudsman investigates complaints from consumers about financial service providers.

Consumers must first make a complaint to the relevant financial institution. If this is not resolved satisfactorily, a complaint can be made to the Financial Services Ombudsman. The service provided by the Ombudsman is free to use and is funded by financial service providers.

The website www.financialombudsman.ie contains information on how to make a complaint, case studies of previous complaints and podcasts.

14.10 Which types of financial service provider does the Ombudsman investigate? List them all.

14.11 Research the website to find out what the time limit is on submitting a complaint about a financial service provider.

Research

KSMIT

The Office of the Ombudsman

The Office of the Ombudsman is responsible for investigating complaints from people who feel they have been unfairly treated by a public body, such as:

> Government departments
> Local authorities
> The Health Service Executive (HSE)
> Publicly funded third-level institutions
> Private and public nursing homes.

The Ombudsman is independent, impartial and provides a free service.

Before making a complaint to the Ombudsman, you must first complain to the relevant public body. If your complaint is not resolved to your satisfaction, you can then complain to the Ombudsman.

**Oifig an Ombudsman
Office of the Ombudsman**

The website www.ombudsman.ie contains information on how to make a complaint, information videos and sample cases.

14.12 Pick one of the case studies on the website www.ombudsman.ie and rewrite it in the form of a newspaper article in the space provided in the Student Activity Book.

Research

KSBC
KSBL

Did you know?

The word *ombudsman* is a Swedish word that means representative or someone appointed to act for another person. The first ombudsman was appointed in Sweden in the early nineteenth century to investigate complaints about the king's ministers.

Ireland's first ombudsman was appointed in 1984.

Small Claims Procedure

The Small Claims Procedure offers a quick, cheap and easy way to resolve a complaint about a faulty good or poor work by a service provider, without having to hire a solicitor.

If you have a complaint of this nature, you should first complain to the retailer or service provider yourself. If you cannot resolve the issue with them, then you can go through the Small Claims Procedure.

You can complain online at courts.ie or by completing an application form and returning it to your local district court.

Research

14.13 What is the fee for using the Small Claims Procedure?

14.14 What is the maximum amount you can claim for?

KSMIT
KSBN

The Small Claims Registrar will inform the business about your claim. The business has fifteen days to reply. If they do not do so, the claim will be undisputed, which means that the district court will direct the business to pay you the amount claimed.

Groupwork

14.15 (a) In your group, draw a flow chart or other type of infographic to inform people of which agency they should use if they have a problem. For example, *Is your complaint about a mobile phone company or broadband? Yes → Complain to ComReg.* Make sure you include all the agencies we have looked at in this chapter.

(b) All groups should display their posters around the room. View other posters and rate them using the template provided in chapter 14 in the Student Activity Book.

KSWwO
KSBC
KSBL
KSMIT

Consumer protection in the media

Newspapers and radio and TV programmes provide information and advice to consumers about their rights.

14.16 In your group, research consumer protection in both local and national media (newspapers, radio and TV). Create a poster or presentation listing the different programmes/newspaper columns and the days they are published/aired. Summarise a particular case that you find interesting. Create a display in your classroom showcasing your research.

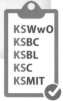

Groupwork

Research

KSWwO
KSBC
KSBL
KSC
KSMIT

14.17 At the end of the exams, eight friends went out for a meal. They had a great time and they all enjoyed their meals. After the first course, Graham said, 'If we complain about a couple of the meals not being cooked through properly, they might give us dessert for free.' Joshua was horrified as everyone had said how much they had enjoyed their meal. What would you say to Graham? Do you all agree with this reaction?

Groupwork

KSC
KSBL
KSMIT
KSMM
KSSW

Think about the impact on:

> the whole dining group
> the waiting staff
> the kitchen staff

> the restaurant business
> other diners who may have overheard
> future visitors to the restaurant.

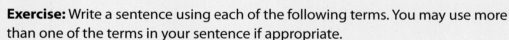

Key Terms

KSBL
KSC
KSMIT
KSBC

You should be able to *define*, *spell*, give *examples* and *apply* to real life each of the following key terms associated with this topic.

Exercise: Write a sentence using each of the following terms. You may use more than one of the terms in your sentence if appropriate.

Commission for Communications Regulation (ComReg)

Commission for Energy Regulation (CER)

Competition and Consumer Protection Commission (CCPC)

consumer

credit note

directive

Financial Services Ombudsman

fit for purpose

guarantee

merchantable quality

ombudsman

redress

refund

repair

replacement

retailer

sample

Small Claims Procedure

unfair commercial practices

warranty

Chapter 15 :: The Impact of Consumer Choices

Learning outcomes

When you have completed this chapter you will be able to:

✔ Consider the role of the consumer in the marketplace and the wider economy

✔ Examine the impact of consumer behaviour on others – locally, nationally and globally

✔ Explore the ways in which consumer choices can influence the provision of goods and services, and how consumer power can change the lives of other people

✔ Outline the concept of sustainability

✔ Explain what it means to be an ethical consumer

✔ Debate the ethical and sustainability issues that arise from consumption of goods and services

✔ Evaluate how you can contribute to sustainable development.

A product's life cycle

'Consumers are increasingly interested in the world behind the product they buy. Life cycle thinking implies that everyone in the whole chain of a product's life cycle, from cradle to grave, has a responsibility and a role to play, taking into account all the relevant external effects. The impacts of all life cycle stages (materials and manufacturing, use by the customer, disposal and handling at end of use) need to be considered comprehensively when taking informed decisions on production and consumption patterns, policies and management strategies.'

Klaus Toepfer, Executive Director, UNEP (United Nations Environment Programme)

Source: https://sustainabledevelopment.un.org/content/documents/846Why_take_a_life_cycle_approach_EN.pdf

Some BIG questions!

Have you ever thought about the type of consumer you are?

> Are you an informed consumer, a responsible consumer, an ethical consumer or perhaps even a 'green' consumer? Do you understand what each of these involves?

> What factors influence your decision to buy a product? Is it the price, the quality, the functionality, or do you simply choose products which are 'new' or which are popular with your friends?

> Do you consider what goes into making the product? Do you know what materials and resources are used to produce it?

> Are you concerned about whether the materials or the finished product are recyclable?

> Do you ever consider where the product comes from, or the many people who are involved in making and delivering that product to you?

> What do you do with products when they no longer meet your needs? Do you make them available for reuse? Do you recycle them? Or do you simply throw them away and replace them with new ones?

These are all very big questions, but many consumers give them very little thought. Our lives are busy and when we go shopping we expect the shops to have the goods and services we need. We simply want to buy those items and just get on with consuming them.

15.1 Give an example from your own experience for each of the following:

(a) Buying something with no thought to its social impact, e.g. buying an item because it was very cheap even though it may have been made abroad by people in very poor conditions.

(b) Buying something with thought to its social impact, e.g. refusing to buy an item that is likely to have been made by people earning very little money.

(c) Buying something with no thought to its environmental impact, e.g. a new phone when your old one was perfectly all right but you wanted a newer model.

(d) Buying something with thought to its environmental impact, e.g. refusing to buy an item that has a lot of unnecessary packaging.

15.2 Have you ever bought something because you really wanted it at the time, but regretted it later as you know that it was not an ethical purchase?

In this chapter you will think about the consumer choices you make, so that as well as being an informed consumer, you will also be a more **responsible**, more **ethical** and more **sustainable** consumer.

In order for this to happen you will need to consider the impact that *your* consumer choices can have at local, national and even at international level. You should also understand that consumers have the power to create **demand** for goods and services, and therefore they have the power to influence the types of goods and services supplied as well as the way in which they are produced.

See Chapter 35

Resources

All goods and services require the use of different types of resources. These may be:

> Natural resources – oil, gas, coal, water, agricultural land, etc.
> Human resources – workers and the labour they provide
> Capital resources – buildings, vehicles, machinery, equipment, etc.
> Financial resources – money.

See Chapter 1

In Strand 3 you will study economics and will examine how these resources give rise to our four basic **factors of production:** land, labour, capital and enterprise. Many of these resources are limited and this often forces us to make choices about how we allocate and use them.

See Chapter 33

The goods and services you consume will have an impact on the use of these resources, and *your* spending habits can have consequences for a large number of people in many parts of the world.

In much the same way as a small stone thrown into a lake can create a ripple effect right across the water, the individual buying decisions that *you* make can have a knock-on effect on the lives of others.

15.3 Think about buying a packet of tomatoes in the local supermarket that were grown in Holland, rather than buying Irish tomatoes loose from the greengrocer. Discuss how this small decision might affect other people as well as the environment.

Discussion

KSWwO
KSMIT
KSC
KSBL

Non-renewable resources

These are resources that are limited in supply or that cannot be replaced. Examples include fossil fuels such as coal, oil and natural gas, which have been formed over millions of years. Since we are using them up at a much faster rate than they can be replenished they will eventually run out.

While we cannot be certain about exact dates and quantities, many experts suggest that at current rates of usage, petroleum may only last a few more decades and coal is likely to be used up in less than 300 years.

15.4 Are we selfish in our use of petrol and diesel for vehicles, or do you think it is acceptable to use the world's resources as we want, and when they run out the scientists and inventors will just have to find replacement fuels? Discuss this in your group.

Discussion

KSWwO
KSMIT
KSC
KSBL

Renewable resources

These are resources that are not limited in supply, that won't run out and that can be regrown, reused or recycled. Examples include wind, sunlight, trees and soil.

15.5 Just because we can grow more trees, is it acceptable to use trees without any thought as to how we are using them and at what rate we are using them? Discuss this in your group.

KSWwO
KSMIT
KSC
KSBL

See Chapter 40

Sustainable consumption

There is a danger that even those resources that can be renewed can be overused to the point of extinction. In order to be truly renewable, these resources must be used **sustainably**.

Sustainability is a process of balancing the social, economic and environmental systems for the wellbeing of individuals now and in the future.

Definition

ONLY WHEN THE LAST TREE HAS DIED AND THE LAST RIVER BEEN POISONED AND THE LAST FISH BEEN CAUGHT WILL WE REALISE WE CANNOT EAT MONEY

There are three core pillars of sustainability:

> Social – people
> Environmental – planet
> Economic – profit.

Sustainable development meets the needs of the present without compromising the ability of future generations to meet their own needs. If everyone in the world had the same standard of living that we have in Europe, we would need the resources of three planet earths.

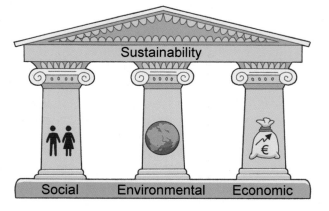

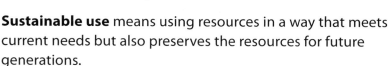

Sustainable use means using resources in a way that meets current needs but also preserves the resources for future generations.

Sustainability involves carefully managing a resource in order to give it time to renew itself. For example, the fishing industry issues licences and also sets limits (called **quotas**)

on the amount of fish that can be caught each year. These measures are designed to protect fish stocks and allow each species time to regenerate. While it would be possible to create more short-term wealth and employment by removing these restrictions, the long-term effect would be the extinction of many species of fish. For that reason unregulated fishing is not sustainable.

Since the choices we make as consumers can affect the lives of so many others, it is important for us to think about our buying habits and to make an effort to become sustainable consumers. **Sustainable consumption** means buying goods and services that do not harm society, the environment or the economy.

In order to better understand the impact of consumer behaviour on both the economy and the environment, let us look at the life cycle of a product.

15.6 In groups, research one of the options below and prepare a presentation for the rest of the class.

Group 1: Research how bananas get from large-scale plantations to Ireland's supermarket shelves. Make sure you provide information on:

KSBC
KSMIT
KSWwO
KSMM
KSBL
KSC

(a) How bananas are grown.

(b) How they are prepared for shipping.

(c) How they are transported to our supermarkets.

(d) How they are stored before reaching the shelves.

Group 2: Research how Fairtrade bananas are grown, prepared for shipping and transported to our supermarkets. Make sure you note the benefits and drawbacks, if any, of Fairtrade bananas over conventionally grown bananas.

Group 3: Research how organic bananas are grown, prepared for shipping and transported to our supermarkets. Make sure you note the benefits of organically grown bananas over non-organically grown bananas.

15.7 When you have seen each group's presentation, discuss as a class:

(a) How do you now feel about buying bananas?

(b) Has this activity changed how you feel about wasting food?

(c) What are reasons why people don't buy Fairtrade or organically grown bananas?

(d) Do you think the workers on large-scale plantations will receive a fair wage for the work they do? How might wages differ depending on where the bananas are grown?

(e) How is eating an Irish-grown apple more beneficial for a sustainable economy than eating a banana grown thousand of kilometres away?

Did you know?

The growth and development of 'fair trade'

The fair trade movement began shortly after the Second World War and developed rapidly during the 1960s. Fair trade means that producers and workers in developing countries are paid a fair price by the developed world for their work. It means they have decent working conditions and fair terms of trade.

The idea continued to grow and resulted in the creation of Fairtrade Labelling Organisations International (FLO) in 1997. This umbrella organisation sets the Fairtrade standards and supports, inspects and certifies producers.

By 2014 the number of Fairtrade producer countries reached 74, while more than 30,000 Fairtrade products were on sale in 125 countries across the world. In that same year global retail sales of Fairtrade products reached €5.1 bn.

The ethical consumer

Ethics and moral values refer to a person's ability to judge right from wrong. While all consumers choose goods and services that meet their needs, *ethical consumers* choose goods and services that meet their needs *and* reflect their moral values.

The problem of course is that not everyone shares the same values and the values we develop depend very much on our culture. Our financial circumstances may create a conflict between our values and the need for value for money. As ever, scarce resources force us to make choices about our consumption.

15.8 The Ethical Consumer is a UK organisation that helps people make informed choices about the products they buy, based on how ethical they are. On their website (www.ethicalconsumer.org), they state five common beliefs about ethical shopping:

Discussion

KSWwO
KSC
KSBL

1 Shopping ethically is just too complicated for me to understand.

2 Shopping ethically doesn't make any difference and is a waste of time.

3 I can't afford to be an ethical consumer – ethical products are always too expensive.

4 Even if it's ethical, shopping is still bad news for the planet – we need to buy less of everything.

5 Ethical shopping is only for radical activists – it's not for me.

Discuss what you think about these statements and how they relate to you personally.

Debunking ethical consumer myths

1 **Shopping ethically is just too complicated for me to understand.**
There are lots of issues to think about when you're out shopping.
The Ethical Consumer magazine produces buyers' guides and recommends best buy companies.

2 **Shopping ethically doesn't make any difference and is a waste of time.**
Not true. Take the example of how the Fairtrade and organic movements hit the big time. Not so long ago Fairtrade and organic goods were only sold in small, specialist shops. It was thanks to thousands of ordinary shoppers going out and demanding that supermarkets stock organic carrots and Fairtrade coffee that the big supermarkets were finally persuaded to stock Fairtrade and organic produce. By acting as part of a much bigger community individuals have a key role to play in bringing about corporate change.

3 **I can't afford to be an ethical consumer – ethical products are always too expensive.**
This isn't always the case. Research carried out by Ethical Consumer has shown that in 28 of our recent buyers' guides, there was an ethical Best Buy amongst the cheapest products in almost half the cases.

4 **Even if it's ethical, shopping is still bad news for the planet – we need to buy less of everything.**
Whilst this is true, everyone still needs to buy food, clothes and other goods. It makes sense then to make sure that the things we buy are ethically sourced.

5 **Ethical shopping is only for radical activists – it's not for me.**
Not true. Growing numbers of ordinary people and families are now thinking about the impact that their shopping has on people and the planet. The latest research suggests that 75% of the population now shop ethically at least some of the time, whether this be buying free-range eggs or shopping locally.

Source: Adapted from www.ethicalconsumer.org/shoppingethically/topethicaltips/
top5ethicalconsumptionmyths.aspx

Figure 15.1 Debunking ethical consumer myths

15.9 Do you agree with the arguments presented in figure 15.1?

KSWwO
KSC
KSBL

The first step in becoming an ethical consumer is to become an **informed consumer** as this will allow you to understand the issues involved and will help you make choices which take into account:

> Your needs   > Your values   > Your financial circumstances.

For example, many people who consume meat products may value and support the humane treatment of animals, but when it comes to purchasing goods, limited availability of cash may mean that they are not willing or able to pay a little extra for free-range brands.

15.10 In pairs, discuss whether you would be prepared to have fewer treats so you could spend extra on something that was a little more expensive, but you know to be ethically produced. For example, would you prefer to buy three cheap T-shirts from a shop known to source their clothes from countries with poor worker conditions, or one T-shirt from a shop that is certified as buying from companies that look after their workers?

Despite differences in values and purchasing power, there are a number of key elements that define ethical goods and ethical consumers.

Ethical goods are produced in a way that is kind to the environment and also to the people who produce them. This means the goods have been manufactured and distributed in a manner that minimises social and environmental damage.

Ethical consumers buy products and services that have been produced under ethical conditions. They:

> Make careful, considered and deliberate choices about the goods and services they buy

> Take responsibility for their buying decisions

> Avoid products and services that have a negative impact on society, on animals or on the environment.

Since many goods are produced by multinational companies that operate in several parts of the world, ethical consumerism also tries to ensure that international labour standards are applied across global supply chains. After all, it is only fair that all workers should be treated with dignity and respect and should receive a fair reward for their efforts.

In the past, campaigns have been launched against several well-known multinational companies including Nike, Gap, Adidas, Primark and Marks & Spencer. Campaigners have highlighted the exploitation of resources and workers used in producing goods.

In some cases consumers were called upon to boycott these companies and their products.

A **boycott** is a voluntary act of protest in which consumers refuse to buy from, or deal with, a particular company.

Did you know?

The word **boycott** entered the English language during the 'Land War' in Ireland (in about 1880). It comes from the name of a land agent, Charles Boycott, who worked for an absentee English landlord in Co Mayo. Following a poor harvest, Boycott refused to lower rents for his tenants and even tried to evict some of them. In protest at his actions, local people shunned him. He was unable to buy or sell anything and even the postman refused to deliver his mail! He was unable to hire workers to harvest his crops. The 'boycott' was widely reported in the newspapers of the time and the word has been used ever since to describe this type of protest action.

As a result of these campaigns and of the growth of ethical consumerism, companies are more aware of the need to behave in a socially responsible manner. Indeed, many commit a lot of resources, including money, to improving their **corporate social responsibility** (**CSR**).

CSR refers to organisations acting to benefit society and/or the environment.

Definition

The impact of ethical consumerism

The growth and impact of ethical consumerism can be witnessed in all of the following areas.

Increased emphasis on CSR

Businesses have come to realise the value of CSR to society and to the business itself, particularly in terms of consumer goodwill and positive public relations.

Increased focus on 'green consumerism'

This takes into account the impact of consumption on the environment. For example, a reduction in the amount of harmful chemicals used in the manufacture of aerosols and fridges, and the increased development and demand for 'green' energy and 'green' cars, etc.

How big is your carbon footprint?

Your carbon footprint – also called an **ecological footprint** – is an approximate measure of all the greenhouse gases emitted either directly by you or on your behalf.

15.11 Use an online carbon footprint calculator to calculate your own personal carbon footprint, or that of your household. Create a poster showing the results of your research.

Research

KSBC
KSMIT
KSMM
KSC
KSBN

The United Nations Millennium Development Goals (MDGs)

These are global objectives that target hunger, poverty, education and environmental sustainability.

15.12 Research the UN's Millennium Development Goals and identify the main targets set out in the initiative. Evaluate how successful countries have been in achieving the targets.

Research

KSMIT

UNDP (United Nations Development Programme)

The production of fair labour-certified garments

Organisations and brands that have this certification seek to improve the pay and conditions of workers and tackle the global 'sweatshops' where vulnerable employees are exploited.

The promotion of animal welfare

Concerns in this area include how animals are used in scientific research, as a source of food or kept in zoos, farms and circuses, etc. Some businesses, including The Body Shop, made a clear commitment not to sell cosmetics that have been tested on animals.

Campaigners also highlight the ways in which human activities affect the welfare and survival of wild species. This includes the destruction of natural habitats.

Enterprise in action

The Body Shop

Anita Roddick started The Body Shop in March 1976, just as Europe was going 'green'. The mission statement of The Body Shop makes an overriding commitment **'to dedicate the business to the pursuit of social and environmental change'**. Its stores and products are used to help communicate human rights and environmental issues.

http://www.thebodyshop.co.uk/content/about-us/aboutus.aspx

The Body Shop International Plc

Sustainable resources and technologies

There is an increased demand for products made using sustainable resources and technologies. Examples include products made from recycled materials or replanted forests.

Reduce, reuse, recycle

The Reduce, Reuse, Recycle campaign has been very successful in reducing waste.

Enterprise in action

See Chapter 17

ReCreate.ie

ReCreate is a social enterprise which collects clean, end-of-line materials from businesses and redistributes them to its members. The concept is known as **creative reuse**, which encourages the public to reuse materials that would normally be thrown away in all kinds of inventive ways.

Members pay an annual subscription fee and in turn have unlimited access to the materials stored in ReCreate's Warehouse Of Wonders, while businesses have their materials collected for free and have the opportunity to avail of a strong CSR programme. This encourages reuse on an industrial scale, which is ReCreate's main aim. Additional income streams include: art workshops, project funding, event management, a complementary shop and team-building programmes.

ReCreate's vision is to continue to be an innovative, dynamic social enterprise inspiring, curiosity, creativity and care for the environment. ReCreate aims to:

> Provide accessible and affordable art materials and educational supplies to all
> Divert materials from landfill and raise environmental awareness around reuse (150 tonnes a year)
> Facilitate social inclusion and social gain, particularly in areas of disadvantage
> Provide quality work experience opportunities for those most distant from the labour market, including those with special needs.

167

ReCreate has learned that by just putting materials on the shelves in its Warehouse of Wonders, the members begin thinking about how they can reuse them. The items' original uses are being reinvented, creatively reused in every way possible from children's art, school murals, sensory projects, festival installations, all the way up to community gardens. The diverse range of materials and alternative / creative opportunities for reusing them really has no limits and ReCreate is making this possible for the whole community.

Source: Information from www.recreate.ie

So what can *you* do?

 'Every time you spend money you're casting a vote for the kind of world you want to live in.'

Anna Lappé, author and educator on sustainable food

1 Engage in life cycle thinking

Consider the environmental and economic impacts of a product over its entire life cycle. The challenges us to be more mindful of the consumer choices we make. It requires us to take responsibility for the impact that our choices have on others.

Issues we should think about include:

> Energy usage
> Working conditions
> Waste production
> Pollution effects
> Destruction of endangered ecosystems.

For example, if you realised that it takes 24 trees to create 50,000 sheets of office paper and 2.3 cubic metres of landfill space to dispose of it, you might choose paper made from recycled material or sourced from sustainably managed forests. Recycled paper creates 75% less air pollution and 35% less water pollution over its life cycle. Better still, only use paper when you really need to.

2 Ask questions

Questions you might want to ask are:

> Where is the product made?
> What is it made of?
> How much energy does it consume?
> How are the workers who made it treated?

15.13 Research the organisations that certify ethical products (e.g. that do not use animal testing or that promote sustainable farming). Create a poster showing the logos and names of these organisations and what their purpose is.

3 Support sustainable businesses

As demand for sustainable goods increases, producers will be more willing to supply them and prices are likely to fall. Consumers have the power to change things as businesses respond to consumer pressure.

4 Reduce, reuse and recycle

Choose goods that are durable and will last a long time. It isn't always necessary to have the latest and most up-to-date products.

5 Consider end-of-life disposal

Before disposing of products that no longer meet your needs, consider the environmental benefits of reuse and recycling. Where this is not possible, be sure to dispose of products in an environmentally responsible manner.

6 Shop local where possible

Buying locally produced goods and services helps reduce some of the environmental damage caused by '**fuel kilometres**' as goods are shipped from around the globe (think back to those bananas!). It also helps sustain Irish jobs and improves the local economy.

Did you know?

Shop local

Buying from locally owned businesses keeps money circulating closer to where you spend. Local shops use local services, accountants, insurance brokers, suppliers as well as employing local people and they also carry a higher percentage of locally produced goods.

Every €10 spent locally on Irish products generates €24 of benefit to the local community.

Forty-five cents of every euro spent is reinvested locally in comparison to only 15 cents for the foreign multiples.

Source: Mark Fielding, Chief Executive of the Irish Small and Medium Enterprises Association (ISME), www.isme.ie

15.14 What are your thoughts on the suggestion that 'every €10 spent locally generates €24 to benefit the local community'? How is this possible?

KSMIT
KSWwO
KSC

In the news

In all fairness: How to consume with a clear conscience

Few big companies fare well when it comes to ethical standards, but change may be in the air

By Conor Pope

Ethics can be hard to hang on to when you're shopping, and once you start looking closely at your purchases you will find few brands that are completely without sin.

By buying Fairtrade products we are doing something to make sure small producers in poor parts of the world are not being exploited.

Sales of Fairtrade products have more than doubled since 2008, because big-name chocolate brands such as Mars and Cadbury started to use Fairtrade on mainstream products.

More support is needed – particularly from the Irish retail sector. Its support of the Fairtrade movement could be, at best, described as partial. Today, three bananas in every 10 consumed in the UK is a Fairtrade one and several retailers have switched 100 per cent of their bananas to Fairtrade. In Switzerland 50 per cent of all bananas sold are Fairtrade. In Ireland the figure is closer to 5 per cent.

In Germany, sales of Fairtrade roses account for more than 30 per cent of the total market but in Ireland that figure is closer to 1 per cent.

Retailer buy-in

'It is not just about consumers making choices, it is about retailers making it easier for consumers to make those choices.'

Awareness of the Fairtrade concept in Ireland is at 82 per cent – the second highest in Europe after the UK. According to Fairtrade Ireland, 95 per cent of Irish people believe companies play an important role in protecting the environment and 89 per cent think companies can reduce poverty through the way they do business. A significant 71 per cent believe shopping choices can make a difference to farmers and workers in poor countries.

Source: Article adapted from the *Irish Times,* 24 Febuary 2014

15.15 Read the newspaper article above. Do you think it is up to the retailers or the consumers to lead ethical consumerism? Discuss your thoughts on this.

Discussion

KSWwO
KSC
KSBL
KSMIT

We do not inherit the earth from our ancestors; we borrow it from our children.

Native American proverb

15.16 What is the proverb above saying to us as modern consumers? Discuss your attitude to this proverb with the class.

Discussion

KSWwO
KSC

Key Terms

KSBL
KSC
KSMIT
KSBC

You should be able to *define*, *spell*, give *examples* and *apply* to real life each of the following key terms associated with this topic.

Exercise: Write a sentence using each of the following terms. You may use more than one of the terms in your sentence if appropriate.

boycott	fair trade
carbon footprint	green consumer
consumer	non-renewable resources
corporate social responsibility (CSR)	renewable resources
ethics	sustainable development

Chapter 16 ::
The Bigger Picture

Learning outcomes

When you have completed this chapter you will be able to:

✔ Explain the term 'globalisation'
✔ Outline the reasons why companies engage in globalisation and foreign trade
✔ Explain what a transnational company is and the reasons why they locate in particular countries
✔ Explain the reasons why ICT has increased globalisation
✔ Identify the impact of global companies and technology on consumer choice and behaviour.

What is globalisation?

Globalisation is the process by which the world becomes interconnected as a result of increased trade and cultural exchange. Many big companies are **transnational corporations** with **subsidiaries** in many countries.

> **Transnational** means operating across national boundaries. A transnational corporation is a company that carries out its business in other countries as well as its own.
>
> **Definition**

> A **subsidiary** is a branch of a business, or a company that is controlled by a parent company.
>
> **Definition**

Globalisation has resulted in:

> Increased international trade
> Greater dependence on the global economy
> Freer movement of capital, goods and services
> Companies such as McDonald's and Starbucks trading throughout the world and treating it as a global market.

See Chapter 41

Development of globalisation

Countries around the world have been trading internationally for hundreds of years. In the last two hundred years this trade has expanded, for a number of reasons:

> In the nineteenth century the industrial revolution made it possible to produce goods cheaply. Rapid population growth worldwide led to increased demand for these goods.

> The construction of the Suez and Panama canals made it quicker and easier to transport goods by sea.

> The invention of the telephone made it easier and quicker for businesses to communicate internationally.

> The invention of aeroplanes allowed for faster transportation of goods and people internationally.

> Increased use of electricity meant that goods could be produced much faster.

> Barriers to international trade were reduced by agreements following the Second World War.

> Widespread use of television created global awareness of and demand for many products.

> The invention of modern technologies such as the computer, the internet and email have made it quicker and easier than ever before to communicate, advertise and sell internationally.

16.1 Which of the developments listed above do you think had the greatest influence on globalisation?

Give reasons for your answer and share these with your partner. Find out if another pair agrees with you.

KSMIT
KSBL
KSC

Reasons for globalisation

The following factors have also helped the globalisation process.

> **Improvements in technology:** The internet and mobile technology have allowed greater communication between people in different countries and allowed businesses to trade internationally very easily.

> **Consumer demands:** As income levels and global awareness increase, consumers are more likely to want goods and services from overseas markets.

> **Economies of scale:** The cost per item reduces when operating on a large scale. The wider you distribute the item, the more you are likely to sell, and the more you make, the cheaper it becomes to produce.

> **Freedom of trade:** Organisations such as the **World Trade Organization (WTO)** encourage free trade between countries, which helps to remove restrictive barriers to trade between countries.

> **Labour availability and skills:** Countries such as India and China have lower labour costs and also high skill levels among their workers. Manufacturing companies in particular will take advantage of this cheap supply of labour.

> **Decreased transport costs:** The cost of transporting goods between countries has decreased, e.g. by using larger cargo ships.

> **Transport improvements:** Goods and people can travel quickly between countries.

Research

KSMIT

16.2 Find out the following about the World Trade Organization:
  (a) Where is the WTO based?
  (b) When was the WTO established?
  (c) How many member countries does the WTO have?
  (d) When did Ireland become a member of the WTO?
  (e) Who is Ireland's current ambassador to the WTO?

Delivery systems

Definition

Delivery systems refers to how the product gets transported from the manufacturer to the consumer.

Improvements in transportation and delivery systems have made it easier for businesses to sell globally.

Commonly used delivery systems are road, rail, sea and air. Table 16.1 looks at the advantages and disadvantages of each.

Table 16.1 Delivery systems

Delivery system	Advantages	Disadvantages
Road	❯ Door-to-door deliveries are possible ❯ Minimum handling of goods	❯ Road works/traffic congestion can cause delays ❯ Not good for the environment due to emissions ❯ Not suitable for bulky goods
Rail	❯ Suitable for bulky goods	❯ Fixed timetable/not flexible ❯ Not every town has a railway station
Sea	❯ Suitable for transporting bulky goods worldwide ❯ Cheaper than transporting by air	❯ Slow ❯ Weather conditions can cause delays ❯ Must link with another form of transport
Air	❯ Fast ❯ Suitable for perishable goods	❯ Expensive ❯ Must link with another form of transport

16.3 There is another method of delivery, drones, which at the time of writing is in its infancy. Do you think it will become a common way of delivering goods? In small groups, research delivery by drones and prepare a presentation, video or podcast to explain it to the rest of the class.

Groupwork

KSWwO
KSBC

Transnational companies

Globalisation has resulted in many businesses setting up or buying operations in other countries. When a foreign company invests in a country, perhaps by building a factory or a shop, this is called **inward investment**, or **foreign direct investment (FDI)**. Ireland has been very successful at attracting inward investment.

When companies have their head office in one country and operate in several different countries they are known as **transnational companies (TNCs)**. The US fast-food chain McDonald's is a large TNC – it has nearly 30,000 restaurants in 119 countries.

Factors attracting TNCs to a particular country include:

> Cheap raw materials
> Good transport links
> Cheap and plentiful labour supply

> Access to markets where goods are sold
> Attractive government policies, e.g. low corporation tax.

Enterprise in action

Microsoft, the world's biggest software company, established an Irish manufacturing facility in 1985 and employed one hundred people. It now employs over 1,200 full-time staff and 700 contract staff in Sandyford, Dublin.

Figure 16.1 Microsoft Ireland is a subsidiary of the US software giant Microsoft, which sells, distributes and markets software globally from Dublin

16.4 Find the names of five Irish companies that are transnational.

16.5 Find the names of five foreign-owned companies that have their headquarters or large subsidiaries in Ireland.

Research

KSMIT

Impacts of globalisation

Globalisation is having a huge effect, both good and bad, on the world economy and on people's lives.

Positive impacts

> **Employment:** TNCs help countries by providing new jobs and skills for local people.

> **Spin-off effects:** TNCs bring wealth and foreign currency to local economies when they buy local resources, products and services, and in doing so they support local businesses. This extra investment results in more tax being paid to the government, and this can be spent on education, health and infrastructure.

> **New experiences:** The sharing of ideas, experiences and lifestyles of different cultures. People can buy foods and other products not previously available to them.

Negative impacts

> **Benefits the rich more than the poor:** Globalisation operates mostly in the interests of the richest countries, which dominate world trade at the expense of poorer ones.

> **Local communities:** There is no guarantee that the wealth from inward investment will benefit the local people where the company operates. Often profits are sent back to the home country of the TNC. This is called **repatriation of profits**. In addition, due to economies of scale, transnational companies may drive small local companies out of business.

16.6 Discuss whether you think it is good that Ireland attracts big companies from overseas to open branches here. Give reasons for your answers.

Are there any negative consequences?

KSBL
KSMIT
KSC
KSWwO

Globalisation means that we can buy goods from and sell goods abroad. This has its advantages, but can mean that we are adding a lot of 'air miles' to goods. For example, if we buy tomatoes from abroad, there are a lot of transport costs involved and the carbon footprint is larger than if we bought Irish tomatoes; and we are not giving the Irish growers our business. If we export live animals abroad instead of their meat, they might be uncomfortable on trucks for many hours. If we create a demand for palm oil (and products made with palm oil), this might mean that rainforests are being destroyed to fulfil this demand.

See Chapter 15

16.7 How important is it to you that your ability to act as a global consumer does not conflict with your responsibilities as an ethical consumer? Do you think we give enough thought to this consequence of globalisation, or do you think there is an 'out of sight, out of mind' mentality when it comes to buying goods?

Discussion

KSWwO

The influence of developments in ICT

Improvements in **ICT** (information and communications technology) have increased globalisation by increasing trade and investment.

Email, the internet, mobile phones and faster phone lines that quickly carry large amounts of information are now considered normal. The internet is a fast and convenient way for businesses all over the globe to communicate with each other, advertise and sell online.

See Chapter 21

This means that a company can have its headquarters in one country and have branches in other countries, e.g. Google's headquarters are in California, USA, but it has more than 70 offices in over 40 countries, including Ireland.

Impact of ICT on consumer choice and behaviour

ICT is a big part of our everyday lives. Our behaviour as consumers is changing as a result of technology.

KSMIT

16.8 How do you and your family use technology to buy goods and services? List items you purchase using technology.

Online booking

Most bookings can be made online, often at much cheaper prices than making the booking in physical outlets.

16.9 What type of bookings can be made online?

16.10 Do you prefer to make bookings online or in person? Why?

16.11 What are the benefits to you and your family of booking online?

16.12 Do you have any worries about booking online?

KSMIT
KSSW
KSMM

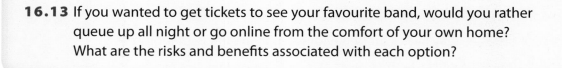

In the news

Tickets for all four U2 Dublin shows sell out in minutes

By Claire Healy

Tickets for Irish shows went on sale at 9 o'clock this morning and were limited to two per person, priced from £30 to £165 for Belfast and €30 to €185 in Dublin.

The band will play four dates at the 3 Arena on November 23, 24, 27 and 28 and fans were up bright and early ahead of tickets going on sale at 9 a.m.

The coveted tickets were sold out within half an hour.

Ticketmaster Ireland said it experienced high demand online as fans scrambled for tickets but the server held up and the site remained online for the duration.

Fans who queued from yesterday outside the 3 Arena were all smiles as they got their hands on tickets for the U2 bonanza. Some fans had queued from 6 p.m. on Sunday for tickets.

Plenty of fans were left disappointed after missing out on tickets this morning.

Source: Adapted from Irish Mirror online, 14 September 2015

16.13 If you wanted to get tickets to see your favourite band, would you rather queue up all night or go online from the comfort of your own home? What are the risks and benefits associated with each option?

KSMIT
KSMM
KSSW

Loyalty cards

Many retailers offer their customers loyalty cards. When the customer takes up this offer, they will supply their name and be given a unique number, which is stored in a database. When the customer buys something in store they are awarded a number of points depending on the amount they spend. The points are stored and can usually be converted into vouchers or discounts in store.

A **database** is a computer program that stores information in a very structured way so that it can be searched for specific details.

See Chapter 21

The loyalty card has benefits for the customer, but it also helps the retailer by providing information about the customer's spending habits.

Electronic commerce

Electronic commerce, or **e-commerce**, is the buying and selling of goods or services over the internet. The advantages for the customer are as follows:

> **Increased convenience:** Consumers can find what they are looking for without leaving their own home.

> **Greater choice:** Consumers are no longer limited to what shops they buy from and can now buy from abroad.

> **Product details**: There is likely to be greater information available online in addition to what a member of staff might be able to provide in store. Consumers are becoming more informed as they can research products online before they buy, and shop around for the best value for money.

See Chapter 13

> **Customer reviews:** There are many websites that customers can use to find out what other people think about a product or service and so make an informed decision when purchasing.

The disadvantages for the customer of buying online are:

> **No human interaction:** Some people prefer to deal with people when buying products or services.

> **Returning goods:** It can be inconvenient and expensive to return products that have been purchased online.

> **Fraud:** A website may take your money but have no intention of delivering the products.

16.14 We are encouraged to 'shop local' and 'shop Irish' but sometimes shopping online and buying something from abroad is cheaper and more convenient. Do you think it is important to shop local, even if it costs a little more? Discuss this and give your reasons for your answer.

KSWwO

Key Terms

KSBL
KSC
KSMIT
KSBC

You should be able to *define*, *spell*, give *examples* and *apply* to real life each of the following key terms associated with this topic.

Exercise: Write a sentence using each of the following terms. You may use more than one of the terms in your sentence if appropriate.

database

delivery systems

economies of scale

electronic commerce (e-commerce)

globalisation

information and communications technology (ICT)

repatriation of profits

transnational company (TNC)

World Trade Organization (WTO)

Strand Two :: **Enterprise**

Chapter 17 :: Enterprise

What is enterprise?

Enterprise is any attempt to start or do something new. It describes the actions of someone who shows initiative by taking the risk involved in setting up, investing in and running a business.

Enterprise is the *ability* of a person or group to:

> Creatively generate and build ideas
> Identify opportunities for innovation
> Turn the opportunities into practical and targeted actions.

Definition

Enterprise in action

Shíofra Ryan, An Tionchar

Transition Year student Shíofra Ryan from Offaly, who won the top prize in the 2015 Student Enterprise Awards, turned her love of camogie into a business idea.

Shíofra's specially designed camogie/hurling boots – 'An Tionchar – The Impact Hurling Boot' – have enhanced ankle supports, shock-absorbent insoles and arch supports.

Shíofra is in discussions with manufacturers to produce her invention on a larger scale.

Figure 17.1 Shíofra Ryan, winner of the 2015 Student Enterprise Awards © BT Young Scientist & Technology Exhibition

Limerick brothers Patrick and John Collison, Stripe

Have you ever bought anything online?

Limerick brothers Patrick and John Collison, who started programming as teenagers, have developed a web and mobile payments company called Stripe, which makes it easier for businesses to accept and manage payments.

Now based in San Francisco, their business is valued at $5 billion and is fast becoming the main payments platform for online businesses. Stripe has a presence in twenty countries worldwide

Figure 17.2 Patrick and John Collison, founders of Stripe and winners of Ernst & Young Entrepreneur of the Year 2015

and has recently linked up with social media firms Twitter, Facebook and Pinterest to help create new 'buy now' buttons on the social networking sites.

Entrepreneurs

> An **entrepreneur** is a person who takes the initiative and risk to set up a business in the hope of making a profit.

Definition

Entrepreneurs are people who put a business idea into practice.

Showing **initiative** is about taking decisions and taking a chance to set up a business. Entrepreneurship is about turning an idea into an *action*.

Shíofra, Patrick and John are entrepreneurs. They have identified business ideas and taken the initiative and risk to turn them into a real business, making a profit in the process.

17.1 Name three other entrepreneurs and the businesses they are associated with. You can choose local, national or international examples.

17.2 Look back at a few issues of your local county or city newspaper. Find an article about an entrepreneur and in your copy write about the person and the business they started. You might need to do a little more research online to get all the information you need about the person.

Research

KSBL
KSMIT

17.3 Local papers are a great way of finding out about entrepreneurs. Throughout this strand, keep a scrapbook or folder (actual or online) of articles, about local entrepreneurs. In each case, summarise the articles, highlighting their reasons for starting a business, the type of businesses they start, and what support they receive.

Characteristics and skills of entrepreneurs

No two entrepreneurs are alike. While Shíofra, Patrick and John are all entrepreneurs, they are very different people. However, entrepreneurs tend to possess certain characteristics and skills which are typically associated with entrepreneurial success.

Characteristics of entrepreneurs

A characteristic is a personality trait that you are born with. Entrepreneurs possess many of the following enterprising characteristics which set them apart from other people.

Realistic risk-takers

Entrepreneurs are willing to risk their money (and time) in setting up a business. Successful entrepreneurs are realistic risk-takers, which means they research carefully and weigh up the risks involved and take a chance only if they have a reasonable hope of success.

Innovative/creative

Being innovative means being able to see problems and opportunities and solving them creatively by doing something in a new or different way. Entrepreneurs are good at coming up with new ideas or new ways of doing things.

Steve Jobs invented the iPhone and it launched in 2007. It wasn't the first mobile phone to access the internet or take photographs, but it was innovative because it was the first to use a large screen and multi-touch display. This enabled it to be used as a mobile computer as well as a phone.

Proactive

Entrepreneurs are proactive, which means they are prepared to use their own initiative and make things happen, rather than waiting for someone else to do something.

Flexible

Entrepreneurs accept change as natural. They learn from their mistakes and failures and can adapt when things don't go according to plan.

Self-confident

Entrepreneurs believe in themselves and in their business idea. They can cope with setbacks.

Decisive

Entrepreneurs have the ability to make decisions quickly and take responsibility for the actions and decisions they make.

Determined/resilient

Entrepreneurs do not give up easily when faced with obstacles and failures. They are good at tackling problems. They stick with a task until it is completed. They are also able to keep going after a setback.

Thomas Edison, the inventor of the lightbulb, famously stated: 'I have not failed. I've just found 10,000 ways that won't work.'

James Dyson developed 5,127 prototype designs before he successfully invented the bagless vacuum cleaner!

17.4 Which four characteristics do you think are most important in an entrepreneur? Write these in your copy. Discuss your choices with another student and find out which characteristics they chose. Try to reach agreement on the top four characteristics and then share these with another pair of students or with the whole class.

KSWwO
KSC
KSMIT

17.5 Discuss whether an entrepreneur has to have *all* the characteristics you have been looking at in class.

KSWwO
KSC
KSMIT

Skills of entrepreneurs

A skill is an ability or expertise that people get through practice, experience, learning or training. Entrepreneurs possess many of the following enterprising skills.

Ability to identify opportunities

Entrepreneurs have the ability to spot a need or gap in the market that is not currently being met and they seize this opportunity. They do this by listening carefully to customers' needs and being aware of future business opportunities.

Ability to make decisions

Entrepreneurs take into account all information available to them when making decisions and make them within a reasonable time.

Ability to plan and set goals

Entrepreneurs learn to set goals for themselves and their business and put plans in place to achieve these goals.

Ability to manage time

Entrepreneurs prioritise their tasks and make the best use of the time available to them each day.

Ability to manage stress

Entrepreneurs can deal with the stress of running a business day to day. They remain calm when faced with deadlines or difficulties.

Human relations skills

Entrepreneurs have the ability to get on with people, e.g. employees, suppliers, investors, customers, and State agencies that provide support to entrepreneurs. They do this by being good communicators and listeners.

Reality perception skills

Entrepreneurs possess the common sense to see things as they are and not as they want them to be.

Ability to assess and manage risk

Entrepreneurs measure the risk involved in a potential course of action and take steps to minimise these risks.

17.6 'Entrepreneurs are born and not made.' Write a short speech arguing for or against this statement.

KSBC
KSBL

17.7 Which four skills do you think are most important in an entrepreneur? Write these in your copy. Discuss your choices with another student and find out which characteristics they chose. Share your decisions with another pair of students or with the whole class.

KSWwO
KSC
KSMIT

17.8 Discuss whether an entrepreneur has to have *all* the skills you have been discussing in class.

KSWwO
KSC
KSMIT

KSBC

17.9 Watch a business programme on TV, particularly one that highlights entrepreneurs. Assess which enterprising characteristics and skills the entrepreneur possesses using the template supplied in the Student Activity Book.

Enterprise in action

From property to pastry: Roll It Hand Made All Butter Pastry

Mairéad Finnegan, a property surveyor, was looking for all-butter puff pastry and was surprised that she could find none made in Ireland, which has a worldwide reputation for producing quality butter. This was the **gap in the market** that Mairéad was looking for, and as work in the building sector was becoming scarce she had the idea of establishing her own business producing hand-made all-butter pastry.

Helped by a friend with a background in marketing and graphic design, she produced samples of her pastry and packaging and displayed them at a food festival near her home in Kells in 2012. She sold them all within hours. This gave her the confidence to approach her local SuperValu supermarket to ask them to stock her product, which they agreed to do.

Mairéad took business courses with Leader and had mentoring and advice from local entrepreneurs through the Co. Meath Local Enterprise Office. She received grants towards equipment, marketing and new packaging.

Mairéad found the advice from her mentor invaluable, especially with preparing business and financial planning. She now provides advice to new food start-ups in her local area and believes it's important to develop a strong local network of entrepreneurs.

Figure 17.3 Mairéad Finnegan: owner of Roll It Hand Made All Butter Pastry

Mairéad says hard work, determination, the ability to cope with inevitable setbacks and confidence in herself and her product were crucial characteristics while establishing her business. Since starting Roll It Pastry, she has developed the skills of time management, juggling production, finances, marketing and deliveries.

Mairéad has entered and won a number of prestigious food awards. Awards are important, as they help her expand her network and keep her in touch with what other producers are doing.

Running her own business gives Mairéad flexibility as it allows her to work from home at times that suit her and her family. She gets a tremendous sense of satisfaction from knowing she has started the business from scratch, and looks forward to expanding her product range and number of sales outlets.

17.10 **(a)** What do think is meant by 'gap in the market'?

(b) What gap in the market did Mairéad take advantage of?

(c) How did Mairéad show initiative?

(d) How was Mairéad innovative?

(e) What characteristics did Mairéad say she needed to make her business work?

(f) What skills did Mairéad get help with (i) when she first started, and (ii) as she grew her business?

(g) What demands on her time does Mairéad have?

(h) What goals has Mairéad set herself?

KSBL
KSMIT

Should entrepreneurial types become entrepreneurs?

Not everyone who has the characteristics and skills of an entrepreneur will want to actually become one. Entrepreneurs may be quite happy working for someone else, in which case their attributes can be used for the benefit of the business or to improve their own career prospects without taking the risk of setting up their own business.

Could you be an entrepreneur?

When deciding whether or not it is wise to become an entrepreneur, you should ask yourself the following questions:

> Am I determined to make this business a success?

> Do I understand the challenges involved and sacrifices I will have to make?

> Am I prepared to work (potentially by myself) for long hours?

> What are the financial risks involved if the business fails?

> Is there a market for my product/service?

> Who are my current competitors?
> Can I provide a better product? A cheaper price? A better service than my competitors?
> Do I have a realistic business plan?

See Chapter 26

17.11 Complete the self-assessment sheets in the Student Activity Book to see how suited you are to becoming an entrepreneur.

17.12 Create a poster aimed at potential entrepreneurs, showing the characteristics and skills they need to be successful. You may include some or all of the questions above.

Rewards and risks of self-employment

There are rewards and risks for an entrepreneur in setting up their own business and becoming self-employed.

Reasons for starting a business

People who start their own business are known as **entrepreneurs**. They see a gap in the market and are willing to take both a personal and a financial risk in order to set up a business. There are many reasons why people might start up in business for themselves. For example:

> They want to be their own boss and get to make all the decisions in the business themselves.

> They spot a gap in the market. Many entrepreneurs start this way, e.g. Roisin Hogan (see Enterprise in Action below).

> They want to keep all the profits of a business for themselves.

> They want to prove something to themselves by showing they can start a business. This will give a great sense of satisfaction.

> They may currently be unemployed. By starting a business they can provide employment for themselves (and possibly others if the business is a success).

> They may have a hobby or interest in something and this may become a business idea, e.g. interest in rugby could lead someone to provide coaching to a local club or to set up a sports shop.

Rewards of self-employment

> You are your own boss.
> You get to make all the decisions in the business.
> You can work flexible hours or have flexible opening hours to suit the needs of your customers.
> You have a great sense of satisfaction if the business is a success.
> You keep all the profit the business makes.

Risks of self-employment

> You may lose the money you invested in the business if it fails.
> You will need to work long hours to get the business up and running and to oversee all aspects of the business.
> You may find it difficult to take time away from running the business.
> Sales may vary each week, so your income is not guaranteed.
> You may not have all the necessary skills to establish and run a business.

Financial enterprise

Many entrepreneurs, like Mairéad Finnegan, and John and Patrick Collison, are **financial entrepreneurs**. This means they establish businesses to make a profit by selling a product or a service. There are other types of enterprise, though, and we look at these below.

Social enterprise

What is social enterprise?

A social enterprise is one that puts **people and community ahead of private and personal gain**. The people who start such enterprises are known as **social entrepreneurs**.

Social enterprises place a strong emphasis on creating jobs, particularly in local communities, and may tackle social, economic or environmental issues that affect the community. Social enterprises are owned by the community or by members. Any profits made are reinvested in the business.

The social enterprise sector in Ireland employs between 25,000 and 33,000 people in over 1,400 social enterprises.

Examples of social enterprise

Credit unions are the best example in Ireland of social enterprise. Other examples include community radio, rural transport schemes, tourism, heritage products and local accommodation.

Some specific examples are:

> **CoderDojo:** Established in 2011, CoderDojo started in Cork and has since expanded throughout the world. Volunteers provide young people with a free introduction to programming/coding, website development and game development.

> **Camara Education:** Established in 2005, Camara provides technology at affordable prices to low-income communities and also provides training and technical support to purchasers. It does this by taking unwanted computers from businesses and refurbishing them for reuse. As well as working in Ireland, Camara has provided IT equipment to disadvantaged students in Africa and the Caribbean.

Enterprise in action

Social enterprise: FoodCloud

According to the Environmental Protection Agency (EPA), approximately one million tonnes of food goes to waste in Ireland each year. A large amount of this food is perfectly edible. Irish retailers have about 87,000 tonnes of surplus food a year, most of which is dumped at a cost of €8.5 million.

To put that in perspective, the Statue of Liberty weighs 204 tonnes, so the amount of food wasted by businesses in Ireland each year is equivalent to over 426 Statues of Liberty!

Social entrepreneurs Aoibheann O'Brien and Iseult Ward used their initiative and creativity to address this problem. They established FoodCloud, a social enterprise that connects businesses that have surplus food with charities that can use the food.

In 2012 Aoibheann and Iseult researched ways of matching businesses and charities and quickly realised that technology was needed to do this efficiently and on a large scale throughout the country and the world.

Figure 17.4 Food wasted in Ireland each year weighs more than 426 Statues of Liberty

They received support, funding and mentoring from, among others, Social Entrepreneurs Ireland. They developed an app and website and launched FoodCloud in October 2013 with some cafés and one Tesco store. By July 2014 they had expanded this to include all Tesco stores throughout Ireland, who now redistribute surplus food to a range of charities around the Republic of Ireland. FoodCloud is also operational in the UK through a partnership with Fareshare and Tesco.

FoodCloud's app allows businesses to upload details of surplus food and a collection time. This sends a text to a local charity and they reply to accept the offer and then collect the food.

There are over 1,100 charities and 500 businesses on board. Since its establishment, FoodCloud has redistributed 1,585,570 kilograms of food (the equivalent of 3,488,253 meals) to charities around Ireland. FoodCloud's charity partners serve over 90,000 people a week. Working with FoodCloud reduces the food bill for charities and allows them to redirect their funds into other important services they provide.

For the businesses involved, it is a socially responsible and environmentally sensitive alternative to wasting good food.

Figure 17.5 Aoibheann O'Brien and Iseult Ward, founders of FoodCloud

KSBL

17.13 (a) What enterprising characteristics and skills have Aoibheann and Iseult shown?

(b) What gap in the market did they seek to fill?

17.14 Aoibheann and Iseult received mentoring, funding and support from Social Entrepreneurs Ireland. In small groups, research this organisation and find out what other social enterprises have received assistance from them. Present your findings to your classmates using a presentation or a poster.

Figure 17.6 Social Entrepreneurs Ireland (SEI) is a registered charity in Ireland, with exclusive copyright of the SEI logo

Groupwork

Research

KSBC
KSMIT
KSWwO

Cultural enterprise

A **cultural enterprise** exists to provide consumers either locally or nationally with access to visual arts, theatre, film, music, radio, festivals or events.

Definition

Cultural organisations are all around us and provide us with access to literature, music, arts and crafts, folklore, language, food and traditional sports. In your local community you may have a library, theatre or arts centre. GAA clubs and Comhaltas Ceoltóirí Éireann support Irish culture through the promotion of Irish sport, music, singing, dancing and language. Other examples include:

> **Abbey Theatre:** Also known as Ireland's national theatre, the Abbey Theatre was established in 1904. It aims to promote Irish writers and artists and to produce a programme of interesting and exciting Irish and international theatre each year.

ABBEY THEATRE AMHARCLANN NA MAINISTREACH

> **Electric Picnic:** Since 2004, this annual music and arts festival has taken place in Stradbally, Co. Laois. It attracts over 42,000 people each year.

> **National Gallery of Ireland shop:** While the National Gallery of Ireland does not charge an entrance fee, it sells a range of goods, e.g. books, greetings cards, umbrellas and stationery, in the Gallery Shop, inspired by the gallery's collections.

> **Rose of Tralee International Festival:** This is one of Ireland's largest and longest-running festivals. The Rose of Tralee has been held annually in Tralee, Co. Kerry since 1959. While you may be familiar with the TV programme shown over two nights in August, the festival itself takes place over five days. It includes a range of family and children's entertainment, including live music, concerts, a fashion show, circus, funfair, fireworks and a Rose Parade. The event attracts over 50,000 people to Tralee each year.

> **Local cultural enterprise events:** These take place throughout Ireland. They tend to be in the form of festivals, which promote the local economy. Examples include the Kilkenny 'Cat Laughs' Comedy Festival and the Cork Jazz Festival.

17.15 Find out about the local cultural events or enterprises in your town or county. What benefits do these events bring to the local community?

KSMIT
KSBL

17.16 Research and profile a local, national or international entrepreneur. Use the template provided in the Student Activity Book. Note the sources you used to find your answers.

KSBC
KSBL
KSMIT

Enterprise is all around us!

Enterprise is not always about business. It can be also be seen in other situations in life, such as the following.

Enterprise in the community:

> People in an area might establish a GAA club, youth club or scout club.

> A community might establish a Neighbourhood Watch scheme or Tidy Towns committee.

> A group of people might establish a Meals on Wheels service for the elderly.

Enterprise in the public service:

> Then Minister for Health Micheál Martin introduced a ban on smoking in the workplace in Ireland in 2004, making Ireland the first country in the world to introduce a total ban in all workplaces. Many countries worldwide have since followed Ireland's lead.

> Coillte was established by the government to develop Irish forests.

> Local Enterprise Offices (LEOs) were established to encourage Irish people to set up their own businesses and create jobs in their local area. LEOs also run the Student Enterprise Awards to promote enterprise in Irish schools.

Student Enterprise Awards

Enterprise while working as an employee:

When employees use their initiative to come up with new ideas for the business they are called **intrapreneurs**. They find a better way to do something to save time or money for the business.

Did you know?

Swan Vesta matches saved thousands of pounds when a factory worker suggested putting sandpaper for striking the matches on only one side of each matchbox. The factory worker got his reward and retired a wealthy man!

Google allows employees to spend 20% of their working week on a personal project, which has led to many of Google's best projects, including one many people use every day: Gmail, which was developed by Paul Buchheit.

17.17 In small groups, brainstorm ideas showing how you could be enterprising in your home, school and in your local community. Brainstorming means getting together to think of ideas – write these down and they will spark new thoughts that you can add to the list.

Groupwork

KSWwO

17.18 In small groups, think of as many business ideas as possible.

KSWwO
KSC

Key Terms

KSBL
KSC
KSMIT
KSBC

You should be able to *define*, *spell*, give *examples* and *apply* to real life each of the following key terms associated with this topic.

Exercise: Write a sentence using each of the following terms. You may use more than one of the terms in your sentence if appropriate.

cultural enterprise

enterprise

entrepreneur

financial enterprise

innovative

intrapreneur

social enterprise

social entrepreneur

Chapter 18 ::
Developing Business Ideas

Learning outcomes

When you have completed this chapter you will be able to:

✔ Outline how entrepreneurs get ideas for businesses
✔ Identify and explain internal and external sources of new product or service ideas
✔ Explain the stages in the new product or service development process.

Sources of business ideas for entrepreneurs and business start-ups

To start in business you obviously need a good idea. In some cases, people will first decide to set up a business and then think about what sort of business they might run. The founders of Innocent drinks, for example, were three friends who met at university and knew that they wanted to go into business together. They engaged in brainstorming until they came up with the idea of smoothies.

Other people might have an idea first and then set up in business. James Dyson was an inventor who came up with the idea of a bagless vacuum cleaner. He pitched it to existing companies, who rejected his idea, and so he set up his own company.

Entrepreneurs may notice a **growing trend in the market** and this allows them to come up with an opportunity for a new product or service. For example, in recent years there has been a major move towards organically produced foods, so there may be opportunities for selling seeds, growing organic food or producing ready meals from organic food.

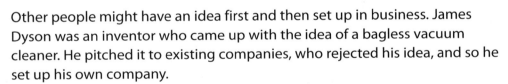

18.1   In small groups, brainstorm different business opportunities which could result from your hobbies and interests. Think about a business by yourself, and a business that could combine the interests of two or more of your group. Share your ideas with the rest of the class, and note any interesting ideas that other groups had.

18.2   What do you think might be the drawbacks and the benefits of turning a hobby into a business?

Groupwork

KSWwO
KSMIT
KSC
KSSW
KSBC

Enterprise in action

Roisin Hogan: HiRo Noodles

By Olive Keogh

Roisin Hogan was a professional accountant. When she gave up smoking, she became much more aware of health and nutrition, but as she worked very long hours she often wanted snacks and quick-cook meals, which tend to be full of sugar and calories.

Figure 18.1 Roisin Hogan, founder of HiRo Noodles

Then she found out about noodles made from konjac flour – a low-calorie, low-carbohydrate vegetable flour. She loved the taste of them and decided to create a business that provided healthy, tasty and convenient meal options that were low calorie, low carb and, above all, tasty and nutritious.

Roisin left her job with a large accountancy firm in 2014 to concentrate on her new business. She had so much faith in her idea that she applied for and was accepted onto the BBC reality series *The Apprentice*. She reached the semi-finals, which helped to get her product noticed and provided her with great skills to take her business forward.

Roisin's start-up costs were about €20,000, which was funded from her own savings and family support. She received first stage feasibility study funding (stage 4 of the product development process) from the Dublin City Local Enterprise Office and took part in the Foodworks programme (a joint initiative between Teagasc, Enterprise Ireland and Bord Bia).

She realised that she would be able to get her products into shops faster by partnering with a well-established food producer and so joined forces with Drogheda-based Nature's Best, which also sells healthy food.

The speciality flour for the noodles is imported from Japan and Roisin started producing four products. Her aim is to grow the business into an international brand and to employ people both through Nature's Best and her own company.

Source: Article adapted from the *Irish Times*, 10 August 2015

Some entrepreneurs may have spotted something working well in **another country** and have brought the idea back to their own country.

18.3 Have you seen or read about something abroad that isn't yet available in Ireland and therefore could be a good business idea for someone here?

Other ideas can come from **family and friends**. For example, an idea could come from hearing a family member complain about not being able to buy a product or service that they need.

Enterprise in action

The entrepreneurs

Bitcove.ie was founded by brothers Peter and James Nagle in 2014. The brothers hold a range of qualifications from University College Cork (UCC) in economics, law, computer science, management information and managerial accounting systems.

Figure 18.2 Peter and James Nagle, founders of Bitcove.ie

James' interests lie in currencies and technology. He quickly became an expert in bitcoin and cryptocurrencies, merging his passions for finance and technology.

Peter had an interest in commodities, and an even greater interest in entrepreneurship and innovation.

Their combined interests and passions led the brothers to develop the Bitcove.ie platform, to meet the increasing demand for bitcoin in Ireland.

Ireland's Premier Bitcoin Exchange

The business

Bitcove.ie is a bitcoin exchange platform that enables its customers to buy and sell bitcoin using euros. The business claims that 'Bitcove ensures that even the most basic computer user can acquire bitcoin securely, comfortably and confidently' with the 'simplicity users expect from other purchase sites such as eBay and Amazon'.

Bitcove.ie is growing strongly, reflecting the increasing interest in bitcoin and digital currencies in Ireland. With the growth of bitcoin, Bitcove is looking into other emerging markets and has recently established a second bitcoin exchange in Greece.

In June 2015 Bitcove won the Bank of Ireland/Ignite Business of the Year award against competition from ten other promising start-ups.

Franchises

Some entrepreneurs choose to become part of an existing business by buying a **franchise**. A franchise is when one firm (*franchisor*) sells the right to use its products and its brand name to another business (*franchisee*).

An example of a franchise business is Supermac's. In return for an initial fee and a percentage of the revenue earned, franchisees can use the Supermac's name and sell Supermac's products. Although the franchisees own the business, they use the methods and products of Supermac's and are subject to strict rules set down by the company. Other popular franchises in Ireland are McDonald's, Subway and Domino's Pizza.

18.4 Search the internet for franchises that are for sale in Ireland. Choose one that appeals to you and write a short report on:

(a) What the business is.

(b) Why you like the idea.

(c) Where you could locate your business and why you have chosen this location.

(d) What skills you could bring to the business.

Advantages of franchises

> **The idea already exists.** The entrepreneur can look at the track record of the existing business and see if the product/service works. This reduces the risk for the franchisee.

> **The brand name may be well established.** If people have heard of the business already, this may make it easier to get customers.

> **The franchisor provides support and training.** This will be valuable to the franchisee as they benefit from the franchisor's guidance, training, products and equipment.

> **Costs such as marketing can be shared between the franchisees.** Promotion of the brand benefits each franchisee as it spreads the cost and allows the business to advertise on national TV and in the national press.

Disadvantages of franchises

> **A negative response to one franchisee might affect all.** If there is a problem with one franchisee, e.g. in relation to quality and service, this will reflect badly on all the other franchisees.

> **Disputes over the balance of power.** There may be disputes between the franchisee and the franchisor. The person selling the franchise might want to keep a high level of control over how things are done. The person buying might want more freedom to make their own decisions.

Forms of business ownership

When establishing a business, an entrepreneur will need to decide on the legal structure of that business. Ownership structures in Ireland include:

> **Sole trader:** This is a form of business that is owned and managed by one person, e.g. if you set up your own business fixing computers you are a sole trader. Setting up as a sole trader is easy to do. You don't need to register with the government or fill in lots of forms. If you have an idea, premises (which might be your own home) and money you can start straight away. This is why it is such a popular form of business ownership and why so many famous entrepreneurs started as sole traders.

- **Partnership:** A partnership is created when two to twenty people set up in business. Partnerships are common with solicitors, doctors, accountants, auctioneers and estate agents, although any business can have partners, such as a shop or a sandwich-making business.
- **Private limited company:** A private limited company is a business set up by between one and 149 people called shareholders. When a business is starting up its shareholders tend to be the business founders, although they may bring in outside investors if they need more funding. The business has Limited or Ltd in its name because the liability of the owners is limited to what they originally invested in the business. It cannot advertise its shares to the general public; if shares are sold this will be done privately.

KSMIT

18.5 Andy has a good business idea. He wants to start a business but he is worried that he doesn't know enough about bookkeeping and promoting the business.

(a) What type of business ownership structure would you recommend to Andy?

(b) What assistance could the Local Enterprise Office provide him?

Sources of new product ideas for existing businesses

Existing businesses also need new ideas to replace or improve existing products.

Business ideas can be generated from inside the business (internally), or ideas may be generated from outside the business (externally).

Internal sources

Sometimes new ideas evolve or come about by accident, but more often businesses have to make some effort to create new product or service ideas. These are some of the ways they might go about it.

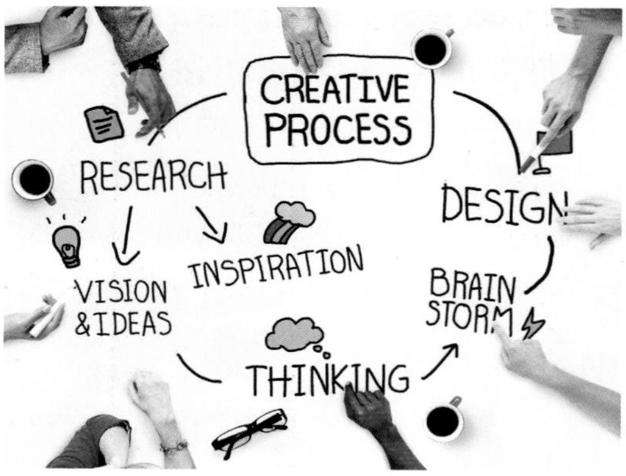

- **Brainstorming sessions:** This involves people coming together and thinking of new ideas. Some of these ideas are rejected while some are given further consideration.
- **Ideas from employees within the business (intrapreneurship):** Employees may be encouraged to think of new ideas and good ideas may be rewarded by a bonus.
- **Sales personnel:** Feedback from sales people who are in touch with the market is a vital source of information about customer needs and wants.
- **The research and development (R&D) department:** Dedicated research and development staff may discover a new product or improve an existing product or service through R&D. In 2013 Intel spent $10.6 billion – 20.1% of their revenue – on R&D.

18.6 Search online using the query 'inventions made by mistake'. Pick five well-known inventions and create a poster with a short paragraph about each, alongside a photo of the product. Note the sources of your information. Put your posters around the classroom for everyone to look at.

Research

KSBC
KSMIT

External sources

Ideas or motivation for new products and services are often driven by people and organisations outside the business.

> **Competitors:** Looking at competitors and copying some of their product or service ideas, while being mindful of patent and copyright law (you cannot copy another business idea while it is protected under copyright or patent). These are known as 'me-too' products.

> **Import substitution:** This is when a product that is currently being imported is substituted by a home-produced product.

> **Customer complaints or feedback:** This could result in changes in or further developments to existing products or services.

> **Market research:** A business could use a market research company that would help to identify gaps in the market and find market trends. The business can then fill these gaps or **niche markets**. Sometimes a business might have a new idea but not be sure that it would work, so they could employ a market research company (or do the work themselves) to ask people specific questions to find out their reactions. (Market research will always be carried out in the development of a new product or service.)

See Chapter 24

A **niche market** is a small, specialised market for a particular product or service. For example, folding bicycles are a niche market: many people want bicycles, but only a small part of that market (e.g. commuters) wants to use a folding bike.

Definition

18.7 Research 'me-too' products in electronics and/or cosmetics. Create a poster or presentation showing the similar products produced by rival businesses.

Research

KSMIT
KSBC

18.8 If you were thinking about starting a car valeting or web design business in your area, who would your competitors be? In pairs, make a list, noting where you found out the information, and then share everyone's information through the teacher.

The product development process

This process helps both entrepreneurs and businesses to develop ideas that have genuine market potential and should ensure that the finished product has the best possible chance of success.

Product development is expensive and risky, so the business needs to take steps to be sure it is not making a mistake. At any point, if major problems arise it may be more cost effective for the business to halt the development process rather than launch a product which will generate losses.

The following steps are involved in the development process for a new product.

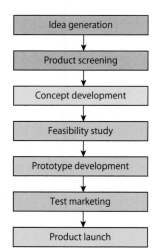

Table 18.1 The product development process

Step	At this stage	Example
1 Idea generation	Think up as many new ideas as possible	Following a brainstorming session a group of students thinks it might be possible to set up a minicompany to produce one of the following: scented candles, cupcakes, T-shirts or wooden ornaments
2 Product screening	The best ideas are considered further and any unworkable ones are discarded	The students realise that their level of skills and resources will make it difficult for them to produce the T-shirts or wooden ornaments, and food hygiene regulations will make the cupcake idea unworkable. They think that the scented candles offer the greatest potential for success
3 Concept development	The chosen idea is developed into a product that will appeal to consumers. It is important to identify a **unique selling point (USP)** for the product to make it different from other products on the market	The students begin to consider the design of the candles and in particular the ingredients, shapes and scents that will distinguish their candles from those of their rivals

4 Feasibility study	A study is carried out to see if the idea is **commercially viable**. This involves finding answers to two key questions: (i) Is it technically possible to make this product? (ii) Can it be produced and sold profitably in current market conditions?	The students research the manufacturing techniques involved and are confident they can achieve it with their own skills and resources. They also look into the costs involved and speak to some potential customers about their willingness to buy the product. Based on their research they decide that the scented candle idea is a feasible one
5 Prototype development	Develop a sample or model of the product. This allows the developer to see exactly how it will be manufactured. The prototype can then be tested and, if necessary, altered to make it better	The students begin to make prototype candles and it takes several attempts to get the correct mix of ingredients and to produce a candle which is good enough to be sold. Their fourth prototype is the most successful and they agree that this should set the standard for all future production
6 Test marketing	A small-scale trial is carried out to identify possible faults and to assess customer reaction. The product is tested on a sample group of potential customers before going into full production	The students produce a batch of five candles, which they sell to neighbours and teachers. They receive very positive feedback on the quality of the candles and the scents. This gives them the confidence to proceed with a larger production run
7 Product launch	The product goes into full-scale production and is introduced to the market. The business will need to select a suitable marketing strategy to persuade consumers to buy the product	The students invest in raw materials to produce fifty candles. They advertise in the school and get some free publicity in a local paper. They launch their product range by taking a stall at a local Christmas market

18.9 Will the stages for the development of a service be the same as for a product? With a classmate, discuss what will be:

(a) The same

(b) Different.

Give reasons for your answers.

KSMIT
KSWwO

Key Terms

KSBL
KSC
KSMIT
KSBC

You should be able to *define*, *spell*, give *examples* and *apply* to real life each of the following key terms associated with this topic.

Exercise: Write a sentence using each of the following terms. You may use more than one of the terms in your sentence if appropriate.

commercially viable

concept development

feasibility study

franchise

idea generation

niche market

partnership

private limited company

product development process

product launch

product screening

shareholders

sole trader

test marketing

USP (unique selling point)

Chapter 19 ::
Types of Employment

Learning outcomes

When you have completed this chapter you will be able to:

✔ Differentiate between work, employment and volunteering
✔ Understand the reasons why people volunteer
✔ Identify the benefits of volunteering to individuals, organisations and society
✔ Discuss different types of employment
✔ Differentiate between employment and self-employment
✔ Explain the benefits of work
✔ Understand what is meant by unemployment
✔ Identify careers relevant to your interests and subjects.

What is work?

In this chapter we will investigate work and the different types of employment.

Work is any productive activity that requires effort. This can be mental and/or physical effort.

You may not be paid for certain types of work, e.g. doing housework, doing your homework, practising a musical instrument and voluntary work.

Employment is work for which a person receives a payment, e.g. a wage or salary.

Employees are people who work for employers in return for a payment.

See Chapter 20

Voluntary work

Volunteering is when people freely offer to carry out some work or activity without payment for their time and effort.

A voluntary/charity organisation is a group of people who come together on a voluntary basis with the aim of helping others (people or animals) or the environment. Voluntary organisations can be local, national or international. Many of these voluntary groups rely on volunteers, and some have paid employees.

Figure 19.1 Local, national and international voluntary groups and organisations in Ireland

19.1 Working in pairs, sort the voluntary organisations whose logos are shown in figure 19.1 under the headings (a) local voluntary groups, (b) national voluntary organisations, and (c) international voluntary organisations.

KSMIT
KSC
KSWwO

19.2 In small groups, investigate what local and national voluntary organisations exist in your locality. Create a poster or presentation about the different organisations, showing the name, logo and purpose of each organisation. Make sure you include at least five organisations.

KSMIT
KSWwO
KSC
KSBC

Why do people volunteer?

There are a number of reasons why people volunteer:

> They are passionate about a cause, e.g. preventing animal abuse, keeping their neighbourhood tidy, preserving a natural habitat.

> They have personal experience of a cause they want to help, e.g. a family member has an illness and they have seen how hard this is for families and so want to help others going through the same thing.

> They have had help themselves and now want to 'give back' and help others in a similar situation.

> They have time available and want to help their community.

> They have a skill that is needed and they want to put it to good use.

> They enjoy the work and get satisfaction from doing it.

19.3 (a) If you do voluntary work, prepare a presentation, explaining what the voluntary body is, what it does, and the work you do. Let people know why you find this work valuable. Include some relevant images. Make your presentation to the rest of your class.
Or,

(b) If you don't currently do voluntary work, think about what you would like to do and why you would like to do it. Research organisations you could do some work for, and prepare a presentation on what the voluntary body is, what it does, and why you would like to work with them.

KSBL
KSBC
KSC
KSMM

Working for a voluntary body

Most people who work voluntarily do so part time, to fit in with their other commitments, such as earning a living, looking after a family, etc. Some people might give their time for one event, others might do one hour a week, others – especially students in Transition Year, or retired people – might devote weeks or months at a time to voluntary work. In some cases this may involve voluntary work overseas.

Voluntary groups will always be grateful for any time and help you can offer them.

Whether you do a one-off voluntary session or work voluntarily full time, you should treat it as you would any job and:

> Be reliable

> Attend any training provided

> Do the tasks assigned to you to the best of your ability

> Do the work in a professional manner, as if you were doing paid work

> Keep information confidential
> Report any unethical behaviour by other volunteers, e.g. accepting payment
> Treat all members/clients of the voluntary body with dignity and respect
> Treat the property of the voluntary body with respect.

19.4 Do you think it is important that people work in a voluntary capacity? Discuss your feelings on giving your time for nothing.

19.5 Discuss the importance of approaching voluntary work in a professional manner, even though you are not getting paid to do the work.

Discussion

KSWwO
KSC
KSMM
KSSW

Benefits of volunteerism

Benefits to the individual volunteer

> A chance to learn **new skills** and an opportunity to put existing skills to work.

> Can lead to paid **employment** in the future and provides an opportunity to get **work experience**.

> It shows **initiative and personal enterprise**. It also highlights a person's willingness to work with and for others. This is likely to impress future employers.

> It offers a chance to make **new friends** and improve **social and interpersonal skills**.

> It enhances **personal satisfaction and wellbeing**. Volunteerism is an activity which provides a 'feel good' factor and which helps improve self-esteem.

Benefits to the organisation

> Volunteers bring a range of **new skills, expertise and ideas** to the organisation.

> Volunteers often carry out work because they are passionate about the issue or the cause. Every organisation benefits from having **passionate and highly motivated people** involved.

> If volunteers are unpaid, more **funds** can be directed towards the organisation's main aims and activities. For example, a homeless charity can use all the money it receives to help reduce homelessness.

> Volunteers may act as 'ambassadors' for the organisation in the wider community. This creates **positive publicity** and helps spread the values and good name of the organisation.

Benefits to society/the economy

> The ideals of 'giving' and **helping others** in order to improve our community lie at the very heart of volunteerism. Communities tend to improve when members work together.

> Many voluntary organisations play an important role in **reducing social isolation**. Examples include sports clubs and charities which assist homeless people or the elderly. Reduced isolation also helps limit the potential for antisocial behaviour.

> Volunteering **gets things done**! Society benefits from the provision of an increased range of community services and activities. These may range from coaching local teams to providing medical services overseas.

> The work of unpaid volunteers **reduces the financial burden on local and national government**. This allows money to be spent on other goods and services. There is an element of opportunity cost involved here.

Employment

Most people work to earn an income. This gives a person a secure standard of living which allows them to buy goods and services to satisfy their needs (e.g. food, shelter) and wants (e.g. luxuries, such as a new car or a holiday).

19.6 What is the current minimum wage in Ireland for a person:

(a) Over 18?

(b) Under 18?

Research

KSMIT

When a person is paid for the work they do, they are known as an **employee**.

Contract of employment

Employees are legally entitled to a **contract of employment** from their employer. This must be signed by both parties within two months of the start date. It will contain the following information:

1 Employer's name and address
2 Employee's name and address
3 Job title
4 Job description
5 Code of conduct expected

6 Date of commencement and duration of contract

7 Remuneration: the salary or wages that you receive, when you receive them, how you receive them, overtime rate

8 Holiday entitlements: employees have a statutory entitlement to 20 days' paid annual leave (although some jobs may give more). There may also be rules about when you can take holidays and details of other statutory leave

9 Duration/length of contract/**probationary period**, if any

10 Any other conditions of job (hours of work/location)

11 Pension arrangements

12 Sick leave entitlements: how many days before a doctor's certificate is needed, details of payment while you are ill

13 Signatures of the employer and the employee

A **probationary period** is a specified period at the start of an employment to see if the employee is suitable for the position. **Definition**

Types of employment

Table 19.1 Types of employment

Types of employment	What this is
Full-time employee	Full-time employees will work a full working week of 35 hours or more. They will receive a full week's wage when working full time. The times might be regular, e.g. 9 a.m.–5 p.m., or change from week to week.
Part-time employee	A part-time employee could work anything up to 30 hours a week. They are paid for the hours they work.
Fixed-term employee	Many more people are now employed on a fixed-term basis (or on specific purpose contracts). Their temporary employment ends when the contract term expires.
Casual employee	Casual workers are on standby to do work as required without fixed hours or attendance arrangements. However, these workers are employees, for employment rights purposes.
Job sharing	Job sharing is when two employees together make up one working week in a particular role. They share the hours in their contract.
Flexitime	Flexitime is when the employee can start work at a time that suits them on each day, as long as they do the hours stated in their contract.
Teleworking	This is when the employee works from home and carries out their duties as if they were working on the business premises. The employee would need to have a phone and an internet connection to respond to email and communicate easily with co-workers, customers, etc.

19.7 (a) Think of two examples of jobs that might have a fixed-term contract.

(b) What benefits might there be to an employee being offered a temporary contract?

19.8 Some casual employees are known as seasonal workers. Give five examples of employment that might be seasonal.

19.9 Why do you think this is called job sharing, rather than it being two part-time jobs?

19.10 (a) If school could be flexitime, and you could work Monday–Friday between the hours of 7 a.m. and 9 p.m. each day, as long as you studied for 30 hours each week, what hours would you choose to do, and why would you choose these hours?

(b) Why do you think schools do not operate on flexitime?

19.11 (a) What are the advantages of teleworking:
(i) To the employer? (ii) To the employee?

(b) What disadvantages of teleworking could you foresee:
(i) For the employer? (ii) For the employee?

KSMIT
KSMM

Self-employment

In addition to the various employment contract types listed above, some people are self-employed and therefore work for themselves. They take their income from the profits they make in the business.

See Chapter 17

Self-employed entrepreneurs may get advice and support or grants from their Local Enterprise Office (LEO) to help them with their business.

19.12 List five different examples of work carried out by self-employed people.

19.13 Discuss in groups the advantages and disadvantages of self-employment.

T-P-S

KSMIT
KSWwO
KSMM

Skills/qualities required by employees

Employers value particular skills and qualities, so if you can demonstrate that you have these, you will have a much better chance of getting a job.

The skills and qualities of a sought-after employee are:

> Hard worker

> Punctual

> Organised

> Problem-solver

> Teamworker

> Good communicator

> Dedicated/enthusiastic

> Honesty.

The perfect
Employee
☑ hard worker
☑ team player
☑ skilled
☑ loyal
☑ honest

19.14 (a) Can you think of any other skills/qualities required by employers?

(b) Provide at least one reason why each of the skills/qualities identified above is necessary for an employee to have.

19.15 Do you think you would be a good employee? What personal skills do you have that you could offer an employer? Give examples of using these skills.

Benefits of work

Whether paid or unpaid, there are several benefits of engaging in work. These are:

> Your self-esteem and sense of achievement is improved as you are engaged in doing something worthwhile.

> Engaging in work can develop your skills and make it more likely that you will be able to get a new job or be promoted in the future.

> Some jobs provide benefits, such as an opportunity to travel, either within Ireland or internationally.

Unemployment

Unfortunately, not everyone in Ireland is employed.

If a person is of working age (over 16 and under 65) and is available for work, but is unable to find employment, they are said to be **unemployed**.

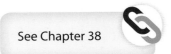
Definition

Unemployment leads to a loss in income. Ireland's unemployment rate increased between 2006 and 2012 but has declined since then.

See Chapter 38

19.16 Research the unemployment rate in Ireland for the past ten years. Create a line graph/bar chart or an infographic displaying this information. What can you deduce from your graph?

KSMIT
KSBC
KSBN

The government has a number of training schemes to help unemployed people to get into or back into employment. Some of these are:

› **An tSeirbhís Oideachais Leanúnaigh agus Scileanna (SOLAS):** This is the further education and training authority in Ireland. It is responsible for funding, planning and coordinating training and further education programmes in Ireland. The training is provided by **Education and Training Boards Ireland (ETBI).**

› **Community Enterprise Scheme (CES):** The Community Employment (CE) programme is designed to help people who are long-term unemployed and other disadvantaged people to get work or get back to work by offering part-time and temporary placements in jobs based in their local communities.

› **Momentum:** This provides access to free education and training projects to help long-term unemployed people access work.

SOLAS
An tSeirbhís Oideachais Leanúnaigh agus Scileanna
Further Education and Training Authority

etbi
Education and Training Boards Ireland
Boird Oideachais agus Oiliúna Éireann

MOMENTUM
FOCUS YOUR TALENT

19.17 What are the advantages of the above employment schemes to:

Groupwork

KSWwO

(a) Unemployed people

(b) Employers

(c) The government?

What job will suit you?

This expression means that our working lives will be more interesting and rewarding if we work in jobs that suit our interests and qualities.

'Find a job you love and you'll never work a day in your life.'

19.18 Look at the example in figure 19.2 of suitable careers for someone who is interested in languages. Using the templates supplied in the Student Activity Book, write down your interests, hobbies and favourite subjects and consider the careers that might suit you.

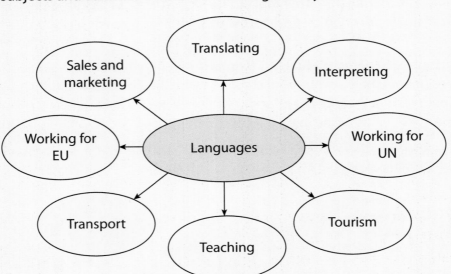

Figure 19.2 Suitable careers for a language expert

Alternatively, you could take an online quiz and see what jobs it recommends for you.

It's never too early to start planning your future career!

Key Terms

You should be able to *define*, *spell*, give *examples* and *apply* to real life each of the following key terms associated with this topic.

Exercise: Write a sentence using each of the following terms. You may use more than one of the terms in your sentence if appropriate.

casual employee	part time
contract of employment	self-employment
employment	teleworking
fixed-term employees	unemployment
flexitime	voluntary work
full time	work
job sharing	

Chapter 20 :: Rights and Responsibilities of Employers and Employees

Learning outcomes

When you have completed this chapter you will be able to:

✔ Outline the rights and responsibilities of employees
✔ Outline the rights and responsibilities of employers
✔ Define industrial relations
✔ Explain why employees might join a trade union
✔ Outline the different types of industrial action
✔ List and briefly explain the laws that protect employees.

In Chapter 19 you learned about employment. In this chapter you will learn about the rights and responsibilities of employees and employers.

An **employer** is a person or business that pays employees for their work.

Definition

We all like to know and receive our rights, but we need to remember that with rights come responsibilities.

A **right** is something you are entitled to receive, e.g. to be treated in a fair, ethical and legal way.

A **responsibility** is a duty or something you should do, e.g. to treat others with respect.

Definitions

Rights and responsibilities can be classified as follows:

See Chapter 42

> **Legal:** As set out by national or EU law, e.g. the right to be treated equally regardless of age, gender, marital status, etc.
> **Social:** The treatment of workers by employers, e.g. payment of a fair wage, prevention of bullying in the workplace, etc.
> **Environmental:** A safe and healthy workplace. In addition, the employer must ensure that they do not damage the local environment.
> **Ethical:** Doing what is right, e.g. fair treatment of employees and suppliers, engaging in fair trade.

In practice, many of the rights and responsibilities are a combination of some or all of the above. For example, discrimination in the workplace is illegal as well as being both socially and ethically wrong.

See Chapters 15 and 40

Rights of employees

Employees are safeguarded by law in a number of employment areas, and employees have the right to:

> Receive a fair day's pay for a fair day's work

> Receive at least the minimum wage

> Receive a contract of employment

See Chapter 19

> Adequate rest breaks

> Holiday pay

> Work in a safe and respectful atmosphere, free from danger, bullying or discrimination

> Join a trade union.

20.1 Some countries do not have laws ensuring that employees are kept safe and receive an adequate income. Discuss whether you think it is right that consumers support this by buying cheap goods made by people in poor conditions receiving a low wage. Compare the rights of people working in Ireland and people working in these conditions.

Discussion

KSC
KSBL
KSMIT

Responsibilities of employees

Employees have the responsibility (either by law or morally) to:

> Carry out their duties as stated in their contract of employment

> Arrive at work on time

> Be loyal to their employer and not disclose confidential business information

> Treat customers, co-workers and the employer with respect and ensure they don't bully or discriminate against other employees

> Follow workplace rules and safety instructions

> Wear any protective equipment and uniform provided to them by the employer

> Attend all training provided by the business.

Rights of employers

Employers have the right to:

> Decide on the objectives of the business.
> Hire suitable staff for their business.
> Dismiss dishonest or unsuitable staff.
> Expect loyalty from their staff.

Responsibilities of employers

The responsibilities of the employer are to:

> Ensure the workplace is safe and has healthy working conditions.
> Provide employees with adequate training (and protective clothing/equipment if necessary).
> Provide employees with statutory holidays and leave, e.g. maternity/paternity/ parental leave.
> Pay agreed wages. They must pay at least the minimum wage to their employees and equal pay to men and women.
> Deduct Pay As You Earn (PAYE), Pay Related Social Insurance (PRSI) and Universal Social Charge (USC) from their employees' pay and keep employment records including Revenue payments for each employee.
> Ensure all employees are treated equally in the business and that bullying/ harassment does not exist. They must not discriminate when advertising, recruiting or promoting staff.
> Comply with all employment law and give employees a written contract of employment.

See Chapter 19

20.2 In groups, create a poster or infographic showing the responsibilities of employers.

KS WwO
KSBC
KSMIT

Employee records

Employers are required to keep records on all their employees. Employee records help an employer make decisions about pay rises, promotions and dismissals. The details they keep are usually as follows:

> Personal details, such as the employee's full name, address, date of birth, PPS number and contact names and telephone numbers in case of emergency.
> Job application form or CV. If an employee completed an application form for the current job, the employer will keep this for their own records.
> Employee's behaviour record. The employer will keep a record of an employee's attendance, punctuality and work performance.
> Timesheets.
> A copy of the employee's employment contract.
> Records of PAYE, PRSI and USC paid.

Industrial relations

Industrial relations refers to the relationship that exists between employers and their employees in the workplace.

If there are good industrial relations, staff will be motivated, hard-working and happy in the workplace, and there will be very few disputes. On the other hand, poor industrial relations can lead to disputes in the workplace, high absenteeism, staff turnover and bad publicity for the business.

Trade unions

All employees have the right to join a trade union.

Workers join trade unions and pay subscriptions to them because their trade union will:

A **trade union** is an organisation that represents workers, protects their rights and negotiates with employers on pay and conditions of work.

> Negotiate with employers for better pay and working conditions for their members

> Represent workers who have disputes with their employers

> Represent employees at discussions about national pay agreements.

The trade union representative in the workplace is known as a **shop steward**. This is an employee elected by the workers to represent them in dealings with the employer.

Examples of trade unions include SIPTU (Services Industrial Professional and Technical Union) and Mandate, which represents retail and bar workers.

20.3 In small groups research one of the following trade unions, or another of your choice, and create a poster or infographic giving the full name, which type of employees it represents and an outline of how it protects the rights of its members.

> Mandate   > IBOA   > INMO   > CPSU

> SIPTU   > IMO   > TEEU   > CWU

KSMIT
KSWwO
KSBC

20.4 In pairs, discuss what you think are the causes of poor industrial relations between employers and employees. Share your thoughts with other pairs of students.

T-P-S

KSMIT
KSC

Types of industrial action

Industrial disputes can result in a range of actions, such as:

An official strike: Employees refuse to work for the employer. The trade union must give the employer one week's notice of the strike action.

Work to rule: Workers do only what is in their job description.

Go-slow: Workers do their work but at a slower pace.

Overtime bans: Workers refuse to do overtime.

Token stoppage: Workers stop working for a short period of time, e.g. for three hours. This can disrupt the flow of work on the day it happens.

20.5 Research recent industrial relations disputes using newspapers or the internet. Find answers to these questions:

Research

KSMIT
KSBL

  (a) In which sector (e.g. retail, medicine) did the dispute take place?

  (b) What trade union was involved?

  (c) Who was the employer?

  (d) Where in Ireland did this dispute take place?

  (e) What was the dispute about?

  (f) How would you suggest the dispute could have been resolved?

Legislation protecting employees

Some of the main laws that protect employees in Ireland are:

> Protection of Young Persons (Employment) Act 1996
> Employment Equality Acts 1998 to 2011
> Unfair Dismissals Act 1977–2007
> Industrial Relations Act 1990
> Workplace Relations Act 2015.

Protection of Young Persons (Employment) Act 1996

This law protects young workers under the age of 18 and prevents young workers engaging in late-night work.

Children aged 14 may do light work outside school term. Children aged 15–16 may also do light work and this may be during school term. In both circumstances there are restrictions on the number of hours that may be worked and when the work may be done, with a complete ban on work between 8 p.m. and 8 a.m.

Young people (those between 16 and 18 years of age) may become employees but there are restrictions on the maximum hours that can be worked and generally the work cannot be between 10 p.m. and 6 a.m.

An employer of a child or young person must:

> See a copy of the employee's birth certificate.

> Obtain a letter of consent from the child's parent / guardian, if the employee is under 16.

> Keep records of the employee's details, such as date of birth, and of the hours worked.

20.6 Create a poster or infographic that could be given to young people from the age of 14, explaining the Protection of Young Persons (Employment) Act 1996. Set out simply the main points of the Act so that a young worker could refer to it to check their work conditions.

Research

KSBC
KSBL
KSMIT

Employment Equality Acts 1998 to 2011

These laws define discrimination as 'the treatment of one person in a less favourable way than another person is, has or would be treated'. Discrimination is outlawed under nine grounds:

> Age

> Gender

> Race

> Sexual orientation

> Religion

> Family status

> Marital status

> Disability

> Membership of the travelling community.

All aspects of employment are covered, including:

> Hiring and training employees
> Equal pay
> Opportunity for promotion

> Dismissal
> Conditions of work
> Advertising for employees.

Unfair Dismissals Act 1977-2007

This law states that **employees cannot be dismissed for the following reasons**:

> Age
> Becoming pregnant
> Religious beliefs
> Political beliefs
> Race
> Sexual orientation

> Being a member of the travelling community
> Being a member of a trade union
> Taking part in an official strike
> Taking legal proceedings against an employer.

Valid reasons for dismissal include:

> Incompetence
> Misconduct
> Redundancy
> Not having the necessary qualifications needed to do the job.

20.7 Using the Venn diagram provided in the Student Activity Book, compare and contrast the reasons for unfair dismissal under the Unfair Dismissals Acts and the reasons for which discrimination is outlawed under the Equality Acts.

KSMIT
KSBN

Industrial Relations Act 1990

This law states that employees engaging in industrial action cannot be stopped or sued by the employer for losses suffered as a result of industrial action, provided the employees held a secret ballot and gave the employer one week's notice of the industrial action.

20.8 Debate as a class why you think it is necessary to have all the laws we do regarding employment. Do you think we have too many laws, or do you think we need to have them to protect employees?

Discussion

KSWwO
KSBL
KSC

Workplace Relations Act 2015

The Workplace Relations Act set up the Workplace Relations Commission, which is an independent statutory body. Its role is to improve workplace relations between employers and employees. It ensures that employers obey all employment law and helps resolve disputes by assisting in talks between employers and employees. This process is known as **conciliation**.

An Coimisiún um Chaidreamh san Áit Oibre
Workplace Relations Commission

Labour Court (LC)

The Labour Court can help resolve disputes that were not resolved by the Workplace Relations Commission. It investigates disputes and recommends a solution in a process known as **arbitration**. It is the **court of last resort** in industrial relations matters.

20.9 Research the functions of the Workplace Relations Commission and the Labour Court.

KSMIT

Key Terms

You should be able to *define*, *spell*, give *examples* and *apply* to real life each of the following key terms associated with this topic.

Exercise: Write a sentence using each of the following terms. You may use more than one of the terms in your sentence if appropriate.

KSBL
KSC
KSMIT
KSBC

arbitration	Labour Court
conciliation	responsibility
employee	right
employer	trade union
industrial action	workplace relations
industrial relations	Workplace Relations Commission

Chapter 21 :: Impact of Technology

'I've come up with a set of rules that describe our reactions to technologies:

1   Anything in the world when you're born is normal and ordinary and is just part of the way the world works.

2   Anything that's invented between when you're fifteen and thirty-five is new and exciting and revolutionary and you can probably get a career in it.

3   Anything invented after you're thirty-five is against the natural order of things.'

Douglas Adams, *The Salmon of Doubt*

An impact is an effect or influence on something. Digital technology's impact on an organisation can be:

> **Positive** – when it benefits the organisation
> **Negative** – when it involves costs or a loss to the organisation.

Digital technology in business

Definitions

Information and communications technology (ICT) refers to the use of technology to send, receive, gather, store, analyse, distribute and communicate information.

Digital technology refers to the use of tools and resources such as computers, tablets, smartphones and apps to create, store, manage and share information.

As consumers, we use our phones, tablets and computers in a variety of ways.

21.1 In just one minute, write down as many uses for technology as you can think of in:

(a) Your home

(b) Your school

(c) A local business you are familiar with.

Consider the quote from the start of the chapter and remember to include technologies that aren't necessarily new. If they've been around for a while, you may just take them for granted! Swap your list with your partner and see how many uses you had in common.

Share your combined list with the whole class.

T-P-S

KSMIT
KSWwO
KSC

Businesses also use technology in a variety of ways:

> To design and produce products
> To conduct market research
> To prepare financial budgets and accounts
> To train staff
> To write reports
> To communicate with suppliers, customers and employees
> To promote and sell their products and services online.

In order to survive and remain competitive, businesses need to invest in and make effective use of technology. Failure to do so can be disastrous. The technology a business employs can affect how the business operates, how orders are processed, stock shortages identified, sales analysed, etc. If it is out of date, business opportunities may be missed, and competitors may gain an advantage.

Technologies used by business

There are many technologies that a business can use to save time and money. Some will be familiar to home users too. Here are some examples.

Word processing for writing reports, letters, business plans, etc.

Spreadsheets for recording employees' wages/salaries, recording cash flow, preparing accounts, creating charts, etc.

Databases for recording employee details, customer details, supplier details, stock items and other relevant data. Databases allow users to store and search for large amounts of information quickly. They can also be used to generate reports that show, for example, best-selling products. They can speed up decision making by making it easy to find information quickly.

Desktop publishing for creating brochures, leaflets, flyers, catalogues, etc.

Presentation packages for creating slideshows for meetings, conferences, etc.

Electronic point of sale (EPOS) for scanning barcodes, printing till receipts, taking payments by debit and/or credit cards, updating stock records, and providing sales reports.

Email for communicating both internally and externally with suppliers, customers, banks and other **stakeholders** (people who are affected by how a business is run).

Internet, a global network connecting computers, tablets and smartphones and allowing them to exchange information. Many financial, social and cultural enterprises have their own website to promote and sell their product/ service and communicate with existing and potential customers. Advertising and selling products through websites has allowed global e-commerce to flourish. Many people use their smartphones to buy products; this is called mobile commerce, or m-commerce.

Cloud computing for saving, storing and accessing information remotely on the internet (the cloud). Enterprises can save money by saving and storing information online. This reduces the need for lots of hardware in the business as well as the number of ICT staff needed to maintain equipment. However, cloud computing requires excellent broadband connections.

Wi-Fi allows computers, tablets, smartphones and other devices to connect to the internet wirelessly. It operates within a certain area range, e.g. a building. Most businesses have broadband, which allows information to be transferred between computers at a high speed. Many consumers expect businesses such as libraries, transport services, shops, cafés, restaurants and hotels to provide free Wi-Fi; businesses that do not may lose customers to competing businesses.

Video conferencing allows two or more people in different locations to communicate using audio and video. Video conferencing reduces the need for travel to meetings, which saves time and money.

21.2 What internet services enable video conferencing?

Research

KSBC
KSMIT

Social media is used by businesses so they can keep in touch with customers quickly and easily and promote products and services to a potential global market.

KSMIT

21.3 **(a)** Name seven different social media platforms.

  (b) Which social media platforms would you recommend to:

  (i) A business selling holidays to 18–30-year-olds?

  (ii) A magazine aimed at teenagers to keep in touch with its readers?

  Provide reasons for your answers.

Tablets are wireless, portable, touchscreen devices, which are smaller than a laptop but larger than a smartphone. Their portability makes them easy to use anytime and anywhere.

Applications (apps) are specialised software programs that perform specific tasks. Many enterprises create apps for their customers or suppliers, e.g. FoodCloud developed an app to link charities and supermarkets with surplus food.

See Chapter 17

21.4 Chris and Claire have decided to open a new restaurant.

    (a) What technologies would you advise them to buy?

    (b) In each case, briefly explain why they would need it and what it will be used for.

    (c) Share your thoughts with a classmate and identify any technologies that you didn't consider.

    (d) Share your combined list with the whole class.

T-P-S

KSMIT KSC

Benefits of using digital technology

Digital technology has many benefits for a business, and these can be categorised as follows:

> Staff
> Market research and marketing
> Production

> Finance
> Administration.

Staff

> Job vacancies can be advertised online, which will increase the number of applicants. Video conferencing can be used to interview shortlisted candidates to reduce travel costs.

> Online shared calendars can be used by employers to view meetings and appointments for staff.

> Email and text messaging can be used to communicate with staff.

> Staff can avail of online training, which they can complete at their own pace.

> Staff might be able to work from home (teleworking) through the use of broadband, email, telephone and video conferencing.

Market research and marketing

> Information on customers' spending habits can be gathered through store loyalty cards, which are swiped when purchasing goods. This allows businesses to target special offers at consumers.

> Field research can be gathered and analysed quickly 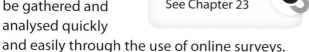 See Chapter 23 and easily through the use of online surveys.

> Customer information stored on databases can be used for direct marketing purposes.

> Products and services can be promoted globally using a company website, while social media can be used to target customers.

> Businesses can sell globally using an e-commerce website.

> Text messages about special offers can be sent to inform those consumers who have opted in to the service.

> Blogs can be used to engage with customers. The business can promote its products and can receive feedback on customer experiences. A blog is an informal type of web page and may take the form of an online chat.

See Chapter 24

See Chapter 16

Production

> Suppliers can be researched online to find the cheapest source of raw materials.

> The information gathered from the EPOS can be used to automatically reorder stock when it runs low.

> CAD (computer-aided design), CAM (computer-aided manufacture) and CIM (computer-integrated manufacturing) can be used to speed up the product development process and produce high-quality products.

Finance

> Spreadsheets can be used to prepare accurate cash flow forecasts and accounts.

> Formulas can be copied to speed up the calculation of accounts.

> Graphs and charts can be created to easily analyse and interpret financial information.

> Presentation software can be used when looking for investment to make financial information more engaging.

Administration

> Decision making is much faster.

> Writing personalised letters and reports is more efficient with word processing and email.

Digital technology and business costs

Investing in technology can be a major cost for businesses. However, using technology can also lead to many cost savings.

Cost increases

> Capital costs when installing new technology.

> Cost of recruitment and training of specialist staff, along with loss of working time while staff are being trained.

> Risk of information loss through staff error or computer **hacking**. Hacking occurs when someone gains unauthorised access to computer data.

> Risk of loss of information if storage is not backed up.

> Cost of designing, maintaining and hosting a website.

> Cost of anti-virus software for business laptops, computers and tablets.

> Health and safety implications for staff, through repetitive strain injury, eye strain, backache, etc. Employees who work on computers/laptops for long periods should take frequent breaks from using the screen to avoid eye strain.

> Cost of technology failure or breakdown. In 2012, Ulster Bank paid compensation to customers and a €3.5 million fine when computer failure prevented customers from accessing their accounts.

> Redundancy cost. The use of technology, including robotics, may displace human workers. Businesses may have to make redundancy payments to staff.

Cost reductions

> A company website can be used to advertise its business and as an online store. The site can be updated on a regular basis, which eliminates the need to produce printed catalogues.

> The use of certain new technologies can reduce the number of workers required, e.g. using robotic equipment instead of people, ATMs reduce the need for bank staff, supermarkets use self-scanning checkouts.

> Teleworking cuts down on costs and reduces the need for large premises.

> Emails can be sent out to many people (who have opted in to the service) much more quickly and cheaply than sending out letters.

Opportunities associated with using digital technology

> The increased use of technology in production allows for standardisation and mass production, resulting in increased output and reduced costs.

> The use of information technology in sales and marketing offers businesses the opportunity to check what consumers are buying in the market and to pick out which sector of the market to focus on.

> **Customer relationship management (CRM)** describes the use of a variety of strategies and technologies to manage interactions with customers. For example, information gathered from websites, blogs, telephone and social media can offer useful insights into a customer's purchase history and preferences.

> Salespeople can have smartphones and laptops, which will help to make them more efficient, as they can access updated information at any time.

> A business can use email and video conferencing to reduce the costs of travel and meetings.

> Technology can reduce the number of people employed in the business or improve the efficiency of those employed.

> Routine tasks can be automated and staff time is available for more creative tasks.

21.5 Do you think any business can survive these days without the use of technology? Discuss this, thinking about a window cleaner, a bank and a farmer, or another business of your choice.

Case Study

A cost–benefit analysis of digital technology in retailing

A clothing retailer with several branches throughout Ireland has decided to rebrand its business in order to appeal to a younger target market. As part of the rebranding it is also considering a large investment in digital technology. The main elements of the plan are as follows:

> Making maximum use of point-of-sale technology for marketing and payment purposes.

> Upgrading the company website to include a new online catalogue and sales facility. The current website is very outdated as it was designed to appeal to an older target audience who have limited interaction with online technology.

> Making use of blogging in an effort to get stay in touch with target market.

Big SALE!

> Investing in iBeacon technology to target individual customers with products. This technology requires customers to download an app to their phone. Once they enter the retail store they receive details of special offers and specific products which they have browsed or 'liked' online.

> Introducing in-store hubs and virtual displays to provide customers with images and information on product lines. In-store hubs make use of touch screen technology and allow customers to view product details including prices, sizes and availability. Customers can also use the technology to order goods which are currently out of stock. The virtual displays are large screens which show the company products to customers as they move around the store.

Cost–benefit analysis of the proposed investment in digital technology

Technology	Costs	Benefits
Point-of-sale technology	> Requires a modest upgrade of existing technology	> Essential for payments in a cashless society > Increases sales of specific products at point of purchase
Website upgrade	> Major investment required and will need to employ specialist staff or engage the services of professional web designer	> The business will have a genuine web presence > Increased interaction with target market > Increased online sales
Blogs	> Developing own blog will be time-consuming and offers no guarantee of success > Making use of an existing fashion blogger may have a more modest cost and a greater appeal	> Increased interaction with target market > Ability to make use of social media as a marketing tool > Ability to get feedback from customers helps with market research
iBeacons	> Costs of developing app and acquiring technology > Risk of annoying some customers with constant push notifications for products	> More targeted advertising and an ability to cater for individual customer needs and preferences > Useful for market research purposes

In-store hubs	› Expensive to program and install the technology › May be time-consuming to maintain and update › May be costly duplication of technology if iBeacon is also in use	› Less intrusive than iBeacon technology › Can encourage customers to order out-of-stock items
Virtual displays	› Cost of purchase, programming, installation and TV licence	› Once installed they are very cheap to update and maintain › Reduce the need to create large in-store displays › Increase availability of revenue-generating floor space
Evaluation and conclusion	Bearing in mind the costs and benefits set out above, management decided: › To upgrade the point-of-sale technology › To update the website and outsource the blog in order to promote the business online › To invest in iBeacon technology and in-store virtual displays › That the benefits of in-store hubs did not justify the costs involved and no investment would be made in this technology.	

Did you know?

The **Internet of Things (IoT)** is a computing concept that describes a future where everyday objects and devices (cars, fridges and traffic signals) will be connected to the internet and be able to interact and share information with other devices. The information they share can be useful for the way we make products or manage transport and healthcare systems.

ICT skills for employees

Being a confident user of digital technologies requires a wide range of knowledge and skills. In table 21.1 you will see a range of common tasks carried out by financial enterprises, social enterprises, cultural enterprises and charities and the skills required to complete these tasks. You may not currently possess all of these skills, but you should aim to develop at least some of them before you leave school/college.

Table 21.1 Skills needed in the workplace

Task	Skills
Web design	› Create websites with images, text and hyperlinks › Create the database that runs an e-commerce website
Social media	› Use social media to promote a business › Use social media to connect and inform clients and customers › Understand how people use social media so you can target the right people on the right platform
Online surveys	› Create, edit and share online surveys for market research purposes with a range of question types › Analyse the information gathered from the survey › Create reports based on the information gathered
Presentations	› Create slides (either from a template or blank slides) › Insert, format and resize text and images › Use animations and transitions
Word processing	› Create business document templates › Input information free from spelling, grammar and punctuation errors › Send personalised letters to individual customers or suppliers › Create notice, agenda and minutes for a meeting › Format and resize text and images
Desktop publishing	› Design brochures, leaflets, posters, catalogues and infographics to communicate with customers
Spreadsheets	› Input data accurately › Format rows and columns › Use formulas to carry out calculations › Create charts with appropriate labels
Database	› Insert, format, edit and delete data › Search records › Sort records › Create reports
Create images	› Create, edit and retouch images to upload to a website or social media
Specialist software	› Be willing to learn a company's or sector's own software that may be new to you

21.6 Look at the list of skills in table 21.1.

(a) Which of these interest you the most?

(b) Which skills do you think will be the most important in the type of work you want to do?

(c) How can you gain the skills you need for working with technology in the workplace?

(d) Complete the self-assessment in the Student Activity Book.

Key Terms

You should be able to *define, spell,* give *examples* and *apply* to real life each of the following key terms associated with this topic.

Exercise: Write a sentence using each of the following terms. You may use more than one of the terms in your sentence if appropriate.

applications (apps)

blog

broadband

cloud computing

customer relationship management (CRM)

digital technology

e-commerce

hacking

hardware

information and communications technology (ICT)

m-commerce

social media

software

stakeholder

tablet

video conferencing

Wi-Fi

Chapter 22 :: Impact of Organisations

Types of impact

An organisation's impact on a community can be:

> **Positive** – when it benefits a community

> **Negative** – when it involves costs or a loss to the community.

Types of organisation

Definitions

A **commercial organisation** has to make a profit. Most businesses – including banks, shops and airlines – are commercial organisations.

A **non-commercial organisation** has *not* been set up for the sole purpose of making a profit. The not-for-profit sector includes many charities and voluntary organisations that provide a range of services and benefits to communities.

Both commercial and non-commercial organisations can be local, national or global.

> **Local organisations** operate in a specific local area. Examples include community groups, local newspapers and shops that operate in one town only.

> **National organisations** operate or have branches all over Ireland. Examples include Dunnes Stores and the GAA.

> **Global organisations** are very large and have operations all over the world. Examples include McDonald's, Coca Cola and the Red Cross.

Economic benefits of organisations

From an economic perspective, the positive impact of an organisation refers to the financial or wealth benefit it brings to a community. These are laid out in table 22.1.

Table 22.1 Positive economic impacts of an organisation

Area impacted	Impact of the organisation
Employment	Direct employment in the organisation as well as jobs in related or spin-off businesses, such as transport, banking, suppliers and cleaning services
Tax revenue	The organisation will contribute to local authority rates and taxes. The money collected is used to develop local **infrastructure**
Improved standard of living	Employees hired by the organisation will have disposable income, which will lead to an improved standard of living
Multiplier effect	Extra income leads to increased spending in the local community, which supports other businesses such as shops and restaurants. The impact of the initial payment is multiplied as it passes around the community
Economic growth	An increase in businesses activity will lead to an increase in the amount of goods produced and services provided from one year to the next. This is an indicator of economic growth See Chapter 38
Balance of payments	An increase in goods and services produced in Ireland may lead to a reduction in imports and a possible increase in exports. In both cases the balance of payments will improve See Chapter 41

Infrastructure refers to the physical (e.g. buildings) and transport (e.g. roads, rail) structures and facilities (e.g. power supplies) needed for a society or enterprise to function.

Definition

The **balance of payments** is the difference in value between a country's total exports and total imports.

Definition

Did you know?

Google, Facebook, Twitter and several other large technology businesses have their EMEA (Europe, Middle East and Africa) headquarters in an area of Dublin known as 'Silicon Docks'. A huge number of cafés, restaurants and bars have opened there to meet the needs of the employees of the technology businesses, which has created more indirect employment in the area.

22.1 In pairs, think of other types of business that exist to meet the needs of the workers in these large technology businesses.

22.2 Think of a business near where you live that has enabled other businesses to exist nearby.

KSMIT
KSWwO
KSC

Social benefits of organisations

From a social perspective, the positive impact of an organisation refers to how it improves the lives of members in the community. Some benefits apply to specific stakeholders and others to the entire community. The positive social impacts of an organisation are shown in table 22.2.

Stakeholders is a collective term to describe all those who belong to an organisation or are affected by its activities. It includes employees, customers, suppliers, investors and the government as well as the wider community in which an organisation operates.

Table 22.2 Positive social impacts of an organisation

Positive impact	How organisations have an impact
More local services	There will be a growth in local services to meet the needs of local organisations (taxi/transport services, banks, credit unions, etc.). Local people can also use these services. Voluntary organisations also provide services for people in need. An example is the Jack & Jill Foundation
Increased choice / lower prices for consumers	New organisations provide extra goods and services as well as greater competition in the marketplace. This generally leads to a wider choice and lower prices for consumers
Promotes enterprise culture	Seeing local entrepreneurs establish businesses can lead to a culture of enterprise in an area and this can encourage more businesses to develop in the local community.
Improved quality of life	Successful social and cultural enterprises such as theatres, libraries, clubs and societies improve community spirit and social interaction. This leads to a better quality of life for local residents and makes the community a better place in which to live

Environmental benefits of organisations

See Chapter 40

From an environmental perspective, an organisation can have a positive impact on the natural resources (land, air, water) or the physical environment of a community. Table 22.3 shows what these impacts are.

Many modern organisations make use of **clean technology**. Clean technologies are designed to be more sustainable and to reduce negative environmental impact. They are found in a range of industries, including manufacturing, energy, water and transportation. Examples include recycling and renewable energy as well as the use of information technology, electric vehicles and energy-efficient lighting.

Table 22.3 Positive environmental impact of organisations

Positive impact	How organisations have an impact
Pollution controls	New developments including factories have to obey strict rules designed to limit pollution. Many high-tech industries use cutting-edge clean technology to minimise pollution and environmental impact
Recycling facilities	Organisations may develop recycling facilities, which serve their own needs or the needs of the wider community. This will reduce waste going to landfill or incineration. Rehab and FoodCloud provide recycling services, which have a positive impact on the natural environment. Some businesses use rainwater harvesting or recycling to reduce their consumption and environmental impact
Energy efficiency	Industry is increasingly using renewable energy, which helps to keep pollution levels low. Building Energy Ratings (BER) have increased awareness and changed building practices
Land usage	Organisations make use of vacant land to develop community services and improve the local landscape. The Tidy Towns organisation works to improve the local environment in this way. Local authorities provide parklands, and sporting organisations develop land to improve local facilities and the physical environment

See Chapter 17

Enterprise in action

What social enterprise can do for you

By Barry Flinn

In 2012 Dublin Fire Brigade won bronze in the most-sustainable government category at the International Green Awards. In 2009 the staff at Kilbarrack Fire Station, in Dublin, were putting in long hours, and morale was flagging. One crew member, Neil McCabe, started encouraging his fellow firefighters to collect and recycle batteries, simply to try to turn the mood around with something constructive.

A social entrepreneur in uniform, McCabe, who is still a full-time fireman, then founded Green Plan. Kilbarrack is thought to be the world's first carbon-neutral fire station, and Green Plan has generated €7.5 million in public-sector savings. Mini wind turbines and other light infrastructure generate more energy than the station uses; fires are put out with harvested rainwater; retired firefighters tend beehives to improve biodiversity, and companies have sprouted up in the area to meet the new demand for green technologies.

Some of these new business owners were previously unemployed, such as John Doyle, director of RainShed, which supplies rain-harvesting systems.

Central to Green Plan's success was ringfencing the savings from Kilbarrack to finance similar activity in Phibsborough, which in turn began the ripple effect throughout the fire brigade. This would have been impossible without a social entrepreneur to lead the way but equally impossible without the firefighters, civil servants and entrepreneurs throughout the organisation and the communities around fire stations.

Social entrepreneurs provide new leadership to society because they introduce ideas that allow people to think and act differently. They change the system.

Source: Article adapted from the *Irish Times,* 13 December 2014
Barry Flinn is a former communications manager for Ashoka Ireland, part of a global network that supports social entrepreneurs. He now works for Fenix Intl, an energy and microfinance social enterprise based in Uganda.

22.3 What steps could your school take to make it more environmentally responsible?

T-P-S

KSWwO
KSSW
KSMIT

22.4 Consider local businesses near you.

(a) How do they support the local community?

(b) How does their support benefit the local community?

Negative impacts of organisations

Unfortunately not all businesses treat their employees, customers and other stakeholders fairly. Table 22.4 gives some examples of negative impacts that may result from a business not behaving responsibly.

Table 22.4 How businesses get a bad reputation

Bad practice	Examples
With customers ❯ Producing poor-quality or dangerous goods ❯ Personal details inadequately protected	In October 2015 the personal details of over 150,000 customers and the bank account numbers of over 15,000 customers of TalkTalk (a UK-based telecommunications company) were accessed by hackers
With employees ❯ Inadequate health and safety training ❯ Unfair wages ❯ Demanding employees work long hours without adequate breaks ❯ Reducing the number of employees ❯ Relocating to another country and making employees redundant	Some well-known fashion retailers produce their clothes in the developing world and pay extremely low wage rates. Some of these producers employ very young workers and do not follow correct health and safety guidelines In 2009, the computer manufacturer Dell relocated from Limerick to Poland, with the loss of 1,900 direct jobs and many more indirect jobs in local suppliers and service industries
With suppliers ❯ Not paying for goods on time ❯ Seeking very large discounts which make sales unprofitable for the supplier	In January 2016, Tesco was ordered to change the way it deals with suppliers after it was found that the supermarket deliberately delayed payments to suppliers, in some cases by up to two years, in order to boost its profits
With government ❯ Not paying appropriate taxes ❯ Disobeying laws	Starbucks paid less than €5,000 in corporation tax in 2014 despite making pre-tax profits of €2.3 million

With society and local community
> Noise pollution through frequent or prolonged exposure to loud noises
> Air pollution caused by harmful chemicals, which can affect public health and damage the environment through the greenhouse effect
> Land pollution and water pollution caused by toxic chemicals and slurry effluent dumped in rivers or seas
> Crowding out competition – large multinationals may dominate market share and make it difficult for smaller, local businesses to compete on price and service levels
> Pressure on housing as employees may choose to live close to their place of work. Increased demand for housing may impact on land rezoning and cause housing and rental prices to rise
> Pressure on local services, since a population increase will also increase demand for community-based services such as waste removal, water and medical services. If there is no increase in supply many people are likely to suffer from reduced levels of service

In Galway in 2007 much of the water supply for the county was contaminated with a parasite called *Cryptosporidium*, which is spread through human and animal faeces. Affected water had to be boiled before use for a period of five months, greatly inconveniencing consumers and adding to the costs for local businesses

In April 2010, an explosion occurred on an oil rig owned by BP in the Gulf of Mexico. The oil gushed for 87 days before it was capped, causing the largest marine oil spill in history. There was extensive damage to wildlife, marine life and the fishing and tourism industries in the area. In July 2015 BP agreed to pay $18.7 billion in fines

22.5 Research newspapers and news websites for a business that has behaved unethically to one of the stakeholders listed above. Create a presentation, poster or infographic showing:

(a) How the business behaved unethically.

(b) Who was affected.

(c) What the consequences/effects were.

Research

KSMIT
KSBC
KSBL
KSC

Judging the success of an enterprise

Profit is one criterion used when assessing the performance of a business. It is, however, a limited way to judge success. Other factors that may be taken into account include:

> **Staff relations** – e.g. a good relationship between employees and employer, low staff turnover, employees paid a fair wage.

> **Customer loyalty** – i.e. do customers return frequently to the business? It's much cheaper to retain customers than to attract new ones.

> **Size of business** – has it grown over time? Has it developed new products? Has it entered new markets?

> **How long the business has survived** – e.g. Coca-Cola started in 1886 and Levi's in 1890.

> **Comparison with competitors** – does the business hold a larger market share than competitors? Is it the best known business in a particular area?

> **Awards** – has the business received awards, e.g. Entrepreneur of the Year, industry awards, etc.?

> **Social and environmental responsibility** – is the business recognised for its positive impact on the environment and the local community? The EU and IBEC (Irish Business and Employers Confederation) give environmental awards to businesses.

Groupwork

KSMIT
KSSW
KSWwO
KSBC
KSBL

22.6 Working in small groups, consider a business, community enterprise or voluntary organisation that operates in your area. It can be a local, national or global organisation. Prepare an oral presentation for your classmates, outlining one of the following:

(a) The benefits of that organisation to the local community.

(b) The negative consequences of that organisation for the local community.

Create an infographic, poster, video or slides to accompany your presentation.

Case Study

Question:

A global hotel operator has announced plans to develop a major hotel and leisure facility on the south-east coast. The plan is to develop an indoor waterpark alongside a 75-bedroom hotel and conference centre. The facilities would be open all year round and would be targeted at local and overseas visitors.

Examine the impact of the proposal from economic, social and environmental perspectives.

Suggested solution:

An evaluation of the impact of a proposed new hotel and leisure facility

Positive impacts	Negative impacts
Economic impact	
The development will create 400 short-term construction jobs and 250 long-term jobs when the hotel and leisure facilities are fully operational. There is strong potential for spin-off jobs and services to meet the needs of staff and visitors	The development may cause the closure of an existing local hotel. This would result in 20 jobs being lost
The development will attract extra tourists to the area and will boost the local economy. It is expected to generate €70m–€80m extra spending in the region each year	There will be a need to upgrade local roads and transport infrastructure. These costs will be roughly €200m and will be met from tax revenues
The local authority will receive additional revenue from taxation and commercial rates	An increase in land prices and housing rental costs is likely
Housing values are likely to increase as the area becomes a more desirable place to live	
The facility will attract overseas visitors and will have a positive impact on the balance of payments	
Social impact	
When fully operational the facility will provide the local community with a range of new leisure services	There may be short-term pressure on some local services as the development is likely to increase the local population
The development and the economic benefits associated with it will improve the quality of life for many local people	Some crowding out of smaller local businesses and tourist attractions may occur
Environmental impact	
The facility will make use of land that has been neglected and unsightly for several years. This will improve the appearance of the local environment. The development will also include some parkland development	Some locals are concerned about the environmental impact of the construction process. The plan also requires a small section of local forest to be cut down
The facility will make use of the most energy-efficient technology and will use solar energy to meet its needs	There are some concerns about the amount of water the facility will require and fears that this will impact on supplies to the wider community
Water harvesting will be a feature of the waterpark development	

22.7 Evaluate the impact of *one* of the developments listed below. Look at it from economic, social and environmental perspectives. Complete the blank template provided in the Student Activity Book.

> A proposal to build a data centre in your local community.

> The impact of a green energy plant on a local community.

> The impact of any other organisation or development on your local community.

Key Terms

You should be able to *define*, *spell*, give *examples* and *apply* to real life each of the following key terms associated with this topic.

Exercise: Write a sentence using each of the following terms. You may use more than one of the terms in your sentence if appropriate.

balance of payments   indirect employment

direct employment   infrastructure

enterprise culture   voluntary organisations

Chapter 23 :: Market Research

Why conduct market research?

As you learned in chapter 18, entrepreneurs find ideas for business in many ways. New products and services are constantly being developed to meet consumer needs. Existing products or services can also be redesigned or updated if necessary.

See Chapter 18

During the new product development process, entrepreneurs have to screen ideas and drop unworkable products. One method of screening is to conduct market research.

What is market research?

Market research is the gathering, recording and analysis of information about consumer preferences for a good or service, in order to make informed decisions about a potential market.

Definition

Businesses conduct market research to help ensure they provide the goods and services that customers need and want and to help them stay ahead of their competition.

Benefits of carrying out market research

Market research helps the business reduce the risk of business failure by finding out:

> Information about customers' needs and wants
> Likely demand for a new product or service
> Consumer reaction to changes to an existing product or service
> Information about the competition
> The best price to charge their customers
> Consumers' response to promotion techniques
> The likely level of sales.

Ultimately, market research helps businesses make **informed decisions** about new products and services or changes to existing products and services.

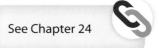
See Chapter 24

23.1 Why do you think people agree to answer questions for market research? Discuss your thoughts with a partner.

T-P-S
KSWwO
KSMIT

Types of market research

There are two main types of market research: field research and desk research.

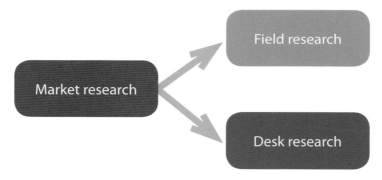

Field research

Field research involves going into the **marketplace** (i.e. to the people who might buy your product or service) to gather information first-hand for a specific purpose. It is also known as **primary research** and is carried out by making direct contact with customers or potential customers.

Table 23.1 Advantages and disadvantages of field research

Advantages	Disadvantages
> Up-to-date information is gathered	> Time-consuming
> Relevant information is gathered for the specific needs of the business	> Expensive
	> Requires skill to conduct

Examples of field research include:

> **Surveys:** Face-to-face or written questionnaires
> **Focus groups:** Meeting with a group of customers to discuss their opinions about a product.
> **Observation:** Looking at customer buying habits.

Surveys

A survey involves questioning consumers in relation to products and services. The responses will be analysed by market researchers. Questions should be clear and they should not be leading (suggesting certain answers). Question types include:

> Closed (requiring a 'yes' or 'no' answer)
> Multiple choice
> Open-ended, which allows the respondents to say what they like rather than be confined to a specific answer. These are useful to gather reactions or opinions. For example, you might ask: Did you like the chocolate bar? The respondent might just say 'No', which isn't much help to you. However, if you ask: 'What did you like and dislike about the chocolate bar?' the respondent might say: 'I liked the taste but the texture was unpleasant, so I wouldn't buy it.'

23.2 Work in small groups. Assume you want to do some research on setting up a business of your choice. Think of one question you could ask for each of the question types:

(a) Closed

(b) Multiple choice

(c) Open-ended.

One person from each group reads out the questions, when asked to do so. Write down any questions that other groups had that your group did not.

Groupwork

KSWwO
KSC
KSBL
KSMIT

'Robin Hoodies' Student Enterprise Market Research Survey

Please indicate your answer by inserting a tick in the appropriate boxes below.

1. *Gender*

    Male ☐   Female ☐

2. *What year are you in?*

    First   ☐   Second ☐   Third ☐

    Fourth ☐   Fifth   ☐   Sixth ☐

3. *Are you interested in buying a school hoodie?*

    Yes ☐   No ☐

4. *If you answered 'yes' to Q3, how much would you be prepared to pay for the hoodie?*

    Up to €15 ☐   Up to €20 ☐   Up to €25 ☐

5. *If you answered 'yes' to Q3, what size would you buy?*

    Small ☐   Medium ☐   Large ☐

6. *What would you like on the hoodie?*

    School name   ☐

    School crest   ☐

    Class signatures ☐

    Other (please specify)

7. *What is your favourite colour?*

Figure 23.1 An example of a survey

The questioning can be done by personal interview, by post, by phone or online. Each method has its advantages and disadvantages (see table 23.2).

It would be impossible to survey all consumers, so market researchers usually select a sample of population to represent all consumers. This is called **sampling**.

Table 23.2 Carrying out surveys

Method	Advantages	Disadvantages
Personal interview Face-to-face interview between market researcher and consumer, using a questionnaire. The interviewer usually fills out the responses on behalf of the consumer	› Allows for detailed responses › Clarification about a question or an answer can be sought	› Time-consuming › Expensive › Consumers may feel uncomfortable answering particular questions face-to-face and may be dishonest in their responses
Postal survey Questionnaires are sent and returned through the post	› Cheaper than a personal interview as there is no interviewer involved › People can answer in their own time	› Very low response rate › Responses may take a long time to be returned
Telephone survey A series of questions is asked over the telephone	› Cheaper than a personal interview › People can be chosen from a wide geographical area › Clarification about a question or an answer can be sought	› Difficult to get people to respond, particularly if you contact them during busy times › People may provide quick responses to get the survey over quickly
Online survey Survey published on a website or sent via email	› Cheapest method (no cost for printing, postage, phone calls or interviewer) › People worldwide can participate › People can answer in their own time › Responses may be analysed automatically	› Many people ignore on-screen pop-ups or ignore the option to complete a survey › The opinions of consumers who are not online are ignored

23.3 Following on from question 23.2, which survey method do you think you will use? Discuss your reasons in small groups. Conduct a survey among the class to identify the most popular choice.

T-P-S

KSWwO
KSC
KSMIT

Focus group

A group of consumers is brought together to discuss a particular product or service.

Advantage: It is an efficient way to gather reactions and opinions from a group of people.

Disadvantage: Some members of the group may dominate the responses and influence the views of other group members.

Observation

This involves watching or viewing consumers in action. For example:

> The number of customers selecting a specific product during a particular period in a store

> The time it takes to select a particular product

> How much attention is given to an in-store display.

This method is often used in retail stores.

Advantages: Large numbers of people can be observed, and it is a relatively cheap method of market research.

Disadvantages: It is time-consuming and provides only limited information. For example, it indicates *what* products are purchased but it might also be useful to know *why* those products were chosen.

Analysing field research findings

When you gather your market research you will need to analyse the findings. Closed questions (e.g. those that require a yes/no or multiple-choice answer) are easier to analyse than open-ended questions (e.g. Q7 in the sample survey in figure 23.1).

If a survey is answered by 75 people, and 50 of those were female and 25 were male, the findings would be as follows:

N = 75 (number of respondents) Female = 50, Male = 25

$$\text{Female} = \frac{50}{75} \times \frac{100}{1} = 66.67\% \qquad \text{Male} = \frac{25}{75} \times \frac{100}{1} = 33.33\%$$

This information can be shown in graph format as a bar chart or pie chart, such as the one in figure 23.2.

Pie charts are suitable when you want to break the answers into different segments to identify which is most popular. **Bar charts** are useful when comparing answers.

Market research results are often displayed using slides at a meeting, e.g. PowerPoint, Prezi, Google Slides, or communicated in a report.

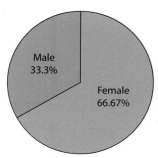

Figure 23.2 Pie chart showing gender of respondents

Did you know?

Businesses use technology to conduct market research. Some retailers gather information about consumers' purchasing habits using their loyalty cards scanned at the electronic point of sale (EPOS).

Many retailers also use social networking sites such as Facebook and Twitter to test customer reactions to products or services.

See Chapter 21

23.4 What drawbacks might there be to using information gathered through social networking sites?

23.5 In activity 18.1 of chapter 18 you thought of a business you might be able to start as a result of a hobby.

Create a survey about the good or service you would sell as part of this business. Think about what you would need to know in order to find out whether people would use this good or service.

Write a variety of relevant questions, using suitable types of questioning, e.g. yes/no, multiple choice, open-ended.

23.6 Pick a minimum of 20 people as your sample to answer your survey. How did you choose these people to answer your survey?

23.7 Present the results of your survey, graphically where possible.

23.8 Create an online version of the survey using one of the free tools available on the internet, e.g. SurveyMonkey or Google Forms.

23.9 Email the survey to 20 people, e.g. friends, family or classmates. Explain that the survey is a school assignment. Analyse the results, graphically if possible.

Desk research

Desk research involves looking at and analysing information that has already been gathered for another purpose or from another source. It is also known as **secondary research** and can be both internal and external.

Table 23.3 Advantages and disadvantages of desk research

Advantages	Disadvantages
› Easy to obtain, as it uses information that is already available › Quick to gather › Cheaper than field research as it does not require trained interviewers	› As the information gathered is not for the specific needs of the business, it may not be as useful or relevant as primary research › Information may be outdated › The researcher may have to read a lot of information to find what they need

Examples of desk research

Table 23.4 Examples of desk research

Example of research	How it might be used
Business sales reports	The examination of all past sales records and reports of the business will help to identify the most and least successful products the business has sold in the past
Newspapers and magazines	Newspaper and magazine articles may contain information about competitors or consumers, e.g. market size, products, international trends
Internet	Checking competitors' products and prices and finding out information about market size and trends
Central Statistics Office (CSO)	The CSO provides information on the population of towns and cities throughout Ireland as well as information on age, gender, marital status, etc. of the population. The Household Budget Survey gives information on the spending patterns of households on different types of goods

KSMIT
KSC

23.10 Which method of desk research do you think would be the best to find information about the following?

    (a) A company's competitors

    (b) Potential customers

    (c) Market size.

23.11 (a) Using the CSO website, www.cso.ie, find the most popular girls' and boys' names for babies born last year.

    (b) Consider what types of business would find this information useful.

An Phríomh-Oifig Staidrimh
Central Statistics Office

23.12 Find an article in a local or national newspaper that contains information that might be of use to a local business. Copy or cut out the article and insert it in your copy. Highlight the most useful information and in your copy say why it is useful.

Uses of market research

Enterprises use market research for the following reasons:

> To identify what is happening in a market, e.g. Apple may want to identify trends in sales of iPads.

> To identify what is likely to happen in the future, e.g. Sunway Travel may research the kinds of holidays people are interested in taking in the next three years so they can provide suitable trips.

> To explain the causes of changes in the market, e.g. Nissan might research why sales of the Qashqai in Europe have declined slightly since 2011, as shown by their sales reports.

> To investigate new market possibilities, e.g. SuperValu could test a new product in stores in Galway to test consumer reaction before launching nationwide.

In the news

Boost as new car sales for January up to 40,000

By Eddie Cunningham

New car registrations for January surged by 10,000 – to nearly 40,000 – and have paved the way for a massive increase in purchases for the year overall.

New figures from the Society of the Irish Motor Industry show a 33.5pc lift to 39,812 (from 29,808 in January 2015).

Hyundai topped the sales charts for the month followed by Toyota, Ford, Volkswagen, Nissan, Renault, Skoda, Opel, KIA and Audi.

And the big-selling models were the Hyundai Tucson, Ford Focus, Toyota Corolla, Ford Fiesta, Volkswagen Golf, Skoda Octavia, Toyota Yaris, Nissan Qashqai, Toyota Auris and Renault Clio.

Commercial sales are also forging ahead – a clear sign of business confidence in the economy.

The phenomenal buying spree has prompted forecasts that we could buy an average of 1,000 new cars a week more than last year.

One top executive is predicting that as many as 170,000 new-car regs will be on the road before the end of the year such has been the surge in buying so far.

That would be an increase of 45,000 on last year and 20,000 more than the most optimistic expert forecasts early in the year.

According to Renault Ireland chief Paddy Magee the original and optimistic estimate of 150,000 will easily be passed.

Source: Article adapted from the Irish Independent, 1 February 2016

23.13 Referring to the news item above, answer these questions.

    (a) Is this an example of field or desk research?

    (b) What types of business might be interested in this information?

    (c) What valuable information is contained in this article?

23.14 Find out about the job of a market researcher. What skills does a market researcher need? Evaluate the importance of a market researcher in an organisation.

Key Terms

You should be able to *define*, *spell*, give *examples* and *apply* to real life each of the following key terms associated with this topic.

Exercise: Write a sentence using each of the following terms. You may use more than one of the terms in your sentence if appropriate.

bar chart	personal interview
desk research	pie chart
field research	postal survey
focus group	primary research
observation	sampling
marketplace	secondary research
market research	survey
online survey	telephone survey

Chapter 24 :: Marketing Mix

What is marketing?

Marketing is the process of identifying and satisfying customer needs and wants while making a profit.

Definition

Market research can be used to gather information about customer needs and wants.

See Chapter 23

Market segmentation

Market segmentation involves dividing the market into segments or parts with the aim of promoting different products or services to each group of customers.

Definition

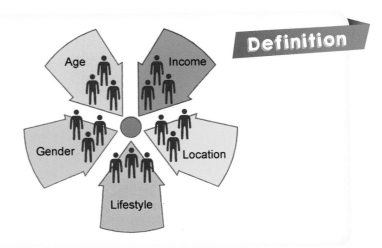

Car manufacturers are experts at this, as they produce a range of different models to suit a variety of budgets and to satisfy the needs of young drivers, families and business executives, etc. Some of the ways markets can be segmented are shown in table 24.1.

Table 24.1 Market segments

Segment	Explanation	Example
Gender	Aiming products at a specific gender (male/female)	Most toiletries are aimed at one gender or another, e.g. Lynx is aimed at men
Age	Aiming products at people of a certain age	Holidays aimed at 18–30-year-olds or families
Income	Aiming products at people with a particular level of income	Some supermarkets have brands aimed at different income levels, e.g. Tesco Value range is aimed at people on low incomes while their Finest range is aimed at people with a higher income
Location	Aiming products at people who live in a particular geographic location	The climate in a country will determine the type of clothing sold in that country. Local radio stations exist in many Irish counties
Lifestyle	Aiming products at people who lead a particular lifestyle	Marks & Spencer has a range of convenience foods called 'Balanced for you', which is aimed at people who are concerned with healthy eating

Selecting a target market

After a business has segmented the market it will choose a particular segment to aim its product at. This segment is known as its target market.

A **target market** is the group of people to whom a business aims to sell its products or services.

TARGET MARKET

24.1 (a) While watching television, listening to the radio, or reading a magazine, take note of five adverts. For each one, name the advert and explain:

> What segment the advert is aimed at, using the headings in table 24.1 above

> What the advert includes to appeal to that segment.

(b) Do you think any of the adverts were aimed at people like you? Did you find these adverts appealing? Explain your answer.

24.2 There are a number of national Irish radio stations. Discuss the following questions with your classmates.

(a) Why do you think there are several different stations, rather than one?

(b) Find out the names and a little about all the different national radio stations and identify the target market for each.

(c) List three examples for each radio station of the type of products or services that would be advertised on that station.

T-P-S

KSWwO
KSMIT
KSC

Marketing mix

The marketing mix is a combination of four elements that can help a business market its products to its target market and helps it achieve the goal of maximising profits. These elements of the marketing mix (also known as the **4Ps**) are:

> Product
> Price
> Place
> Promotion.

The goal is to combine these elements in a way that increases customer satisfaction and product sales.

Think of the marketing mix like a recipe: it is important to get the right **mix** of ingredients or it will not be totally successful.

Product

A **product** is an actual item (either a physical good or a service) provided to meet consumers' needs.

Definition

In the marketing mix, the product element includes:

> Design
> Product life cycle
> Branding
> Unique selling point (USP).

Design

Design is the first stage in making a product. Well-designed products are attractive, easy to use, long lasting and useful.

Product life cycle

Most products have a limited lifespan, due to changes in fashion, consumer taste and new inventions. While products last for different lengths of time, they all tend to move through a product life cycle, which contains five stages:

1 **Introduction:** The new product is launched. Sales will be slow until consumers become familiar with it.

2 **Growth:** Sales increase rapidly as more consumers get to know about the product.

3 **Maturity:** Sales growth increases at a slower pace and may start to level off, often due to competition.

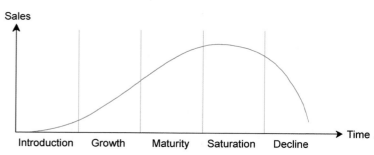

Figure 24.1 The product life cycle

4 **Saturation:** Sales reach their peak, due to many competitors in the market. Also, most consumers in the target market already have the product. This makes it difficult to increase sales as there are fewer 'new' customers available.

5 **Decline:** Sales fall due to changes in taste/fashion or the introduction of a new or better product. Eventually the product will be withdrawn from the market.

24.3 Draw the product life cycle diagram in the space provided in the Student Activity Book. Don't forget to label both axes.

The life cycle for a product can be extended by:

> Introducing a new, improved version of the product
> Selling the product in a new market or in new outlets
> Changing the price of the product
> Launching a new advertising campaign.

24.4 (a) Think of five products you are familiar with. In your group research the products using a variety of sources, e.g. newspapers, magazines, internet, and decide where each of the products appears on the product life cycle. Draw a product life cycle diagram and mark the name of the product on it.

(b) Create a presentation showing:

> The name and a picture of the product.
> Your product life cycle diagram showing where your product fits.
> Reasons, backed up by reference to your research, why you know it falls in this part of the life cycle.

Branding

A **brand** is a name, symbol, design or other feature that makes it easy to recognise and distinguishes the product(s) from competing products.

Definition

24.5 In pairs, think of five examples of brands and discuss what distinguishes them as a brand.

T-P-S

KSWwO
KSMIT
KSC

Most brands are developed by the producer and while developing a brand can be expensive, it has the following **advantages**.

> Branding helps a business to increase sales.
> Branding makes products easy to recognise, which means it is easier to introduce new products with a brand name (e.g. the Apple watch is successful because Apple already has a good reputation for making other products).
> Branding encourages customers to buy upgrades or new products from the same brand (known as **brand loyalty**).
> Higher prices can be charged for branded products, as consumers often associate them with better quality and are willing to pay extra for this.

Own branding

Some large shops have their own brand products, e.g. Tesco Finest, Dunnes Stores Simply Better.

Own label brands are generally developed or commissioned by a retailer rather than by a producer.

24.6 Think of the last time you bought runners or a mobile phone. Discuss and write down your responses to the following questions with your partner.

(a) Did the brand influence the choice of product you bought?

(b) Can you name other brand names of competing products?

(c) Why did you choose the brand you did?

T-P-S

KSWwO
KSMIT
KSC

Unique selling point

A business will identify the unique selling point (**USP**) of its product or service. This is what makes the product different from the competition and will be highlighted particularly during promotion of the product. For example, Volvo's USP is safety, and Toyota's is reliability.

Price

> The **price** refers to the amount of money a seller charges a customer for a product or service.

Definition

The price for a product is often determined by supply and demand. Other factors that a business may consider when setting price include:

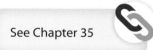
See Chapter 35

> The cost of making the product
> The amount of profit the business wants to make
> Where the product is in its life cycle
> The price charged for competing products
> The target market for the product.

Pricing strategies

Businesses use different pricing strategies to decide how to price their products or services. They are:

> **Cost-plus pricing:** The business calculates how much it costs to produce a product and then adds a percentage mark-up to make a profit. For example, if a product costs €4 to produce and the manufacturer wants a 30% mark-up, they will sell the product for €4 + 30% (€1.20) = €5.20.

> **Loss leaders:** The business deliberately sells products below cost price in order to attract customers. It hopes that the customers will buy higher-priced products while buying loss leaders.

> **Premium pricing:** The business charges a permanently high price to convey an image of exclusivity, e.g. BMW cars.

> **Penetration pricing:** The business charges a low price when a product is new to the market, to get consumers interested in it. Once the product becomes known, the business may increase its price.

24.7 Think of a recent purchase you made. Identify what type of pricing strategy was used. Give a reason for your answer.

Place

Place refers to where customers will buy the product and the channel of distribution used to get the product to this location.

This element of the marketing mix involves the distribution of the product in order to ensure it is conveniently available to the consumer.

Channels of distribution refers to the way in which the product gets from the manufacturer to the consumer.

There are four main ways the product can get from the manufacturer to the consumer. They are:

1 The **manufacturer** sells directly to the **consumer**, e.g. farm shops, mail order, internet shopping.

2 The **manufacturer** sells to **large retailers**, e.g. Dunnes and Tesco, who can buy in bulk, and who will distribute to their own branches and sell to consumers.

3 The **manufacturer** sells in bulk to **wholesalers** who sell in smaller quantities to **retailers**. Many goods are sold in this way and this is the traditional channel.

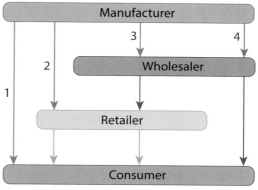

Figure 24.2 Channels of distribution

4 The **manufacturer** sells to the **wholesaler**, who then sells directly to the **consumer**, e.g. buying a book from Amazon.

The channel used depends on:

> The **product** itself – some products such as fresh fruit have a short shelf life, so they need to be delivered to retailers quickly.

> **Legal requirements** – some products must be sold through a certain channel, e.g. certain medicines can be sold only by a pharmacist.

> **Image** of the product – some products have a high-quality image which means they will be sold only via an exclusive retailer, e.g. Brown Thomas.

Different types of retailer

Department stores sell a wide range of products, through different departments such as women's clothing, menswear, children's wear, accessories, cosmetics, household goods, etc. Examples include: Debenhams, Arnotts, Brown Thomas.

Chain stores usually specialise in a type of product and have many different branches throughout the country. Examples include: River Island, Oasis, Eason, Boots.

Supermarkets sell a wide range of products, including food, drink, cleaning products, toiletries, etc. Examples include: SuperValu, Dunnes, Tesco.

Discount retailers sell products at a reduced price. Examples include: Dealz, EuroGiant.

Franchises operate using a licence from a franchisor. Examples include: McDonald's, Subway.

Independent retailers are small businesses, usually owned by a sole trader. Examples include: local boutique, small newsagent, village shop.

Online stores are shops set up on the internet. Sometimes they are only on the internet and sometimes physical shops also sell online. Examples include: Amazon, Tesco.

KSMIT

24.8 Think of the main, or one of the main, streets in your nearest town or city. List the shops and note what kind of retailers they are.

24.9 Mark on your list those shops that also sell online.

24.10 Think of five items you or your family bought recently. Which type(s) of retailer did you purchase from?

24.11 Many businesses use technology to sell directly to consumers, either through a website or through an app. Some businesses sell exclusively online, e.g. ASOS and Ryanair. Think of two advantages and two disadvantages of an online shop for:

(a) The business

(b) The consumer.

Promotion

> **Promotion** refers to raising customer awareness of the product or brand in order to increase sales and create brand loyalty.

Definition

Businesses use promotion to:

> Launch a new product
> Increase sales of existing products
> Improve the image of the business.

The **promotion mix** is the combination of promotional activities used by a business to communicate with existing and potential customers. It includes:

> Advertising
> Sales promotion
> Public relations

> Sponsorship
> Personal selling
> Social media

> Celebrity endorsement
> Product placement.

Advertising

> **Advertising** involves communicating with the public to let them know about a product and get them interested in buying it.

Definition

Advertising is the promotion method that we are probably most familiar with. Advertising is paid for by businesses and is directed at a large audience rather than individual consumers. Adverts follow the **AIDA** model as they:

> **A** – attract **attention**
> **I** – capture the **interest** of the consumer
> **D** – stimulate **desire** for the product
> **A** – lead to **action**, i.e. purchasing the product.

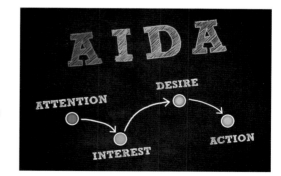

Adverts can reach a large number of potential consumers across a range of target markets.

There are five different categories of advertising:

1 **Informative advertising:** Provides information about a product or service to the general public.

2 **Persuasive advertising:** Convinces/persuades people that they need a particular product or service.

3 **Competitive advertising:** Used by businesses to convince people that their product is better than their competitors' products.

4 **Reminder advertising:** Used to simply remind customers that a product is still available and continues to represent good value for money.

5 **Generic advertising:** Firms in an industry work together to produce an advertisement to persuade people to buy that particular type of product, e.g. milk is advertised by the National Dairy Council (NDC).

24.12 Look through magazines and newspapers to find at least one example of each of the five different categories of advertising. Copy these or (if it belongs to you) cut out the advertisement and stick it in your copy. Write notes by the side of the advert to explain what message the advert is trying to convey.

Advertising media

The medium used for advertising will depend on:

> The target market for the product
> The advertising budget available.

The most common media for advertising are television, radio, newspapers, magazines, cinema, billboards and internet. The medium used will depend on the target market for the product and the advertising budget available. Table 24.2 shows the advantages and disadvantages of each medium.

Table 24.2 Advertising media

Medium	Advantages	Disadvantages
Television	> Can reach a national or global audience > Can provide a demonstration of the product > Can target specific audiences during particular TV shows	> Expensive to produce and put on TV, especially during popular programmes > Some people skip the adverts, while others channel hop to avoid adverts
Radio	> Cheaper than TV advertising > Can target specific audiences based on radio programme, radio station > Local radio adverts are suitable for local businesses > More captive audience than TV, people are less likely to switch stations > Jingles can make adverts memorable	> There's no option to rewind or listen again on radio > Lack of images makes it impossible to demonstrate the product

continued

Newspapers	❯ Full-page adverts are attention-grabbing ❯ Can provide lots of information which can be re-read ❯ Can target specific markets, depending on the newspaper chosen ❯ Local newspapers are suitable for local businesses	❯ National full-page adverts are expensive ❯ Newspapers contain lots of adverts so it can be difficult to stand out ❯ No sound or video content to demonstrate the product ❯ A short shelf life means that adverts may not be visible for very long.
Magazines	❯ High visual impact as they are usually printed in colour on quality paper ❯ Can target specific markets ❯ Are kept by readers for a longer time than newspapers so may be viewed repeatedly	❯ No sound or video content to demonstrate the product ❯ Competitors may advertise in the same publications
Cinema	❯ Shown to a more captive audience than TV adverts ❯ Can provide a demonstration of the product ❯ Can target specific audiences during particular movies, e.g. toys advertised during Disney movies	❯ Limited audience of cinema-goers ❯ Expensive to produce
Billboards	❯ Visual impact ❯ Can be displayed in busy locations ❯ Useful for short messages	❯ Are ignored by many people ❯ Can only convey a limited amount of information
Internet/ websites	❯ Relatively cheap to create and share ❯ Sound and video can be used ❯ Some online adverts go viral and can reach a global audience ❯ The number of times an advert is viewed online can be monitored ❯ Detailed information can be placed on a business website and can be read at a time convenient to the consumer	❯ Internet users increasingly shut down pop-up ads or skip adverts at the start of videos

24.13

(a) What is figure 24.3 called?

(b) With which of the advertising media in table 24.2 would you find these?

(c) Why are they included on adverts?

(d) Where else, other than adverts, could you find them?

(e) In your copy explain what this is, and why it is used. Provide instructions for using the code. (If you don't know, ask someone in your class to demonstrate to you.)

KSMIT
KSC
KSBC
KSBL

Figure 24.3

Did you know?

The cost to air a 30-second TV advert during the Super Bowl, the most high-profile TV event in the United States, was $5 million in 2016. That doesn't even include the cost of making the advert, which can also run into millions of dollars. The reason businesses are prepared to pay so much is because the adverts will be viewed by at least 114 million people in the United States alone and many more worldwide. Super Bowl adverts are also often posted online, providing further exposure for the business.

24.14 From your own experience or by talking to other people, find out what kinds of adverts are shown during different programmes at various times and on various days. What does this tell you about the target market? Compare your results with your classmates'. From your research, write a short report on targeted advertising on TV.

Research

KSBC
KSMIT
KSBL

Advertising ethics

Adverts should not mislead customers or make false claims about products or services.

See Chapter 14

The **Advertising Standards Authority of Ireland** (**ASAI**) is a body set up and financed by the advertising industry that ensures that all marketing communications are **legal, decent, honest and truthful**. The ASAI investigates complaints made by the public. Its website contains a list of recent complaints.

ASAI

24.15 Class debate: Do you think adverts for toys and sweets should be shown during children's television programmes?

Discussion

KSC
KSWwO

Sales promotion

Sales promotions are incentives offered to customers to attract them to buy products. These incentives often include short-term tactics to improve sales, such as:

> Free samples

> Buy one, get one free (BOGOF)

> Gifts with purchase

> Bonus packs, e.g. 50% extra free

> Loyalty card schemes

> Money-off vouchers/coupons

> Competitions

> Point-of-sale materials, e.g. posters, displays.

24.16 (a) What are the benefits of sales promotions to the consumer?

(b) What are the disadvantages of sales promotions to the consumer?

KSMIT

See Chapter 13

Public relations/publicity

The role of public relations is to portray a positive image of the business to the public. This may be achieved by organising charitable events, giving back to the local community or by minimising any negative story about the business.

Businesses often create press releases to inform the media of new products.

24.17 How is publicity different from advertising?

24.18 Although publicity isn't paid for directly in the same way as advertising, in what ways will it cost the business money?

Sponsorship

Businesses sometimes sponsor events, sports competitions, teams or venues. They do this by providing financial support in return for promoting the business and/or its products. Businesses can benefit from the success of those they sponsor and can become popular with customers who support/visit the sponsored event, team, competition or venue.

24.19 In your copy, list five examples of sponsorship. Include local, national and international examples.

Personal selling

Personal selling involves salespeople selling directly to new or existing customers. This form of promotion uses the specialist knowledge of the salespeople to inform and encourage the customer to buy the product.

The message used can be personalised to the individual customer. Personal selling is frequently used to sell high-priced products, e.g. cars, cosmetics in large department stores, specialist machinery and financial services such as insurance and pension products.

Social media

Social media provides businesses and organisations with a very quick, cheap and easy way to promote products and services to a potentially global audience. Most businesses now have at least one social media account, e.g. Snapchat, Facebook, YouTube, Twitter, Instagram, to share photos or videos of new products to existing and potential customers.

Social media can promote interactive communication with customers and businesses can gather feedback on potential new products.

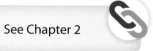
See Chapter 2

Celebrity endorsement

Businesses often use celebrities to promote their products by providing them with free samples to use or wear or by paying them to appear in an advert. If a celebrity is seen with a product, it can raise the appeal of that product very quickly and effectively.

24.20 List celebrities you know who appear in adverts for products. Name the products and businesses involved. Compile a class list.

24.21 Would you buy a product because it had a celebrity endorsement? Why would their involvement encourage you to buy the product?

KSMIT
KSWwO

Product placement

Businesses often pay significant amounts of money for their latest products to feature or be seen in TV programmes or movies, e.g. the Sony Xperia Z5 featured in the James Bond film *Spectre*. The product is not brought to the attention of the viewer, but its presence can be enough to persuade people to buy it because they like the show or the actor, or just because continually seeing it makes them recognise it.

KSMIT

24.22 Look out for product placement when you watch a movie or a TV programme. What product was used? If you can't spot this, search on the internet for items about product placement to find out what programmes or movies have shown products.

KSMIT
KSBC

24.23 For a product or service of your choice, create a suitable marketing mix using the template provided in the Student Activity Book.

24.24 Do you have a business or product idea? Identify the potential target market for this product and plan the marketing mix for it.

Key Terms

KSBL
KSC
KSMIT
KSBC

You should be able to *define, spell*, give *examples* and *apply* to real life each of the following key terms associated with this topic.

Exercise: Write a sentence using each of the following terms. You may use more than one of the terms in your sentence if appropriate.

advertising

Advertising Standards Authority of Ireland (ASAI)

branding

channels of distribution

competitive advertising

cost plus pricing

ethics

generic advertising

informative advertising

loss leader

market segmentation

marketing mix

media

penetration pricing

persuasive advertising

place

premium pricing

price

product

product life cycle

promotion

public relations

reminder advertising

retailer

social media

sponsorship

target market

unique selling point (USP)

wholesaler

Chapter 25 ::
Financial Planning for Business

Learning outcomes

When you have completed this chapter you will be able to:

✔ Assess the major short-term, medium-term and long-term financial needs of a business

✔ Distinguish between short-, medium- and long-term sources of finance

✔ Describe and evaluate the major sources of finance for business

✔ Outline the factors that will influence a business when choosing a source of finance

✔ Explain the concept of working capital

✔ Explain the importance of effective working capital management

✔ Prepare and analyse a cash flow forecast for a business.

Financial needs of businesses

Businesses need finance for a variety of reasons:

Short-term needs are the most immediate and involve items of expenditure that must be paid within the current financial year, such as raw materials, wages, light and heat, telephone, advertising, insurance and transport costs. Since these are ongoing costs that must be paid regularly and repeatedly, they are generally classified as **current expenditure**.

Medium-term needs involve spending on items that are likely to last beyond the current financial year, such as the purchase of vehicles and ICT (information and communications technology) equipment that typically have a working life of up to five years. These are also examples of **capital expenditure** as the items will be owned and used by the business for several years.

Long-term needs include the purchase of items that will provide benefits to the business over a more extended period of time, usually in excess of five years, such as premises and machinery. These are also examples of capital expenditure.

25.1 Discuss with your partner whether each of these is a short-, medium- or long-term need.

(a) A packaging machine for a factory

(b) A fridge for a restaurant

(c) A telephone bill

(d) Furniture for reception

(e) Marketing leaflets

(f) A stable for a horse riding school

The **matching principle** ensures that businesses use a source of finance that is most suited to their specific needs, i.e. that short-, medium- and long-term needs are financed (or matched) with short-, medium- and long-term sources of finance.

Factors that influence the source of finance

Business managers have to consider the following when choosing a suitable source of finance.

The purpose of the finance: Is it for day-to-day purposes (working capital) or is it to fund long-term goals or the purchase of **fixed assets**? (Fixed assets are items owned by the business and intended for long-term use, e.g. premises, equipment and vehicles.)

 See Chapter 10

The amount of finance required: Long-term sources tend to be more suitable for large amounts as this allows a business to spread the cost of borrowing over a longer time period. This will reduce monthly repayments, which will help with monthly cash flow (**liquidity**).

Cost of finance: Borrowers should compare the APR of each possible source and lender.

 See Chapter 9

Control: How will the source of finance impact on business ownership and control? For example, issuing new shares will allow new shareholders to have a say in how the business is run.

Security required: What **collateral** will be required to protect the lender in case of non-payment? Some sources of finance, including mortgages, may require business assets to be set aside in the event of default. If the borrower fails to repay the loan the lender can claim the assets and sell them to recover the money owed to them.

 See Chapter 10

Sources of finance

Sources of finance are categorised based on the repayment period involved:

> Short-term finance will be repaid within one year

> Medium-term finance will be repaid between one and five years

> Long-term finance will be repaid over a period longer than five years.

This is known as the matching principle.

Some finance comes from a business's own resources (**internal sources**) while other types of funding come from other businesses or financial institutions (**external sources**).

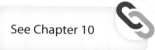
See Chapter 10

Internal sources of finance tend to be quite limited and rely on the business's ability to cut costs, sell assets or generate profit for reinvestment.

External sources provide businesses with access to a wider variety of finance options but they often carry increased risks and costs. There are two types: debt capital and equity capital.

Definitions

Debt capital is money borrowed from an external source and it must be repaid with interest.

Equity capital is money received by selling shares.

Debt capital allows a business with limited financial resources to operate and expand.

Equity capital is a cheap source of finance and does not have to be repaid. Shareholders do, however, have a say in how the business is run and will expect to receive a share of the annual profits in the form of a dividend.

Table 25.1 gives a summary of common business needs and suitable sources of finance.

Table 25.1 Common business needs and suitable sources of finance

Short-term needs	Short-term sources of finance (repaid within 1 year)
Stock Raw materials Wages Transport Light and heat Insurance Advertising	❭ Cash ❭ Bank overdraft ❭ Accrued expenses and deferred payment ❭ Credit card ❭ Trade creditors ❭ Factoring*/invoice discounting
Medium-term needs	**Medium-term sources of finance (repaid 1–5 years)**
Vehicles Computers and ICT equipment Fixtures and fittings	❭ Leasing ❭ Hire purchase ❭ Medium-term loan
Long-term needs	**Long-term sources of finance (repaid 5+ years)**
Premises Land Machinery Expansion	❭ Share capital/equity ❭ Venture capital ❭ Retained profit* ❭ Grants ❭ Sale and leaseback* ❭ Debentures / long-term loan ❭ Mortgage ❭ Crowdfunding

* Not suitable for start-up business.

Borrowing in any form can be costly and risky. For each potential source of finance, business managers will need to consider:

❭ The costs

❭ The benefits

❭ The potential risks.

25.2 Taking costs and risks into account, do you think it is better for a business to source finance internally, externally or through a combination of both? Share your answer with another student and reach agreement on a shared answer. Share your combined answer with another pair.

T-P-S

KSMIT
KSWwO
KSC

Short-term sources of finance

Table 25.2 Short-term sources of finance

	Explanation	Cost/risk
Cash	Using existing cash reserves to pay for day-to-day business expenses	None (other than opportunity cost)
Bank overdraft	Similar to personal bank account. Account holder can withdraw more money from their current account than they have in it. The overdraft must be arranged in advance. The bank will set a limit to the amount that can be withdrawn	Interest will be paid on the amount overdrawn. The lender can recall or terminate the overdraft facility at short notice
Accrued expense	The business has the use of certain expenses for up to two months before it needs to pay for these, e.g. electricity, phone, broadband If the delay in payment is part of a formal agreement with a creditor, this is called a **deferred payment**	If the bill is not paid on time, the service could be disconnected. Failure to pay bills could damage the credit rating of the business
Trade creditor	A creditor is a person or business to whom a business owes money. Many suppliers sell on credit, which allows the business to buy now and pay later	Cash discounts for prompt payments will be lost. There may be interest charged on overdue accounts
Credit card	Allows the card holder to buy now and pay later. They are not suitable for all business purchases, but may be used to pay for some staff expenses, e.g. travel costs, fuel, accommodation, meals	Interest is charged on the balance outstanding
Invoice discounting	A form of factoring that allows a business to borrow money against its outstanding sales invoices. Unlike factoring, the business is responsible for collecting payments from its debtors and will forward payment to the bank	Interest is charged on the amount borrowed
Factoring debt	When a business sells goods on credit, it will be owed money by its debtors. It may not receive the cash in time to meet its ongoing payments. Factoring allows the debt to be sold for less than its value, but the cash will be received quickly	Very expensive as debts are often sold at a big discount

An example of factoring

Elite Ltd is owed €100,000 by Thrifty Ltd for goods sold on credit. Thrifty Ltd is slow in paying the debt and Elite Ltd approaches a factoring company which agrees to take over the total debt of €100,000 but at a discounted price of €80,000. Elite Ltd no longer has an outstanding debt and has improved its cash position with an immediate payment of €80,000.

The factoring company will receive €100,000 when it collects the debt and will earn a €20,000 profit on the deal. Most commercial banks offer factoring services to their business customers.

25.3 Megan and Julie run a restaurant on the coast. They have an overdraft facility on their bank account, but don't use this all the time.

(a) Why do you think they have the facility when they seem not to need it?

(b) Are there times of year when they might need it more than others?

25.4 What are the alternatives to deferred payments if a business does not have money available to pay a creditor?

T-P-S

25.5 Galvin's sells veterinary products to veterinary practices around the country. Each of their ten salespeople has a business credit card for when they are on the road.

(a) What do you think the sales team use their credit cards for?

(b) What are the benefits of using business credit cards to:

  (i) The salespeople?

  (ii) The business?

25.6 Some large businesses require long credit terms from small suppliers. What problems could this cause for the smaller businesses?

T-P-S

25.7 In the case of factoring, who does the factoring company have to credit-check?

Medium-term sources of finance

Table 25.3 Medium-term sources of finance

	Explanation	Cost/risk	Impact on control	Security required?
Leasing	Renting an asset over a number of years. The lease agreement, which is a legally binding contract, allows a business to have possession and use of the asset provided they make fixed regular payments to the leasing company	Expensive. Over a long time the cost will be greater than the purchase price of the asset. Ownership is never transferred and the asset remains the property of the leasing company	None	None, as ownership remains with the leasing company
Hire purchase (HP)	The purchaser pays an initial deposit and a finance company pays the balance to the seller. The purchasing business then pays back the finance company with an agreed number of fixed regular payments	Expensive. The APR may be in excess of 20%. Failure to meet the repayment schedule will result in the assets being repossessed	None	None, as ownership is not transferred until the final payment is made
Medium-term loan	Accessible from banks and credit unions. Borrowers make fixed repayments (which cover repayment of the loan plus interest) over an agreed time period, usually between one and five years	APR is usually cheaper than a bank overdraft. Failure to repay the loan can result in legal action and a poor credit rating	None	Collateral may be required

25.8 Why is hire purchase often used as a last resort by businesses?

25.9 Why do you think interest payments on loans are considered a business expense?

Long-term sources of finance

Table 25.4 Long-term sources of finance

	Explanation	Cost/risk	Impact on control	Security required?
Share capital	Capital is money invested into a business by its owners. The owners are called shareholders. In return for their investment a profitable business may pay them a dividend (a portion of profits paid to shareholders)	There are no fixed interest payments involved in selling shares. Shareholders may receive dividends, but the business is not obliged to pay them	Issuing new shares will reduce the control of existing shareholders. Each share provides a shareholder with a vote in running the business	None
Venture capital	Venture capitalists invest in new or high-risk businesses. They often take shares and a seat on the board of directors. The 'dragons' on *Dragon's Den* are venture capitalists. Many banks have venture capital divisions that specialise in financing business start-ups	Venture capitalists will look for a significant return on investment. This may be in the form of a shareholding in the business and dividend payments	If the venture capitalist takes shares they will have some control over the business	None
Retained profit	A portion of the annual profits is put back into the business. Reinvesting the profits can be used to purchase fixed assets or to fund expansion	Cheap, as the money already belongs to the business. Minimises the level of external debt required	None	None, as the business's own money is being used
Grants	Money provided by the government, local authority or EU. May be used to pay for staff training, purchase of machinery, create employment. Start-up businesses may also receive grants to fund a feasibility study	Free from interest charges and usually don't have to be repaid, as long as they are used for their intended purpose	None, but the agency providing the grant may attach strict conditions on the use of the grant	None

Sale and leaseback	A business may decide to 'cash in' on the value of its premises by selling it to an investor and simultaneously signing a long-term lease with the new owner. This allows the business to keep using the premises while providing a large amount of extra capital	Annual rent charge. Loss of future increase in value of the premises	The business will lose control over the asset once it is sold. This will reduce the value of the fixed assets of the business	None
Debentures	A long-term loan with a fixed interest rate and a specific repayment date, e.g. a €5 million 7% debenture (2025) allows a business to borrow €5 million immediately and repay 7% interest per year with the lump sum due for repayment in 2025	Fixed interest payments must be paid each year and the business must generate enough income to pay these. The amount borrowed must be repaid in full by the due date; failure to do so may lead to loss of assets	None	Collateral will be required in the form of fixed assets, e.g. title deeds of property
Mortgage	Specifically used to purchase property. Typically repaid over 20–30 years	If the borrower cannot repay the debt the lender can sell the property and recover the money owed	While the lender will not have control over the business they have a legal claim to the property. This may limit the ability of the business to sell or dispose of this asset	The lender will secure a legal claim on the property and may repossess it in the event of non-payment by the borrower
Crowdfunding	Seeking small amounts of funding from a large number of people. The investors will receive a reward for investing in the business depending on how much they invest, e.g. early access to products or shares in the business	Need to find a large number of individual investors to reach the target	In the case of equity-based funding, the investors will be entitled to a shareholding in the business. This will entitle them to a share of profits and a say in running the business	None

25.10 Why might a company find it difficult to sell more shares?

25.11 Venture capitalists tend to be people that the business owner does not know in advance. What kinds of problems do you think this could cause?

Figure 25.1 *Dragon's Den* © Ruth Medjber

25.12 Why is it a good idea for any business to put some of its profits back into the company to make cash available for purchases?

25.13 **(a)** Research what organisations in your local area offer grants to start-ups.

(b) What grants do they provide?

(c) Apart from grants, what other types of support do these organisations provide to start-ups?

25.14 What are the advantages to a business of being able to continue trading from the same premises after selling them to someone else?

25.15 Why are factoring debts, retained earnings and sale and leasehold not available for start-up businesses?

25.16 Do you think the interest payments from debentures will have to be paid before or after dividends are paid to the shareholders? Why is this?

25.17 Research crowdfunding websites and find a business that has raised money in this way. Prepare a presentation for the rest of the class. Include:

(a) Details about the business.

(b) Why it needs the capital.

(c) What rewards are available for investors.

(d) Whether or not the campaign has been successful.

(e) What happened after the funding was received.

Loan applications for businesses

A business that requires a loan will approach lenders to request one.

The lender will consider a number of factors before agreeing to loan money to a business. These will include:

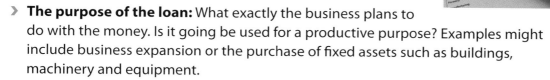

> **The purpose of the loan:** What exactly the business plans to do with the money. Is it going be used for a productive purpose? Examples might include business expansion or the purchase of fixed assets such as buildings, machinery and equipment.

> **The business's ability to repay:** The potential borrower has to show they will be able to repay their loan. Businesses seeking loans will need to provide audited accounts for several years as well as a realistic cash flow and a **business plan**, which will outline future sales projections, planned expenditure and profit forecasts.

 See Chapter 26

> **Collateral (security):** Lenders need some means of recovering their money if borrowers default.

> **Credit history:** Financial institutions are required to check the credit history of all applicants.

> **Own investment:** Lenders are more likely to lend to businesses if the risk is shared. This usually requires the borrower to part-finance the project with some of their own money.

See Chapter 10

25.18 What do you think are (a) the similarities and (b) the differences between an individual requesting a loan from a bank and a business requesting a loan from a bank?

Working capital management and cash flow forecasts

Working capital is the money a business has available to fund its day-to-day expenditure.

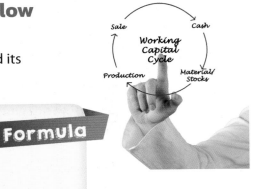

Formula

working capital = current assets − current liabilities
(cash, debtors, stock, etc.) (bank overdraft, creditors, expenses due, etc.)

Businesses need working capital for liquidity.

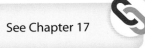

Definition

Liquidity measures the ability of a business to pay its day-to-day expenses and debts. It is about cash flow.

Poor liquidity is the single biggest reason for business failure, so keeping a balance between total income and total expenditure should be a key priority for business managers.

Many businesses get into financial difficulty because they try to grow too quickly. For example, entrepreneurs often try to increase their profit by selling more goods, usually on credit.

See Chapter 17

Discussion

25.19 What do you think we mean by a business 'growing too quickly'?

25.20 How can growing too quickly cause a business to get into financial difficulty?

KSWwO
KSMIT
KSC

The business operating cycle

As you can see from figure 25.2, there is often a time delay between payment of expenses (cash outflows) and receipts from sales and debtors (cash inflows). Businesses therefore need to find a way of continuing to operate despite this temporary shortage of cash. They need to manage their working capital very carefully; this requires them to manage debtors, stock and cash.

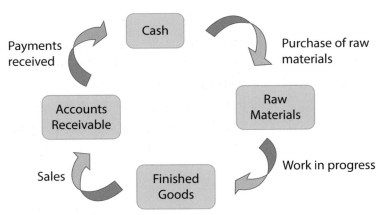

Figure 25.2 The business operating cycle

Managing debtors

Debtors are people who owe money to a business. Most businesses sell goods on credit and this means there is a delay between the sale of goods or services and the receipt of payment for them. Thirty days is a common period of credit, but in some cases it may be longer. Since a business must continue to pay its operating expenses (raw materials, wages, transport, light and heat, etc.) it is important to make sure cash is being received from debtors on a regular basis.

25.21 Think of three types of business that do not provide credit to customers.

25.22 Do you think that businesses that don't offer credit have cash flow problems? Give reasons for your answer.

KSWwO
KSMIT
KSC

Managing stock

Businesses should always aim to keep the optimum amount of stock. This means not having too much or too little stock, but having just the right amount to meet the demands of the market. A business that has too little stock will be unable to meet customer demands and is likely to lose potential sales. As well as the immediate loss of sales, there is also the danger that customers will take their business elsewhere.

25.23 What are the costs of having more stock than you need in a business?

KSMIT
KSWwO

Managing cash flow

A **cash flow forecast** is a business version of a household budget. It is a financial plan that shows expected monthly income and planned expenditure. Cash flow forecasts also help identify future surpluses and deficits.

Definition

See Chapter 5

Once identified, managers can make plans to deal with excess income or expenditure. For example, the business may need to arrange for a short-term loan to cover cash shortfalls or may invest cash surpluses to earn deposit interest.

Cash flow forecasts are useful for predicting future cash flow problems.

Cash flow forecasts

Cash flow forecasts focus on two specific areas:

> Receipts (income)

> Payments (expenditure).

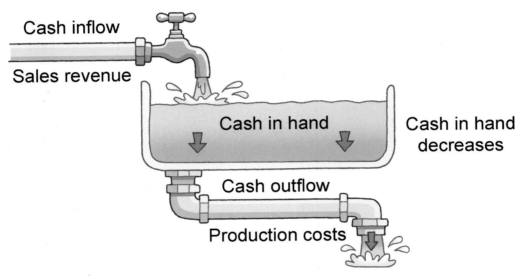

Figure 25.3 Representation of cash flow

Sources of **income** for businesses	Areas of **expenditure** for businesses
> Sales income	> Purchase of raw materials
> Investment income/deposit interest	> Purchase/rental of fixed assets
> Receipts from debtors	> Dividends to shareholders
> Income from grants	> Taxation (VAT, import duty, etc.)
> Borrowings	> Payments to creditors
> Share capital	> Overheads (including wages)
> VAT refunds	> Loan repayments

Preparing a cash flow forecast

A cash flow forecast of ABC Ltd is shown below; this outlines receipts and payments of this company.

Cash flow forecast of ABC Ltd

	May €	June €	July €	August €	Total (May–Aug) €
RECEIPTS					
Cash Sales	70,000	70,000	90,000	100,000	330,000
Grant	45,000				45,000
Total receipts (A)	**115,000**	**70,000**	**90,000**	**100,000**	**375,000**
PAYMENTS					
Cash purchases	28,000	28,000	42,000	28,000	126,000
Wages	16,000	16,000	16,000	16,000	64,000
Light & heat	4,600		7,400		12,000
ICT equipment		35,000			35,000
Delivery costs	6,000	6,000	6,000	6,000	24,000
Rent	5,500	5,500	5,500	5,500	22,000
Machinery			75,000		75,000
Insurance	800	800	4,800	800	7,200
Total payments (B)	**60,900**	**91,300**	**156,700**	**56,300**	**365,200**
Net cash (A − B)	54,100	(21,300)	(66,700)	43,700	9,800
Opening cash	12,000	66,100	44,800	(21,900)	12,000
Closing cash	66,100	44,800	(21,900)	21,800	21,800

Interpreting cash flow forecasts

> Cash flow forecasts will highlight 'problem months' for the business. A figure in brackets is a minus amount and represents a deficit, i.e. a net cash outflow for that month. This is never an ideal situation for any business, but it may be sustainable in the short term, provided the deficit can be made up from available cash reserves (opening cash), e.g. in June in the cash flow forecast of ABC Ltd.

> ABC Ltd's cash flow forecast indicates that the business expects to receive more income in May and August than they plan to spend. This will leave them with net cash surpluses of €54,100 and €43,700 respectively.

> In June and July, however, the company expects a net cash deficit. In June the planned overspend of €21,300 can be met out of opening cash reserves, but in July the deficit of €66,700 is greater than the available opening cash. This means that ABC Ltd will face an overall (closing cash) shortfall of €21,900 at the end of July.

> A closing cash deficit is *always* a problem for a business, since this money will need to be made up from borrowing. A business that has an ongoing liquidity problem of this type will have trouble paying bills and will be very reliant on short-term borrowings.

> Fortunately for ABC Ltd, their liquidity problems are for a short time only and the cash flow forecast indicates that they will have overcome the deficit by the end of August. The bank will want to see this cash flow forecast if ABC Ltd decides to apply for an overdraft.

25.24 Look at the cash flow forecast for Active Ltd and answer the questions below.

Cash flow forecast for Active Ltd

	August €	Sept €	Oct €	Nov €	Total (Aug–Nov) €
RECEIPTS					
Cash sales	90,000	90,000	110,000	140,000	430,000
Receipts from debtors	15,000	22,000	28,000	35,000	100,000
Total receipts (A)	**105,000**	**112,000**	**138,000**	**175,000**	**530,000**
PAYMENTS					
Cash purchases	38,000	38,000	47,000	68,000	191,000
Wages	19,000	19,000	21,000	24,000	83,000
Light & heat	4,600		7,400		12,000
Vehicles		55,000			55,000
Delivery costs	6,000	6,000	8,000	10,000	30,000
Rent	5,500	5,500	5,500	5,500	22,000
Machinery			95,000		95,000
Insurance	800	800	4,800	800	7,200
Total payments (B)	**73,900**	**124,300**	**188,700**	**108,300**	**495,200**
Net cash (A − B)	31,100	(12,300)	(50,700)	66,700	34,800
Opening cash	22,000	53,100	40,800	(9,900)	22,000
Closing cash	53,100	40,800	(9,900)	56,800	56,800

(a) What are the reasons Active Ltd would prepare a cash flow forecast?

(b) Identify two examples of capital expenditure in the above cash flow forecast.

(c) According to the cash flow forecast, in which month(s) will Active Ltd experience cash flow problems?

(d) Suggest two possible solutions to these liquidity problems.

(e) Create a bar chart/trend graph to show total receipts and total payments for August–November for Active Ltd.

Key Terms

KSBL
KSC
KSMIT
KSBC

You should be able to *define, spell,* give *examples* and *apply* to real life each of the following key terms associated with this topic.

Exercise: Write a sentence using each of the following terms. You may use more than one of the terms in your sentence if appropriate.

accrued expenses

bad debts

business operating cycle

capital expenditure

cash flow forecast

crowdfunding

debentures

debt capital

debtors

deferred payment

equity capital

factoring

grant

hire purchase

issued share capital

leasing

liquidity

overheads

sale and leaseback

venture capital

working capital

Chapter 26 :: Writing a Business Plan

The business plan

As we saw in chapter 25, when a business goes to a financial institution to request a loan, the lender will want to see their business plan, which will provide information about:

See Chapter 25

> The history of the firm
> What type of business it is

> Where it gets its income from
> Its ability to repay a loan.

Anyone starting up a business is advised to write a business plan, even if they are not looking for finance, as it is a good way of looking at:

> Where the business is now
> Where it is heading
> How it will get there.

Planning

Planning involves setting goals for the business and deciding on ways to achieve these goals. When setting goals, always remember that they should be **SMART**:

S	Specific	Target an exact and clear goal
M	Measurable	It must be possible to measure whether or not the goal has been achieved
A	Achievable	It must be possible to reach the goal within the time frame
R	Relevant	The goal must be worthwhile for the success of the business
T	Timed	This gives the goal a target date to be achieved

SWOT analysis

Before writing a business plan it may be useful to carry out a SWOT analysis.

A **SWOT analysis** identifies the *strengths* and *weaknesses* of a business and identifies *opportunities* and *threats* facing it.

Definition

Strengths and weaknesses are internal factors, which the business has control over, while opportunities and threats are external factors, over which the business has no control.

Completion of a SWOT analysis forces a business to consider its strengths and weaknesses at present along with the opportunities and threats it may face in the future. Sometimes it will be carried out for the business as a whole, sometimes for a department, and sometimes at project level.

Strengths and opportunities are positive factors, while weaknesses and threats are negative factors.

	Helpful	Harmful
Internal	Strengths	Weaknesses
External	Opportunities	Threats

Businesses may consider asking employees, managers, customers and suppliers to identify factors for each element of the SWOT.

26.1 Why might businesses ask for other people's input into the SWOT analysis?

KSMIT

Let's take an example of a SWOT analysis for McDonald's.

SWOT analysis for McDonald's

Strengths	Weaknesses
> Strong brand name > Global recognition	> High staff turnover, which means spending money on hiring and training new staff > Over-reliance on fast food, which does not have a reputation for being healthy
Opportunities	**Threats**
> Offering healthier food options > Opening new branches	> Competition from new fast food businesses > Government introducing a sugar tax on soft drinks

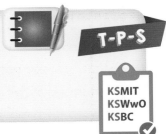

26.2 Working in pairs, identify a business you are familiar with (local, national or international). Using the template supplied in the Student Activity Book, complete a SWOT analysis for this business. Aim to have a minimum of two examples for each element.

KSMIT
KSWwO
KSBC

26.3 It is not just businesses that carry out SWOT analyses; individuals do too. At what points of life might an individual carry out a SWOT analysis?

KSMIT
KSC

The business plan

A **business plan** is a written description of a business's future aims, strategies, markets and financial forecasts. It is a document that explains what the business plans to do and how it plans to do it.

Definition

A business plan will be required if external finance is needed, either for a start-up business or to fund expansion for an existing business.

A business plan is also useful to help the entrepreneur(s) identify the resources and finance that are needed to start the business, as well as the marketing and production needed to ensure the business is a success.

The purpose of a business plan is to:

> Establish whether the business is likely to succeed
> Help the business raise the finance it needs
> Force the entrepreneur to focus on the goals of the business
> Anticipate problems and identify possible solutions
> Set targets to be achieved.

A business plan will contain the following headings:

Section 1: Background of the business

> Details of the aims and objectives of the business, i.e. what it is set up to do.
> The name and address of the business.

Section 2: The business team

> The people involved in the business, including their educational details and past experiences.

Section 3: Market and marketing

> A brief description of the market.

> The current and potential size of the market.

> The number of competitors already in the market.

> The marketing mix strategy, i.e. product, price, place and promotion.

See Chapter 24

Section 4: Production

> A breakdown of all premises and equipment available to the business.

> The production process to be used, i.e. job (single/one-off products), batch (group of similar products) or mass (products produced in very large quantities).

Section 5: Costings and finance

> How much it costs to produce the item (cost price) and what mark-up/profit margin will be added on to get the price it will be sold at (selling price).

See Chapter 25

> Details about any existing loans that the business has.

> The amount of finance required and the purpose for which it is required.

> How the finance is to be repaid.

> Detailed cash flow forecasts and projected profits for two or three years.

Section 6: Structure of the business

> The legal structure of the business (sole trader, partnership or private limited company).

See Chapter 18

Example: Luxury Furniture Ltd

Luxury Furniture Ltd has been operating for ten years in Co Carlow. It manufactures luxury tables and chairs for the Irish market. A bank loan is needed for expansion. The company managers have prepared a business plan in support of their application.

Business Plan – Luxury Furniture Ltd

Section 1: Background of the business

The business, Luxury Furniture Limited, has headquarters in Market Street, Tullow, Co Carlow.

The objective of Luxury Furniture Ltd is to make and sell high-quality tables and chairs for the Irish market.

Section 2: Team

The shareholders of the company are Michael O'Neill and Grainne O'Neill.

Michael is responsible for production and design. He holds an engineering degree from UCD and has been working in furniture manufacturing for over 20 years. He has invested €30,000 in the business.

Grainne qualified in business management and administration in IT Carlow in 2009 and had several years' managerial experience in the manufacturing sector. She is the managing director and finance manager. She too has invested €30,000 in the business.

Section 3: The market

It is estimated that the market for luxury furniture is growing and is worth around €10 million. There are currently seven competitors based throughout the country. The product is a luxury brand, therefore the price charged is a premium price. The main form of promotion is advertising on local radio stations and in newspapers. The products are sold through a national network of furniture retailers.

Section 4: Production

The fixed assets of the business are the premises in Market Street, Tullow (which consists of production, office, showroom and display areas), industrial saws, equipment and two delivery vans.

The company produces the tables and chairs in batch production.

Section 5: Costings and finance

The cost price per chair is €100 and with a mark-up of €50 each one has a selling price of €150.

The cost price per table is €700 and with a mark-up of €300 each one has a selling price of €1,000.

The company has no existing borrowings (loans) and wishes to borrow €100,000 in order to finance expansion. This money will be used to:

> Build an extension to the premises
> Purchase an additional delivery van
> Update the company website to allow for increased sales both within Ireland and internationally.

The loan is required for ten years and will be paid for out of existing income.

Section 6: The structure of the business

Luxury Furniture Limited is a private limited company.

Signed:

Michael O'Neill

Grainne O'Neill

Date: 30/12/17

26.4 Using the template in the Student Activity Book, write a business plan for Lightbody's Bakery Ltd using the details supplied.

Key Terms

You should be able to *define*, *spell*, give *examples* and *apply* to real life each of the following key terms associated with this topic.

Exercise: Write a sentence using each of the following terms. You may use more than one of the terms in your sentence if appropriate.

business plan

SMART plans

SWOT analysis

Chapter 27 ::
Business Documents

Learning outcomes

When you have completed this chapter you will be able to:

✔ Explain the importance of record-keeping in business
✔ Identify and complete the documents used by businesses when buying and selling goods
✔ Analyse the information in business documents
✔ Define the different terms associated with business documents
✔ Outline the procedures for dealing with incoming and outgoing business documents.

The importance of business documents

Nearly everything that happens in a business relies on some sort of documentation. When you receive wages, you get a payslip; when all the staff need to know something, they are sent a memo; when a client needs to be contacted, they are sent a letter. Even if a telephone call is made it can generate a document in the form of a note outlining the conversation.

Sometimes the document is electronic, but it is still considered a document.

In this chapter we will look at the documents that are involved in buying and selling goods.

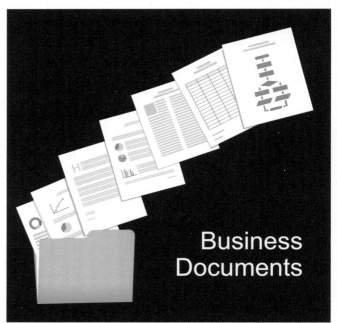

Business Documents

27.1 Why do businesses use documents when buying and selling goods?

Table 27.1 is a summary of all the documents that may be used by firms for selling goods.

Table 27.1 Summary of transaction documents

	Document	Sender		Receiver
1	Letter of enquiry	Buyer	→	Seller
2	Quotation	Seller	→	Buyer
3	Order	Buyer	→	Seller
4	Delivery note	Seller	→	Buyer
5	Invoice	Seller	→	Buyer
6	Credit note	Seller	→	Buyer
7	Debit note	Seller	→	Buyer
8	Statement of account	Seller	→	Buyer
9	Payment	Buyer	→	Seller
10	Receipt	Seller	→	Buyer

1 Letter of enquiry

An individual will usually buy an item from a shop, or over the internet, or they might phone a supplier to get a price. When a business wants to buy from another business (known as **B2B**), they will often write a letter of enquiry, particularly if they haven't dealt with the business before. This isn't always the case – they might find it easier to telephone the business – but a letter or email will help a business keep a record of the enquiry.

The buyer might contact several different businesses, requesting availability of goods, prices and the terms of sale.

Figure 27.1 B2B means business to business

The **terms of sale** are the conditions attached to a sale, such as who pays for delivery, what discount is available, and when the invoice has to be paid.

Definition

KSMIT

27.2 Why would a business be advised to write a letter of enquiry to at least three businesses that offer the same goods for sale?

Figure 27.2 shows a typical letter of enquiry.

O'BRIEN ELECTRICAL LTD
12 MAIN STREET
TRIM
CO MEATH
TEL: (046) 1234566/FAX (046) 9876544
EMAIL: OFFICE@OBRIENELECTRICAL.IE
WWW.OBRIENELECTRICAL.IE

02/11/2016

Downtown Wholesalers Ltd
Water Street
Clonakilty
Co Cork

Dear Sir/Madam

Re: Quotation request

Please quote your best price and terms of sale for the following goods:

10 Windspool dishwashers
15 Windspool washing machines
50 Meteor electric blankets

Yours faithfully,

James O'Brien

James O'Brien
Purchasing Manager

Figure 27.2 Example of a letter of enquiry

Dealing with the letter of enquiry

Seller (incoming)	Document	Buyer (outgoing)
On receipt of a letter of enquiry: > Check stock and prices > Prepare quotation > File the original for reference	**Letter of enquiry**	Before sending a letter of enquiry: > Check name and address of seller > Check quantities quoted > File a copy for reference

27.3 You have just set up a business selling sports kit and equipment. Decide on your business name and address. Research three sportswear suppliers and write a letter of enquiry to one of them, using the contact details you have found online, requesting 10 each of your county GAA kits in sizes small, medium and large, and 40 footballs.

KSC
KSBC
KSBL

2 Quotation

When the enquiry is received, the seller will check the current prices and prepare a quotation.

The **quotation** is a written document that is sent by a seller to a potential buyer and shows the price of the goods and any terms of sale.

Definition

Terms of sale

The terms of sale are the conditions attached to a quotation and subsequent sale. They might include:

> **Delivery:** If the quotation says 'Carriage paid', the seller of the goods will cover the cost of delivering the goods to the buyer. Otherwise, they will give a cost for postage or a courier.

> **E&OE:** This stands for **errors and omissions excepted**. This means that the business will not be held responsible if an error has been made and can alter the price in the case that it has.

> **Price held:** The prices quoted might be valid for only a limited time. This encourages the customer to order quickly.

> **Trade discount:** This is a reduction of the selling price given to business customers. It is subtracted before the VAT is added on.

> **Cash discount:** An extra discount may be given if the goods are paid for in a short period of time. For example, cash discount 5% for fourteen days. Sellers offer this extra incentive to encourage quick payment by buyers.

> **VAT:** This is a tax on goods and services. It must be charged on each transaction in the channel of distribution.

> **CWO (cash with order):** Payment must be made when the order is placed for the goods.

> **COD (cash on delivery):** Payment for the goods must be made when they are delivered.

> **Payment terms:** This is where details of the credit and payment terms are given, e.g. a buyer may have up to thirty days to pay for the goods.

27.4 Businesses offer different terms of sale. For example, one business may require CWO, while another may offer customers thirty days' credit. Likewise, businesses may offer different levels of trade discount. Discuss why you think this happens.

When the buyer has received all the quotations asked for, they will compare them and make a decision about who to purchase from.

27.5 Discuss in groups what factors other than price buyers will take into account when deciding which supplier to buy from.

Figure 27.3 shows a typical quotation.

Quotation   No. 0076

Downtown Wholesalers Ltd

Water Street
Clonakilty
Co Cork
Tel: (091) 6543276/Fax (091) 7896543
Email: office@downtownwholesalers.ie
www.downtownwholesalers.ie

06/11/2016

To: O'Brien Electrical Ltd
12 Main Street
Trim
Co Meath

Quantity	Description	Model no.	Unit price €
10	Windspool dishwashers	DW500	200.00
15	Windspool washing machines	WM350	150.00
50	Meteor electric blankets	EB776	50.00

These prices are valid for orders within 21 days.

All goods include a 5% trade discount. Carriage paid.

VAT rate: 20%

Payment terms for first order: Cash on delivery

Subsequent orders may be given 30 days' credit on receipt of bank and trade references.

Signed: *Robert Walsh*

Sales manager
E&OE

Figure 27.3 Example of a quotation

27.6 Who is the buyer and who is the seller in this quotation?

27.7 Why do you think that payment is COD for the first order, but the buyer may be given credit for orders made in the future?

Dealing with the quotation

Buyer (incoming)	Document	Seller (outgoing)
On receipt of a quotation: ❯ Check against letter of enquiry ❯ Check prices and availability of goods ❯ Compare to other quotations ❯ File the original for reference	**Quotation**	Before sending out a quotation: ❯ Check details against letter of enquiry ❯ Check all prices and terms of sale ❯ File a copy for reference

27.8 The price of goods is usually given in a quotation. For services, however, an estimate might be given rather than a quotation. A quotation is an amount that is fixed, but an estimate is a figure that shows the likely price but it may change.

Why do you think goods are quoted for but services are sometimes estimated rather than quoted?

3 Order

Once the buyer has decided which business offers the best prices and terms, they will place an order for the goods. They may order all the items on the quotation, or just some of them.

An **order** is a written document sent by a buyer to a seller requesting the supply of a quantity of goods listed.

Definition

The order might be made by telephone, email, on an order form or by letter. A record should be kept of the order.

An order might look similar to the one shown in figure 27.4.

Order		Order No.: 554

O'Brien Electrical Ltd
12 Main Street
Trim
Co Meath
Tel: (046) 1234566/Fax (046) 9876544
Email: office@obrienelectrical.ie
www.obrienelectrical.ie

10/11/2016

To: Downtown Wholesalers Ltd
Water Street
Clonakilty
Co Cork

Please supply the following goods as per your Quotation No. 76.

Quantity	Description	Model no.	Unit price €
10	Windspool dishwashers	DW500	200.00
15	Windspool washing machines	WM350	150.00
50	Meteor electric blankets	EB776	50.00

Signed: *James O'Brien*

James O'Brien, Purchasing Manager

Figure 27.4 Example of an order

Dealing with the order

Seller (incoming)	Document	Buyer (outgoing)
On receipt of an order: ➤ Deal with it quickly to avoid losing custom ➤ Check all goods are in stock ➤ Check details of prices and terms against the quotation ➤ File the original for reference	**Order**	➤ Check quantities and product details ➤ Check quotation to ensure seller has goods in stock ➤ File a copy for reference

Effective purchasing

Effective purchasing is about buying the right goods, at the right time, at the right price, in the right quantity and of the right quality.

Stock control

An efficient business must engage in **stock control** and will try to ensure the optimum stock level at any given time. This simply means that they do not have too much or too little stock.

When deciding on the right level of stock to keep, a business should consider the following factors:

> **Storage:** Does the business have enough space to hold the required level of stock?

> **Costs:** Carrying greater levels of stock will mean that insurance costs will increase.

> **Level of customer demand:** A business may have to stock up on extra products, e.g. at Christmas.

> **Lead time:** How long does it take for an order to be delivered from their supplier? The longer the delivery time, the more stock a business will have to hold.

> **Type of stock:** That is, whether it is perishable or durable. If a product will go off quickly e.g. vegetables, milk, etc., a business will be able to carry only a limited amount of stock at any given time.

The major cost associated with having too little stock (known as a **stockout**) is potential for loss of sales.

4 Delivery note

Once the sale has been agreed, the seller will then start to complete the order and prepare a delivery note and invoice.

> **Definition**
>
> The **delivery note** is a document sent by the seller to the buyer that lists the items being delivered.

When the goods are delivered to the buyer's address, the person making the delivery will ask the buyer to sign the delivery note. This will act as proof, if required, that the goods were delivered.

Figure 27.5 shows an example of a delivery note.

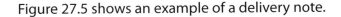

Delivery Note   No. 0124

Downtown Wholesalers Ltd

Water Street
Clonakilty
Co Cork
Tel: (091) 6543276/Fax (091) 7896543
Email: office@downtownwholesalers.ie
www.downtownwholesalers.ie

15/11/2016

To: O'Brien Electrical Ltd
12 Main Street
Trim
Co Meath

Quantity	Description	Model no.	Unit price €
10	Windspool dishwashers	DW500	200.00
15	Windspool washing machines	WM350	150.00
50	Meteor electric blankets	EB776	50.00

Comment: *Received the goods in excellent condition.*

Signed: *James O'Brien*

James O'Brien, Purchasing Manager

Figure 27.5 An example of a delivery note

Dealing with the delivery note

Buyer (incoming)	Document	Seller (outgoing)
On receipt of a delivery note: ❯ Compare with order to ensure correct goods delivered ❯ Check quantities actually delivered match the delivery note ❯ Check that goods are in perfect condition ❯ Sign delivery note and return to delivery driver ❯ File the copy for reference	**Delivery note**	Before sending out a delivery note: ❯ Check the goods being delivered match the order ❯ Check all goods are in perfect condition ❯ Check the delivery address ❯ File the original for reference

5 Invoice

An invoice will be sent either with the delivery or by post.

The **invoice** is a document sent by the seller to the buyer with the goods or shortly after the delivery of them. It gives details of the quantity, price of the goods being sent, terms of sale and details about carriage.

The invoice acts as the final bill for the goods delivered.

The invoice must contain the following information:

❯ The name and address of the supplier
❯ The name and address of the buyer
❯ A unique invoice reference
❯ The date the invoice was issued
❯ A complete list of the products or services provided
❯ The net amount owed for the goods (i.e. not including VAT)
❯ The total amount of the invoice
❯ The payment terms of the invoice, including details of cash discounts. This discount is an extra reduction if the buyer pays within a short time period, e.g. 5% in 14 days.

Figure 27.6 shows an example of an invoice.

Invoice

No: 10524

Downtown Wholesalers Ltd
Water Street
Clonakilty
Co Cork
Tel: (091) 6543276/Fax (091) 7896543
Email: office@downtownwholesalers.ie
www.downtownwholesalers.ie
VAT registration no. IE494037J

Date: 15/11/2016

To: O'Brien Electrical Ltd
12 Main Street
Trim
Co Meath

Your order number 554

Quantity	Description	Model no.	Unit price (€)	Total (€)
10	Windspool dishwashers	DW500	200.00	2,000.00
15	Windspool washing machines	WM350	150.00	2,250.00
50	Meteor electric blankets	EB776	50.00	2,500.00
	Total (excluding VAT)			6,750.00
	Discount at 10%			675.00
	Subtotal			6,075.00
	VAT at 20%			1,215.00
E&OE	Invoice total **COD**			7,290.00

Downtown Wholesalers Ltd, registered no. 494037J, registered at Water Street, Clonakilty, Co Cork

Figure 27.6 An example of an invoice

Some businesses send a copy of the invoice via email instead of posting it.

Dealing with the invoice

Buyer (incoming)	Document	Seller (outgoing)
On receiving an invoice: > Check against the delivery note > Check the prices are the same as on the quotation > Check calculations > Record details in the (purchases) accounts > File the original for reference	**Invoice**	Before sending out an invoice: > Match the goods listed against the order > Check the prices match the quotation > Check the discounts and terms of sale > Check the customer's name and address > Check calculations > Record details in the (sales) accounts > File a copy for reference

27.9 What are the advantages to the seller of sending an invoice by email?

KSMIT

6 Credit note

Definition

A **credit note** is a document that is sent by the seller to the buyer to decrease the amount owed. It is issued when goods that have been purchased on credit are returned to the seller and it would not be appropriate to provide a cash refund.

The credit note is sent if any of the following situations arise:

> The amount charged was too much
> The wrong goods were delivered
> The goods were damaged or of poor quality
> Some of the goods have to be returned for some reason.

Figure 27.7 shows a credit note.

Credit Note   No. 886

Downtown Wholesalers Ltd

Water Street

Clonakilty

Co Cork

Tel: (091) 6543276/Fax (091) 7896543

Email: office@downtownwholesalers.ie

www.downtownwholesalers.ie

VAT registration no. IE494037J

16/11/16

To: O'Brien Electrical Ltd

12 Main Street

Trim

Co Meath

Ref. Invoice number 10524

Quantity	Description	Model No.	Unit price (€)	Total (€)
3	Windspool dishwashers (damaged)	DW500	200.00	600.00
	Total (excluding VAT)			600.00
	Trade discount 10%			60.00
	Subtotal			540.00
	VAT 20%			108.00
E&OE	Total (including VAT)			648.00

Downtown Wholesalers Ltd, registered no. 494037J, registered at Water Street, Clonakilty, Co Cork

Figure 27.7 An example of a credit note

Dealing with the credit note

Buyer (incoming)	Document	Seller (outgoing)
On receiving a credit note:	**Credit note**	Before sending out a credit note:
› Check the details match the returned goods		› Check details match the returned goods
› Check calculations		› Check calculations
› Record the reduction in amount owed to creditors in the accounts		› Record the reduction in amount owed by debtor in the accounts
› File the original for reference		› File a copy for reference

7 Debit note

> A **debit note** is sent by the seller to the buyer and will increase the amount owed. It is used when there has been an undercharge on an account.

The debit note is issued if either of the following situations arise:

> If the buyer has been undercharged
> If the buyer received goods but was not charged for them on the invoice.

Figure 27.8 shows a debit note.

Debit Note   No. 88

Downtown Wholesalers Ltd

Water Street
Clonakilty
Co Cork
Tel: (091) 6543276/Fax (091) 7896543
Email: office@downtownwholesalers.ie
www.downtownwholesalers.ie
VAT registration no. IE494037J

18/11/16

To: O'Brien Electrical Ltd
12 Main Street
Trim
Co Meath

Ref. Undercharge on Invoice No. 10524

Quantity	Description	Model No.	Unit price (€)	Total (€)
50	Meteor electric blankets	EB776	5.00	250.00
	Total (excluding VAT)			250.00
	Trade discount 10%			25.00
	Subtotal			225.00
	VAT 20%			45.00
E&OE	Total (including VAT)			270.00

Downtown Wholesalers Ltd, registered no. 494037J, registered at Water Street, Clonakilty, Co Cork

Figure 27.8 An example of a debit note

Dealing with the debit note

Buyer (incoming)	Document	Seller (outgoing)
On receiving a debit note: > Check calculations > Record the increase in the amount owed to creditors in the accounts > File the original for reference	**Debit note**	Before sending a debit note: > Check calculations > Record the increase in the amount owed by debtors in the accounts > File a copy for reference

8 Statement of account

> A **statement of account** is sent by the seller to the buyer and is a summary of all the transactions between the two firms over a particular period of time. It shows the full amount owed and will act as a demand for whatever payment is still owed.

The method used in the statement of account is known as the **continuous balancing method**.

The statement works on the following rules/assumptions:

> The balance shown at the start of the month/period is the amount owed by the buyer to the seller at that date.

> Any entry in the debit column will increase the amount owed and is added to the previous balance in order to get the new balance.

> Any entry in the credit column will decrease the amount owed and is subtracted from the previous balance in order to get the new balance.

> The last balance represents the amount owed as on that date.

> The phrase '4% 14 days' means that the buyer will get a 4% discount if they pay in full within 14 days of receiving the statement.

An example of a statement of account is shown in figure 27.9.

Statement of Account   No. 229

Downtown Wholesalers Ltd

Water Street
Clonakilty
Co Cork
Tel: (091) 6543276/Fax (091) 7896543
Email: office@downtownwholesalers.ie
www.downtownwholesalers.ie
VAT registration no. IE494037J

30/11/16

To: O'Brien Electrical Ltd
12 Main Street
Trim
Co Meath

Date	Details	Debit €	Credit €	Balance €
1/11/16	Balance			3,200.00
15/11/16	Invoice No. 10524	7,290.00		10,490.00
16/11/16	Credit Note No. 886		648.00	9,842.00
18/11/16	Debit Note No. 88	270.00		10,112.00

E&OE

Terms: 4% 14 days

Downtown Wholesalers Ltd, registered no. 494037J, registered at Water Street, Clonakilty, Co Cork

Figure 27.9 An example of a statement of account

Dealing with the statement

Buyer (incoming)	Document	Seller (outgoing)
On receiving a statement: > Check the opening balance > Check against invoices/credit notes/debit notes received > Check all payments have been recorded > Check calculations (and closing balance) > Pay the amount due by the due date > File the original for reference	**Statement**	Before sending out a statement: > Check the opening balance > Check invoice amounts > Check debit and credit note amounts > Check payments have been recorded > Check calculations and closing balance > File a copy for reference

27.10 If O'Brien Electrical Ltd pays the outstanding amount from their October statement on 15 November, will they be entitled to the cash discount? Explain your answer.

27.11 If the outstanding amount from the October statement is paid on 15 November, how much will O'Brien owe to Downtown Wholesalers:

(a) At 15 November?

(b) At 30 November?

9 Payment

When goods are sold for cash, payment may be made when the order is made (CWO) or when the goods are delivered (COD). The payment may be made in cash or through other forms of payment such as a cheque or bank credit transfer.

If immediate CWO or COD are not required, payment should be made within the credit terms given, e.g. thirty days.

10 Receipt

Receipts should be filed away safely as they may be required as proof of payment in the future.

An example of a receipt is given in figure 27.10.

> **Definition**
>
> A **receipt** is a written document stating that the goods have been paid for. It is signed by the seller and given to the buyer.

Receipt   No.: 375

Downtown Wholesalers Ltd
Water Street
Clonakilty
Co Cork
Tel: (091) 6543276/Fax (091) 7896543
Email: office@downtownwholesalers.ie
www.downtownwholesalers.ie
VAT registration no. IE494037J

Date: 03/12/2016
Received from: O'Brien Electrical Ltd

The sum of: Seven thousand two hundred and ninety euro (€7,290.00) for payment of invoice number 0010524.

With thanks: *Steven Monahan*
Accounts Manager

Figure 27.10 An example of a receipt

Dealing with the receipt

Buyer (incoming)	Document	Seller (outgoing)
On receiving a receipt: ➤ Check the figure matches the payment ➤ Record the payment in the creditors account ➤ File the original for reference	**Receipt**	Before sending out a receipt: ➤ Check the figure matches the payment ➤ Record the payment in the debtors account ➤ File a copy for reference

27.12 In pairs, create an infographic or poster showing the documents that might be created as part of the buying/selling process between two businesses. Use table 27.1 as a guide.

27.13 What documents might be used if a service is being purchased rather than goods, e.g. an accountant hired to do work for a business?

KSWwO
KSBC
KSC
KSMIT

Key Terms

KSBL
KSC
KSMIT
KSBC

You should be able to *define*, *spell*, give *examples* and *apply* to real life each of the following key terms associated with this topic.

Exercise: Write a sentence using each of the following terms. You may use more than one of the terms in your sentence if appropriate.

B2B	effective purchasing
carriage paid	invoice
cash discount	letter of enquiry
COD (cash on delivery)	quotation
credit note	receipt
credit transfer	statement of account
CWO (cash with order)	stock control
debit note	terms of sale
delivery note	trade discount
E&OE (errors and omissions excepted)	VAT

Chapter 28 ::
Double Entry Bookkeeping

Learning outcomes

When you have completed this chapter you will be able to:

✔ Understand the term 'double entry bookkeeping'
✔ Prepare an analysed cash book, post to the ledger and extract a trial balance
✔ Account for VAT on sales and purchases.

Why keep accounts?

It is important that a business keeps an accurate and up-to-date record of all its business transactions. In this chapter we will briefly revise the rules for recording transactions in the analysed cash book (Record Book 1). We will also look at general ledger accounts (prepared in Record Book 3), before illustrating how both record books combine to create a system of double entry bookkeeping. The abbreviation A/C is used for account.

See Chapter 6

The information contained in the analysed cash book and ledgers comes from the business documents. For example, invoices received contain information used to write up the purchases and VAT amounts in the general ledger.

See Chapter 27

The analysed cash book

Cash transactions are a specific type of financial transaction where cash is used to settle a transaction on the same date that it takes place. In bookkeeping, we use an analysed cash book (ACB) to record receipts of money coming into the business and payments of money going out of a business. The rule that is used when entering transactions in the ACB is as follows:

Cash book rule

Debit (Dr) money received by the business	**Credit (Cr)** money paid out by the business

Rule

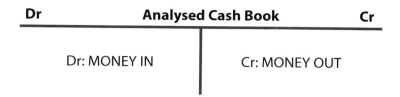

Dr   **Analysed Cash Book**   **Cr**

Dr: MONEY IN   Cr: MONEY OUT

Opening cash and bank balances

The opening balance refers to the cash or bank balance at the beginning of an accounting period. In some months a business may have cash left over from a previous month. This is shown as a Balance b/d on the debit side of the ACB.

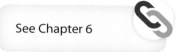

See Chapter 6

Example 1:

This is a Cash A/C which has an opening balance of €2,500 on 1 January 2016.

Dr							Cr
Date	**Details**	**F**	**Amount**	**Date**	**Details**	**F**	**Amount**
1 Jan 2016	Balance b/d		€2,500				

Record Book 1

If the business has overdrawn its account and has a bank overdraft, it owes money to the bank. This is recorded as a Balance b/d on the credit side of the ACB.

Example 2:

Here is a Bank A/C which has an opening bank overdraft of €3,000 on 1 January 2016. Note that the opening balance appears on the credit side.

Dr							Cr
Date	**Details**	**F**	**Amount**	**Date**	**Details**	**F**	**Amount**
				1 Jan 2016	Balance b/d		€3,000

Ledgers

Ledgers are recorded in Record Book 3 and are the books in which all individual **accounts** are recorded.

These accounts are used to bring together:

> The transactions involving a particular business or person, or
> The transactions involving a particular income or expense.

Therefore we could have an account called Michael O'Neill A/C or Electricity A/C or Wages A/C, etc.

As we are dealing with cash transactions only, we will be using the **general ledger (GL)**. This is used to record all the expenses that are involved in running a business, e.g. rent and electricity. As part of a double entry system of bookkeeping, the information in the ACB must also be **posted to** (recorded in) the ledgers.

Double entry bookkeeping

As its name suggests, double entry bookkeeping requires that every transaction be entered *twice* in the accounts. This is because there is both a giving element and a receiving element, i.e. one account gives something and another account receives something.

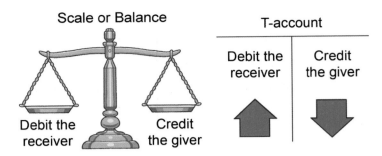

Scale or Balance

Debit the receiver — Credit the giver

T-account

Debit the receiver | Credit the giver

When dealing with cash transactions, this will require:

> **One entry in the analysed cash book**
> **One entry in the appropriate general ledger account**.

Example 3:

O'Connor Ltd paid a €400 bill for light and heat by direct debit from its bank account on 6 April 2016.

The €400 payment from the bank account is recorded on the credit side of the ACB (the Bank account is the 'giver').

The transaction is also entered on the debit side of the Light & Heat A/C in the general ledger (the Light & Heat account is the receiver).

The entry in the Bank A/C shows:

> The date of the transaction (6 April 2016)
> Where the money went/the name of the other account involved (Light & Heat)
> A reference or **folio** to indicate where the corresponding double entry is (GL)
> The amount of the transaction (€400).

There is a corresponding entry in the Light & Heat A/C. The two accounts are shown below.

Dr   **Bank A/C (ACB)**   **Cr**

Date	Details	F	Amount	Date	Details	F	Amount
				6 April 2016	Light & Heat	GL	€400

Record Book 1

Dr   **Light & Heat A/C (in GL)**   **Cr**

Date	Details	F	Amount	Date	Details	F	Amount
6 April 2016	Bank	ACB	€400				

Record Book 3

The entry in the Light & Heat account shows:

> The date of the transaction (6 April 2016)
> Where the money came from/the name of the other account involved (Bank A/C)
> A reference or folio to indicate where the corresponding double entry is (ACB)
> The amount of the transaction (€400).

As we post from the ACB to the GL we follow the rule:

Double entry rule

A **debit entry in the ACB** will be posted to the **credit side in the ledger**.

A **credit entry in the ACB** will be posted to the **debit side in the ledger**.

This is because for every debit there is an equal and opposite credit.

Rule

Accounting for sales, purchases and VAT

In accounting terms, **sales** refers to money received when a business sells goods which are part of its normal day-to-day business activity. For example, any revenue a greengrocer earns from selling fruit and vegetables would be classified as sales and entered in the Sales A/C in the general ledger. Money generated from the sale of an old delivery van would **not** be regarded as sales revenue since the greengrocer is not in the business of selling vehicles.

Example 4:
On 21 April 2016 O'Connor Ltd sold goods for €650 cash. For the purposes of this example we are assuming there is no VAT involved. The double entry needs to record this transaction as follows:

Dr: Cash A/C in ACB; **Cr:** Sales A/C in GL.

This is what it will look like:

Dr   **Cash A/C (in ACB)**   **Cr**

Date	Details	F	Amount	Date	Details	F	Amount
21 April 2016	Sales	GL	€650				

Record Book 1

Dr   **Sales A/C (in GL)**   **Cr**

Date	Details	F	Amount	Date	Details	F	Amount
				21 April 2016	Cash	ACB	€650

Record Book 3

Similarly, the term **purchases** refers specifically to goods which a business buys and intends to resell as part of its normal day-to-day business activity. For example, if a greengrocer buys a box of apples, this would be entered into the Purchases A/C in the general ledger.

KSMIT

> **28.1** If the grocer buys a replacement delivery van, would this be entered in the Purchases A/C? Explain your answer.

Example 5:

On 15 April 2016 O'Connor Ltd bought goods for resale. The cost of these goods was €500 and O'Connor paid for the goods by cheque. For the purposes of this example we are again assuming there is no VAT involved. The double entry needs to record this transaction as follows:

Dr: Purchases A/C in GL; **Cr:** Bank A/C in ACB.

This is what it will look like:

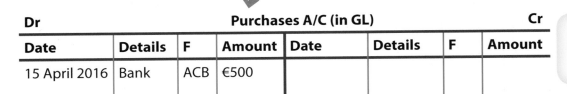

Dr				Bank A/C (in ACB)			Cr	
Date	**Details**	**F**	**Amount**	**Date**	**Details**	**F**	**Amount**	
				15 April 2016	Purchases	GL	€500	

Record Book 1

Dr				Purchases A/C (in GL)			Cr	
Date	**Details**	**F**	**Amount**	**Date**	**Details**	**F**	**Amount**	
15 April 2016	Bank	ACB	€500					

Record Book 3

Note: When working with these types of transaction, deal with the ACB entry first, remembering to debit money in, and to credit money out. Once you have correctly worked out this entry, put the general ledger entry on the opposite side.

How the VAT system works

Value added tax (VAT) is a tax on consumer spending. It is charged at every stage of sale where the supplier is registered with Revenue for VAT and the good or service is liable for the tax.

For example, a manufacturer sells a mobile phone to a wholesaler for €100 plus VAT at 23%. The wholesaler pays €123 to the manufacturer, which keeps €100 and pays €23 to Revenue.

The wholesaler sells the mobile phone to a retailer for €200 plus VAT at 23%. The retailer pays €246 to the wholesaler, which keeps €200 and owes €46 to Revenue; but the wholesaler may also reclaim the €23 VAT that was paid to the manufacturer and so pays Revenue €46 − €23 = €23.

The retailer sells the mobile phone to a consumer for €300 plus VAT at 23%. The consumer pays €369 to the retailer, which keeps €300 and owes €69 to Revenue; but the retailer may also reclaim the €46 that was paid to the wholesaler and so pays Revenue €69 − €46 = €23.

The consumer can't reclaim the VAT and has paid €69 tax for their good. The government via Revenue has received 23% of the cost of the mobile phone, but it has been paid in stages: €23 from the manufacturer + €23 from the wholesaler + €23 from the retailer.

The VAT for all sales and purchases will be recorded in a single VAT account and paid to or reclaimed from Revenue at certain dates. The VAT element of both sales and purchases transactions should not be included as part of sales or purchases figures in the respective ledger accounts.

Example 6:

On 2 June 2016 O'Connor Ltd bought goods for resale and paid by cheque. The cost of the goods was €300 plus €60 VAT. The entries needed to record this transaction are as follows:

1 Dr: €300 to the Purchases A/C in GL

2 Dr: € 60 to the VAT A/C in GL

} = €360 debit

3 Cr: €360 to the Bank A/C in ACB = €360 credit

Total debits equals total credits

The total of the two debit entries (purchases + VAT) is €360 and this is equal to the amount credited to the Bank A/C. This is in keeping with the rule that **every debit entry must be matched by a corresponding credit entry**.

This is what it will look like:

Dr   **Purchases A/C (in GL)**   **Cr**

Date	Details	F	Amount	Date	Details	F	Amount
2 June 2016	Bank	ACB	€300				

Record Book 3

Dr   **VAT A/C (in GL)**   **Cr**

Date	Details	F	Amount	Date	Details	F	Amount
2 June 2016	Bank	ACB	€60				

Record Book 3

Analysed cash book (credit side only):

Date	Details	Folio	Bank	Purchases	VAT
2 June 2016	Purchases	GL	€360	€300	€60

Record Book 1

Accounts commonly found in the general ledger include:

> Share Capital A/C

> Sales A/C

> Purchases A/C

> Carriage In A/C

> VAT A/C

> Vehicles A/C

> Machinery A/C

> Carriage Out A/C

> Wages A/C

> Light and Heat A/C

> Rent A/C

> Advertising A/C

> Bad Debts A/C

The trial balance

A business will have many accounts to prepare and mistakes can be made. Therefore it is important to check that all accounts have been prepared correctly. In bookkeeping, we use the trial balance to carry out this check.

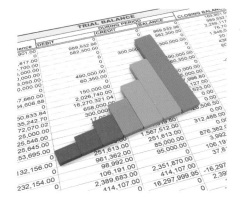

> A **trial balance** is simply a list of ledger balances. In the trial balance (Record Book 2), we take all the balances b/d from the ledger accounts (including the cash/bank balance) and list them. In doing this, we use the following rule:
>
> A **debit balance in the ledger** will appear as a **debit in the trial balance**.
>
> A **credit balance in the ledger** will appear as a **credit in the trial balance**.

Rule

If the rules for double entry bookkeeping have been followed correctly the trial balance should balance. This means that the total of the debit balances matches the total of the credit balances.

If the trial balance totals do not match, a mistake has been made somewhere in the accounts and will have to be corrected.

Once the trial balance has been correctly completed, the information can be used to prepare the firm's final accounts.

See Chapters 29–31

Example 7:
This is the ACB, ledger and trial balance.

Byrne Ltd had the following bank transactions. You are required to enter these in the analysed cash book, post to the ledger and extract a trial balance as at 31/1/16. Use the following analysis columns in the analysed cash book:

Dr: Sales, VAT, Capital
Cr: Purchases, VAT, Wages, Insurance

Bank transactions:

3 January 2016	Cash sales lodged, Receipt no. 1, €20,000 plus VAT €4,600
7 January 2016	Cash purchases, cheque no. 1, €7,500 plus VAT €500
8 January 2016	Paid wages, cheque no. 2, €2,000
12 January 2016	Shareholders invested €50,000 and this was lodged
18 January 2016	Paid insurance, cheque no. 3, €3,500

Suggested solution:

Analysed cash book for Byrne Ltd for January 2016

(Dr)   (Cr)

Date	Details	Rcpt	F	Bank	Sales	VAT	Capital	Date	Details	Chq	F	Bank	Purchases	VAT	Wages	Insurance
2016				€	€	€	€	2016				€	€	€	€	€
03/01	Sales	1	GL	24,600	20,000	4,600		07/01	Purchases	1	GL	8,000	7,500	500		
12/01	Capital		GL	50,000			50,000	08/01	Wages	2	GL	2,000			2,000	
								18/01	Insurance	3	GL	3,500				3,500
								31/01	Balance c/d			61,100				
				74,600	20,000	4,600	50,000					74,600	7,500	500	2,000	3,500
01/02	Balance b/d			61,100												

General Ledger

Sales A/C

(Dr)								(Cr)
Date	**Details**	**F**	**Total**	**Date**	**Details**	**F**	**Total**	
2016			€	**2016**			€	
				03/01	Bank	ACB	20,000	

Capital A/C

Date	**Details**	**F**	**Total**	**Date**	**Details**	**F**	**Total**
2016			€	**2016**			€
				12/01	Bank	ACB	50,000

VAT A/C

Date	**Details**	**F**	**Total**	**Date**	**Details**	**F**	**Total**
2016			€	**2016**			€
07/01	Cash purchases	ACB	500	03/01	Cash sales	GL	4,600
	Balance c/d		4,100				
			4,600				4,600
				07/01	Balance b/d		4,100

Purchases A/C

Date	**Details**	**F**	**Total**	**Date**	**Details**	**F**	**Total**
2016			€	**2016**			€
07/01	Bank	ACB	7,500				

Wages A/C

Date	**Details**	**F**	**Total**	**Date**	**Details**	**F**	**Total**
2016			€	**2016**			€
08/01	Bank	ACB	2,000				

Insurance A/C

Date	**Details**	**F**	**Total**	**Date**	**Details**	**F**	**Total**
2016			€	**2016**			€
18/01	Bank	ACB	3,500				

Trial Balance of Byrne Ltd as on 31 January 2016

Date	Details	F	Dr	Cr
2016			€	€
31/01	Capital	GL		50,000
	Sales	GL		20,000
	Purchases	GL	7,500	
	Wages	GL	2,000	
	Insurance	GL	3,500	
	VAT	GL		4,100
	Bank	ACB	61,100	
			74,100	74,100

Key Terms

You should be able to *define*, *spell*, give *examples* and *apply* to real life each of the following key terms associated with this topic.

Exercise: Write a sentence using each of the following terms. You may use more than one of the terms in your sentence if appropriate.

analysed cash book (ACB)

double entry bookkeeping

ledger

opening balance

trial balance

VAT

Chapter 29 ::
Income Statements 1
(The Trading Account)

Learning outcomes

When you have completed this chapter you will be able to:

✔ Explain what is meant by the term 'final accounts'
✔ Outline the reasons why businesses prepare final accounts
✔ Outline the purpose of the income statement
✔ List and explain the key elements of an income statement
✔ Prepare a trading account in order to calculate gross profit.

Introduction to final accounts

Every year, a business needs to answer two very important questions:

1 How much profit (or loss) did we make this year?
2 How much is this business worth?

To find the answers to these questions the company will prepare a set of accounts.

The answer to the profit or loss question can be found by preparing an **income statement**.

The question about company value can be answered by preparing a **statement of financial position**.

See Chapter 31

Collectively these are referred to as **final accounts**.

Companies are required by law to prepare a set of final accounts at the end of each financial year.

The income statement

An **income statement** is made up of a **trading account** and a **profit and loss account**.

Definitions

The **trading account** section calculates the gross profit or loss the business has made from selling its products or services.

See Chapter 30

The **profit and loss account** section calculates the net profit after deducting expenses from the gross profit figure.

If the company is profitable it will also need to prepare a **profit and loss appropriation account**, which shows how the profit will be distributed. It also shows the amount of financial reserves that the company has at year end.

The trading account is used by a business to calculate gross profit or gross loss on its core activities. This is the profit (or loss) generated by a business as a result of making and selling its products. It does not include expenses, such as electricity or wages.

Gross profit = Sales − Cost of sales

Cost of sales may also be known as cost of goods sold.

Consider the following simple example:

> Imagine you went to a supermarket and bought some baking ingredients and the total cost of your purchases came to €40.
> You then used all of these items to make cupcakes, all of which you sold to family, friends and neighbours for €90.
> Your gross profit in this situation would be €50 as this is the difference between your sales revenue and the cost of your purchases (i.e. €90 − €40 = €50 gross profit).

This simple example illustrates the concept of gross profit. It does, however, make certain assumptions which may not be realistic. For example, it assumes:

> You had no goods to begin with (opening stock) and since you sold all of the goods you purchased, you had no goods left over at the end (closing stock).
> There were no other costs associated with purchasing, making or selling the goods.

Since all of these are real possibilities for a business, it will be necessary to consider how each possibility will impact on our calculation of gross profit.

First, we'll define the key terms that you will come across.

Sales is the value of the goods sold by the business.

Opening stock is the cost of goods held in stock at the beginning of the financial year. This may be stock of finished goods or raw materials.

Purchases is the cost of goods bought during the year. These goods are bought with the specific intention of reselling them.

Carriage inwards is the cost of having purchases delivered to the business.

Customs duty is a tax paid on purchases from countries outside the EU. This item may also appear as **import duty**.

Closing stock is the value of goods held in stock at the end of the financial year. This may be stock of new materials or finished goods.

Cost of sales / Cost of goods sold is the cost to the business of selling goods.

You will need to *learn* the items that appear in an income statement and also the order in which they appear. You will also need to *practise* preparing income statements as this is the only way to make sure you can correctly calculate gross profit or loss.

The most basic income statement will have just four items, and they will appear in the following order:

1 Sales

2 Opening stock

3 Purchases

4 Closing stock

Example 1: Basic income statement

Prepare an income statement for the year ended 31/12/2016 from the following information:

> Sales €450,000

> Purchases €280,000

> Opening stock €5,000

> Closing stock €11,000

Income Statement for year ended 31/12/2016

	€	€
Sales		450,000
Less cost of sales:		
Opening stock	5,000	
+ Purchases	280,000	
Cost of goods available for sale	285,000	
– Closing stock	11,000	
Cost of goods sold		274,000
Gross profit		**176,000**

Record Book 2

Subtract cost of goods sold from sales

Points to note:

> The cost of sales takes account of the opening stock held by the business at the start of the year plus the additional goods purchased during the year.

> It is also necessary to deduct the value of the closing stock that remains unsold at the end of the year. Since these goods will not be sold until the next financial year, we need to subtract them from this year's accounts. The closing stock for this financial year will become the opening stock for next year.

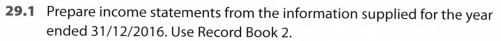

29.1 Prepare income statements from the information supplied for the year ended 31/12/2016. Use Record Book 2.

(a)

Sales	€550,000
Purchases	€290,000
Opening stock	€15,000
Closing stock	€17,000

(b)

Sales	€930,000
Purchases	€680,000
Opening stock	€8,000
Closing stock	€12,000

(c)

Sales	€850,000
Purchases	€480,000
Opening stock	€15,000
Closing stock	€16,000

(d)

Sales	€435,000
Purchases	€265,000
Opening stock	€15,000
Closing stock	€16,000

Example 2: Income statement with carriage inwards and customs duty

Prepare an income statement for Zing Ltd for the year ended 31/12/2016 from the following information:

> Sales €450,000
> Purchases €280,000
> Carriage inwards €4,000
> Customs duty €2,000
> Opening stock €5,000
> Closing stock €11,000

Income Statement of Zing Ltd for year ended 31/12/2016

	€	€
Sales		450,000
Less cost of sales:		
Opening stock (01/01/2016)	5,000	
+ Purchases	280,000	
+ Customs duty	2,000	
+ Carriage inwards	4,000	
Cost of goods available for sale	291,000	
− Closing stock (31/12/2016)	11,000	
Cost of goods sold		280,000
Gross profit		**170,000**

Record Book 2

Subtract

Point to note:

> In this example the cost of sales is increased due to the payment of transport (carriage in) and importation costs (customs duty). Since both of these items increase the cost of purchasing goods, they are added to purchases.

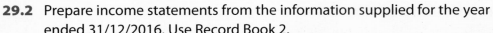

29.2 Prepare income statements from the information supplied for the year ended 31/12/2016. Use Record Book 2.

(a)			(b)		
Sales	€355,000		Sales	€685,000	
Purchases	€280,000		Purchases	€483,000	
Carriage inwards	€14,000		Carriage inwards	€1,650	
Customs duty	€12,000		Customs duty	€8,000	
Opening stock	€5,000		Opening stock	€15,000	
Closing stock	€11,000		Closing stock	€19,700	

(c)			(d)		
Sales	€480,000		Sales	€630,000	
Purchases	€380,000		Purchases	€570,000	
Carriage inwards	€5,000		Carriage inwards	€26,200	
Customs duty	€8,000		Customs duty	€18,800	
Opening stock	€4,000		Opening stock	€5,000	
Closing stock	€10,000		Closing stock	€16,000	

(e)			(f)		
Sales	€922,000		Sales	€502,000	
Purchases	€670,000		Purchases	€348,000	
Carriage inwards	€6,500		Carriage inwards	€5,500	
Customs duty	€8,900		Customs duty	€6,370	
Opening stock	€11,000		Opening stock	€9,570	
Closing stock	€14,000		Closing stock	€13,920	

(g)			(h)		
Sales	€700,000		Sales	€644,000	
Purchases	€474,000		Purchases	€304,000	
Carriage inwards	€8,500		Carriage inwards	€16,500	
Customs duty	€7,800		Customs duty	€12,400	
Opening stock	€15,000		Opening stock	€19,000	
Closing stock	€19,000		Closing stock	€13,200	

Remember ...

If you are having trouble remembering the contents of the trading account section of the income statement and the order in which they appear, remember that 'Some Old People Can Drive Cars In Space!'

Sales	Some
Opening stock	**O**ld
Purchases	**P**eople
Customs **D**uty	**C**an **D**rive
Carriage **I**n	**C**ars **I**n
Closing **S**tock	**S**pace!

29.3 Think up your own saying to remember the contents and order in which they appear on the trading account section of the income statement.

KSBC
KSBL

Key Terms

KSBL
KSC
KSMIT
KSBC

You should be able to *define*, *spell*, give *examples* and *apply* to real life each of the following key terms associated with this topic.

Exercise: Write a sentence using each of the following terms. You may use more than one of the terms in your sentence if appropriate.

carriage inwards	import duty
closing stock	income statement
cost of goods sold	opening stock
customs duty	purchases
final accounts	sales
gross profit	trading account

Chapter 30 ::
Income Statements 2 (The Profit and Loss Account)

Income statement

Remember:

An **income statement** is made up of a **trading account** and a **profit and loss account**.

See Chapter 29

Accounting for expenses

In addition to the direct costs of sales outlined in the previous chapter, it is likely that a business will have other expenses which will reduce their overall level of profit. These expenses, also called **overheads**, include a range of additional costs involved in operating a business. Examples include rent, wages, insurance, advertising and delivery costs.

These items will be included in the company's profit and loss account. **This section of the income statement is used to calculate the net profit (or net loss) for the financial year.**

This section lists all administration, financial, sales and distribution expenses for the year.

All expenses are subtracted from gross profit.

Net profit = Gross profit − Expenses **Formula**

If the expenses are greater than the gross profit, this will result in a **net loss** for the trading period.

30.1 What net profit/net loss do the following result in?

    (a) Gross profit €125,000; Expenses €47,500

    (b) Gross profit €250,000; Expenses €53,000

    (c) Gross profit €75,000; Expenses €91,300

Capital expenditure versus current expenditure

Capital expenditure refers to money spent on the purchase of items that will last the business for several years. These items are called **fixed assets** and examples include buildings, vehicles, machinery and equipment.

Capital expenditure is *not* recorded in the income statement. It is, however, recorded in the statement of financial position.

See Chapter 31

Current expenditure (also called **revenue expenditure**) refers to expenses incurred in the day-to-day running of the business. Examples include advertising and fuel costs for vehicles.

Current expenditure items *are* included in the income statement. Note that the day-to-day operating and maintenance costs associated with fixed assets are regarded as current expenditure and are therefore included in the profit and loss account. For example, the purchase of a vehicle is not recorded in the income statement, whereas the running costs of the vehicle are recorded in the expenses section of the income statement.

30.2 Which of these are capital expenditure, and which are current expenditure?

    (a) A telephone bill.

    (b) A new telephone cabling system for the whole factory.

    (c) Servicing of the fleet of cars.

    (d) A new car for the sales representative.

    (e) An oil tank for the heating oil.

    (f) Filling the tank with oil.

Expenses

Table 30.1 shows some of the most common business expenses appearing in the income statement.

Table 30.1 Business expenses appearing in the income statement

Administration	Selling and distribution	Financial	Depreciation
Wages and salaries	Wages of sales people	Interest on loans	Depreciation of fixed assets[4]
Insurance	Advertising	Bank overdraft interest	
Light and heat	Carriage outwards[2]		
Telephone	Selling expenses		
Rent and rates	Vehicle operating expenses		
Postage and stationery	Marketing expenses		
Audit fees[1]	Bad debts[3]		
Repairs			
General expenses			
Office expenses			
Cleaning expenses			
Travel expenses			

> This is a guide to help classify business expenses. It does not include all possible expenses that a business may incur.

Notes

1 **Audit fees:** The role of auditors is to examine company accounts in order to ensure that they have been properly prepared and that the accounts present a true and fair picture of the financial position of the business.

2 **Carriage outwards:** The transport and delivery costs associated with selling goods to customers. This expense is different from carriage inwards, which is entered in the trading account.

3 **Bad debts:** This is when a debtor is unable to repay the debt and the money is written off as a non-recoverable loss. It is treated as an expense in the income statement.

4 **Depreciation:** This is a reduction in the value of a fixed asset due to age, usage and wear and tear. Businesses generally 'write off' a portion of the assets value each year. For example, a new vehicle that is expected to have a working life of five years would be depreciated by 20% each year.

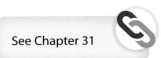

See Chapter 31

Example 1: Basic income statement with expenses

Use the following information provided by Intra Ltd to prepare a profit and loss account for the year ended 31/12/2016.

> Gross profit €180,000 > Carriage outwards €3,000
> Wages €56,000 > Advertising €8,300
> Rent €12,000 > Office expenses €2,000
> Light and heat €4,700

Record Book 2

Income Statement for Intra Ltd for year ended 31/12/2016

	€	€	€	Notes
Gross profit			180,000	P&L section of the income statement begins with Gross profit
Less expenses:				
Administration				
Wages	56,000			
Rent	12,000			
Light and heat	4,700			
Office expenses	2,000	74,700		
Selling and distribution				
Carriage outwards	3,000			
Advertising	8,300	11,300	86,000	Subtract total expenses
Net profit			94,000	Net profit = Gross profit – Expenses

The profit and loss account begins with gross profit (or loss) and ends with the calculation of net profit (or loss). In practice it is really just an extension of the trading account. Remember that these two sections together make up the income statement.

This question will give you practice in preparing profit and loss accounts.

30.3 Use the information provided to prepare a profit and loss account for Benny & Hughes for the year ended 31/12/2016. Use Record Book 2.

Gross profit	€230,000	Carriage outwards	€3,000
Wages	€66,000	Advertising	€6,300
Rent	€16,100	Office expenses	€2,500
Light and heat	€9,700		

Stages in the record-keeping process

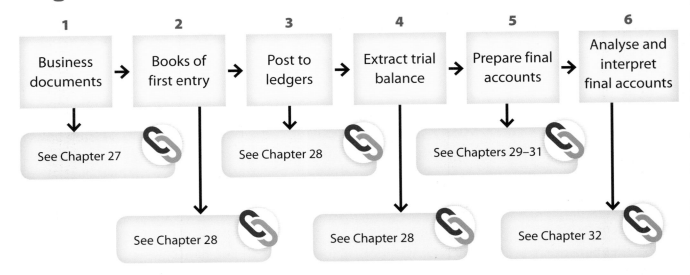

Notes:

> The information from the business documents (invoices, credit notes, etc.) is posted to the books of first entry (analysed cash book).

> The system of double entry bookkeeping requires that figures from the analysed cash book are also posted to the ledger accounts.

> Accounts are balanced and totalled and a trial balance is extracted.

> Figures from the trial balance are used to prepare the final accounts.

> The accounts must be analysed to get a better understanding of the underlying financial position of the business.

From trial balance to net profit

At the end of the financial year, the ledger accounts and analysed cash book will be balanced off and totalled. A **trial balance** will be drawn up. This is simply a list of ledger and cash book balances at the end of the accounting period. These figures will be used to prepare the final accounts for the business.

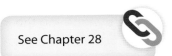

See Chapter 28

Example 2: Income statement with combined trading and profit and loss account

Use the following information to prepare an income statement for Fresh Ltd for the year ended 31/12/2016.

Trial Balance of Fresh Ltd on 31/12/2016

	DR €	CR €	Notes	
Sales		234,500	T	Record Book 2
Purchases	155,000		T	
Opening stock	16,000		T	
Carriage inwards	4,000		T	
Customs duty	2,500		T	
Salaries	25,000		Exp	
Carriage outwards	8,000		Exp	
Rent and rates	6,700		Exp	
Light and heat	12,000		Exp	
Office expenses	3,300		Exp	
Depreciation on equipment	2,000		Exp	
	234,500	**234,500**		

Closing stock (as at 31/12/2016) €11,500 (T)

Points to note:

> Closing stock is not included in the trial balance, but is listed as an extra item below the trial balance. It needs to be included in the trading account.

> Before preparing the income statement it is helpful to identify each item in the trial balance and make a note of where it will appear in the final accounts.

> In this example, the following abbreviations are used:

> > T = Trading account item

> > Exp = An expense in the profit and loss account. Subtract from gross profit.

Here is the completed income statement:

Income Statement for Fresh Ltd for year ended 31/12/2016

	€	€	€
Sales			234,500
Less cost of sales			
Opening stock (01/01/2016)		16,000	
Purchases		155,000	
Customs duty		2,500	
Carriage inwards		4,000	
Cost of goods available for sale		177,500	
– Closing stock (31/12/2016)		11,500	
Cost of goods sold			166,000
Gross profit			68,500
Less expenses			
Administration			
Salaries	25,000		
Rent and rates	6,700		
Light and heat	12,000		
Office expenses	3,300	47,000	
Selling and distribution			
Carriage outwards		8,000	
Depreciation			
Depreciation on equipment		2,000	57,000
Net profit			11,500

Record Book 2

Remember!

Some

Old

People

Can Drive

Cars In

Space

This question will give you practice in preparing income statements.

30.4 Use the information provided to prepare an income statement for Wright Brothers Ltd for the year ended 31/12/2016. Use Record Book 2.

Sales	€820,000	Wages and salaries	€55,000
Purchases	€440,000	Carriage outwards	€6,600
Opening stock	€8,000	Rent and rates	€8,400
Closing stock	€6,000	Light and heat	€3,750
Carriage inwards	€3,000	Office expenses	€4,500
Customs duty	€9,000	Repairs	€7,100

The profit and loss appropriation account

This final section of the income statement is used to show how the annual profit is distributed. Some of the profit might be used to pay a dividend to shareholders, with the rest being held as retained profits (also known as revenue reserves) and used for future investment in the business, e.g. to expand the business or purchase new assets.

The P&L appropriation account contains the following entries:

> Any dividends paid by the business during the current financial year. These are subtracted from the net profit or loss.

> Any reserves or retained profits carried forward by the business from previous years. These are added to the net profit or loss.

Net profit – Dividends paid + Opening reserves = Reserves (retained profits)

Example 3: Profit and loss appropriation account

The layout of a typical profit and loss appropriation account is as follows.

Profit and loss appropriation account of Fresh Ltd for year ended 31/12/2016

	€	€	Notes	
Net profit		11,500		
– Dividends paid		10,000	Portion of profit paid to shareholders	
		1,500		
+ Opening reserves (01/01/16)		30,000	Retained profit from previous years	
Reserves (retained profit) 31/12/16		31,500	Retained profit at the end of this financial year	

Points to note:

> If dividends have already been paid to shareholders they will be listed in the trial balance as **dividends paid**.

> The opening reserve (if one exists) will be listed in the trial balance.

> The closing reserve represents the retained profit or **reserves** at the end of the current financial year.

These questions will give you practice in preparing profit and loss appropriation accounts.

30.5 Use the information provided to prepare a profit and loss appropriation account for Jackson and Perkins Ltd for the year ended 31/12/2016.

Net profit	€325,000
Dividends paid	€16,000
Opening reserve (01/01/2016)	€42,000

30.6 Use the information provided to prepare a profit and loss appropriation account for Christopoulos Pharmaceutical Ltd for the year ended 31/12/2016.

Net profit	€714,000
Dividends paid	€35,000
Opening reserve (01/01/2016)	€57,000

Example 4: Complete income statement (trading, P&L and appropriation account)

From the following information prepare an income statement for Sunny Ltd for year ended 31/12/2016.

> Cash sales	€420,000	(T)
> Cash purchases	€225,000	(T)
> Opening stock	€23,000	(T)
> Customs duty	€2,000	(T)
> Closing stock	€13,750	(T)
> Carriage inwards	€6,000	(T)
> Rent	€12,800	(Exp)
> Light and heat	€3,250	(Exp)
> Wages	€65,000	(Exp)
> Carriage outwards	€4,000	(Exp)
> Telephone	€5,150	(Exp)
> Depreciation on vehicles	€10,000	(Exp)
> Opening reserves (01/01/2016)	€50,000	(App)
> Dividends paid	€6,000	(App)

Income Statement of Sunny Ltd for year ended 31/12/2016

	€	€	€
Sales			420,000
Less cost of sales			
Opening stock (01/01/2016)		23,000	
Purchases		225,000	
Customs duty		2,000	
Carriage inwards		6,000	
Cost of goods available for sale		256,000	
– Closing stock (31/12/2016)		13,750	
Cost of goods sold			242,250
Gross profit			177,750
Less expenses			
Administration			
Wages	65,000		
Rent	12,800		
Light and heat	3,250		
Telephone	5,150	86,200	
Selling and distribution			
Carriage outwards		4,000	
Depreciation			
Depreciation on vehicles		10,000	100,200
Net profit			77,550
Less dividends			6,000
			71,550
Add opening reserves (01/01/2016)			50,000
Reserves (retained profit)			121,550

Record Book 2

Remember!

Some

Old

People

Can **D**rive

Cars **I**n

Space

These questions will give you practice in preparing an income statement.

30.7 Use the information provided to prepare an income statement account for Grace Fashions Ltd for the year ended 31/12/2016.

Cash sales	€385,000
Cash purchases	€175,000
Opening stock	€13,500
Closing stock	€13,750
Carriage inwards	€3,200
Rent	€16,000
Depreciation on machinery	€8,000
Light and heat	€5,250
Wages	€32,000
Carriage outwards	€7,000
Telephone	€7,950
Opening reserves (01/01/2016)	€41,000
Dividends paid	€17,000

30.8 Use the information provided to prepare an income statement for Film & Vinyl Ltd for the year ended 31/12/2016.

Cash sales	€970,000
Cash purchases	€645,000
Opening stock	€43,000
Closing stock	€23,450
Carriage inwards	€7,600
Customs duty	€900
Rent	€16,000
Depreciation on vehicles	€7,000
Light and heat	€5,250
Repairs	€6,000
Wages	€72,000
Carriage outwards	€1,200
Telephone	€1,150
Opening reserves (01/01/2016)	€82,000
Dividends paid	€25,000

Key Terms

You should be able to *define*, *spell*, give *examples* and *apply* to real life each of the following key terms associated with this topic.

Exercise: Write a sentence using each of the following terms. You may use more than one of the terms in your sentence if appropriate.

bad debt	fixed assets
capital expenditure	net loss
carriage inwards	net profit
carriage outwards	overheads
current expenditure	profit and loss account
depreciation	profit and loss appropriation account
expenses	reserves (retained profit)

Chapter 31
The Statement of Financial Position

Learning outcomes

When you have completed this chapter you will be able to:

✔ Outline the purpose of a statement of financial position and list its main elements

✔ Distinguish between fixed assets, current assets and creditors falling due within one year

✔ Explain the term 'working capital' and understand its significance

✔ Distinguish between authorised and issued share capital

✔ Prepare a statement of financial position

✔ Understand the impact of adjustments to final accounts

✔ Prepare a complete set of final accounts

✔ Prepare a set of final accounts for a not-for-profit organisation.

The statement of financial position

The statement of financial position illustrates the year end value of a business's assets and creditors (liabilities), as well as outlining details of its capital structure.

Whereas the income statement illustrates yearly totals ('for year ended'), the statement of financial position reflects the financial status of a business on a *given day*.

What's in the statement of financial position?

The following will be in the statement of financial position:

1 Fixed assets

2 Current assets

3 Creditors falling due within one year

4 Working capital

5 Total net assets

6 Capital employed.

1 Fixed assets

These are items owned by a business and intended for long-term use, e.g. premises, equipment, vehicles, etc. They may depreciate over time and their valuations in the statement of financial position will need to reflect this reduction.

31.1 Write a definition of depreciation.

31.2 How does depreciation impact on the value of assets?

See Chapter 30

31.3 Why is it necessary to list assets at their current market value rather than their cost price?

2 Current assets

Cash, or any asset that can be converted to cash in the short term (i.e. within one year).

Examples in this category include:

> Cash
> Bank deposits
> Money owed to the business by debtors
> Stock of goods.

The term **debtor** refers to someone who owes money to another person or business. In a business context the term debtor usually refers to another business who owes us money because we have sold them goods on credit. This means we have supplied them with the goods now and expect them to pay for them at an agreed future date, usually in thirty days.

3 Creditors falling due within one year

These are short-term debts owed by the business. Examples include:

> Bank overdraft
> Unpaid bills (accruals)
> Money owed to creditors, i.e. people or other businesses to whom the business owes money.

4 Working capital

> Working capital = Current assets − Creditors falling due within one year

Formula

Working capital provides a good indication of a business's short-term liquidity. **Liquidity** refers to cash flow and shows whether the business can generate enough short-term income to pay its short-term debts.

For example, if a business has current assets valued at €100,000 and creditors falling due within one year of €70,000 it will have a positive working capital of €30,000. This suggests its short-term liquidity is not a problem.

We will look in more detail at the significance of these issues in the next chapter.

See Chapter 32

5 Total net assets

This is also called **net worth**. It shows what the business would be worth if it were to sell its assets and pay its short-term debts.

> Total net assets = Fixed assets + Working capital **Formula**

6 Capital employed

This is the total of the **Financed by** section of the balance sheet, and sets out the capital structure of a business.

This section of the balance sheet contains:

> ❯ Details of the business's share capital.
> ❯ Long-term loans taken out by the business. These are creditors falling due after more than one year and will not be repaid during the current financial year.
> ❯ Retained profits or reserves held by the business for future reinvestment.

Capital is money invested into a business and used to generate income. Capital comes from two main sources: investments by shareholders (**equity capital**) or borrowings (**debt capital**).

See Chapter 32

Authorised vs issued share capital

When a company is being set up, its owners must set an upper limit for the amount of share capital that it can issue. This maximum limit is called the **authorised share capital**.

See Chapter 25

For example, Flash Ltd may have an authorised share capital of €700,000, made up of 700,000 individual shares with a **nominal value** of €1 each. This nominal value represents the original value of the shares when they are issued. Over time the actual value of these shares (their market value) may rise or fall.

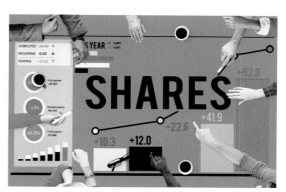

The **issued share capital** of a company indicates the number of shares it has actually issued (sold) to date. For example, Flash Ltd may have an issued share capital of €300,000 comprising 300,000 €1 shares.

KSBN

31.4 From the information provided above, calculate how many extra shares Flash Ltd may choose to issue in the future if it needs to raise extra capital.

Example 1: Preparing a statement of financial position

Use the following information to prepare a statement of financial position for Kahouna Ltd as at 31/12/2016. The company has an authorised share capital of €700,000.

Premises €320,000

Machinery €170,000

Bank (deposits) €23,000

Closing stock €14,000

Debtors €18,000

Bank overdraft €7,500

Creditors €9,500

Issued share capital €440,000

Long-term loans €78,000

Reserves €10,000

Record Book 2

Statement of Financial Position of Kahouna Ltd as at 31/12/2016

	€ Cost	€ Depreciation	€ Net book value	Notes
Fixed assets	Cost	Depreciation	Net book value	These headings apply to the fixed assets section only
Premises	320,000	–	320,000	Assets have not depreciated in value
Machinery	170,000	–	170,000	
Total fixed assets	490,000	–	490,000	Book value of fixed assets
Current assets				
Bank	23,000			
Closing stock	14,000			
Debtors	18,000	55,000		Total current assets
Less creditors falling due within one year				
Bank overdraft	7,500			
Creditors	9,500	17,000		Total creditors falling due within one year
Working capital			38,000	CA – CFD*
Total net assets			528,000	Total fixed assets + Working capital
Financed by:				
Creditors falling due after more than one year (long-term loan)			78,000	
Capital and reserves	*Authorised*	*Issued*		
Ordinary share capital	700,000	440,000		Must show both authorised and issued share capital
+ Reserves		10,000	450,000	
Capital employed			528,000	This matches the Total net assets

*CA = current assets; CFD = creditors falling due within one year

Point to note:

As with the income statement, it is important to use the standard layout for a statement of financial position.

31.5 In which part of the statement of financial position (fixed assets, current assets, creditors falling due within one year or financed by) will you find the following?

(a) Premises

(b) Machinery

(c) Bank (deposits)

(d) Closing stock

(e) Debtors

(f) Bank overdraft

(g) Creditors

(h) Issued share capital

(i) Long-term loans

Adjustments to final accounts

We have already seen that the figures used to prepare a business's final accounts are contained in the trial balance. Sometimes, however, there may be additional information available, which is not contained in the trial balance, but which needs to be included in the final accounts. These items are usually listed below the trial balance and are treated as 'adjustments' to final accounts.

See Chapter 30

There are two specific adjustments to final accounts:

> Closing stock
> Depreciation.

Each of these adjustment items **need to be entered twice** in the final accounts: once in the income statement, and then in the statement of financial position.

Closing stock appears:

> In the income statement (trading account section).
> As a current asset in the statement of financial position.

Depreciation appears:

> As an expense in the income statement.
> In the fixed assets section of the statement of financial position. Depreciation should be subtracted from the asset's cost price in order to calculate its net book value.

Example: Machinery that cost €50,000 is to be depreciated by 20%.

Depreciation is calculated as follows: €50,000 × 20% = €10,000.

This €10,000 will first be included in the list of expenses contained in the income statement. It will also appear in the statement of financial position as follows:

Statement of financial position extract (as at 31/12/2016)

Fixed asset	Cost €	Depreciation €	Net book value €	Notes
Machinery	50,000	10,000	40,000	NBV = Cost price – Depreciation

Point to note:

The net book value (NBV) represents the current value of the fixed asset and reflects the impact of age and wear and tear. If no account is taken of depreciation and assets are included at their original cost price, this will have the effect of over-stating the actual value of the assets and would give a false impression of the financial strength of the business.

Example 2: Preparing final accounts, including adjustments

Here is a fully worked example of final accounts, including adjustments.

Use the information below to prepare an income statement of Speed Ltd for the year ended 31/12/2016. Prepare a statement of financial position on that date also.

Speed Ltd has an authorised share capital of 400,000 €1 ordinary shares.

The following abbreviations are used in this example to indicate where each item appears in the final accounts.

> T = Trading account section of the income statement.

> Exp = An expense in the income statement (P&L section).

> App = Appropriation account section of the income statement.

> SFP (FA) = Statement of financial position (Fixed assets section).

> SFP (CA) = Statement of financial position (Current assets section).

> SFP (CFD) = Statement of financial position (a creditor falling due within one year).

> SFP (Fin) = Statement of financial position (Financed by section).

Trial Balance of Speed Ltd as at 31/12/2016

Record Book 2

	€	€	Notes
	Dr	**Cr**	
Cash sales		380,000	T
Cash purchases	200,000		T
Carriage inwards	1,100		T
Rent	13,200		Exp
Opening stock	4,000		T
Wages	48,000		Exp
Customs duty	1,200		T
Telephone	4,000		Exp
Dividends paid	14,000		App
Light & heat	11,500		Exp
Carriage outwards	3,000		Exp
Premises	160,000		SFP (FA)
Vehicles	40,000		SFP (FA)
Office expenses	1,800		Exp
Cash in hand	4,000		SFP (CA)
Machinery	90,000		SFP (FA)
Creditors		12,000	SFP (CL)
Debtors	11,000		SFP (CA)
Bank overdraft		8,000	SFP (CL)
Advertising	4,200		Exp
Issued share capital		150,000	SFP (Fin by)
Reserves (P&L balance)		37,000	App
Five-year loan		24,000	SFP (Fin by)
	611,000	**611,000**	

The following additional information is provided on 31/12/2016:

> Closing stock (31/12/16) €10,000 – T, and SFP (CA).

> Vehicles are to be depreciated by 20% – Exp and SFP (FA).

Income Statement of Speed Ltd for year ended 31/12/2016

Record Book 2

	€	€	€	Notes
Sales			380,000	Some
Less cost of sales:				
Opening stock		4,000		Old
+ Purchases		200,000		People
+ Customs duty		1,200		Can Drive
+ Carriage inwards		1,100		Cars In
Cost of goods available for sale		206,300		
− Closing stock		10,000		Space
Cost of goods sold			196,300	
Gross profit			183,700	
Less expenses:				
Administration				
Wages	48,000			
Telephone	4,000			
Light and heat	11,500			
Office expenses	1,800			
Rent	13,200	78,500		
Selling and distribution				
Advertising	4,200			
Carriage outwards	3,000	7,200		
Depreciation				
Depreciation on vehicles		8,000	93,700	Depreciation = 20% of €40,000
Net profit			90,000	
− Dividends paid			14,000	
			76,000	
+ Opening reserves			37,000	
Closing reserves			113,000	

31.7 Prepare Browne Ltd's final accounts from their trial balance. Browne Ltd has an authorised share capital of €350,000. Use Record Book 2.

Trial Balance of Browne Ltd on 31/12/2016

	DR €	CR €
Cash sales		250,000
Cash purchases	120,000	
Opening stock (01/01/2016)	1,500	
Carriage inwards	5,000	
Insurance	6,000	
Rent	6,000	
Office expenses	3,000	
Advertising	4,500	
Dividends paid	15,000	
Premises	210,000	
Machinery	39,000	
Debtors	7,500	
Creditors		11,000
Bank overdraft		9,000
Cash	2,500	
Issued share capital		150,000
	420,000	**€420,000**

Note: Stock on 31/12/2016 was €15,000.

We provide a number of other trial balances in the Student Activity Book for you to practise preparing the final accounts. Do as many as you need to until you feel confident with your work.

Final accounts of not-for-profit organisations

Not-for-profit organisations such as clubs, charities and community groups also need to prepare final accounts. These accounts are used to support applications for loans and grants and also to show members how money was received and spent during the year.

Since these accounts are not required to show profitability they will look a little different from those prepared by companies and other commercial organisations. Commercial organisations are those whose main aim is to make a profit.

Not-for-profit organisations will record all money received or paid out in an analysed cash book and these figures will eventually be used to prepare a set of final accounts.

See Chapter 6

Any extra income (revenue) over expenditure will be recorded as an operating **surplus** and this money will be reinvested into the organisation to help achieve its aims. For example, if a homeless charity records a surplus income it will be used to fund higher levels of service for homeless people.

If annual expenditure is greater than income, this will be recorded in the accounts as a **deficit**.

Expenses related to the goals of the organisation are listed in the income statement as **programme expenses**. The type of expenditure will depend on the type of not-for-profit organisation. For example, a community development association is likely to spend money supporting local issues such as small business development, youth groups and restoration projects. A sports club or a charity would have different programme expenses to reflect their different goals.

Table 31.1 sets out the major differences between the final accounts prepared by companies and those prepared by not-for-profit organisations.

Table 31.1 Final accounts prepared by companies and not-for-profit organisations

Company accounts	Not-for-profit organisations
Main goal is to make a profit Profits belong to shareholders, who may receive a dividend	**Making a profit is *not* the main goal** Surplus income is reinvested to help achieve organisational goals or to benefit members
Accounts prepared by **accountants** and double checked by **auditors**	Accounts prepared by **finance officer** or **treasurer** and may be checked by an auditor
Income > Expenditure = **Profit** Expenditure > Income = **Loss** These are recorded in the income statement	Income > Expenditure = **Surplus** (excess income) Expenditure > Income = **Deficit** (excess expenditure) These are recorded in the income statement
Sales are the main source of income or revenue	**Subscriptions/donations/grants** are major sources of income or revenue
Issued share capital is recorded in statement of financial position	**Accumulated fund is** recorded in statement of financial position

Example 3: Final accounts of a not-for-profit organisation

Barrtown Community Development Association prepared the following final accounts for the year ended 31/12/2016.

Income Statement of Barrtown Community Development Association for year ended 31/12/2016

	€	€
Revenue:		
Donations	18,000	
Grants	27,000	
Fundraising income	6,800	51,800
Less expenditure:		
Programme expenses	29,000	
Rent	3,100	
Insurance	4,300	
Light and heat	8,400	
General expenses	2,700	
Depreciation on equipment	2,000	49,500
Surplus income		**2,300**

Statement of Financial Position of Barrtown Community Development Association as at 31/12/2016

Fixed assets	Cost €	Depreciation €	Net book value €
Equipment	20,000	2,000	18,000
Current assets			
Cash	900		
Debtors	3,100	4,000	
Creditors falling due within one year			
Bank overdraft	1,300		
Creditors	1,700	3,000	
Working capital			1,000
Total net assets			19,000
Financed by:			
Accumulated fund		16,700	
Surplus income (reserves)		2,300	
Capital employed			19,000

Key Terms

KSBL
KSC
KSMIT
KSBC

You should be able to *define*, *spell*, give *examples* and *apply* to real life each of the following key terms associated with this topic.

Exercise: Write a sentence using each of the following terms. You may use more than one of the terms in your sentence if appropriate.

authorised share capital

capital employed

creditors falling due after more than
  one year

creditors falling due within one year

current assets

debt capital

debtor

deficit

depreciation

equity capital

fixed assets

issued share capital

net assets/net worth

programme expenses

statement of financial position

surplus

working capital

Chapter 32 :: Analysing and Assessing Financial Accounts

Ratio analysis

In the previous chapters we learned how to prepare final accounts for a company. In this chapter we will take a closer look at those final accounts and we will dig a little deeper in order to get a better understanding of the financial story being told.

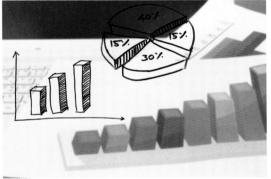

To help us with this investigation we will make use of **ratio analysis**.

Ratios are helpful because they focus on financial performance in **percentage terms** rather than in monetary terms.

Ratios are most useful when they are used to **compare performance over a long period of time** or **against other businesses in the same industry**. This makes it easier to compare different companies and different years.

There are three main categories of accounting ratio:

1 **Profitability ratios** analyse the profit made during the financial year. These ratios measure the relationship between profits, sales and capital employed.

2 **Liquidity ratios** measure the ability to pay short-term debts. Poor liquidity is a major cause of business failure.

3 **Gearing ratios** measure the proportion of the business's capital that has come from external sources. This is long-term debt and must be repaid with interest.

Users of financial information

Stakeholders is a collective term used to describe all those who are involved in or affected by the activities of an organisation.

Although their reasons for doing so may be different, the following business stakeholders will have an interest in analysing financial information.

1 Employees and managers:

> Interested in all financial aspects of the business, because their long-term job security depends on the business remaining profitable and **solvent**.

> All employees, including managers, may be rewarded for high levels of profitability, either through wage increases or the payment of performance-related bonuses.

A business is **solvent** when the value of its total assets is greater than its external debt. This means the business can pay *all* its debts.

External debt (or **liabilities**) refers to money that is owed to people outside the business, i.e. all creditors.

Definitions

2 Shareholders:

> As the owners of the business, shareholders will mainly be concerned with profitability and the payment of dividends.

> Potential shareholders will also be interested in return on investment.

3 Lenders:

> All existing and potential lenders will be concerned with liquidity as this measures the ability of the business to repay its debts.

> Lenders will also be concerned with ability to repay debts and **gearing**. High levels of external debt increase the pressure on a business to make repayments and increase the likelihood of non-payment or default.

Gearing measures the level of a business's debt compared to its equity capital such as shares and reserves.

Definition

4 Suppliers:

> Liquidity will be the primary concern for suppliers, especially those who supply goods on credit. A business that is having cash flow problems may struggle to pay its bills on time. This increases the likelihood of bad debts for suppliers.

5 Government:

> The government collects tax on company profits (corporation tax) and will therefore be interested in profitability levels.

> Organisations also submit a variety of other taxes and charges, including VAT, PAYE and PRSI.

Calculating ratios

In the examples that follow, all information will be taken from the accounts of Euro Ltd, whose final accounts for the year ended 31/12/2016 are set out below. For comparison purposes, the company has also provided a copy of its key figures for the previous four years' trading. Where relevant, the industry average is also provided.

Summarised Income Statement of Euro Ltd for year ended 31/12/16

	€
Sales	350,000
Less cost of sales	178,000
Gross profit	172,000
Less expenses	82,000
Net profit	90,000
– Dividend paid	14,000
	76,000
+ Opening reserves (01/01/16)	37,000
Closing reserves (31/12/16)	113,000

Statement of Financial Position of Euro Ltd as at 31/12/2016

	€	€	€
Fixed assets	Cost	Depreciation	Net book value
Premises	160,000	–	160,000
Vehicles	40,000	8,000	32,000
Machinery	90,000	–	90,000
	290,000	8,000	282,000
Current assets			
Cash in hand	4,000		
Debtors	11,000		
Closing stock	10,000	25,000	
Creditors falling due within one year			
Bank overdraft	8,000		
Creditors	12,000	20,000	
Working capital			5,000
Total net assets			**287,000**
Financed by:			
Creditors falling due after more than one year (5-year loan)			24,000
Capital and reserves	*Authorised*	*Issued*	
Ordinary share capital	350,000	150,000	
Reserves		113,000	263,000
Capital employed			**287,000**

Profitability

We will look at some of the ways profitability can be measured.

Gross margin

Profitability can be measured by the **gross margin**, which is also known as the **gross profit percentage**.

$$\text{Gross margin} = \frac{\text{Gross profit}}{\text{Sales}} \times \frac{100}{1}$$

Formula

The 2016 gross margin for Euro Ltd is therefore:

$$\frac{172,000}{350,000} \times \frac{100}{1} = 49\%$$

This means that Euro Ltd makes 49c gross profit from every €1 of sales revenue it receives from customers.

This figure can be measured against the gross margin for previous years and against the industry average for this year:

Euro Ltd gross margin (previous four years)

2012	2013	2014	2015
35%	30%	35%	40%
2016 INDUSTRY AVERAGE		42 %	

The trend graph for the five-year period 2012–2016 is shown in figure 32.1.

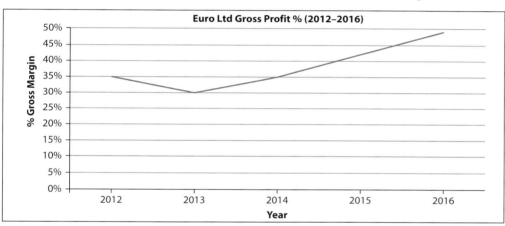

Figure 32.1 Trend graph, Euro Ltd 2012–2016

Commentary and evaluation

With the exception of a drop in profitability in 2013, Euro Ltd has seen a gradual improvement in its gross profit margin over the five-year period. The 49% figure in 2016 represents a five-year high and suggests that sales (turnover) have improved and the cost of sales is under control. The result is also well above the industry average for 2016 and represents a very positive outcome.

KSBN
KSC
KSMIT

32.1 Use the information provided to calculate the gross profit percentage for each of the three businesses. Comment on the results.

Alpha Ltd	Beta Ltd	Gamma Ltd
Gross profit €360,000	Gross profit €275,000	Gross profit €360,000
Sales €800,000	Sales €500,000	Sales €1,200,000

Net margin

Profitability can be measured by the **net margin**, which is also known as the **net profit percentage**.

$$\textbf{Net margin} = \frac{\text{Net profit}}{\text{Sales}} \times \frac{100}{1}$$

Formula

The 2016 net margin for Euro Ltd is, therefore:

$$\frac{90,000}{350,000} \times \frac{100}{1} = 25.7\%$$

This means that Euro Ltd makes 25.7c net profit from every €1 of sales revenue that it received from customers.

The figure for net margin can be measured against the net margin for previous years and against the industry average for this year:

Euro Ltd net margin (previous four years)

2012	2013	2014	2015
11%	10%	14%	17%
2016 INDUSTRY AVERAGE		20 %	

32.2 Using the information provided above, draw a trend graph in your copy to illustrate Euro Ltd's net margin for the five-year period 2012–2016. Round the 2016 figure to the nearest whole number.

Commentary and evaluation

Euro Ltd has seen a year-on-year improvement in net margin between 2015 and 2016 with the figures rising from 17% to 25.7%. This maintains a positive trend since 2013, which has seen a steady increase over the period. The result is also above the industry average for 2016.

32.3 Use the information provided to calculate the net margin for each of the three businesses. Comment on the results.

Alpha Ltd	Beta Ltd	Gamma Ltd
Net profit €200,000	Net profit €175,000	Gross profit €360,000
Sales €800,000	Sales €500,000	Expenses €180,000
		Sales €1,200,000

Return on capital employed

Profitability can be measured by the **return on capital employed (ROCE)**, which is also known as the **return on investment (ROI)**.

$$\text{Return on capital employed} = \frac{\text{Net profit}}{\text{Capital employed}} \times \frac{100}{1}$$

The 2016 return on capital employed for Euro Ltd is, therefore:

$$\frac{90{,}000}{287{,}000} \times \frac{100}{1} = 31.36\%$$

ROCE is useful when comparing profitability between companies, because it gives an indication of how well the business is using its capital to generate income.

By comparing the ROCE available on different investment options, potential investors can choose the best possible option.

It is also useful to compare the ROCE from a business investment with the return on a (risk-free) investment in a financial institution.

For example, if money can be invested in a bank for a guaranteed 5% return, with no risk to their capital, an investor might avoid the higher risk associated with a possible 6% return on a business investment where their capital is not guaranteed to be returned.

Euro Ltd return on capital employed (previous four years)

2012	2013	2014	2015
20%	20%	28%	25%
2016 INDUSTRY AVERAGE		22 %	

32.4 Using the information provided, draw a trend graph to illustrate Euro Ltd's return on capital employed for the five-year period 2012–2016. Round the 2016 figure to the nearest whole number.

KSBN
KSC
KSMIT

Commentary and evaluation

Euro Ltd has seen a year-on-year improvement in its return on capital employed, from 20% in 2012 to 31.36% in 2016. This figure is well above the 'risk free' rate of return currently available from financial institutions. It is also well above the industry average for the year and is therefore a positive result which will be especially pleasing to managers and investors.

32.5 Research the best available rate on offer from Ireland's major financial institutions for an investor with €100,000 and a willingness to leave the money on deposit for up to:

(a) One year.

(b) Three years.

(c) Five years

KSMIT
KSBN

32.6 Use the information provided to calculate the return on capital employed for each of the three businesses. Comment on the results.

KSBN
KSC
KSMIT

Alpha Ltd	Beta Ltd	Gamma Ltd
Net profit €200,000	Net profit €275,000	Gross profit €360,000
Capital employed €1,000,000	Capital employed €900,000	Expenses €180,000
		Capital employed €600,000

Liquidity

We will look at some of the ways liquidity can be measured.

Working capital ratio (current ratio)

This ratio is really asking the following question:

Does the business have enough short-term assets available to generate the cash it needs to pay short-term debts?

Working capital ratio = Current assets : Creditors falling due within one year

The 2016 working capital ratio for Euro Ltd is, therefore:

$$25,000 : 20,000 = 1.25 : 1$$

This indicates that Euro Ltd should be able to generate enough short-term cash to pay its short-term debts. The result is, however, well below the **recommended level of 2:1**.

Euro Ltd current ratio (previous four years)

2012	2013	2014	2015
1.8 : 1	1.2 : 1	2.5 : 1	3 : 1
2016 INDUSTRY AVERAGE		2.3 : 1	

Commentary and evaluation

When we consider the five-year trend, it is clear that Euro Ltd has generally improved its cash flow position between 2013 and 2016.

The 2016 figure of just 1.25:1 is below the recommended minimum of 2:1 and also represents a major disimprovement since last year. It is also below the industry average, which suggests the liquidity problem is unique to Euro Ltd and is not a reflection of overall market conditions.

> **32.7** Use the information provided to calculate the current ratio for each of the three businesses. Comment on the results.
>
> KSBN
> KSC
> KSMIT
>
> | Alpha Ltd | Beta Ltd | Gamma Ltd |
> |---|---|---|
> | Current assets €400,000 | Current assets €700,000 | Current assets €800,000 |
> | Creditors falling due within one year €200,000 | Creditors falling due within one year €400,000 | Creditors falling due within one year €900,000 |

Acid test ratio (or quick ratio)

This ratio is a stricter test of liquidity than the working capital ratio and accounts for the fact that some current assets, especially stock, can take time to convert to cash.

The most common current assets in order of liquidity are:

> Cash – is already cash!

> Bank deposits – are 'near cash' and can usually be withdrawn on demand, or at short notice.

> Debtors – will typically be given thirty days to pay, but may pay sooner if required or if offered discounts. There is also the option to avail of factoring if cash is urgently required.

> Closing stock – it may take quite a long time to sell large amounts of stock and this may require huge discounting of prices. For this reason the acid test ratio excludes the closing stock figure from the current assets and asks the question: Does the business still have enough short-term assets available to repay short-term debts?

Acid test = (Current assets − Closing stock) : Creditors falling due within one year   **Formula**

The 2016 acid test for Euro Ltd is therefore:

(€25,000 − €10,000) : €20,000

= 15,000 : 20,000

= 0.75   : 1

Euro Ltd acid test ratio (previous four years)

2012	2013	2014	2015
1.4 : 1	1 : 1	1.9 : 1	2.5 : 1
2016 INDUSTRY AVERAGE		1.4 : 1	

Commentary and evaluation

The ideal or benchmark figure for the acid test ratio is **1:1**. Euro Ltd has achieved this target in each of the previous four years but its 2016 figure of just 0.75:1 is below both the required level and the industry average. This sharp decline in liquidity is a worrying sign and suggests the business may have a large portion of its available cash tied up in stock. This can create liquidity problems if there is a need to generate cash quickly.

32.8 Use the information provided to calculate the acid test for each of the three businesses. Comment on the results.

Alpha Ltd	Beta Ltd	Gamma Ltd
Current assets €400,000	Current assets €700,000	Current assets €900,000
Closing stock €150,000	Closing stock €100,000	Closing stock €200,000
Creditors falling due within one year €200,000	Creditors falling due within one year €400,000	Creditors falling due within one year €800,000

Solvency

Solvency is a measure of whether a business can pay its total debts.

A business that does not 'pass' the solvency test is said to be **insolvent**. A business that is insolvent is likely to be declared bankrupt, unless it can find a solution to its debt problem.

The test for solvency is:

Total assets > External liabilities

The 2016 solvency test for Euro Ltd is, therefore:

Total assets		External liabilities	
Fixed assets	€282,000	Creditors falling due within one year	€20,000
Current assets	€25,000	Long-term loan	€24,000
Total assets	€307,000	Total external liabilities	€44,000

Commentary and evaluation

Since total assets greatly exceed external debt Euro Ltd is *solvent* as at 31/12/2016.

32.9 Use the information provided to calculate whether each of the three businesses below is solvent. Comment on the results.

Alpha Ltd	Beta Ltd	Gamma Ltd
Total assets €700,000	Current assets €700,000	Current assets €900,000
External liabilities €350,000	Fixed assets €600,000	Fixed assets 700,000
	External liabilities €800,000	Creditors falling due within one year €800,000
		Long-term loans €950,000

Gearing

Gearing focuses on the **capital structure** of the business and compares the proportion of finance provided by debt to the proportion of finance provided by equity (or shareholders).

Debt capital includes all long-term loans (debentures, mortgages, etc.).

Equity capital includes issued share capital and reserves.

> If **debt capital > equity**, the business is **highly geared**.
>
> If **equity capital > debt capital**, the business is **lowly geared**.

Low gearing is less risky since the business is under less pressure to meet fixed interest repayments.

High gearing is associated with a greater level of risk, as the external debt must be repaid with interest. During periods of slow growth or economic downturn, a business may struggle to generate the levels of income required to meet these repayments.

Businesses that are highly geared may also find it more difficult to raise extra funding, since potential lenders and investors may be unwilling to loan money to a business that already has high levels of debt.

Debt capital : Equity capital

Euro Ltd's 2016 gearing position is as follows:

Debt capital			Equity capital	
Long-term loan	€24,000	:	Issued share capital	€150,000
		:	Reserves	€113,000
=	€24,000	:	€263,000	
=	0.09	:	1	

Commentary and evaluation

In 2016, Euro Ltd is very lowly geared and the vast majority of its capital comes from equity. This means that the business will not be under any pressure to generate high levels of income to repay debt.

32.10 Use the information provided to calculate the gearing for each of the three businesses. Comment on the results.

Alpha Ltd	Beta Ltd	Gamma Ltd
Equity capital €650,000	Equity capital €400,000	Equity capital €550,000
Debt capital €350,000	Debt capital €500,000	Debt capital €350,000

32.11 Study the information extracted from the final accounts for Omega Ltd and answer the questions that follow.

Final accounts	2014	2015
Income statement (summary)	€	€
Sales	220,000	340,000
Gross profit	100,000	120,000
Net profit	75,000	105,000
Statement of financial position (summary)	€	€
Current assets (including closing stock)	380,000	570,000
Creditors falling due within one year	190,000	400,000
Closing stock	60,000	85,000
Reserves	85,000	95,000
Issued share capital	320,000	340,000

(a) Calculate the gross profit margin and the net profit margin for 2014 and 2015. Comment on the trend.

(b) Calculate the acid test ratio for 2014 and 2015. Comment on the trend.

Report writing

A **report** is a written document used to communicate information from which conclusions and recommendations can be drawn.

Reports are quite structured and contain many common elements. They must be accurate, brief and clear, especially as they will most likely be used as a basis for decision making.

Having used ratio analysis to assess the financial performance of a business it may be appropriate to prepare a report to provide stakeholders with relevant information.

This report template will ensure you include all the information needed.

Report template

1 **Title:** A Report On …..

2 **To:** For whom is the report written?

3 **From:** By whom is the report written?

4 **Date:** Sets a timeframe for the report and its contents.

5 **Terms of reference:** What is the report about? What was the writer asked to investigate?

6 **Introduction:** Introduces topic and explains how the investigation was carried out.

7 **Main body of report:** Detailed analysis of the topic under investigation.

8 **Conclusions/recommendations:** What are the main findings and what action should now be taken?

9 **Signature of author:** The person who wrote the report should sign it.

Report writing example

Orla Power is an investment broker and financial consultant. The directors of Euro Ltd have asked her to analyse and assess the financial performance of their company for the year 2016. They have specifically requested feedback on profitability, liquidity and solvency and have also asked Orla to present her findings in a written report.

Orla examined the final accounts of Euro Ltd (as given throughout this chapter) and carried out a detailed ratio analysis of the figures. She has prepared the report shown in figure 32.2 for the company directors, based on the template above.

① A Report on the Financial Performance of Euro Ltd in 2016

② To: The Directors of Euro Ltd

③ From: Orla Power, financial consultant

④ Date: 4 March 2017

⑤ Terms of reference: To analyse the final accounts of Euro Ltd and present a detailed assessment of its financial performance for the year ended 31/12/2016.

⑥ I have examined the final accounts of the company for 2016 and carried out a detailed ratio analysis. I have presented my main findings below under the following headings:

> Profitability
> Liquidity and Solvency.

⑦ Profitability for 2016:

> The gross profit margin for the year is: 49%
> The net profit margin for the year is: 25.7%
> The return on capital employed is: 31.36%

Comment: All of these figures are very positive and represent an improvement in profitability levels since 2015. They are also above the industry average figures for profitability.

Liquidity and solvency for 2016:

> The working capital ratio for the year is: 1.25 :1
> The acid test ratio for the year is: 0.75:1
> The company was solvent at the end of 2016.

Comment: While the company remains solvent at the end of the financial year, there has been a worrying decline in liquidity since 2014. The liquidity figures are below the recommended minimum.

⑧ Conclusions/recommendations

The overall profitability position of the business is very strong. It continues to grow and is well ahead of rivals in the industry. Management should try to ensure that this positive trend is maintained, although they need to be careful of overtrading. This means carrying out a level of trading that is beyond the financial scope of the business. The worsening liquidity position highlighted by my analysis may suggest that current profitability levels are not sustainable.

I suggest that the business attempts to increase its level of cash sales, reduce its overall stock levels and make sure that it collects cash on time from debtors. All of these actions should help improve liquidity in the year ahead.

⑨ SIGNED: *Orla Power*

Orla Power, Financial Consultant

Figure 32.2 Example report on accounts

32.12 **(a)** What three things does Orla Power suggest that Euro Ltd does to improve liquidity?

(b) How will each of these three things help improve liquidity?

Key Terms

You should be able to *define*, *spell*, give *examples* and *apply* to real life each of the following key terms associated with this topic.

Exercise: Write a sentence using each of the following terms. You may use more than one of the terms in your sentence if appropriate.

acid test ratio	liquidity
current ratio	lowly geared
debt capital	net margin
dividends	profitability ratios
equity capital	quick ratio
gearing	solvent
gross margin	terms of reference
highly geared	working capital ratio
insolvent	

Accounting ratios

Gross margin $= \dfrac{\text{Gross profit}}{\text{Sales}} \times \dfrac{100}{1}$ **Formula**

Net margin $= \dfrac{\text{Net profit}}{\text{Sales}} \times \dfrac{100}{1}$ **Formula**

Return on capital employed $= \dfrac{\text{Net profit}}{\text{Capital employed}} \times \dfrac{100}{1}$ **Formula**

Working capital ratio = Current assets : Creditors falling due within one year   **Formula**

Acid test = (Current assets − Closing stock) : Creditors falling due within one year   **Formula**

Solvency

Total assets > External liabilities   **Formula**

Gearing

If **debt capital > equity**, the business is **highly geared**.

If **equity capital > debt capital**, the business is **lowly geared**.

Debt capital : Equity capital   **Formula**

Strand Three ::
Our Economy

Chapter 33 :: Scarcity and Choice

Learning outcomes

When you have completed this chapter you will be able to:

✔ Define economics
✔ Explain the term 'economic resources'
✔ Identify and explain each of the factors of production
✔ Describe how a business uses each of the factors of production to create goods, services and wealth
✔ Explain how scarcity, choice and opportunity cost impact on the production of goods and services
✔ List the rewards association with each factor of production.

What is economics?

Economics is the study of how people, businesses and governments with limited resources make choices in order to satisfy their needs.

`Definition`

Economic resources are the factors or inputs used to produce and distribute goods and services.

`Definition`

There are two important points here:

1 Resources are scarce.

2 Society must use these scarce resources efficiently.

When making choices about limited resources, we must distinguish between needs and wants.

Needs, wants and choices

All people have both needs and wants.

See Chapter 1

A **need** is something that is necessary for survival, e.g. food, water, shelter.

A **want** is anything that we would like to have but do not need to survive, e.g. a holiday, a car.

There are two costs involved when we buy goods and services: the financial cost and the opportunity cost. As we all have a limited income (scarce resources) and don't have enough money to buy all the things that we would like, we have to make choices. The **financial cost** is the price of the item you choose to buy and the item that you *don't buy* is the **opportunity cost**.

 See Chapter 1

33.1 Think of the last time you didn't have enough money to buy everything you wanted and had to make a choice.

T-P-S

(a) What items did you have to choose between?

(b) What was the opportunity cost?

(c) What was the financial cost?

(d) What influenced your final decision about which item to choose? Explain your choice to your partner.

KSWwO
KSMIT
KSC

Businesses and governments have scarce resources too. This forces them to make choices between alternatives and also gives rise to opportunity costs. For example:

› A business wants to expand and has €100,000 retained earnings. It must decide whether to hire more employees or invest in research and development.

› The minister for finance must decide whether to spend money on building a new school to cater for the expanding population, or a new road to cut travel times between two cities.

In the news

Cork–Limerick motorway plan 'too expensive' says transport minister Paschal Donohoe

By Daniel McConnell

Transport minister Paschal Donohoe has defended the shelving of the proposed M20 motorway between Cork and Limerick, insisting the proposed project was too expensive.

Mr Donohoe said he took the decision to park the motorway plan in preference of smaller 'targeted' projects.

'This is a €1bn project. If you look at the sum total of all the projects I have announced that were targeted, the sum total of all of them is less than the total cost of that single road,' he said.

'As things stand, I had to make a choice because of the cost of the project and because of how we can spend scarce additional resources.'

Mr Donohoe rejected criticisms, saying he had a choice to make given the cost of the road. 'That is why we had to make choices as to what we could do,' he said.

Source: Article adapted from the *Irish Examiner*, 3 January 2016

Individuals, businesses and governments make rational choices when faced with scarce resources. A rational choice is one where the expected gains outweigh the expected losses.

When choosing between two or more alternatives, we will choose the one that will provide us with the greatest benefit or satisfaction from our limited resources. For example, if we are shopping for a new phone, we will make the rational choice to purchase from the shop that is selling the phone we want at the cheapest price.

33.2 If you were minister for finance and had to make choices about government spending, what would you prioritise? Go to www.peoplesbudget.ie and decide how you would make the best use of limited resources. Write a paragraph on how you made your decisions.

33.3 In a class discussion, debate the choices you have made. Would other people have made different choices? Why?

KSBC
KSMIT
KSC
KSMM
KSBL

Factors of production

Definition

The **factors of production** are the economic resources needed to produce goods and services.

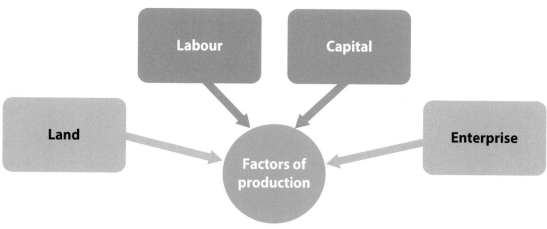

Figure 33.1 Factors of production

Land

Land refers to the things provided with the help of nature that are used to produce goods and services. Examples include: sea, fields, rivers, mines, forests and climate.

Some resources are non-renewable, which means that they are limited in supply, e.g. oil, coal.

Other resources are renewable, e.g. solar power, wind energy, water. The **reward** for this factor is **rent**.

Labour

Labour refers to the people involved in producing a good or service, e.g. teachers, electricians, carpenters, factory workers, games developers. Labour is scarce as it is limited to people who are available to work and have the skills required by business. The **reward** for this factor is **wages**.

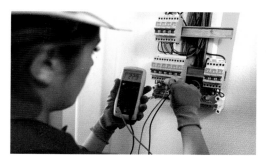

Capital

Capital refers to the physical items used in the production of goods or services, e.g. buildings, machinery, vehicles, computers, etc. The **reward** for this factor is **interest**.

Enterprise

Enterprise is the factor of production that brings together land, labour and capital to produce a product or a service. It involves a person having an idea and taking a personal and financial risk in setting up a business. This person is known as an entrepreneur. Enterprise is scarce as not everyone possesses the skills and characteristics needed to start and run their own business successfully. The **reward** for this factor is **profit**.

See Chapter 17

Every business needs to bring these four factors of production together to produce goods and services.

For example, the factors of production for Ben and Jerry's ice cream will be:

Land	Cows that produce the milk graze on the land, while sugar beet and fruit are grown to make flavourings for the ice cream
Labour	Ben & Jerry's employ staff to produce ice cream
Capital	Machinery and equipment are required to make the ice cream, while delivery vans are needed to deliver it to shops
Enterprise	Ben Cohen and Jerry Greenfield founded the business by investing $12,000 and opening a shop in a former gas station in Vermont, USA in 1978 after they completed a course in ice cream making

33.4 Choose an entrepreneur or business you are familiar with, which may be local, national or international. Using the template provided in the Student Activity Book, show how the entrepreneur or business has used each factor of production to produce a good or service. Using the template, create a poster, infographic, presentation or video to present your results to your classmates.

KSBC
KSMIT
KSC
KSWwO

Scarcity

Economic resources have three things in common:

> They have value
> They have alternative uses
> They are scarce or limited in supply.

We do not have endless supplies of land, labour, capital or enterprise to meet the wants, or indeed the needs, of all people.

As resources are scarce, choices must be made about:

> **What** will be produced. This may depend on supply of raw materials and demand for products.

> **How** it will be produced. In the past most goods were produced by people, but increasingly goods are produced by machinery.

> **Where** it will be produced. This is influenced by the availability of factors of production, including raw materials and labour.

> **Who** will receive the goods and services.

See Chapter 35

Most people in the developed world have similar needs and wants: for goods such as clothes, food, houses, furniture and electrical equipment, and services/service providers such as electricians, satellite TV and broadband. As consumers, we depend on different sectors of the economy to supply us with these goods and services.

33.5 List the needs and wants a person may have at different times in their lives, e.g. going to college, getting married, buying a house, having a baby, retirement. Divide these needs and wants into goods and services.

33.6 What are the needs and wants of people living in:

(a) A drought-stricken country?

(b) A war-ravaged country?

KSMIT

Key Terms

KSBL
KSC
KSMIT
KSBC

You should be able to *define*, *spell*, give *examples* and *apply* to real life each of the following key terms associated with this topic.

Exercise: Write a sentence using each of the following terms. You may use more than one of the terms in your sentence if appropriate.

capital	land
economics	needs
enterprise	opportunity cost
factors of production	rational choice
financial cost	scarcity
labour	wants

Chapter 34 :: Distribution of Economic Resources

What is an economy?

An **economy** refers to the way in which goods and services are made, sold and used in a country or area. The goal of an economy is to make the most effective use of available resources. This involves making choices about how best to maximise output and benefits while minimising costs. Sometimes, poor choices and improper use of resources can cause businesses, and even entire economies, to fail.

Economic resources

In this chapter we will focus on the way in which economies choose to allocate and distribute available resources in order to maximise outputs and minimise costs.

Economic resources are the inputs that are used to create things or provide services, i.e. land, labour, capital and enterprise.

See Chapter 33

Economic systems

Countries have to make the best use of their scarce resources. Choices have to be made about:

> What goods and services are to be produced
> Who will produce them, and
> Who will receive them.

The amount of choice that individuals have depends on the economic system in the country.

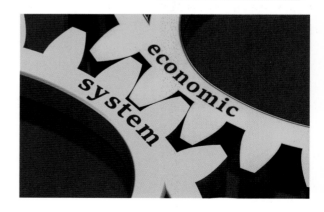

An **economic system** is the method by which countries distribute economic resources and trade goods and services.

Definition

An economic system deals with:

> Allocation of scarce resources
> Production of economic outputs (goods and services)
> Distribution of goods and services across the economy
> The role of the government and non-government sectors of the economy.

There are a number of different economic systems and each country must make a choice about which is most suited to its economic needs, values and preferences.

The three most common economic systems are:

> A centrally planned economy
> A free market economy
> A mixed economy.

Centrally planned economy

A centrally planned economy is one where the government has a lot of control over economic resources and decision-making.

Communism is the most extreme example of a centrally planned economy. Under this economic model the state controls all of the factors of production and makes all the decisions about what goods and services will be produced. All firms are owned by the government and private citizens have no involvement in business ownership. North Korea and Cuba are examples of centrally planned economies.

Figure 34.1 Havana, Cuba: a centrally planned economy

Free market economy

A free market (or **capitalist**) economy is one where private individuals control resources, own businesses and make all decisions about what goods and services will be produced. Prices are determined by the level of demand from consumers and the willingness of businesses to supply goods and services. The USA is an example of a free enterprise economy.

See Chapter 35

Figure 34.2 Washington DC, USA: a free enterprise economy

Mixed economy

A mixed economy is one that combines elements of the free market and centrally planned systems. It involves sharing the production of goods and services between government and private individuals. Ireland is an example of a mixed economy.

Figure 34.3 Bus services in Ireland: a mixed economy

While most goods and services are produced by private businesses, there is still significant government involvement in services such as security, health and education, as well as other services. For example, if a consumer wishes to travel to Galway from Dublin by bus, they can use Bus Éireann (public sector), GoBus or Citylink (both of which are private sector).

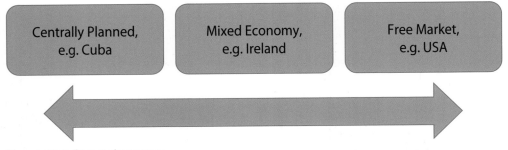

Figure 34.4 Economic systems

Centrally planned and free market systems lie at opposite ends of the economic spectrum while a mixed economy, with elements of both of these systems, lies somewhere in the middle.

In reality, there are no examples of purely free market or centrally planned economies in the world today and every country combines both systems to some degree. Countries that have 'big government' involvement are socialist in nature. Examples include China, Denmark and Sweden. These economies have:

> High personal taxation

> A high level of state services

> A more equal distribution of wealth and resources.

As we move towards the free market end of the spectrum, the level of government involvement decreases. Examples of countries that operate this type of economic system include the USA, Hong Kong and Singapore. These economies have:

> Lower levels of taxation

> Lower levels of public services

> A less equitable distribution of wealth and economic resources

> A huge income gap between the rich and the poor in society.

34.1 Research some examples of centrally planned and free market economies in the world today. Think about the benefits and drawbacks of each system. Write a report on your findings and make conclusions.

Research

KSMIT
KSBL
KSC

34.2 Discuss with a partner which economic system you think is best. Justify your answer with examples.

Sectors of the economy

In Ireland, goods and services are produced and distributed through three sectors:

> Public sector
> Private sector
> Third sector.

Public sector

The public sector is the part of the economy that is owned and controlled by the government. It provides services to the public that may not be provided by the private sector. It consists of local and national government and state-owned organisations.

Sectors of the economy

Public — National government
Public — Local government
Public — State-owned businesses

Private — Sole traders
Private — Partnerships
Private — Limited companies

Third — Social enterprises
Third — Non-profit-making organisations

Local government

Ireland has thirty-one local authorities. These provide a range of public services locally. Local authorities promote the interests of the local community, and provide:

> Housing
> Planning services
> Road maintenance
> Fire services
> Pollution control
> Local environment protection
> Facilities and services to support art, culture, sports, leisure, libraries and recreation.

34.3 What is the name of your local authority?

34.4 What is:

(a) The website address of your local authority?

(b) The postal address of your local authority?

34.5 Create a poster with the title 'Know your local authority' to explain how it serves the community.

National government

Government departments provide a range of services. Table 34.1 shows some examples.

Table 34.1 Government departments and what they do

Department	Services provided
Department of Health	Hospitals, treatment, surgeries, healthcare
Department of Education and Skills	Education and training, schools, examinations
Department of Agriculture, Food and the Marine	Support services to agriculture, fisheries, food and forestry
Department of Arts, Heritage, Regional, Rural and Gaeltacht Affairs	Conserves, preserves, protects and presents Ireland's heritage and culture and promotes regional development
Department of Communications, Climate Action & Environment	Responsible for the telecommunications and broadcasting sectors and regulates, protects and develops Ireland's natural resources

34.6 Search the government's website, www.gov.ie and research the services provided by the other government departments. In the search box on the website enter 'Departments of state'. Create a poster showing all the government departments and the services they provide, using table 34.1 as a template.

Research

KSBC
KSMIT
KSBL
KSC

State-owned organisations

State-owned organisations are organisations established by the government. There are two categories:

> **Commercial**, which charge for their product or service
> **Non-commercial**, which provide services free of charge that are seen as necessary to develop the country.

Table 34.2 shows some examples of commercial and non-commercial state-owned organisations.

Table 34.2 Examples of commercial and non-commercial state-owned organisations

Commercial state-owned organisations	
Transport	> Bus Éireann > Irish Rail > Dublin Bus > Dublin Airport Authority
Entertainment	> RTÉ
Communications	> An Post
Energy	> Electric Ireland > Ervia (formerly known as Bord Gáis)
Natural resources	> Coillte > Bord na Móna
Non-commercial state-owned organisations	
Regulation	> Environmental Protection Agency > Health and Safety Authority
Marketing	> Fáilte Ireland > Bord Iascaigh Mhara > Bord Bia
Development of business	> Enterprise Ireland > Local Enterprise Offices > IDA Ireland

Private sector

The private sector refers to businesses owned by individuals that produce and sell goods and services with the aim of making a profit. Private sector businesses can be classified as

See Chapter 17

> Sole traders   > Partnerships   > Limited companies.

Table 34.3 Private sector businesses

Business	Logo	Sector
Eir	eir	Telecommunications
Ryanair	RYANAIR	Transport

34.7 Create a poster showing the names and logos of ten private sector businesses. Make sure to include local and national examples.

Research

KSMIT
KSBC

Third sector

The third sector consists of social enterprises and not-for-profit organisations such as charities and voluntary organisations. These not-for-profit, citizen-based groups that operate independently of government are often referred to as **non-governmental organisations (NGOs)**.

Not-for-profit organisations

Charities are set up to benefit others by raising money, either through collections, events or charity shops. They depend largely on volunteers. The aims of charities depend on the cause for which they were established, but include: relieving poverty, helping the vulnerable, and providing funding for animal welfare and medical research. Table 34.4 shows some examples of national charities.

See Chapter 19

Table 34.4 Examples of national charities

Charity	Logo	Aim
Oxfam	OXFAM Ireland	To reduce poverty
ISPCA (Irish Society for the Prevention of Cruelty to Animals)	ISPCA CARING FOR ALL ANIMALS	To prevent cruelty to all animals, through education, legislation and ongoing support for its 20 affiliated societies
Focus Ireland	FOCUS IRELAND	Works to support people who are homeless or are at risk of losing their homes across Ireland
Irish Cancer Society	Irish Cancer Society	Provides free, nationwide services for cancer patients and their families, funds innovative cancer research to find better ways of diagnosing and treating cancer, advocates for cancer patients at a public policy level

34.8 In pairs or small groups, research a charity local to you and identify:

(a) Who they support

(b) What services they provide

(c) How they raise money.

Present your findings as a poster or presentation and display it for the rest of the class.

KSMIT
KSC
KSBC
KSWwO
KSBL

Voluntary organisations

Voluntary organisations provide services for their members. They raise finance by charging a membership fee and sometimes by organising fund-raisers. They are managed and run by an elected committee, with help from volunteers. Examples include golf clubs, GAA clubs, tennis clubs and Scouts Ireland.

34.9 In small groups, research local clubs.

(a) Create a map of your local area and indicate where each club is located.

(b) Create a poster with a brief outline of local clubs, which can be used to inform people who move to your area.

KSMIT
KSC
KSBC
KSSW
KSBL
KSWwO

Social enterprises

Social enterprises, unlike private sector businesses, have a social or environmental aim. While they are run in a business-like way, they aim to make a profit to benefit a specific cause rather than the owners.

See Chapter 17

34.10 Choose a social enterprise that you know of, or find one through an internet search.

Find out:

(a) The name of the social enterprise

(b) The name of the entrepreneur(s) involved

(c) The aims of the social enterprise

(d) The products it sells or service it provides.

KSMIT
KSC
KSBC
KSBL

Present your findings to your classmates in an infographic or presentation.

Research

KSBC
KSMIT
KSC
KSBL

34.11 The following are examples of third-sector organisations:

> DSPCA

> Irish Cancer Society

> ISPCC

> Jack and Jill Foundation

> GAA.

Select one of these organisations or a local example you know of. Write a short report on your chosen organisation under the following headings:

(a) History of the organisation

(b) Aims and objectives

(c) Sources of finance

(d) Services provided.

The circular flow of income

The circular flow of income illustrates the movement of economic resources and wealth throughout the economy.

In a simple closed economy (which has no imports or exports) households provide businesses with factors of production (land, labour, capital and enterprise). In return for these resources, businesses will pay households a reward.

KSMIT

34.12 What is the reward for each of the following?

(a) Land   **(c)** Capital

(b) Labour   **(d)** Enterprise

This flow of resources and rewards between households and businesses is illustrated in figure 34.5.

Businesses use these factors to produce goods and services, which they sell to households.

Households in turn spend money on the goods and services produced by firms. This money is then used by firms to pay households for their work.

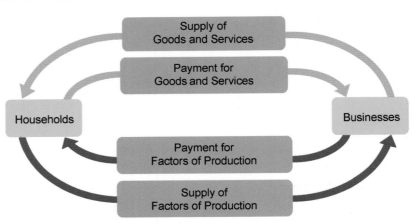

Figure 34.5 Circular flow of income A

This process repeats itself and creates a circular flow of income in the economy. The circular flow of income diagram in figure 34.5 illustrates that expenditure on goods and services is equal to the income received by households. As a result we can say that:

$$National\ income = National\ expenditure$$

In an economy where households do not spend all their income, savings will create a leak from the circular flow. Banks will in turn lend this money and it will be returned or injected back into the economy in the form of investment.

In an economy where the government plays a role, some of the income leaks from the circular flow as households and businesses pay taxes to government. In most economies, this money is returned to the circular flow through government spending.

In an open economy like Ireland, which is heavily involved in international trade, imports and exports impact on the circular flow of income. Money spent on imports is a leakage from the circular flow, while revenue generated by exports injects money back into the economy.

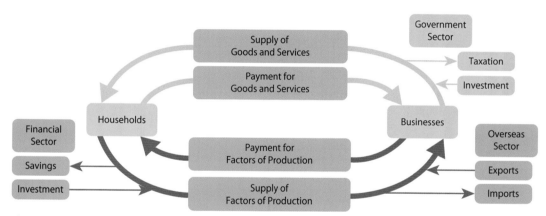

Figure 34.6 Circular flow of income B

Key Terms

KSBL
KSC
KSMIT
KSBC

You should be able to *define*, *spell*, give *examples* and *apply* to real life each of the following key terms associated with this topic.

Exercise: Write a sentence using each of the following terms. You may use more than one of the terms in your sentence if appropriate.

centrally planned economy

circular flow of income

factors of production

free market economy

mixed economy

private sector

public sector

third sector

Chapter 35 :: Demand and Supply

What is a market?

A **market** is a place where buyers and sellers interact in order to trade or exchange goods and services.  **Definition**

Most markets are actual locations where buyers and sellers meet and exchange goods and services (e.g. supermarkets and farmers' markets). These are known as **final markets** as they are where finished goods and services are bought and sold.

Other markets include:

› **Factor markets**, where the factors of production are bought and sold. This includes the property market, labour market, money market and stock market.

See Chapter 33

› **Commodities markets**, where raw materials used in the production of goods and services are bought and sold, e.g. agricultural products, energies (oil, gas, etc.) and metals (gold, silver, copper, etc.).

In each case it is the presence of buyers and sellers that creates a market.

Consumer behaviour

Economists make the following assumptions about consumer behaviour:

1 Consumers are rational, which means that they will choose the cheaper option if offered two similar goods at different prices.

2 Consumers will have to make choices to get the best use out of their limited resources.

3 Consumers will try to get as much benefit (known as *utility* in economics) as possible from their limited resources.

4 The benefit a consumer receives from consuming a good or service reduces over time. This is known as the *law of diminishing marginal utility*. For example, you will enjoy one bar of chocolate and perhaps two, but the more chocolate you consume, the less you will enjoy each bar.

Demand

Demand refers to the quantity of a product that consumers are willing to buy at a given price.

Definition

We have seen how businesses carry out market research to gather information about the market for their goods and services. As part of that research they try to find out how much of a particular product consumers are willing to buy. They also try to discover how much consumers are willing to pay for the product. This type of research helps a business to establish the level of demand for their goods and services.

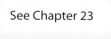
See Chapter 23

Effective demand is a willingness to buy, backed up by an ability to pay. Effective demand is real or actual demand.

Demand for a product is rarely fixed and will tend to change over time.

> **35.1** Think of products that were strongly in demand a few years ago, but for which there is very little demand nowadays. What factors have caused the level of demand for these products to change?
>
> **35.2** Identify products or services for which the level of demand is seasonal, i.e. demand varies depending on the time of year. Does the price of these goods vary at different times of the year? Explain or justify your answer with relevant examples.

KSMIT
KSBL
KSC

Many factors influence the level of demand for a product, but its **price** is the most important.

Price refers to the amount of money expected or paid for a product or service. Sometimes the price is set by the seller alone; in some markets it is agreed between the buyers and sellers.

In general, lower prices will increase demand for a product. This is because a lower price makes the product more attractive for buyers.

The opposite is also true and higher prices will tend to reduce demand for a product. When the price increases, buyers may choose to stop buying a product entirely, or they may switch to buying an alternative product instead.

> For most goods and services:
>
> › Demand will increase when price is reduced.
> › Demand will fall when price increases.

There are many real-world examples that illustrate this relationship between demand and price:

› Elite professional sports stars are in great demand and have the highest transfer prices and wage levels.

› In the housing market, increased demand for family homes in the Dublin area has caused prices to rise.

› Ticket prices for very popular sporting and music events will be higher than less popular ones and this reflects the expected level of demand.

› Hotel and flight prices generally increase during school holidays as this is a peak season for family holidays or travel. In the winter many hotels offer reduced price 'special offers' in an effort to create extra demand during the off season.

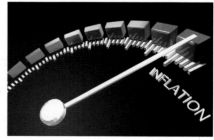

These examples illustrate that an increase in demand creates inflationary pressure and causes prices to rise in the market.

Inflation is a sustained increase in the general level of prices from one period to another.

See Chapter 38

Definition

Demand schedule

A demand schedule shows the number of goods demanded by customers at different price levels.

Here is a demand schedule for a mobile phone Sonix424. It shows the number of phones that customers would buy per month at various prices.

The demand schedule indicates that a price increase from €50 to €100 will see a fall in the number of mobile phones demanded per month (from 200 units to 160 units).

Table 35.1 Demand schedule

Price	Quantity demanded
€50	200
€100	160
€150	120
€200	80

Demand curve

We can use the information from the demand schedule to plot a demand curve for the Sonix424 mobile phone. See figure 35.1.

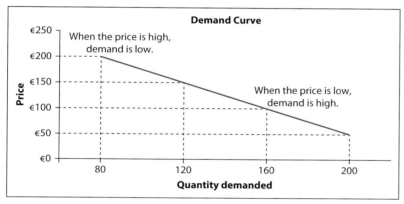

Figure 35.1 Demand curve for a Sonix424 mobile phone

A **demand curve** is a graph that illustrates the expected demand for a product at various price levels.

When drawing a demand curve, the horizontal (x) axis indicates the number of products demanded at a given price, while the vertical (y) axis shows the various prices that may be charged.

Figure 35.1 illustrates that a small quantity is demanded at higher prices whereas demand increases when the price is reduced.

Figure 35.1 also illustrates that price changes cause movements *along* a demand curve.

Under normal market conditions *a business cannot control both price and demand*. For example, if the price of the Sonix424 mobile is set at €200 the level of demand is decided by consumers. And as we have seen, they will tend to reduce their demand for the product at higher prices.

35.3 From the point of view of *sales revenue*, can you explain whether a retailer of Sonix424 mobile phones would be better off with a selling price of €50 or €100? Explain your answer.

KSBN
KSMIT

Other factors affecting demand

Demand for a product can be affected by other factors apart from price.

A change in these factors will cause the demand curve to shift left or right. An improvement in demand conditions will cause the demand curve to shift to the right. A negative change in demand conditions will cause the demand curve to shift to the left. This is shown in figure 35.2.

These factors include the following.

Figure 35.2 Shifts in a demand curve

1 Price of substitute products

When the price of beef increases, so too does the demand for substitute products, such as chicken and pork, as people switch to cheaper alternatives.

2 Price of complementary goods

A complementary good is a product that is used with another product, e.g. apps and a mobile phone. If the price of the complementary product decreases, demand for the original product will increase.

3 Fads and fashions

As consumer tastes change, demand for products will also change. Those goods or brands that are fashionable will see a sharp increase in demand while those that are unfashionable will experience reduced levels of demand.

Social factors often play a big part in creating demand for certain products. For example, your demand for social media applications (Facebook, Snapchat, WhatsApp, etc.) is very much driven by the choices of your friends and peers. If you wish to connect to them you'll need to choose the same apps, but if they stop using a particular app, your demand for it will probably decline also.

4 Advertising

Products that are heavily advertised may see an increase in demand. This in turn is likely to create extra demand in the medium term.

5 Changes in population or market size

An increase in the birth rate will lead to increased demand for baby products. In a similar way, population trends can also impact on demand for housing and public services.

6 Seasonal factors

Demand for some products changes depending on the time of year. Obvious examples include chocolate products at Christmas and Easter, ski clothing in winter, ice cream in summer.

7 Price expectations of buyers

If buyers expect future prices to increase they may increase current demand to try to beat the price rise. If, on the other hand, buyers expect future prices to fall, they may delay their purchase in order to avail of lower prices. This will reduce current demand.

8 Income levels

Demand for **normal goods** rises when income rises. If a person's income increases they will be able to buy more expensive goods and services. They may, for example, choose to buy more expensive cuts of meat, more premium-brand clothing, or a more expensive car.

With **inferior goods**, demand falls when the income rises. Cheaper cuts of meat and own-brand products are examples of inferior goods as consumers will tend to demand less of them when their income increases. For many consumers, buying generic or own-brand goods is a sensible choice when income levels decline and is in keeping with the guidelines for effective household budgeting.

See Chapter 5

The term **inferior** does not refer to the quality of the goods but simply reflects the affordability of the goods. It is an economic term that indicates that these goods will experience a drop in demand when income increases.

35.4 In pairs, discuss the following list of goods and services. Decide which are examples of normal goods and which are examples of inferior goods.

> Instant noodles
> Diamonds
> Gym memberships
> Sony plasma screen TVs
> Potatoes
> Generic MP3 players
> Bread
> BMW cars

> Public transport
> Sausages
> Foreign holidays
> Organic fruit and vegetables
> Second-hand cars
> Own-brand breakfast cereal

Supply

Supply refers to the quantity of a product that producers are willing to make available for sale at a given price.

Most producers are willing to supply more of a good when its price increases. This is because there is potential to sell more goods and at greater profit margins.

See Chapter 33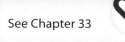

Less efficient producers who are unable to compete at lower prices are also likely to enter the market when the selling price is higher. This will also increase the supply of goods available in the market.

> For most goods and services:
>
> › Supply will increase when price is increased.
> › Supply will reduce when the selling price drops.

There are many real-world examples that illustrate this relationship between supply and price:

› Global oil and gas prices fell when countries with these commodities produced more oil. The increase in supply resulted in lower gas and oil prices for households and businesses.

› A very warm summer may lead to a bumper crop of strawberries. To get rid of the excess supply, farmers will need to lower the price of strawberries. This lower price should encourage consumers to buy more strawberries.

› Following a bad spell of weather there may be a shortage of wheat available. The price of wheat will increase dramatically.

› If a large number of new workers arrive in a city, the supply of labour may be greater than the number of jobs available. This excess supply of labour is likely to drive wages down, especially if the new arrivals are willing to accept low-wage employment.

Supply schedule

A supply schedule shows how much a firm will be willing to supply at particular prices

The supply schedule shown in table 35.2 illustrates the quantity of mobile phones (model Sonix424) that the producer is willing to supply (per week) at various prices.

Table 35.2 Supply schedule

Price	Quantity supplied
€50	80
€100	100
€150	120
€200	140

Supply curve

We can use the information from the supply schedule to plot a supply curve for the Sonix424 mobile phone.

> A **supply curve** is a graph that illustrates the quantity of a product that a seller is willing and able to supply at a series of price points.

Definition

Figure 35.3 illustrates that changes in price will cause movements *along* the supply curve.

Other factors affecting supply

As we saw with demand, other factors apart from price can impact on the quantity of goods supplied. These factors will cause the supply curve to *shift* right or left at a given price. An improvement in supply conditions will cause the supply curve to shift to the right. A negative change in supply conditions will cause the supply curve to shift to the left (see figure 35.4). The following factors can all affect supply.

1 Environmental conditions

Weather can impact on the supply of crops available. For example, a very wet summer may reduce the wheat harvest and will cause the supply curve to shift to the left. This indicates a reduced level of supply at each price point.

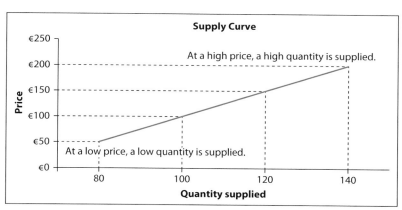

Figure 35.3 Supply curve for a Sonix424 mobile phone

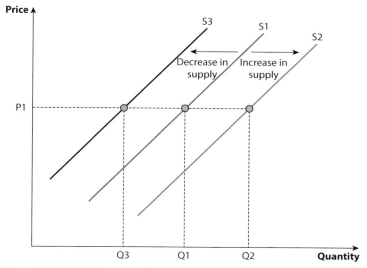

Figure 35.4 Shifts in a supply curve

Since wheat is an important commodity and is used as an ingredient in many other products, a poor harvest is also likely to lead to price increases and will have knock-on effects across a whole range of industries including confectionery and brewing.

A **commodity** refers to a raw material or primary agricultural product that can be bought and sold. Other examples include copper and coffee.

35.5 List three other products or commodities that have similar knock-on effects across a range of industries.

2 The price of related goods

Changes in the price of substitute and complementary goods can impact on the supply of a product.

For example, an increase in the price of rival mobile phones (substitute products) will increase the supply of Sonix424s made available, whereas a decrease in the price of rival phones will reduce the supply of Sonix424 phones made available across a range of prices.

> **35.6** Why do you think substitute goods have this effect on supply?

A reduction in mobile usage charges (a **complementary service**) will see an increase in mobile phone usage and an increase in the supply of Sonix424 mobile phones. An increase in mobile usage charges will have the opposite effect and will see fewer Sonix424 phones being supplied.

> **35.7** Why do you think complementary goods have this effect on supply?

> **35.8** Outline your understanding of the terms 'substitute goods' and 'complementary goods' by giving an example of a substitute product and a complementary product for each of the following goods and services:
> - **(a)** A Zanussi dishwasher.
> - **(b)** Nescafé coffee.
> - **(c)** Potatoes.
> - **(d)** A train ticket to Galway.

3 Production and development costs

Producers of goods and services will incur costs. These costs include product development, manufacturing costs, wages, raw materials and transport costs. When costs are low, more goods will be supplied at all different price levels.

See Chapter 18

4 Technology

Technology tends to improve business efficiency and productivity. As a result of increased use of technology (robotics, for example) production costs may be reduced and this will lead to an increased level of supply.

See Chapter 21

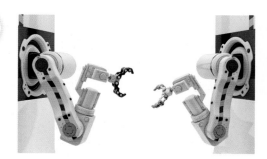

5 The number of suppliers

If new suppliers enter a market, supply will increase and prices will fall. The Irish retail sector experienced this effect with the arrival of many overseas supermarket chains, such as Aldi and Lidl. The entry of Ryanair into the marketplace also saw increased capacity (supply) and lower prices on flights between Ireland and Europe.

6 Expectations of sellers

If sellers expect prices to increase, they may store current supplies in the hope of selling them at a higher price in the future. The opposite will happen if suppliers think that prices will fall.

7 Government intervention

Taxes and government regulations can all impact on quantities supplied. Higher taxes and regulations will increase costs and reduce supply. Supply will also be reduced where quotas are applied.

> A **quota** is a limit on the number of goods made available for sale. For example, the fishing industry has a quota for the number of fish they may catch.

Finding a balance between supply and demand

In the marketplace, supply and demand interact until a balanced or **equilibrium** position is reached. At this price-point, the quantity supplied will equal the quantity demanded. This should mean that sellers can sell all that they produce and buyers can buy all that they want.

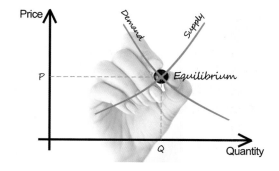

If we plot our supply and demand curves (from figures 35.1 and 35.3) on the same axis we can see the market equilibrium price level for the Sonix424 mobile phone as shown in figure 35.5.

The diagram clearly shows that supply will equal demand at a market price of €150. At this market equilibrium price, monthly demand is 120 units and this is also the quantity that sellers are willing to make available for sale.

When there is either excess supply or excess demand, the market

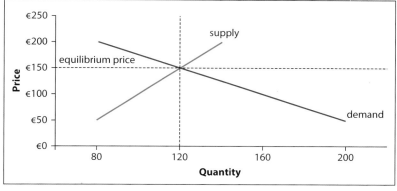

Figure 35.5 The market equilibrium price level for the Sonix424 mobile phone

will not be in an equilibrium position. The market is said to be in **disequilibrium**. When this happens the interaction of supply and demand will tend to create market pressures that will eventually force the market back into equilibrium.

For example, if there is excess supply, there are more goods available for sale than there is actually demand for, and so:

> In order to sell more of these goods, sellers will need to reduce their price.

> Sellers may also reduce production levels.

> As the price reduces, demand should increase as more consumers will be able to afford the items, while others may switch from competing products.

> Eventually the market will reach an equilibrium price at a point where supply equals demand.

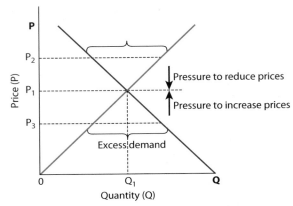

Figure 35.6 An excess of supply or demand

Similarly, when demand exceeds supply (excess demand), sellers can afford to charge a higher price because they realise that some buyers are willing to pay more to ensure they get goods that are in short supply. For example, many rare or limited-edition music releases carry a higher or premium price, which reflects their scarcity. Tickets for 'sold out' music or sporting events are likely to fetch very high prices on auction websites or the 'shadow market' (i.e. trading outside the law).

35.9 Discuss the 'shadow market' with a partner and share your answers with the class.

(a) Give examples of products that are often sold on the shadow market.

(b) Outline your understanding of the shadow market.

(c) Explain how this type of market has a negative impact on the legitimate or official economy.

The **law of supply and demand** explains how the interaction of supply and demand affects the price of goods and services.

We have already seen that high levels of demand for a good will cause the price of that good to rise. Equally, if there is a large supply of a good but not enough demand, the price of that good will fall.

Let's now examine how the law of supply and demand operates in the property market and how the interaction of supply and demand will set an equilibrium price for property.

Supply and demand in action

Interaction of supply and demand in the property market

Each housing transaction involves a buyer and a seller. When there is high demand for property in a particular area and good-quality housing is in short supply, house prices will tend to rise.

During the Irish property boom (2000–2006) an increase in demand led to strong price inflation over a number of years. This extra demand was caused by the interaction of several factors, including:

> **Income levels:** Wage and employment levels in a booming economy were on the rise. Low interest rates made borrowing cheaper, so buyers in general had more money to spend.

> **Price of alternatives:** Increases in housing rental costs encouraged many people to consider buying their own property.

> **Fads and fashions:** Home ownership became 'trendy' and homes in some locations were extremely desirable. This caused very large price increases in many areas, particularly near major towns and cities. It was also quite common for people to own investment properties (properties they let out for the rental income) and this further fuelled demand.

> **Changes in population and market size:** There was a large increase in the number of new buyers entering the property market. Increased demand for investment properties and easy access to mortgage finance encouraged many new consumers to consider home ownership.

> **Price expectations of buyers:** As market prices continued to rise, consumers began to see this as an inevitable trend. Many looked to get on the 'property ladder' as they expected future price rises to make property unaffordable for them.

> **Advertising:** Property was heavily advertised and mentioned in the media. This helped heighten the significance or fashionability of home ownership.

On the supply side, there was an initial shortage of good-quality family homes and also a shortage of available land on which to build them. Over time the land shortage became less of a problem as more land was rezoned for housing.

In this climate of strong demand and rising property prices it was very much a **sellers' market** and many houses were sold for prices that exceeded the original asking price. Many sellers held auctions to ensure that they achieved the best possible price for their property.

Prices in the Irish property market peaked in 2006.

By 2007 property prices levelled out and the market reached an equilibrium position. Rising prices and a weak economy reduced demand, and supply increased as property developers speculated on future profit potential.

From 2007 to 2013, demand for Irish property declined enormously and there was a large oversupply of property in some areas. Mortgage approvals also declined by nearly 75%.

In keeping with the law of supply and demand, Irish property prices crashed. In some areas of the country house prices fell by over 50% between 2007 and 2010. Prices of apartments fell by even greater amounts.

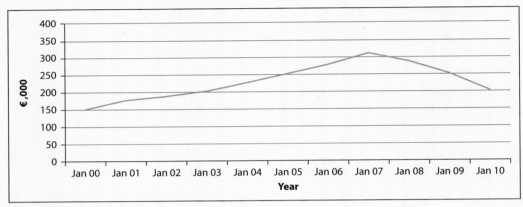

Figure 35.7 House prices in Ireland (2000–2010)

This example illustrates how the constant interaction of supply and demand impacts on market prices. It also illustrates clearly that demand, supply and price are all market variables.

Discussion

Answer these questions based on the discussion in the Supply and Demand in Action panel.

35.10 Discuss the interaction of supply and demand at an auction. Suggest a reason why sellers of property or rare antiques often use auctions to sell their goods.

35.11 What might be the reasons for the prices of apartments to fall more quickly than the prices of houses?

KSWwO
KSMIT
KSBL
KSC

Key Terms

You should be able to *define*, *spell*, give *examples* and *apply* to real life each of the following key terms associated with this topic.

Exercise: Write a sentence using each of the following terms. You may use more than one of the terms in your sentence if appropriate.

commodity	market
complementary goods	market equilibrium
demand	normal goods
demand curve	quota
equilibrium	substitute goods
inferior goods	supply
inflation	supply curve

KSBL
KSC
KSMIT
KSBC

Chapter 36 :: The Purpose of Taxation

Learning outcomes

When you have completed this chapter you will be able to:

✔ Explain the term 'taxation'
✔ Outline the principles of a fair tax system
✔ Examine the purpose of tax from a financial, social, legal and ethical point of view.

What is taxation?

Taxation is the process by which the government collects money from citizens and businesses to pay for public services.

> The **Office of the Revenue Commissioners** (Revenue for short) is the state body responsible for the assessment and collection of all taxes and duties in the Republic of Ireland.

Definition

Citizens and businesses must pay a range of different taxes and duties, for example:

› Tax on the income of employed people is deducted from their pay, collected by the employer through the PAYE system, and paid over to Revenue.

› Corporation tax on business profits is paid directly to Revenue.

› VAT on goods and services is included in the price of most products and services. It is collected by the supplier and paid over to Revenue.

› Excise duty is charged on tobacco products, alcohol products, petrol, diesel, cars and bets.

Revenue
Cáin agus Custaim na hÉireann
Irish Tax and Customs

See Chapters 12 and 37

The money collected is used to provide services to people living in Ireland, for example to build schools, hospitals and roads, and to pay the wages of teachers, nurses and gardaí.

Principles of a fair tax system

While few people *want* to pay taxes, most realise that they are necessary and provide benefits.

Taxes must be fairly imposed on all people living in a country. Adam Smith, an economist who lived in the eighteenth century, described principles of taxation (which he called the canons of taxation) in his book *The Wealth of Nations*. Although this was published in 1776, these principles are still used by governments when imposing taxes.

A fair tax system should have the following principles:

> **Equality:** The amount of tax that a person has to pay should be related to their ability to pay, i.e. those who earn more should pay more.

> **Certainty:** The amount of tax a person must pay should be clear and predictable.

> **Economy:** The cost of collecting a tax should be less than the amount that will be collected.

> **Convenience:** It should be easy for each person to pay their taxes when they fall due. For example, VAT is easy for an individual to pay since the tax is included in the price we pay for a good or service.

AN

INQUIRY

INTO THE

NATURE AND CAUSES

OF THE

WEALTH OF NATIONS.

By ADAM SMITH, LL.D. F.R.S.

WITH

A LIFE OF THE AUTHOR.

ALSO,

A VIEW OF THE DOCTRINE OF SMITH,

COMPARED WITH THAT OF THE FRENCH ECONOMISTS; WITH A METHOD
OF FACILITATING THE STUDY OF HIS WORKS; FROM
THE FRENCH OF M. GARNIER.

IN THREE VOLUMES.

VOL. I.

EDINBURGH:

PRINTED FOR STIRLING AND SLADE, ADAM BLACK, AND FAIR-
BAIRN AND ANDERSON, EDINBURGH; LACKINGTON AND CO.
J. CUTHELL, R. PRIESTLY, R. SCHOLEY, G. COWIE AND CO. T.
AND J. ALLMAN, G. MACKIE, AND J. BUMPUS, LONDON.

Along with Smith's canons of taxation, **tax should *not act as a disincentive***. This means that if taxes are too high, people may decide that it is not worthwhile working as the Revenue may take most of their income. Likewise, if corporation taxes are too high, it may discourage people from being entrepreneurial and prevent existing businesses expanding. Excessively high taxes can lead to the emergence of a shadow economy, where people evade tax.

See Chapter 12

The government uses tax to **redistribute income**. A fair tax system should be used to collect money from those who earn higher incomes in order to look after those in our society who need help, e.g. to provide unemployment benefit to those who do not have a job.

36.1 Discuss whether each of the following taxes follow the principles of (i) equality, (ii) certainty, (iii) economy, (iv) convenience.

Discussion

KSWwO
KSMIT

(a) Income tax (PAYE)

(b) VAT

(c) Capital gains tax

(d) Capital acquisitions tax

(e) Corporation tax.

36.2 In small groups, research answers to the following.

Groupwork

Research

KSMIT
KSBL
KSC
KSWwO

(a) Identify three taxes that the government collects from individuals.

(b) Identify three taxes that the government collects from businesses.

(c) List three different services provided by money raised through taxes in Ireland.

(d) Identify two new taxes that have been introduced in Ireland in recent years.

The purpose of taxation

Taxes are imposed for a variety of reasons, which can be classified under four main headings:

> Financial   > Social   > Legal   > Ethical.

Financial reasons

> **Financing the work of government:** The government uses the money to pay for the various services that it provides to people living in Ireland, e.g. education, health, policing, social welfare payments.

> **Meeting economic objectives:** Taxes may be used to control inflation. For example, if the prices of goods and services are increasing too quickly, the rate of PAYE may be increased so that take-home pay is less and people's disposable income is reduced, meaning they have less money to spend.

> **Assisting enterprise:** Money collected from taxes is used to encourage and help entrepreneurs. State bodies such as Enterprise Ireland and Local Enterprise Offices provide grants or services to entrepreneurs or businesses.

> **Servicing the national debt:** Interest and repayments have to be made on money borrowed by the government.

36.3 Research how much the Irish government pays each year on the interest on the national debt.

36.4 Calculate how much each person living in Ireland has to contribute to pay the interest on the national debt each year.

Research

KSMIT
KSBN

Social reasons

> **Redistributing wealth and income for the common good:** A major function of taxation is to transfer money from those on high incomes to those on lower or zero incomes. This allows the government to provide for those in our society who need help to bridge the gap between their actual income and what their income needs to be in order to have a reasonable standard of living.

> **Meeting social objectives:** Taxes are used to discourage people from engaging in certain behaviour that is bad for their health or bad for the environment. For example, excise duty is placed on tobacco and alcohol as their consumption can seriously harm a person's health.

Legal reasons

> **Fulfilling a legal requirement:** The payment of taxes due is compulsory under Irish law. Severe interest and penalties are due to those individuals and businesses who do not pay their taxes.

Ethical reasons

> **Fairness:** Tax must be fair and apply to everyone, depending on their ability to pay. The income lost to the state as a result of tax evasion reduces the amount available to be spent on essential services. This can lead to higher tax rates being imposed in order to collect more revenue.

See Chapter 12

In the news

Panama Papers show morals matter little – and only the little people pay their taxes

By Shane Phelan

The late US hotelier and real estate investor Leona Helmsley was once overheard uttering the immortal line that paying taxes was 'only for the little people'. She had time to reflect on this when she was jailed for filing incorrect tax returns back in the 1980s. While Helmsley's crime was relatively unsophisticated, systems for reducing, avoiding or illegally evading tax have evolved significantly since then. The use of offshore accounts in tax havens with deliberately poor disclosure and transparency laws has long been a way for the rich and powerful to hide their wealth.

But the disclosures made in the Panama Papers – over 11 million files leaked from the law firm Mossack Fonseca – reveal how the practice of concealing wealth is now being conducted on a truly industrial scale.

And while systems adopted by Western governments to combat tax dodgers have greatly improved, Helmsley's infamous statement still has more than a ring of truth to it.

The Panama Papers reveal how secretive offshore tax packages were created for world leaders, their associates, politicians and celebrities.

Billions of euro have been shielded from the view of tax authorities in this way.

One example was in Uganda, where a company wanted to sell an oil field and paid Mossack Fonseca to help it avoid paying $400m in taxes. The method used by the law firm to achieve this was simple: it moved the company's address from one tax haven to another.

The $400 m that should have been paid would have been more than Uganda's annual health budget. The Ugandan government tried unsuccessfully to have the tax paid. In the meantime, hospitals near the oil field lack equipment and infant mortality is high.

Source: Article adapted from the *Irish Independent*, 5 April 2016

36.5 In chapter 12 you learned about the difference between tax avoidance, which is legal, and tax evasion, which is not legal. Do you think that tax avoidance by individuals or businesses is ethical? Explain your reasons to your partner. Debate this with the rest of the class.

T-P-S

KSMIT
KSSW
KSBL
KSC

Key Terms

KSBL
KSC
KSMIT
KSBC

You should be able to *define*, *spell*, give *examples* and *apply* to real life each of the following key terms associated with this topic.

Exercise: Write a sentence using each of the following terms. You may use more than one of the terms in your sentence if appropriate.

certainty	PAYE
convenience	redistribution of wealth
economic objective	social objective
economy	standard of living
equality	tax
fairness	tax avoidance
inflation	tax evasion
Office of the Revenue Commissioners	taxation

Chapter 37 :: Government Revenue and Expenditure

The national budget

The role of the government is to run the country. Providing public services is an important part of this task. Ireland has a **mixed economy**, which means that some goods and services are provided by the private sector while the government (or public sector) provides many others.

 See Chapter 34

The government will need to make use of available **resources** to provide the best possible level of public services. Since the government doesn't have enough resources to meet all demands for public services, it will need to *prioritise* some services over others. This requires the government to make *choices* which will have both financial and opportunity costs.

For example, if the government chooses to spend €200 million on a new hospital, this money is not available for spending on schools, roads or museums. Those schools, roads and museums which cannot now be built represent the opportunity cost of building the hospital.

 See Chapter 1

Before making these kinds of choices the government will need to consider the revenue (or income) available to it.

Government revenue

Government revenue refers to all money received by the government.

 Definition

Government revenue can be divided into two distinct categories:

> **Current revenue** – money received by the government on a regular or day-to-day basis. The vast majority of this income comes from taxation.

See Chapter 36

> **Capital revenue** – money received on an irregular or once-off basis.

Major sources of government current revenue

> **Income tax:** Taxes on wages and salaries.

> **Universal Social Charge (USC):** Another tax on income.

See Chapter 12

> **Pay Related Social Insurance (PRSI):** Insurance paid by employers and employees, which is used to fund social welfare payments, such as illness benefit and maternity benefit.

> **Value added tax:** Tax on the value added to goods at each stage of their production. The burden of this tax falls on the consumers who buy the finished goods.

> **Corporation tax:** Tax on company profits.

> **Excise duty:** Tax charged on goods such as alcohol, tobacco and fuel products.

> **Customs duties:** A tax on goods coming into Ireland from countries outside the EU.

> **Local property tax:** Tax on residential properties.

> **Central Bank surplus income:** The role of the Central Bank is to manage the nation's money supply and to act as a 'lender of last resort' to banks during a financial crisis. If the Central Bank makes a profit on its operations, this money will be transferred to the government.

> **Capital gains tax (CGT):** Tax on the profits earned from investments. These profits usually arise from an increase in the value of shares or investment properties.

> **Capital acquisitions tax (CAT):** Tax on gifts and inheritances.

> **Dividends from State companies:** As the sole or major shareholder, the State is entitled to receive a share of any profits earned by State companies such as the ESB and An Post.

> **Stamp duty:** A tax for registering legal documents.

37.1 The table gives the government's budgeted figures for income in 2016.

(a) Calculate the percentage of overall revenue that each of the sources in the table represents.

(b) Create a pie chart or bar chart from this data.

(c) Do any of these figures surprise you? Comment on the figures.

(d) In pairs, create an infographic to display these figures.

Revenue source	Amount of revenue €m
Income taxes (including USC)	18,994
Value added tax (VAT)	12,860
PRSI	8,491
Corporation tax	6,614
Excise duties	5,643
Stamp duties	1,320
Central Bank surplus income	983
Capital gains tax (CGT)	589
Local property tax	438
Capital acquisitions tax (CAT)	375
Customs duties	391
Dividends	263
National Lottery surplus	203
Other sources	3,599
Total planned revenue	**60,763**

KSBN
KSMIT
KSWwO
KSBC
KSBL

Major sources of government capital revenue:

> **Sale of State-owned companies:** For example, in 2015 the government sold its 25% stake in Aer Lingus to the IAG group for €335 million.

> **Borrowings:** Our government borrows money from other governments or from financial institutions in order to fund its spending plans.

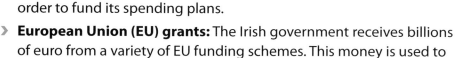

> **European Union (EU) grants:** The Irish government receives billions of euro from a variety of EU funding schemes. This money is used to support important economic and social projects.

See Chapter 42

Government expenditure

> **Government expenditure** refers to all money spent by the government.

Definition

Government expenditure can be divided into two categories:

> **Current expenditure:** money spent by the government on a regular or ongoing basis. The majority of government current expenditure involves the day-to-day provision of essential public services. Operating costs and wages for public sector workers account for a large portion of government current expenditure.

> **Capital expenditure:** spending on 'once-off' projects or on infrastructure that will have long-term benefits for the country.

> **Infrastructure** refers to the basic facilities, structures and services needed for a country to function. It includes water, power lines, transport, communications systems, schools and hospitals.

Definition

Examples of government current expenditure

> **Social protection:** Payments and income supports such as pensions, child benefits and jobseekers' benefits.

> **Healthcare:** Expenditure on the day-to-day running costs of hospitals and healthcare facilities, e.g. staff wages, buying medicines, and light and heat.

> **Education:** Expenditure to enable schools and colleges to be run efficiently, e.g. teachers' salaries, light and heat, and maintenance of school buildings.

> **Justice:** Expenditure to ensure our legal and judicial systems operate, e.g. judges' wages, garda wages and operating costs of prisons.

> **Agriculture:** Expenditure to help farmers and ensure this important sector is maintained, e.g. income supports to farmers and funding for a wide variety of rural development schemes.

> **Defence:** Expenditure to maintain defence of our country, e.g. wages to members of the defence forces and civilians working for the sector, maintenance of facilities, training costs, etc.

> **Transport and tourism:** Money spent on maintaining our existing transport systems as well as providing funding for tourism promotion agencies such as Fáilte Ireland.

Examples of government capital expenditure

› **Public transport:** Building new rail networks, buying new trains and buses.

› **Health:** Building new hospitals, buying new equipment and ambulances.

› **Education:** Building or extending schools, buying furniture and ICT equipment for schools.

37.2 The table gives the government's budgeted figures for expenditure in 2016 (with the department names correct at the time of the budget).

(a) Calculate the percentage of overall expenditure that each of the amounts in the table represents.

(b) Create a pie chart or bar chart from this data.

(c) Do any of these figures surprise you? Comment on the figures.

(d) In pairs, create an infographic to display these figures.

KSBN
KSMIT
KSWwO
KSBC

Expenditure	Amount spent €m
Social Protection	19,627
Health	13,175
Education & Skills	8,524
Justice & Equality	2,264
Agriculture, Food & the Marine	1,134
Children & Youth Affairs	1,113
Environment, Community & Local Government	957
Public Expenditure & Reform	940
Defence	837
Transport & Tourism	722
Foreign Affairs & Trade	694
Finance	430
Communications, Energy & Natural Resources	325
Jobs, Enterprise & Innovation	297
Art, Heritage & the Gaeltacht	234
Taoiseach	201
Total planned expenditure	**51,474**

Preparing a national budget

An Roinn Caiteachais Phoiblí
agus Athchóirithe
Department of Public
Expenditure and Reform

An Roinn Airgeadais
Department of Finance

The **national budget** is the government's financial plan for the year ahead.

The **Department of Finance** and the **Department of Public Expenditure and Reform** work together to ensure that the government has enough money to run the country. Each year the government must make a financial plan for the year ahead. It estimates how much money each government department will need in order to provide its services. It must also decide how to raise the income required to pay for these services. (See the tables in activities 37.1 and 37.2.)

See Chapter 36

The Department of Public Expenditure and Reform assesses each department's request for money and sanctions all government spending. The Department of Finance authorises all taxes and government borrowing.

Each year, the minister for finance outlines the government's financial plan for the coming year when the national budget is announced in the Dáil.

As with a household budget, the national budget sets out all the income that the government expects to receive. It also includes details of the government's spending plans.

A balanced budget

If the government expects that planned revenue will be equal to planned expenditure it will be a **balanced budget**.

The following figures illustrate a balanced budget situation:

Planned revenue (2019)	€52,876 million
Planned expenditure (2019)	€52,876 million
Balance	€0

In this situation the government is taking money out of the economy through taxation but is returning the same amount of money to the economy via spending on public services. For this reason a balanced budget is also called a **neutral budget**.

A budget surplus

If revenue is expected to be *greater* than planned expenditure, the government will have a **budget surplus**.

Just as with household budgeting, a budget surplus indicates that the government is living within its means and has some scope to cut taxes or increase the level of services it plans to provide.

See Chapter 5

The following figures illustrate a budget surplus:

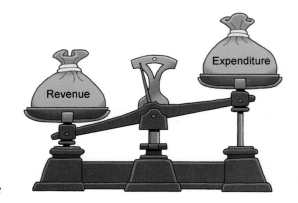

Planned revenue (2019)	€52,876 million
Planned expenditure (2019)	€50,000 million
Budget surplus	€2,876 million

In a surplus situation the government is taking more money out of the economy (through taxation) than it is putting back in (through spending). This will reduce the overall level of money and spending in the economy. Since it has the effect of making the economy smaller it is said to be a **contractionary budget**.

The government may choose to use this type of approach if it is concerned about inflation or the economy growing too quickly.

See Chapter 38

A budget deficit

If planned revenue is *less* than planned expenditure, the government will be facing a **budget deficit**. This indicates that the government is living beyond its means and will have to increase taxes, cut spending or borrow money to finance its plans.

The following figures illustrate a budget deficit:

Planned revenue (2019)	€52,876 million
Planned expenditure (2019)	€53,680 million
Budget deficit	(€804 million)

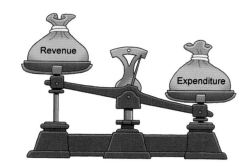

A budget deficit is generally seen as a negative outcome and often arises because the government has failed to meet its income targets or because public expenditure is out of control.

As a member of the EU, Ireland must also follow strict financial rules that aim to control budget deficits. For these reasons the government will try to keep its budget deficits to a minimum.

37.3 Look at the budget figures for 2016 in activities 37.1 and 37.2. Did the government expect to have a budget surplus, a balanced budget or a budget deficit in that year? Illustrate and explain your answer.

Figure 37.1 illustrates the pattern of budget surpluses and deficits in Ireland during a ten-year period (2006–2015).

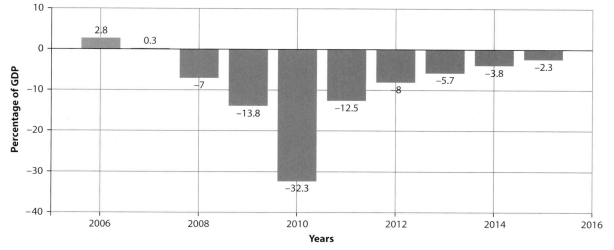

Figure 37.1 Ireland's budgets 2006–2015

37.4 In your group, discuss/comment on the trends and suggest possible reasons for them.

37.5 How does the figure you calculated for 2016 follow the trends you identified in activity 37.4?

KSWwO
KSMIT
KSBN
KSBL
KSC

In some circumstances, having a budget deficit, especially a small one, may be a deliberate and positive economic policy choice by the government.

See Chapter 39

A deficit means the government is injecting more money into the economy (through spending) than it is taking out (through taxation). A deliberate decision to do this is known as an **expansionary budget** because it will result in extra money and spending in the economy. The government may use this approach if it wishes to boost the level of economic growth.

Solutions to a budget deficit

There are three possible ways of reducing or eliminating a budget deficit and governments tend to use a combination of all three:

> **Increase planned revenue** – by raising taxation levels or selling state assets.
> **Reduce planned expenditure** – by cutting the level of public services.
> **Borrow money** – to bridge the gap between revenue and expenditure. This is a short-term solution since paying interest and repaying borrowings will impact on future budgets.

37.6 Discuss why a government would use a combination of all three strategies to resolve a budget deficit.

KSWwO
KSBL
KSMIT

Key Terms

KSBL
KSC
KSMIT
KSBC

You should be able to *define*, *spell*, give *examples* and *apply* to real life each of the following key terms associated with this topic.

Exercise: Write a sentence using each of the following terms. You may use more than one of the terms in your sentence if appropriate.

balanced budget

budget deficit

budget surplus

capital expenditure

capital revenue

current expenditure

current revenue

Department of Finance

Department of Public Expenditure
  and Reform

infrastructure

national budget

Learning outcomes

When you have completed this chapter you will be able to:

✔ Identify and explain each of the major economic indicators
✔ Describe the effects of the economic indicators on Ireland's households, businesses and the economy
✔ Calculate the rate of inflation
✔ Calculate the rate of economic growth.

Economic indicators

Economic indicators provide useful insights into the direction in which an economy is going, or is likely to go in the future.

These indicators are **pieces of economic information that highlight the condition of the economy** and allow economists to assess its overall health.

Depending on how well the economy is performing, the government may wish to continue with existing policies or adopt new ones to improve the situation.

In this chapter we will consider six economic indicators and will discuss their impact on households, businesses and the economy. They are:

> Inflation
> Employment levels
> Interest rates

> National debt
> National income
> Economic growth.

Inflation

Definition

Inflation is the increase in the general level of prices of goods and services from one year to the next.

The official rate of inflation is measured by the **consumer price index (CPI)**.

In Ireland, the Central Statistics Office (CSO) collects approximately 53,000 prices every month and compares these to the corresponding prices from the previous month to find out the CPI.

An Phríomh-Oifig Staidrimh
Central Statistics Office

Calculation of inflation

Calculation of rate of inflation

$$\frac{\text{Difference in cost of living between Year 1 and Year 2}}{\text{Cost of living in Year 1}} \times 100$$

Formula

Example

The cost of living for a household in 2015 was €8,500 and the cost of living in 2016 was €8,755. Calculate the rate of inflation.

Solution:

2016 Cost of living	€8,755
2015 Cost of living	€8,500
Difference =	€255

$$\frac{\text{Difference in cost of living between Year 1 and Year 2}}{\text{Cost of living in Year 1}} \times 100$$

$$\frac{255}{8,500} \times 100 = 3\%$$

38.1 The following are the inflation rates in Ireland for the years 2011–2015.

KSBN
KSMIT
KSC
BSBL

Year	2011	2012	2013	2014	2015
Inflation rate (%)	2.6%	1.72%	0.48%	0.2%	−0.3%

(a) Draw a trend graph to illustrate Ireland's inflation rate for the years 2011–2015.

(b) Consider the 2015 inflation rate and answer the following:

   (i) What does this tell us about the change in price levels?

   (ii) What do you think this type of situation is called?

   (iii) Do you think this is a positive development for you and your household? Explain your answer.

   (iv) Do you think this is a positive development for the Irish economy? Explain your answer.

What are the causes of inflation?

Inflation is caused by any of the following.

> When the cost of producing goods increases, e.g. because the cost of wages or raw materials rises, the cost price increases and this is likely to be passed on to the consumer. This is called **cost-push inflation** since the extra costs push up the price of goods.

> If the cost of imported raw materials increases, the price of the finished goods using these raw materials will rise. This is called **imported inflation**.

> An increase in indirect taxes, e.g. VAT or excise duties, will automatically increase the price of a product.

> If the demand for goods or services is greater than the supply, then the price will rise. Consumers will have to compete with each other for the items that are scarce and this will drive up the price. This is known as **demand-pull inflation** since the excess demand pulls the price upwards.

KSMIT

38.2 Answer these multiple-choice questions in your copy.

  (a) Inflation could be caused by the VAT rate:
   (i) Being reduced.
   (ii) Being increased.
   (iii) No longer being applied to electrical goods.

  (b) Cost-push inflation could be caused by:
   (i) The minimum wage being raised by €1.50.
   (ii) The price of electricity going down.
   (iii) Tax on profits being reduced by 2%.

  (c) Imported inflation could be caused by:
   (i) Increased ferry charges between the UK and Ireland.
   (ii) An exceptionally bad wheat harvest in the USA increasing the price of this product.
   (iii) The price of oil remaining steady.

  (d) Demand-pull inflation could be caused by:
   (i) An increase in wages for construction workers.
   (ii) An increase in building costs.
   (iii) An increase in the number of people who want to buy a home.

The impact of high inflation on households, businesses and the economy

Table 38.1 How high levels of inflation affect households, businesses and the economy

Households	Businesses	Economy
› Inflation reduces the purchasing power of money. Consumers will not be able to buy as many goods and services as they did previously and this will result in a lower standard of living › Inflation tends to stop people from saving money if the rate of interest is less than the rate of inflation. This is because the interest received will not match the price increase of goods and services	› Workers may demand wage increases so they can afford the same amount of goods and services as they did before inflation. This will increase business costs and will result in lower profits or higher prices. If the wage increase isn't paid, workers may go on strike › Rising business costs will discourage expansion and investment	› Irish-made goods and services will be more expensive and it will become more difficult to sell them abroad. This may result in job losses and rising unemployment › The higher cost of Irish-made goods will result in cheaper imported goods and services. This has a negative impact on our balance of payments and may also cause job losses See Chapter 41 › Government spending may increase due to rising costs and increased social protection payments

Consider this example:

Declan has €100 and can use all this money to buy a new pair of football boots. He decides to postpone the purchase and instead puts his money in a savings account that pays 2% APR. When he withdraws his money in a year he will have €102.

If the rate of inflation in the economy is 5%, the price of the football boots will have risen to €105 and Declan will no longer have enough money to buy the boots.

In money terms Declan is better off (he now has €102 rather than €100) but the purchasing power of his money has been reduced and it will buy him fewer goods than it did a year ago.

38.3 (a) Find out the current rate of inflation in Ireland.

(b) How does it compare to the average rate of inflation across the European Union (EU)?

 Research

 KSMIT KSBN

Employment levels

The **labour force** refers to all those people of working age (16–65) who are willing and able to work. This definition does not include retired people, full-time students or those who have an illness or disability that prevents them from working.

> **38.4** Use the CSO website to find out the current size of Ireland's population and labour force. Express the labour force figure as a percentage of the total population.

Research

KSMIT
KSBN

Members of the labour force who are able to find work are said to be **employed**, whereas those who cannot find work are classified as **unemployed**. The levels of employment and unemployment in an economy are important indicators of its economic wellbeing. A healthy and growing economy will tend to have low levels of unemployment.

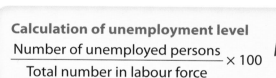

UNEMPLOYED

Those who are unemployed usually receive some form of financial payment from the Department of Social Protection. This money is designed to help them meet their daily needs and to provide short-term financial support until they succeed in finding a job.

> **Calculation of unemployment level**
> $$\frac{\text{Number of unemployed persons}}{\text{Total number in labour force}} \times 100$$

Formula

The aim of all governments is to have as many people in employment as possible. This will increase government revenue (due to higher tax revenue) and reduce government expenditure (less social welfare payments).

Full employment refers to a situation where almost all members of the labour force are employed. In Ireland an unemployment rate of around 4% is regarded as full employment.

> **38.5** The following are the unemployment levels in Ireland for the years 2011–2015.
>
> | Year | 2011 | 2012 | 2013 | 2014 | 2015 |
> |------|------|------|------|------|------|
> | **Unemployment rate (%)** | 14.5% | 14.7% | 12.5% | 10% | 9.5% |
>
> **(a)** Draw a trend graph to illustrate the unemployment rate in Ireland for the years 2011–2015.
>
> **(b)** Research online the unemployment rate for each year since 2015. Continue your trend graph with this information.
>
> **(c)** What can you say about the unemployment rate from 2011 to present?

Research

KSBN
KSBL
KSMIT

The effect of high unemployment for households, businesses and the economy

Note that if the unemployment rate falls, the opposite effects to those listed in table 38.2 are likely.

Table 38.2 How high unemployment affects households, businesses and the economy

Households	Businesses	Economy
› There will be a decrease in consumer demand for goods and services as people lose their jobs and their income levels fall › Many households will have a lower standard of living. Those facing long-term (i.e. twelve months or more) unemployment may suffer from poverty and may find it difficult to maintain their skills and find new employment › Some workers may have to emigrate to find employment	› It may be harder to attract extra finance as investors will be less willing to invest at a time of falling demand › There may be a reduction in sales and profits as consumers have less disposable income	› There will be reduced economic activity due to a reduction in disposable income › Social problems may increase and the shadow economy may grow › The emigration of highly qualified or skilled workers makes Ireland a less attractive location for foreign direct investment (FDI). This loss of important and talented workers is often called the **brain drain**

Interest rates

Low interest rates will encourage people and businesses to borrow more and will reduce the cost of existing borrowings. This is likely to increase the level of spending and investment in the economy.

People will be less inclined to save when interest rates are low.

Because Ireland is a member of the euro area, interest rates in Ireland are controlled by the European Central Bank (ECB).

Interest rates are the cost of borrowing money or the reward for money saved.

See Chapter 42

The effect of low interest rates for households, businesses and the economy

Note that high interest rates will have the opposite effects to those listed in table 38.3.

Table 38.3 How low interest rates affect households, businesses and the economy

Households	Businesses	Economy
› Access to cheaper finance will result in more borrowing and more spending › Those with existing loans will have more disposable income as repayment costs are reduced. A reduction in the cost of mortgages will be a huge benefit to households › Increased borrowing will increase the level of household debt	› Expansion and new product development will be easier because of cheaper loans. This will lead to increased profitability and employment › Repayments on any existing loans will fall, leading to lower business costs. The business may become more competitive and therefore sales, exports and profits should increase	› Increased borrowing and spending will lead to an increase in (VAT) revenue for the government › Increased investment will help reduce unemployment and the level of social welfare payments › The cost of servicing the national debt will be reduced › Very low interest rates may discourage householders from saving their money. The extra consumer spending will lead to increased business profits

National debt

National debt is the total amount of money that a country's government has borrowed.

Definition

Over the last number of years, Ireland's national debt has risen from €65 billion in 2008 to €184 billion in 2016.

This increase arose from the government's need to fund large budget deficits and to provide financial support to the banks.

Debt servicing is the term used to describe the payment of interest on our national debt.

The state body that manages the national debt is the **National Treasury Management Agency (NTMA)**.

Gníomhaireacht Bainistíochta an Chisteáin Náisiúnta
National Treasury Management Agency

38.6 (a) What is the current amount of Ireland's national debt?

(b) Which country in Europe has the highest national debt?

(c) Which country in the world has the highest national debt?

Research

KSMIT
KSBN

The impact of national debt on households, businesses and the economy

Table 38.4 How the national debt affects households, businesses and the economy

Households	Businesses	Economy
› Taxes may increase to help fund the repayment on the government's loans › Government spending may be reduced, which will impact the level of public services being provided	› Taxes may increase to help fund the repayment on the government's loans › Consumers with less disposable income will buy fewer goods and services › Reduced consumer demand may lead to job losses › A negative economic climate will reduce business investment	› Borrowing money in order to pay essential public services (teachers, gardaí, nurses, etc.) is not sustainable. As a result these services are likely to be cut back › Debt has a significant opportunity cost. Money spent on debt servicing is not available for other important needs, including infrastructure and public services provision

National income

> **National income** is the total value of all new goods and services produced within a country in a year.

Definition

National income is normally expressed as either gross domestic product or gross national product.

> **Gross domestic product (GDP)** measures the total value of the goods and services produced within a country in one year. This includes goods and services produced by indigenous (native or local) and foreign-owned businesses.

> **Gross national product (GNP)** is the total value of the goods and services produced by a country (either in that country or overseas) in one year.

GDP is seen as the best indicator of economic health because it doesn't include income from overseas investment.

When the Central Statistics Office (CSO) compiles the national income figures it needs to be aware of the impact of inflation on the value of goods and services produced. For example, an increase in the *value* of output may simply be as a result of rising prices rather than greater efficiency and productivity. For this reason the CSO removes the effect of inflation and calculates national income in *real terms*.

The result is GDP (or GNP) 'at constant prices' and this allows us to compare changes in national income from one year to the next. It is this year-on-year change that is used to measure the level of growth in an economy.

Economic growth

Economic growth occurs when there is an increase in the amount of goods and services produced in an economy from one year to the next.

Definition

Calculation of economic growth

GROWTH

Calculation of rate of economic growth

$$\frac{\text{Difference between Year 1 and Year 2}}{\text{Production in Year 1}} \times 100$$

Formula

Example

The total value of goods produced (at constant prices) in 2014 was €80,000 and in 2015 it was €85,000. Calculate the rate of economic growth.

Solution:

2015	€85,000	$\dfrac{\text{Difference between Year 1 and Year 2}}{\text{Production in Year 1}} \times 100$	$\dfrac{5,000}{80,000} \times 100 = 6.25\%$
2014	€80,000		
Difference	€5,000		

The economic cycle

The **economic cycle** is the term used to describe the way in which **the level of economic activity changes over time**.

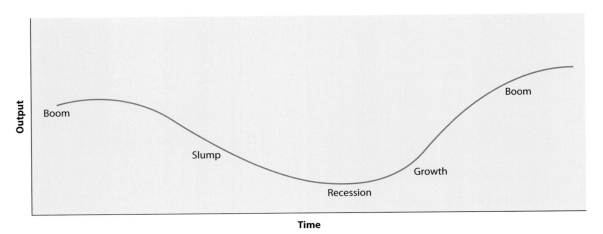

Figure 38.1 The economic cycle

> **Economic growth** occurs when the amount of goods and services produced in the economy increases from one year to the next. Economic growth is likely to increase when taxation and interest rates are low and investment and employment levels are high.

> **Economic boom** describes a *continuous period of rapid economic growth*. Ireland experienced an economic boom during the 'Celtic Tiger' years (1995–2006).

> A **recession** represents a *general slowdown in the level of economic activity*. Officially, an economy that experiences negative economic growth in two consecutive quarters (six months in a row) is said to be in recession. During a recession, GDP, demand for goods and services, investment, household incomes, business profits and inflation all fall.

> An **economic depression** occurs when a recession is very severe and continues for a sustained period of time.

Economic growth in Ireland

The economic cycle can be seen if we examine the last decade in Ireland. Figure 38.2 shows that Ireland's economic growth:

> Was high and remained so until 2007 (during the Celtic Tiger economy)

> Declined sharply as the recession began in 2008 and remained negative until 2010

> Increased at a slow pace until 2013

> Was much stronger in 2014.

Economic growth continued strengthening in 2015.

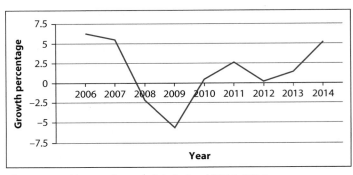

Figure 38.2 Economic growth in Ireland 2006–2014

38.7 The following figures show the GDP growth rate year on year for 2011–2015.

Year	2011	2012	2013	2014	2015
GDP growth rate (%)	2.2%	0.2%	3.4%	4.8%	5.2%

Note: the 2011 growth rate of 2.2% followed three consecutive years of negative growth. Ireland was in a recession during this period.

(a) Draw a trend graph to illustrate the growth rate of GDP in Ireland for the years 2011–2015.

(b) Research online the rate of economic growth for each year since 2015. Continue your trend graph with this information.

KSBN
KSMIT

KSBN
KSMIT
KSBC

38.8 The table shows the figures for economic growth for Ireland (as shown in figure 38.2) and for the world from 2006 to 2014.

	Economic growth	
Year	Ireland (%)	World (%)
2006	6.3	4.1
2007	5.5	3.9
2008	−2.2	1.5
2009	−5.6	−2.1
2010	0.4	4.1
2011	2.6	2.8
2012	0.2	2.3
2013	1.4	2.4
2014	5.2	2.5

(a) Draw a line graph plotting these two series of figures (choose your own scales).

(b) Comment on economic growth, comparing Ireland to the rest of the world.

The effects of economic growth on households, businesses and the economy

Table 38.5 How economic growth affects households, businesses and the economy

Households	Businesses	Economy
› There will be increased employment and this will lead to an improved standard of living	› **Multiplier effect:** As more money is spent in the economy, demand increases and this will encourage production. This will lead to increased employment, which will lead to increased demand › **Rise in government income:** If the government is able to collect more taxation, it may be able to run a budget surplus that could allow lower tax rates, which generally would have a positive effect on business See Chapter 37	› It may result in strong economic growth and inflation. When the economy grows rapidly, some resources become scarce and this causes prices to rise

In the news

Ireland remains fastest growing economy in the euro zone

New forecasts from the European Commission show Ireland will continue to remain the fastest growing country in the euro zone this year.

In its latest economic forecast, the Commission said the Irish economy will grow on the back of improving public finances and sustained employment growth.

For 2016 and 2017, GDP growth is expected to continue towards 'more sustainable rates' of about 4.5% and 3.5% respectively.

In its latest forecasts, the Commission said that government debt is also set to continue falling.

It is expected to drop to 98.4% of GDP in 2015, down from 107.5% in 2014. By 2017, government debt is projected to fall to 91.5% of GDP.

On inflation, the Commission said the very subdued rate of consumer price growth is expected to gradually increase during the year, mainly due to the expected recovery in wages.

Unemployment is also set to continue falling with job creation remaining broad-based across all sectors of the economy and across all regions of the country.

'In line with the projected moderation to GDP growth in 2016–2017, the unemployment rate is also expected to decline more slowly to 7.5% at the end of 2017.'

'Economic fundamentals are robust and point to more sustainable but still strong GDP growth rates in 2016 and 2017. Government finances are improving as strong revenue growth more than offsets increases in expenditures,' it added.

Source: Article adapted from *RTÉ News online*, 4 February 2016

38.9 Is the information given in the above 'In the news' item positive or negative for Ireland? Pick out four phrases from the article to support your answer.

KSBL
KSC
KSMIT

Key Terms

KSBL
KSC
KSMIT
KSBC

You should be able to *define*, *spell*, give *examples* and *apply* to real life each of the following key terms associated with this topic.

Exercise: Write a sentence using each of the following terms. You may use more than one of the terms in your sentence if appropriate.

consumer price index (CPI)

cost-push inflation

debt servicing

demand-pull inflation

economic boom

economic cycle

economic depression

economic growth

employment

gross domestic product (GDP)

gross national product (GNP)

imported inflation

inflation

interest rates

multiplier effect

national debt

National Treasury Management Agency (NTMA)

recession

unemployment

Chapter 39 :: Government Economic Policy

What is government economic policy?

A **policy** sets out proposed actions and principles for an organisation to follow. All organisations write their own policies. Some are required by law (e.g. a health and safety policy) and some are created by choice (e.g. an internet usage policy). Your school will have a number of policies – they set out how your school complies with laws or wishes its pupils and teachers to behave.

> **Definition**
>
> **Government economic policy** refers to all the ways in which the government tries to have an impact on the economy.

39.1 Your school will have many policies. Why do you think it has:

(a) A code of behaviour policy?

(b) An anti-bullying policy?

BULLY FREE ZONE

> **Discussion**

KSWwO
KSBL
KSC
KSMIT

Governments also have a number of policies, including ones that are designed to deal with the economy of the country.

The main aim of government economic policy is to create a stable economic climate that promotes:

> Full employment
> Low inflation
> Increased economic growth

> Industrial and regional development
> Social and income equality.

While many government policies have an economic impact, we will confine our discussion to the following major ones:

> Fiscal policy
> Monetary policy

> Industrial policy
> Direct intervention policy.

Fiscal policy

Fiscal policy is how the government sets the levels of taxation and spending in the economy. We saw in chapter 37 that this is achieved through national budgets. Fiscal policy also deals with the redistribution of wealth and resources.

See Chapter 37

For example, the government may decide to increase income tax rates for higher earners and use some of this money to increase public services for the less well off.

Monetary policy

Monetary policy is used to control the supply of money available in an economy at a particular time it is also used to set interest rates and to help control inflation.

See Chapter 38

For example, higher interest rates and reductions in the supply of money will tend to reduce borrowing and spending. This will help keep prices under control.

The European Central Bank (ECB) sets the interest rates and controls the supply of money in all euro area countries, including Ireland. In effect this means that the Irish government has little or no control over monetary policy.

See Chapter 42

Industrial policy

The government's industrial policy encourages the development and growth of the three sectors of the economy (primary, secondary and tertiary). The government encourages both **indigenous** (local) businesses and **foreign direct investment** (FDI), as they create employment in the economy.

Direct intervention policy

The government's direct intervention policy deals with setting up semi-state companies to provide goods and services that are not produced or supplied by the private sector. These companies provide jobs in the public sector, which are paid for by the taxpayer. Examples are Electric Ireland and Fáilte Ireland.

39.2 List three other examples of semi-state companies in Ireland.

Research

KSMIT

Evaluating government economic policy

Government economic policies have an impact on the success of the economy as a whole, the taxes paid by households and the public services available to citizens. For this reason you should keep up to date with important economic developments and debates.

39.3 Create a scrapbook (actual or digital) to which you can add news articles about topical economic issues and policies. This useful resource will enable you to keep up to date with ongoing developments and help with future evaluation of government policy.

Researching economic issues

When evaluating economic issues, use the questions in table 39.1 to guide you. The answers to the questions will inform your opinions and may in the future help determine the actions of the organisation you work for.

Table 39.1 Questions to consider

Question	Reason
What is the economic issue?	You need to be clear on the issue and the impact it might have
What caused the economic issue?	Understanding the cause may highlight the solution or help avoid future problems
What is the government doing about it?	How the government is dealing with the issue will impact on you. You need to know whether there is already an economic policy in place or whether there is going to be one. If there is, when was it introduced, and has it started having an effect yet?
Do other countries have a similar economic policy?	If so, how successful has it been? Your answer to this question will help you decide how effective our government's policy might be.
What are the benefits of the economic policy?	Who will/does it benefit and how will they benefit?
Are there any costs associated with the policy?	Who will bear the cost?
Do you agree with the economic policy that is in place? If not, how would you deal with the issue?	Can you see the benefits of the policy for Ireland, for its citizens, for you personally, for your organisation? If it benefits one sector but has costs for another, is this acceptable for the overall good of the country?

39.4 What sources will help you research government economic policy? Between you, create a list of sources – TV and radio programmes, newspapers, magazines, websites, social media accounts – that you can refer to.

39.5 How can you decide whether these sources are reliable and trustworthy?

Discussion

KSMIT
KSWwO
KSBL

In the news

Global examples feed arguments for and against sugar tax

By Mark Hilliard

No 'robust' evidence to show what effects policies have on consumption and health

Britain will introduce a dual-band sugar tax in 2018. Several countries have already introduced such a tax with varied policies, but there is no robust evidence to show what effects these policies have on consumption and health.

Both sides of the sugar-tax debate point to the international experience as a reason for and against the introduction of a levy in Ireland.

With varied policies and success, health strategies around the world have included everything from sugar-sweetened drinks to chocolate, ice-cream and jam.

The policy accompanies a growing appreciation of the dangers of sugar consumption, obesity and the kinds of chronic diseases associated with poor diets.

The UK's duel-band policy on sugar-sweetened drinks will target sugar content in products above both 5 g and 8 g per 100 millilitres and aims to raise about €662 million a year.

Research by Public Health England found increasing the price of high-sugar products reduced purchase levels proportionate to the tax rate.

It found tax-related reductions in sales in Norway, Finland, Hungary and France.

A 10 per cent tax in Mexico led to an average 6 per cent reduction in sales of sugar-sweetened drinks in 2014. The figure was about 9 per cent for lower socioeconomic households.

However, there is no 'robust' evidence to show what effects existing tax policies have on consumption or health. There are just 'some indications' of relative decreases in purchasing of between 4 and 10 per cent.

Campaigners against 'fat tax' look to the Danish experience. Its policies were repealed in 2012 after just one year.

Irish lobby against tax

'Our view is that it's certainly very, very patchy,' said Paul Kelly, director of the Food and Drink Industry Ireland, of the international experience. It promises to fight similar moves in Ireland. 'There are a lot of problems with it. Where there has been an impact it has been very, very small.'

The Danish system fell, he said, 'because people were going across the border to Germany and food trade unions identified job losses.'

Source: Article adapted from the *Irish Times*, 18 March 2016

39.6 Divide into groups and research one of the following.

Research

KSWwO
KSBC
KSBL
KSMIT

  (a) The policies governing the 'sugar tax' in different countries: what they are and how they are implemented.

  (b) The arguments for a sugar tax in Ireland based on research and other countries' successes.

  (c) The arguments against a sugar tax in Ireland based on research and other countries' failures.

Each group should present to the rest of the class.
Refer to the questions listed in table 39.1.

39.7 Do you think Ireland should introduce a sugar tax? How could the government's economic policy help ensure the success of such a tax? Do you think this tax would have the desired effect? Explain your answer, bearing in mind the questions listed in table 39.1.

Discussion

KSWwO
KSBL

Assessing government economic policies

Any policy needs to be assessed from time to time in order to see if it is effective in achieving its goals. If it is not working, it may be necessary to change or abandon it. When a policy is written, a date may be set for reviewing it to ensure that it is assessed and reviewed regularly. The government will do this for its policies, but you can also assess a policy to measure its impact on you, your family (and the organisation you work for in the future).

A cost-benefit analysis

The first stage in making an assessment of any economic policy is to carry out a **cost–benefit analysis**. This weighs up all the costs associated with the policy and balances them against the potential benefits. The benefits should outweigh the costs.

BENEFITS   COST

These are the steps for carrying out a cost–benefit analysis:

1 **Gather evidence and information** about the policy. This may require you to use several sources of information and to consider several points of view. (Think about the activity you carried out for question 39.6.)

2 **Calculate the costs involved** and who will have to pay them. Financial and opportunity costs need to be taken into account.

3 **Examine the benefits** and try to work out who will receive them.

4 **Balance the costs against the benefits** in order to see the overall impact of the policy.

5 **Consider whether the policy is equitable.** This examines whether a policy is 'fair' and is normally judged by looking at the likely impact of a policy on society. It considers whether the new policy will be ethical or 'morally just' and also how the costs and benefits will be shared by different sections of the population. Ideally they will be spread evenly.

6 **Consider whether the policy is sustainable.** This examines whether it will be possible to continue with a policy in the long term, without having a negative impact on society or the resources available to us. For example, a decision to offer 'tax breaks' to property developers might help increase the supply of available housing, but in the long term it is likely to drive land and property prices upwards. It was this type of unsustainable policy that created the 'boom and bust' in the Irish property market between 1999 and 2007.

7 **Make an evaluation** of the policy based on the issues raised in points 1–6 above.

What are the costs, and who bears them?

Every policy decision will involve both a **financial cost** and an **opportunity cost**. For example, a decision to spend €650 million (financial cost) on a national children's hospital will mean that this money is not available for spending on schools or social housing (opportunity costs).

See Chapter 34

Before introducing a new policy it is *vital* that the government considers the costs involved as well as the impact these costs will have on the country and its citizens.

Taxpayers usually bear the costs of government policy, either through increased taxation or cutbacks in public services. Even if the money is borrowed, future tax revenue will be used to service the debt and make loan repayments.

Some policy decisions impact more heavily on specific groups of citizens and these people will bear the greatest cost.

Some examples are:

> A decision to introduce residential property tax impacts on home owners.

> A decision to impose the Universal Social Charge impacts on all those in employment.

> A decision to increase the national minimum wage increases wage costs for all employers.

39.8 Who do the following decisions affect?

 (a) Cutting the rate of child benefit.

 (b) Increasing the pupil–teacher ratio.

What are the benefits, and who receives them?

Some citizens may **benefit directly** from government economic policy whereas others may **benefit indirectly**.

As with costs, it is essential that the government considers the impact of these benefits before introducing or changing economic policy.

Some examples that illustrate the benefits of government economic government policy include:

> A decision to provide grants for FDI will impact *directly* on those who get jobs with these overseas employers. Extra corporation tax collected from FDI companies will have *indirect benefits* for many citizens as the government may be able to reduce income tax or increase spending on public services.

> A decision to cut income tax rates will *directly benefit* all employees. Businesses may receive *indirect benefits* when these workers choose to spend their additional disposable income.

A cost–benefit analysis of a proposed 'sugar tax'

What is the economic issue?

> The negative impact of obesity on our society and the increasing costs associated with poor diet and ill health.

> This is a socioeconomic issue. This means that it impacts on the wellbeing of both our society and our economy.

What caused the economic issue?

> An increase in the marketing, availability and subsequent consumption of food and drink products that have a high sugar content. This has led to greater levels of ill health. A large number of people suffer from obesity, heart disease, diabetes and other diet-related problems.

> This obesity epidemic has resulted in huge economic costs. A 2012 study* into the economic cost of obesity in the Republic of Ireland estimated the annual cost to be **€1.13 billion**. This figure includes direct treatment and healthcare costs as well as indirect economic costs such as absence from work and premature death.

*Source: Safefood

What is the government doing about it? Is there an economic policy in place?

> There is currently no economic policy in place to deal with this issue. The government is considering introducing a 'sugar tax', which will increase the price of high-sugar drinks and thereby (it is hoped) reduce their consumption.

> The tax should also raise some revenue for the government and this can be used to fund education programmes designed to promote healthy eating.

Do other countries have a similar economic policy? If so, how successful has it been?

Several other countries have introduced sugar taxes, with mixed results:

> Mexico successfully introduced a sugar tax which resulted in a 6% reduction in purchases of sugary drinks. Norway, Finland and France have also successfully introduced sugar taxes.

> Denmark introduced a tax on fatty foods in 2011 and had plans for a 'sugar tax'. It scrapped both taxes after a year because many consumers engaged in cross-border shopping in Germany in order to avoid the levy. There are fears that a similar trend could occur on the island of Ireland. If this were to happen, this would make the policy unsustainable. However, the UK government has announced that it will introduce a sugar tax in 2018.

What are the proposed benefits of the economic policy?

> Savings on direct healthcare costs, including doctors' fees and medicines, of €398 million per year.

> Indirect economic benefits, due to higher productivity and lower mortality, of €728 million per year.

> Total financial benefit to the economy of €1.13 billion per annum.

> It is estimated that a 20% tax would raise about €122 million* in revenue and would reduce obesity levels by around 1.25% (or 10,000 people).

*Source: Irish Times, 23 December 2015

Are there any costs?

> Cost of collection: the Office of the Revenue Commissioners has expressed concern that it may cost more to introduce the tax than it will generate in tax revenue.

> Possible loss of FDI: it has been suggested that the introduction of the sugar tax will make Ireland a less attractive location for multinational soft drinks companies to locate in Ireland.

> Cross-border shopping may result in loss of revenue for Irish businesses near the border, although the introduction of a sugar tax in the UK would reduce this risk.

Do you agree with the economic policy? If not, how would you deal with the economic issue?

Evaluation

> The cost–benefit analysis above indicates that the economic cost of obesity is very high and needs to be reduced. Previous attempts, using education alone, have not worked and it seems reasonable that another approach should be taken.

> Despite concerns over collection costs and the regressive nature of a flat tax, which is likely to fall most heavily on low-income families, the analysis suggests that the introduction of the sugar tax has potential to increase tax revenues and reduce government spending on healthcare.

> For these reasons I would be happy to recommend the introduction of a 'sugar tax' on the understanding that its effectiveness will be monitored year by year.

39.9 Consider the costs and benefits associated with one of the following government economic policy proposals and complete the cost–benefit analysis template in the Student Activity Book, following the example we have given for the sugar tax. Think of this (i) from the government's point of view and (ii) from your own and your family's point of view.

KSMIT
KSC
KSBL

(a) Decentralisation: a proposal to move some government services and departments away from major cities like Cork and Dublin and relocate them in large rural towns.

(b) A decision to scrap the Universal Social Charge.

(c) A decision to build enough social housing to eliminate 'social housing lists'.

(d) A proposal to provide free state-funded childcare for all pre-school children.

(e) A proposal to introduce a 'wealth tax' for all those with incomes over €100,000 per annum.

(f) A decision to privatise a major public sector business such as An Post or Córas Iompair Éireann (CIÉ).

(g) A proposal to re-introduce college fees for all students.

(h) A decision to provide a medical card for all children under 18 years of age.

(i) Any other economic policy decision of your choice – it may be something that has a direct impact on you or your family, or be something that is topical.

Economic changes

You may need to review your opinions and reactions to government policies for the same reasons that governments themselves regularly have to review them. These reasons are outlined in table 39.2.

Table 39.2 Economic changes that affect government policy

Economic change	Reason	Example
The economy is dynamic	› Economies are not stable and Ireland's economic climate is likely to change over time. Policies need to change in order to reflect this	› If house prices rise very quickly, fewer people will be able to buy their own house. This affects the rental market and has a knock-on effect on wages and housing support
Priorities and policies change	› Governments change, and so do their priorities and available resources › Your own priorities and views change over time at and different stages of your life, too, and so the impact of a particular government policy will also be different	› During a recession a government may have limited financial resources. It may then promote industrial development and economic growth › During an economic boom, the government may change its priorities to control inflation and try to ensure greater income equality
Conflicting goals	› Some economic goals are mutually exclusive. This means that it may not be possible to improve one thing without having a negative effect on another	› Cutting interest rates and taxes will increase the amount of disposable income available to households. This will lead to greater spending on goods and services, increased employment, and higher levels of economic growth › These positive outcomes may lead to high levels of inflation › In this case economic growth and low inflation may be mutually exclusive and the government will need to prioritise one over the other
Ireland is a small open economy	› This means that our rates of economic growth are greatly affected by growth in world trade and the economic performance of our major export markets. The actions of the Irish government alone cannot influence every aspect of our economy and some policies may be ineffective due to external factors	› If a competitor country reduced its cost of manufacture, it may take over a large market share of our export market in that product so less money would be coming into Ireland and the workers in that sector might lose their jobs › The UK decision to leave the EU may require changes to Irish economic policy

Key Terms

You should be able to *define, spell,* give *examples* and *apply* to real life each of the following key terms associated with this topic.

Exercise: Write a sentence using each of the following terms. You may use more than one of the terms in your sentence if appropriate.

economic policy

industrial policy

fiscal policy

monetary policy

foreign direct investment (FDI)

policy

indigenous firms

Chapter 40 :: Sustainable Development

Learning outcomes

When you have completed this chapter you will be able to:

✔ Identify the positive and negative effects of economic growth on society and the environment

✔ Appreciate the necessity for sustainable development

✔ Understand what is meant by business ethics

✔ Suggest ways in which the government can influence the impact of business on society and the environment.

Economic growth and its effects on society and the environment

Previously you learned that an enterprise in a local area will lead to increases in employment and in the standard of living in that area. Similarly, on a national scale, when a country has economic growth there are positive and negative impacts on society and the environment.

See Chapter 22

Positive effects

> If economic growth is high, **employment** will increase and this will lead to a decrease in government spending (less money spent on social protection) and an increase in government revenue (more money collected in income tax).

See Chapter 38

> The extra money available through increased employment will be spent on goods and services, which will lead to further economic growth.

> An increase in economic growth will lead to an improvement in the **standard of living** for employees. An increase in living standards has a positive effect on life expectancy.

Did you know?

In Ireland in 1915 the average life expectancy was just over 49 years for both men and women, while currently it is just over 78 for Irish men and just over 82 for Irish women.

> Economic growth leads to an **increase in demand for higher education**, as people have more money to spend on education. Interestingly, there is also a positive relationship between higher education standards and economic growth, as businesses tend to locate near a supply of well-educated workers.

> Countries with high economic growth spend more money on **infrastructure**, such as transportation, telecommunications, supply of water, electricity and gas. This in turn leads to further increases in economic growth as better infrastructure makes it easier for businesses to trade.

40.1 In pairs, discuss why an increase in living standards has a positive impact on life expectancy. Share your reasons with the whole class and listen to your classmates' reasons.

T-P-S

KSMIT
KSC
KSWwO

Negative effects

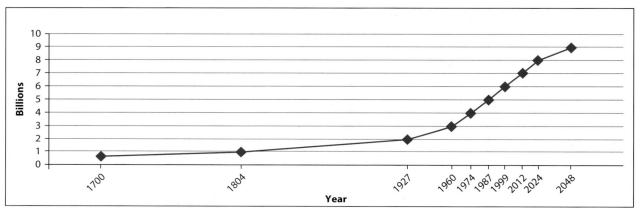

Figure 40.1 World population since 1700 and projected to 2048

> Increasing living standards have led to an **increased life span**. There are now more people alive than at any point in history, and the numbers are growing. As economic resources are scarce, food production and supply may not be able to keep up with demand from a growing population.

See Chapter 33

> An increase in living standards can lead to people spending money on convenience foods, which cause **obesity** when consumed to excess.

Did you know?

Over two-thirds of Irish people are overweight or obese. The annual cost of obesity in Ireland is over €1 billion. Almost 40% of this is in direct healthcare costs, while the remainder is indirect costs, e.g. lost productivity and absenteeism.

> Over-reliance on a particular industry. For example, during the period of the Celtic Tiger economy, the Irish economy was over-reliant on the construction sector and when the economic crash occurred there was very high unemployment in this sector.

> Destruction of natural habitats to build factories.

> Increased pollution, e.g. air pollution caused by fossil fuels required by planes and cargo ships used to export goods around the world.

> Traffic congestion caused by delivery of goods. Congestion in turn increases exhaust emissions, adding to pollution and greenhouse gases.

> More and bigger landfill sites required for large amounts of consumer waste.

> Climate change – since the Industrial Revolution in the late eighteenth century, business activity has contributed to climate change, due to the increased use of fossil fuels (coal, oil, gas) which release carbon dioxide into the atmosphere. This has increased greenhouse gases, causing the surface temperature of Earth to rise. China and India are two of the most densely populated countries in the world with over 36% of the world's population between them. As these economies develop, they will use increasing amounts of already limited fossil fuels.

Did you know?

The Kyoto Protocol of 1997 is an international treaty that established legally binding commitments to reduce greenhouse gases. There are financial penalties for countries that fail to achieve their targets. Ireland signed this protocol and must abide by it.

> Income inequality – the gap between the rich and poor has increased significantly in recent decades.

Did you know?

The USA has 5% of the world's population but consumes 30% of the world's resources and generates 30% of the world's waste. If all countries consumed at US rates, we would need three to five planets!

> Destruction of landmarks and sites of historical importance.

In 2013, a Mayan pyramid was destroyed in Belize. The pyramid, called the Noh Mul temple, which was approximately 2,300 years old, was destroyed by a construction company for use as gravel for road filler. Only a small part of the pyramid was left standing.

40.2 Discuss how it makes you feel when you read or hear stories like the Mayan temple being bulldozed. Should profit *ever* come before heritage and environment? Should the people responsible for this destruction be penalised lightly or heavily?

Discussion

KSWwO
KSBL
KSMIT

Sustainable development

Definition

Sustainable development is development that meets the needs of the present without compromising the ability of future generations to meet their own needs.

Sustainable economic growth requires countries to create conditions where the economy is stimulated without harming the environment. Job opportunities and decent working conditions are also required for the whole working-age population.

See Chapter 15

The United Nations has 17 sustainable development goals to transform the world, including one on economic growth. Some of the targets include:

SUSTAINABLE DEVELOPMENT GOALS

> An increase of 7% in GDP in the least developed countries

> Stopping forced labour, human trafficking and child labour

> Protecting workers' rights

> Promoting safe and secure working environments for all workers

> Achieving full and productive employment for all men and women, including persons with disabilities, by 2030

> Reducing the proportion of young people not in employment, education or training by 2020.

In recent years, consumers and businesses have become aware of the need to be socially responsible and take the environment into account when producing goods and services. Examples of this include:

> Using sustainable raw materials
> Replanting raw materials
> Recycling waste products
> Increasing the use of environmentally friendly products
> Decreasing pollution
> Using renewable energies, e.g. solar panels, wind power.

Did you know?

Velvet, the toilet tissue brand, replaces three trees for every one they use to make their toilet tissue. To date they have planted over seven million trees around the world.

40.3 Research how Dundalk, Co. Louth, became Ireland's first sustainable energy zone in 2007. Create an infographic to show:

> What a sustainable energy zone is
> How Dundalk is managing this
> What its aims are.

Research

KSBC
KSMIT
KSSW

Producing sustainable products

As natural resources continue to be consumed and depleted, businesses are under increased pressure – from governments, consumers and retailers – to produce sustainable products. Many have begun to adopt a 'total lifecycle' approach to the issue and now examine the environmental cost of the product across *all* stages of its production and disposal.

See Chapter 15

The cradle to grave approach to sustainability

The total lifecycle approach looks at sustainability 'from cradle to grave'. This requires businesses to consider all of the following.

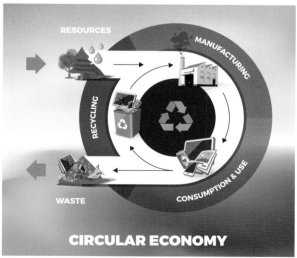

Figure 40.2 A product lifecycle approach to sustainability

Production and sourcing of raw materials

The questions that need to be asked are:

> Are they sourced in an ethical way and from sustainable sources?
> What is the impact on the workers, communities and economies involved in the production of raw materials?

Product manufacturing processes

Many businesses have changed how they produce goods to reduce the social and environmental costs of their activities. **Social costs** refer to the costs to society of business activity. Cutting down rainforests and environmental pollution are examples of social costs because everyone in society suffers the consequences of these actions.

The impact of product distribution

Production facilities should be located close to the source of raw materials and/or consumers in order to minimise transportation and its environmental impact. Modes of transport that rely on fossil fuels should be eliminated or reduced.

The impact of product usage by consumers

This used to be seen as beyond the control of a business. Attitudes have changed recently and more businesses are designing and marketing their products to reduce the social and environmental costs associated with their use.

The makers of all electrical goods are required to display an 'energy rating' for each of their products. This helps consumers to make an informed choice when buying products about which product provides the greatest energy efficiency during use.

Figure 40.3 All electrical goods have to display an energy rating

40.4 Discuss whether an energy rating score is a good or bad thing for producers and consumers. Would you like to see rating scales applied to other goods? Explain your answer.

Discussion

KSWwO
KSC
KSMIT

The impact of product disposal

Producers may try to influence consumer attitudes and behaviour through the use of recyclable materials and packaging. They may also support efforts or policies designed to promote sustainable disposal of product waste. Examples in this area include the use of refills for many products and the promotion of the 'reduce, reuse, recycle' campaign.

In some industries the government may take action to make producers accountable for product disposal.

For example, WEEE Ireland helps members meet their producer responsibility through the collection, recovery, and recycling of waste electrical and electronic equipment and batteries.

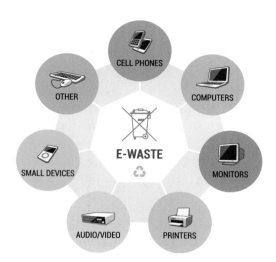

40.5 What does WEEE stand for?

40.6 Who does WEEE work for?

40.7 How does WEEE work with schools? Create a poster that could go on the wall in schools to encourage them to work with WEEE. Display these in your classroom or school.

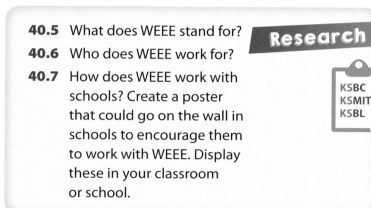

KSBC
KSMIT
KSBL

The benefits of the lifecycle approach

The lifecycle approach to sustainability offers the following benefits.

Taking a longer-term view

Decisions made at individual or industry level should aim to promote long-term sustainability. The use of quotas in the fishing industry is a good example of this type of long-term thinking. The industry realises there is little point increasing short-term production and job creation if the long-term consequences would lead to the extinction of some species and the eventual demise of the industry.

See Chapter 15

Focus on the bigger picture

Our decisions are not without consequence and we see how the actions we take can impact on others at different stages of the lifecycle. This wider focus should also prevent stakeholders at one stage of the lifecycle taking actions that simply push the problem or the negative consequences to another stage. This also emphasises interdependence and shared responsibility.

Promotes positive action and sustainable behaviour

Since we are aware of all of the negative consequences, we are in a better position to take steps to reduce or eliminate them. The growth of the 'fair trade' campaign is a good example and it began when retailers and consumers supported the calls for a fairer share of wealth and better working conditions, especially for producers and suppliers of raw materials.

Corporate social responsibility

Many businesses now have a corporate social responsibility (CSR) policy. CSR sets out how the organisation will act to benefit society and/or the environment. A CSR policy brings the following benefits:

> The reputation of the business will improve as it reduces its negative impact on the environment and society.

> Customers who care about the environment are likely to buy from the business.

> The business can attract top-quality staff who share their aims.

Did you know?

Dell is an American computer manufacturer that produces and sells PCs and laptops direct to the consumer through its company website. Each order can be customised to the consumer's specific requirements. Dell employs over 100,000 people worldwide and has a comprehensive CSR policy.

Dell minimises negative impacts on the environment by reducing waste and preventing pollution in its factories. All boxing materials are made from recycled materials. Its products are designed to reduce air pollution and consumers can recycle used computers, monitors and printers for free when they purchase a new Dell product.

Research

40.8 Use Dell's website to research their CSR policy and identify what steps it takes to reduce its impact on the environment and local communities.

40.9 Croke Park became the first stadium in Ireland and the UK to be certified for sustainability and environmental protection. Research the steps Croke Park takes to minimise its impact on the environment and identify whether your local GAA grounds could adopt similar steps.

40.10 Consider a manufacturer located near you. Find out whether it has a CSR policy and, if so, what it prioritises.

Business ethics

Definition

Business ethics are moral principles that influence the way a business behaves to consumers, suppliers, employees, shareholders, the government and society.

By behaving ethically, a business can attract consumers and staff who agree with its aims. The business may also receive awards for being ethical.

An ethical business will behave responsibly towards those it affects:

Consumers	Providing high-quality goods and services
Suppliers	Paying them on time
Employees	Fair pay, equal pay to all employees, adopt health and safety procedures
Shareholders	Run the business in the best interests of the shareholders, provide a fair return on investment
Government	Pay all taxes on time, obey laws
Society	Ensure the business does not negatively affect the local environment

Did you know?

In November 2015, Nestlé (which produces a range of products such as Cheerios breakfast cereal, Nescafé coffee, Rowntree sweets and pet foods) commissioned an investigation of their supply chain and found that slave labour was being used to produce seafood in Thailand. Nestlé has since taken steps to protect workers.

40.11 Discuss as a class whether we each have a moral duty to make every effort to find out whether goods we buy are produced or sourced ethically, or whether this responsibility should be on suppliers alone.

Groupwork

KSWwO

Role of government in reducing negative impacts of business on society

Central and local government have a clear role to play in reducing the negative impact of business and economic growth on society and the environment. They can do this by:

> Passing laws such as the Safety, Health and Welfare at Work Act 2005 and the Consumer Protection Act 2007 to ensure that workers and consumers are protected from unsafe business practices.

> Refusing planning permission to a business that wishes to build a factory that would harm the environment or the health of local people, or would cause traffic congestion in an area.

> Introducing a charge to limit damage caused by pollutants and waste, for example the charge for plastic shopping bags, which was introduced in 2002 to reduce the consumption of disposable plastic bags.

Did you know?

The plastic bag charge introduced in 2002 had an immediate effect on consumer behaviour. Usage dropped from an estimated 328 bags to 21 bags per person per year.

40.12 Research the website of your local authority to see if any planning applications have been made that could have a negative impact in your local area.

Government organisations that protect consumers and the environment

Competition and Consumer Protection Commission (CCPC)

When a business becomes very large it may expand by buying its competitors and become the only supplier of a product or service. (This is known as a **monopoly** in economics.) In that case, the business can control supply of the product (think back to supply and demand, which we looked at in chapter 35). This has the following effects for consumers:

See Chapter 35

> Reduced choice
> Increased price
> Possible poor-quality customer service.

The CCPC enforces Irish and European competition law in Ireland and conducts investigations into possible cartels.

See Chapter 14

A **cartel** is an illegal agreement between a group of producers to regulate supply of a particular good or service in an effort to manipulate prices.

Definition

The purpose of a cartel is to make a profit at the expense of the consumer by reducing choice. This arrangement also limits genuine competition and leads to higher prices for consumers.

Environmental Protection Agency

The Environmental Protection Agency (EPA) is a public body established in 1992. It helps protect Ireland's environment by providing advice to businesses through publishing reports and guidance on air quality, biodiversity, climate change, green business, waste, drinking water, noise, and genetically modified organisms (GMOs). It also enforces environmental law, monitors, analyses and reports on the environment, and conducts environmental research.

Sustainable Energy Authority of Ireland (SEAI)

Established in 2002, SEAI is Ireland's national energy agency. It aims to promote sustainable energy by:

> Developing renewable sources of energy
> Improving energy efficiency
> Reducing the impact of energy use on the environment
> Providing advice to consumers
> Managing grants for home improvement to reduce energy consumption.

Key Terms

KSBL
KSC
KSMIT
KSBC

You should be able to *define*, *spell*, give *examples* and *apply* to real life each of the following key terms associated with this topic.

Exercise: Write a sentence using each of the following terms. You may use more than one of the terms in your sentence if appropriate.

business ethics

cartel

Competition and Consumer Protection Commission (CCPC)

corporate social responsibility (CSR)

Environmental Protection Agency (EPA)

sustainable development

Sustainable Energy Authority of Ireland (SEAI)

Chapter 41 :: International Trade and Globalisation

What is international trade?

International trade is the buying (**importing**) and selling (**exporting**) of goods and services between different countries. Ireland is one of the most open economies in the world. This means that Ireland is an economy that engages in international trade. Ireland exports approximately 80% of what it produces.

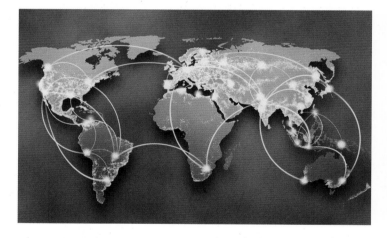

International trade is divided into visible and invisible trade:

> **Visible trade** deals with *physical products* that can be seen going out of and coming into Ireland, e.g. food, cars.

> **Invisible trade** deals with *services*. No physical product can be seen going out of or coming into Ireland as a result of the sale or purchase of services, e.g. insurance, banking, tourism.

What is importing?

Importing is buying products or services from other countries. This means that money leaves the country.

Definition

Imports are divided into visible and invisible imports:

> **Visible imports** are the *physical products* that Ireland *buys* from other countries, e.g. cars, oil, coal and fruit.

> **Invisible imports** are *services* that Ireland *buys* from other countries, e.g. Irish people going on holidays abroad, foreign music bands performing in Ireland, Irish students going abroad on school tours, giving a foreign firm the contract to build our roads, and Irish people buying services from foreign businesses, e.g. insurance and transport.

41.1 List ten goods that Ireland imports. Share your list with your partner and then as a class.

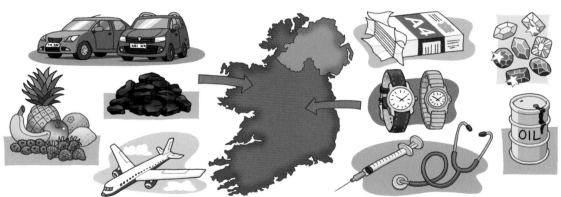

Figure 41.1 Some of Ireland's visible imports

Why does Ireland import goods and services?

Ireland is not self-sufficient for the following reasons:

> **Climate:** Ireland does not have the right climate to grow certain products, e.g. oranges, bananas, coffee.

> **Raw materials:** Ireland lacks the essential raw materials or natural resources that would enable it to produce certain goods, such as oil, coal and steel.

> **Choice for consumers:** Irish consumers want to have a variety of goods and services that they can buy and choose from. They would like to have a choice, e.g. fruit.

> **Natural skills:** Certain countries have people with the skills to make certain products, e.g. French wine. There is a lack of skills and tradition in producing some goods or services and this is a limiting factor in production.

> **Cost:** Foreign goods may be cheaper than comparable Irish goods.

> **Small domestic market:** Due to the small Irish market certain products cannot be produced economically and so must be imported, e.g. cars.

What is exporting?

> **Exporting** is selling goods or services to other countries. Money comes into the country.

Exporting is divided into visible and invisible exports:

> **Visible exports** are the *physical products or goods* that Ireland *sells* to other countries, e.g. meat, dairy products, live animals.

> **Invisible exports** are *services* that Ireland *sells* to other countries, e.g. Spanish students coming to Ireland to learn English and an Irish band performing in another country.

41.2 List ten goods that Ireland exports. Share your list with your partner and then as a class.

T-P-S

KSWwO
KSC
KSMIT

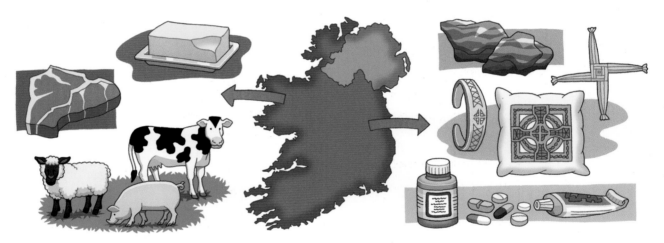

Figure 41.2 Some of Ireland's visible exports

Why does Ireland export goods and services?

Ireland exports goods and services for the following reasons:

> **Earn foreign currencies:** The receipt of foreign currencies can boost our country's reserves and provides the finance to help pay for imports.

> **Increased sales/profits:** Irish firms can increase their sales and profits by exporting their excess output to a foreign market.

> **Employment creation:** Exporting helps to maintain jobs in Ireland. The more we sell, the more people we need to make the goods.

> **Demand:** There is demand for Irish products by consumers abroad, such as our food products, e.g. beef and butter.

KSMIT

41.3 Some items might appear on both export and import lists, e.g. clothes and ICT equipment. Why might Ireland both import and export ICT equipment?

41.4 What other items might be both imported and exported?

Ireland's main trading partners

Ireland is a small open economy, which means that we rely heavily on trading (importing and exporting) with other countries.

Table 41.1 Ireland's exports and imports

	Exports	Imports
Trading partners	› United States › United Kingdom › Belgium › Germany › Switzerland › France › The Netherlands › Spain	› United Kingdom › United States › Germany › China › The Netherlands › France › Japan › Switzerland
Goods and services	› Machinery and equipment › Computers › Chemicals › Medical devices › Pharmaceuticals › Food › Animal products	› Petroleum and petroleum products › Cars › Machinery › Textiles and clothing
Value (2014)	€89 billion	€53.5 billion

41.5 (a) Research the most recent figures for the value of goods imported from Ireland's main trading partners.

(b) Carry out the same exercise for the exports.

(c) Compare the two sets of figures graphically.

(d) What do these figures tell you?

How is international trade measured?

The **balance of payments** is the difference between total exports and total imports over a period of time, usually one year.

The balance of payments shows the flow of money coming into and going out of a country.

Balance of payments = Total exports – Total imports

Total exports > Total imports = Balance of payments surplus

Total imports < Total exports = Balance of payments deficit

Balance of trade

> The **balance of trade** is the difference between visible exports and visible imports.

> **Balance of trade = Visible exports − Visible imports**
> Visible exports > Visible imports = Balance of trade surplus
> Visible exports < Visible imports = Balance of trade deficit

How to calculate the balance of trade and balance of payments

Question:

The following data relates to the international trade of a country for 2015:

	€
Visible imports	1,150 million
Invisible exports	1,380 million
Visible exports	1,250 million
Invisible imports	1,300 million

(a) From the above data, calculate the balance of trade and the balance of payments.

(b) Indicate in each case whether it is a surplus or a deficit balance.

Solution:

(a) *Balance of trade* € (m)

Visible exports	€1,250
− Visible imports	− €1,150
(b) Surplus	€100

(a) *Balance of payments*

Total exports	€2,630 (€1,380 + €1,250)
− Total imports	− €2,450 (€1,150 + €1,300)
(b) Surplus	€180

41.6 The following data relates to the international trade of a country for 2016:

	€
Visible imports	1,570 million
Invisible exports	1,620 million
Visible exports	2,050 million
Invisible imports	1,950 million

(a) From the above data, calculate the balance of trade and the balance of payments.

(b) Indicate in each case whether it is a surplus or a deficit balance.

Benefits of international trade for Irish businesses

> **Increased sales:** With less than five million domestic consumers, the Irish market is quite small. By exporting, Irish businesses can increase sales.

> **Spread risk:** A business can spread the risk by not relying on their local market only.

> **Raw materials:** Irish businesses need to import some raw materials as we do not produce them in Ireland, e.g. oil.

> **Lower costs:** Irish businesses have to increase production to satisfy demand from abroad. The more products that are made, the cheaper it becomes to make each one. This is known as **economies of scale**.

Challenges of international trade for Irish businesses

> **High costs:** As Ireland is an island, transportation is more difficult and more expensive for Irish exporters as goods can only be transported abroad by plane or ship.

> **Languages:** Irish exporters may need to make their websites available in many languages to appeal to customers in different countries, e.g. Ryanair.

> **Exchange rates:** If the euro increases in value, the price of Irish products in countries that do not use the euro will become more expensive. This may lead to a reduction in demand for Irish exports. However, if the euro decreases in value, it will be more expensive for Irish importers to buy raw materials from countries that are not in the euro area.

> **Getting paid:** Trying to collect payments from businesses in other countries can be more difficult than at home.

> **Competition from low-cost economies:** Irish wages are quite high by international standards. This means that it is much cheaper to produce goods in other countries, particularly in Asia and Africa. It is difficult for Irish manufacturers to compete against goods manufactured in low-wage economies.

Free trade

This is when countries can buy and sell without any trade barriers or restrictions in place, e.g. customs duties on goods.

The member countries of the European Union (EU) enjoy free trade.

See Chapter 42

The World Trade Organization (WTO) has 164 members (July 2016). It helps governments sort out trade problems and encourages the removal of barriers to trade.

Barriers to trade

Examples include:

> **Tariff:** This is a tax that a country adds to imports to make the products more expensive and less attractive for customers to buy in their country, e.g customs duties and import duties. It encourages consumers to buy home-produced products.

> **Quota:** Countries put a limit on the amount of a good that can be imported into their country. This should increase demand for domestically produced goods and services.

> **Embargo:** A country can put a complete ban on goods being imported from a certain country. Consumers will have no choice but to buy the home produce.

> **Subsidy:** This is a direct payment to a producer. It will reduce the cost of production and make exports cheaper. It boosts employment and improves the balance of trade, e.g. Irish farmers obtain direct farm payments from the EU.

Reasons countries impose barriers to free trade

The reasons governments impose barriers to free trade in their country are:

> **To protect their domestic industries:** New industries may have difficulty competing with established industries from other countries and so the government may choose to protect them by limiting these imports.

> **To protect domestic employment:** Foreign competition costs people their jobs. Limiting imports helps protect jobs.

> **To protect against 'cheap labour' economies:** Domestic firms may not be able to compete with those countries that gain their advantage by paying their workers low wages. A government might restrict imports from these countries.

> **National security:** Free trade can result in the spread of animal diseases. For example, if there is an outbreak of the devastating foot and mouth disease abroad, the government will ban the importation of cattle to protect this vital industry.

Enterprise Ireland

Enterprise Ireland is the state agency that assists Irish businesses that want to sell their products or services to other countries.

> It provides market research information on foreign markets to Irish businesses.

> It organises **trade fairs** and exhibitions for Irish businesses to show their products to foreign buyers.

> It provides advice on everything to do with foreign trade, including all documentation, how to get paid, labelling of goods, etc.

Globalisation

Globalisation is the process by which the world becomes interconnected as a result of increased trade and cultural exchange.

See Chapter 16

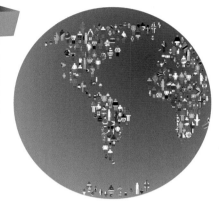

Definition

A **global business** sees the world as one market and production location. It provides the same product worldwide. It uses a global marketing strategy, which involves the same marketing mix of product, price, place and promotion (the 4Ps) throughout the world to build a global brand.

The growth in globalisation and global firms, with their quality produce at cheap prices, is a challenge for Irish exporters. Irish exporting firms will have to become more efficient and provide products with a unique selling point (USP) to survive the competitive threat from global firms.

KSMIT

41.7 List five examples of global businesses.

41.8 List three examples of Irish global businesses.

Reasons for the development of global companies

> **Increased sales:** To increase sales and to make higher profits. The business's home market is saturated: they cannot increase their sales any more in their home market.

> **Mass production:** This allows the company to have economies of scale. This means the more they produce, the lower the cost per unit.

> **Developments in ICT:** Communication is faster and easier with the use of video conferencing, email, etc. This has made it easier to manage global businesses.

See Chapter 21

Global marketing

A global business will sell the same product in the same way all over the world using the global marketing mix (the 4Ps). The global business will concentrate on similarities across world markets. They will use a **standardised marketing mix** wherever possible. We looked at the 4Ps of the marketing mix in chapter 24; here we will look at them in the context of a global market.

See Chapter 24

Global product

The company will try to use the same brand name worldwide and they will try to have the same product design all over the world. The product may need to be adjusted to reflect technical, legal and language requirements, e.g. a left-hand drive car; packaging may need to be changed to cater for the needs of the local market. For example, McDonald's adjusts its menu to fit local tastes. India is the only country where McDonald's doesn't serve beef products, as Hindus believe the cow is sacred and don't eat its meat.

Global price

Global firms attempt to have the same price in each market, but there may be factors that mean the price is different in different countries. These factors are:

> A higher standard of living in some countries, which may lead to the company charging a higher price as customers have more disposable income.

> More expensive transport costs to get the product into the country may lead to a higher price.

> More competition may lead to lower prices.

> Exchange rate fluctuations may cause the price to change.

Global promotion

The company will try to have the same advertising all around the world, but this may not always be possible because of differences in language and culture. For example, in Italy a campaign for Schweppes Tonic Water translated into 'Schweppes Toilet Water'.

Global place

This is how the global company gets their product to the market. The company could sell directly to customers or use a distribution agent. Many global businesses will rely on local agents and distributors to deliver their products. For example, Coca-Cola distributes its product through 250 bottling partners worldwide.

Key Terms

KSBL
KSC
KSMIT
KSBC

You should be able to *define*, *spell*, give *examples* and *apply* to real life each of the following key terms associated with this topic.

Exercise: Write a sentence using each of the following terms. You may use more than one of the terms in your sentence if appropriate.

balance of payments	import substitution
balance of trade	importing
economies of scale	international trade
Enterprise Ireland	invisible trade
exporting	open economy
global marketing (4Ps)	trade barriers
globalisation	visible trade

Chapter 42 ::
The European Union

Origin and aims of the EU

The European Union (EU) was established shortly after the Second World War in an attempt to prevent future conflict between former enemies. Originally it was known as the European Economic Community (EEC) and had just six members. Many other countries have since joined, including Ireland in 1973.

42.1 How many countries are currently in the EU? List them in your Student Activity Book.

The EU is a kind of 'club' for European countries. Its members agree to join and to follow club rules. Each member must pay a fee and in return they receive certain benefits, including the support and co-operation of fellow members. Club members share ideas and resources and work together to achieve common goals. Member countries also work collectively to promote and improve the position of the EU globally.

The European Union has three main aims:

› To establish European citizenship. This means protecting human rights and freedoms.

› To ensure freedom, security and justice for EU citizens.

› To promote economic and social progress. This involves the single market, the euro, environmental protection and social and regional development.

As it currently exists the EU is based on the idea of **shared sovereignty**. This means that each country is willing to give up control over some parts of its government in order to work with others to achieve common goals, standards and laws.

In June 2016 the majority of citizens in the United Kingdom voted to leave the EU. The term 'Brexit' was coined to describe Britain's exit from the EU. This exit is expected to happen by 2018 and to have major socio-economic consequences for many countries. The impact of Brexit on Ireland will be discussed later in this chapter (see page 467).

European Union institutions

While each member country still has the power to make most of its own laws, a number of EU institutions play an important role in enacting and enforcing EU law. These EU rules apply to all member countries and may take priority over domestic laws.

The European Council

The European Council meetings are summit meetings held regularly by EU heads of state. These meetings take place at least twice a year and are used to set out priorities and a general strategy for the development of the EU.

These meetings usually discuss major issues facing the EU, for example debt problems, migration and security concerns.

Once the overall agenda has been set by the Council, responsibility for day-to-day decision-making in the EU lies with its three main institutions:

› The European Commission

› The European Parliament

› The Council of the European Union.

Together, these are known as the EU's institutional triangle.

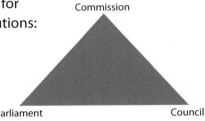

Figure 42.1 The EU's institutional triangle

The European Commission

Commissioners are responsible for the day-to-day management of the EU. Each member state has a commissioner who is given responsibility for a particular area of EU policy, e.g. agriculture or transport. The job of a commissioner is similar to that of a government minister in Ireland.

The main functions of the European Commission are:

> Proposing new laws. The Commission works very closely with the Parliament and the Council of the EU to achieve this aim.
> Enforcing EU law.
> Managing the EU's budget.
> Representing the EU internationally. For example, the EU trade commissioner attends World Trade Organization (WTO) talks, and the environment commissioner attends international conferences on climate change.

Figure 42.2 The European Commission building in Brussels

42.2 Find out the name of the current European commissioner for Ireland. Identify the portfolio he/she is responsible for.

Research

KSMIT

European Parliament

Members of the European Parliament (MEPs) are directly elected by EU citizens.

Each member state has a set number of MEPs, based on its population. Elections take place every five years.

42.3 How many MEPs does the Republic of Ireland have?
42.4 How many members does the European Parliament have?
42.5 What proportion of the Parliament are Ireland's MEPs?
42.6 Where is the Parliament located?

Research

KSMIT
KSBN

The role of the European Parliament

The main functions of the European Parliament are:

> To represent EU citizens
> To help introduce legislation
> To approve the EU budget.

Figure 42.3 The European Parliament

42.7 For European Parliamentary elections, Ireland is divided into electoral regions called constituencies.

(a) What are the names of these constituencies?

(b) How many MEPs does each of these constituencies have?

(c) What are the names of the MEPs currently elected to represent your area of the country?

Council of the European Union

Council members are government ministers from EU member states. The membership of the Council depends on the topic being discussed, e.g. finance ministers discuss budget issues, agriculture ministers debate agricultural policy.

The main functions of the EU Council are:

> Goal setting and policy co-ordination
> Passing legislation
> Approving the EU budget
> Signing international agreements.

Court of Auditors

The role of the Court of Auditors is to monitor EU spending to ensure that taxpayers' money is not being wasted. It checks that money allocated to member states is used for the purpose intended and presents the European Parliament and the Council with an annual report each year.

EU Court of Justice

Each member state of the EU appoints a judge to the Court of Justice, which makes sure that EU laws are applied fairly and consistently in all member states. The Court has the power to force governments and businesses to comply with EU laws.

Figure 42.4 European Court of Justice

European Central Bank (ECB)

The ECB:

> Sets the monetary policy of the EU
> Ensures that the euro is seen as a safe and secure currency
> Is responsible for issuing euros
> Is responsible for keeping the level of inflation in the **euro area** under control.

Figure 42.5 Eurozone members (2016)

The **euro area** (also known as the **eurozone**) is the collective name for the EU member states that share a common currency, the euro.

42.8 Which EU member states are in the eurozone? List them and identify them on a map.

Benefits of EU membership for Ireland

The benefits to Ireland of EU membership can be divided into economic benefits and social benefits.

Economic benefits of EU membership

> The creation of a **single European market (SEM)** allows for free movement of goods, services, capital and citizens.

> The removal of customs barriers has **reduced costs for importers and exporters**.

> The EU provides a **larger market for exports**, which allows Irish businesses to reach 510 million consumers compared with a domestic population of under 5 million.

Table 42.1 Destinations of Irish exports

	1973	2015
UK	55%	16%
Other EU countries	21%	44%
USA	10%	23%
Rest of the world	14%	17%

> Ireland is **less dependent on the UK** than it once was as a market for exports, as you can see from table 42.1.

See Chapter 41

> Ireland shares a common currency with eighteen other member states in the euro area. This **eliminates exchange rate risk** when Irish businesses export to these countries.

> Ireland receives huge amounts of **EU funding** which has helped to develop our infrastructure and transformed our economy from one of the poorest to one of the wealthiest in Europe.

> **Lower interest rates** have made it cheaper for Irish businesses to expand.

> Ireland is an attractive location for **foreign direct investment**. Many foreign businesses have chosen to locate their European headquarters in Ireland so that they can access the SEM.

Did you know?

Ireland has received over €6 billion from the EU's social cohesion fund for investment in education and infrastructure. The social cohesion fund aims to reduce economic differences between different regions of the EU.

> The Common Agricultural Policy (CAP) is a major source of funding for the Irish **agricultural sector**. CAP invested €11.7 billion into Irish farms and rural economies between 2007 and 2013. A further €11 billion will be invested by 2020.

> Irish businesses can bid for government contracts worth over €50,000 in other member states. This is known as **public procurement**.

Figure 42.6 Foreign direct investment in Ireland

Did you know?

Even though Ireland has only 1% of Europe's population, it attracts nearly 25% of all US **greenfield industrial investment** in the EU. A greenfield investment occurs when a parent company starts a new venture in a foreign country. Overseas firms exported €124.5 billion from Ireland in 2013.

Figure 42.7 Europe's Common Agricultural Policy

Social benefits of EU membership

> EU social policy has **strengthened the rights of Irish consumers**. For example, producers of processed food must provide consumers with nutrition and allergy information. Goods sold in the EU are subject to strict safety requirements and must have CE marking.

> EU social policy has **improved the rights of workers** by improving health and safety, setting minimum wage levels, better working conditions and holiday entitlements.

> Irish workers enjoy a **better standard of living** due to higher income levels.

> EU countries have **improved social conditions** and rate highly on the Human Development Index (HDI). This measures life expectancy, education and standard of living.

Did you know?

The letters CE are the abbreviation of the French phrase *Conformité Européenne*, which means 'European Conformity'. This is the manufacturer's proof that the product has been checked against EU safety criteria.

> The **European Social Fund (ESF)** funds projects to improve the skills of the unemployed, and helps to reduce poverty, social exclusion and discrimination. Over €500 million will be allocated to projects in Ireland between 2014 and 2020.

European **Social** Fund

Did you know?

In 1973 Irish income levels (GDP per capita) were 65% of the EU average. By 2010 this had risen to 120% of the EU average.

> EU laws on **workplace equality** have ensured that men and women are entitled to equal pay for equal work. Women are entitled to paid maternity leave and men are entitled to paid paternity leave. These measures have helped increase the number of women in the Irish labour force.

Did you know?

When Ireland joined the EU in 1973, women made up just 25% of the Irish workforce, and married women were barred from working in public service jobs such as teaching. In 2015, 55% of Irish women were employed outside the family home.

> **Consumers have greater choice** as they can shop in any EU country without paying import duties.

> **EU citizens can travel and work freely** in all member states without the need for visas or travel permits.

> EU roaming costs have **reduced the costs of receiving and making calls** when travelling in EU countries.

> The European Health Insurance Card (EHIC) provides **healthcare access** to Irish citizens when travelling in the EU. The card entitles you to the same healthcare benefits as local citizens in EU member states.

> Almost two million young people have **studied in another EU member state** with the help of the Erasmus+ programme, an EU exchange programme for students.

42.9 Research the Erasmus+ programme and create a presentation/ poster or infographic explaining what it is, who can apply, which universities participate, and so on. Present your findings to the rest of the class.

KSC
KSBC
KSWwO
KSBL

42.10 How do you think you personally have benefited by Ireland being in the EU? Can you imagine what life would be like if we were not in the EU? Does everyone in the class agree on the benefits?

KSC
KSMIT

Challenges of EU membership for Ireland

Economic challenges of EU membership

> The SEM means that Irish businesses face **increased competition from lower-cost economies** in some other member states. This has resulted in job losses in some Irish industries.

> As Ireland's wealth grows, we will need to **make larger contributions to the EU budget**.

> The **ECB controls monetary policy for all euro area countries**, including Ireland. This removes our control of interest rates and we cannot reduce them independently to encourage economic growth or increase them to prevent inflation.

> **Ongoing reform of the CAP and Common Fisheries Policy** will have consequences for Irish agricultural and fishing industries. Fishing boats from other EU member states can fish off Irish waters. These reforms may reduce income levels and the ability to create jobs in these industries.

Social challenges of EU membership

> Complying with EU laws on consumer and employee rights has **increased costs for Irish businesses**.

> **Increasing the number of member states** increases the diversity of the population of the EU, which means more language and cultural differences. This can make it difficult to get agreement on, for example, social policy.

> The protection of Irish culture in the European Union with shared sovereignty will be a challenge. There needs to be a **balance between integration and independence**.

> Turf cutting is a traditional activity in rural Ireland and is a low-cost source of solid fuel in many Irish homes. The **EU has banned turf cutting** to protect the bog areas. Although this is an environmental benefit, it creates financial challenges for some people.

> Europe is facing a **refugee crisis** on a scale not seen since the Second World War. Balancing human compassion with security and employment concerns is challenging.

> The EU has a **Common Security and Defence Policy (CSDP)**, which enables the EU to take a leading role in peacekeeping operations, conflict prevention and strengthening international security. Ireland's position as a neutral country may come under threat if this policy is expanded to provide for an EU army.

> Many **different languages are spoken** in the twenty-eight EU member states. This can make communication difficult. While English is one of the main languages of international trade, we need to learn other languages if we want to remain competitive.

42.11 Listen to or watch the news on radio or TV or read it online once a day for the next two weeks. What EU challenges are being highlighted at the moment?

Research

KSMIT
KSBL

42.12 Having learned about the benefits and challenges of EU membership for Ireland, hold a class debate evaluating Ireland's membership and what life would be like if we had not joined the EU in 1973.

Discussion

KSMIT
KSBL
KSC

Impact of Brexit on Ireland

Ireland has a very close relationship with the UK for the following reasons:

> The UK is our closest trading partner and Ireland and Britain trade over €1 billion worth of goods and services each week.

> Overall, approximately 16% of Irish exports go to the UK, but this figure rises to 43% for indigenous exports.

> The UK is the biggest export market for Irish food and drink products.

> UK citizens are the biggest customers for Ireland's tourism industry, with approximately three million UK visitors each year.

Economic consequences of Brexit for Ireland

> A fall in the value of sterling will make Irish exports more expensive in Britain and will make British imports cheaper in Ireland. This is likely to have a negative impact on Ireland's balance of payments since Irish-produced goods will be less affordable to UK customers and UK imports will provide increased competition for Irish businesses.

> Similarly, the tourism industry may suffer from a weaker pound, as British tourists will find it more expensive to visit Ireland.

> As a small open economy Ireland is likely to feel the negative effects of any slow-down in the level of economic growth in Britain or the EU.

> If the UK is outside the EU's free trade area, this will impact on the free movement of goods, services, capital and people. This is likely to increase business and travel costs and may see the reintroduction of tariffs and border controls.

> The UK may decide to cut its rate of corporation tax to enable it to compete more aggressively for foreign direct investment (FDI).

> As the only English-speaking member of the EU and the euro area, Ireland may be in a stronger position to attract FDI from businesses that are keen to locate their operations in the EU. For example, some financial services businesses may relocate from the City of London to the International Financial Services Centre in Dublin.

42.13 **(a)** Research the current position with regard to the new trading relationship between Britain and the EU. Share your findings with a partner or small group.

(b) Use your research findings to assess the impact of Brexit on Ireland. Evaluate whether the impact will be mostly positive or mostly negative and share your evaluation with the class.

Research

KSMIT
KSWwO
KSC

Key Terms

KSBL
KSC
KSMIT
KSBC

You should be able to *define*, *spell*, give *examples* and *apply* to real life each of the following key terms associated with this topic.

Exercise: Write a sentence using each of the following terms. You may use more than one of the terms in your sentence if appropriate.

Brexit

Common Agricultural Policy (CAP)

Council of the EU

Court of Auditors

European Central Bank (ECB)

European Commission

European Court of Justice

European Parliament

eurozone

foreign direct investment (FDI)

Member of the European Parliament (MEP)

shared sovereignty

single European market (SEM)

Index

Abbey Theatre 192
acid test ratio 361–2
accounts, keeping 312
accrued expense 275
actuary 115
Adams, Douglas 223
Adidas 164
advertising 263–6
    ethics 266
    media 264–5
Advertising Standards Authority of Ireland
    (ASAI) 266
AER (annual equivalent rate) 84, 89
AIDA model 263
air pollution 241
American Express 79
An Post 63, 85–7
    Prize Bonds 87
    Savings Bonds 85
    Savings Certificates 85
An Tionchar 183
analysed cash book 24, 41, 49–52
    benefits 55
    checking against bank statement 74
    columns 50–1
animal welfare 166
apps (applications) 226
APR (annual percentage rate) 104, 272
    calculating 104–5
arbitration 222
assets 93, 282
ATM (automated teller machine) 67, 68
average clause 119

B2B 295
balance 52
    of payments 236, 451–2
    of trade 452
balancing an account 52–6
bank
    accounts 64–7
    draft 71
    fees and charges 67, 71–2
    overdraft 56–7, 95, 275
    statement 64, 72–4
banking see internet banking, online
    banking, telephone banking
banks, commercial 63, 86, 98
barcode 138, 225
basic pay 13
batch production 291
benefits in kind 11
best before date 138
billboards 265
bills, checking 23
bitcoin 198
Bitcove 198
blog 228
Body Shop 166–7
bonus 11, 13
books of first entry 332
boom 422
Bord Bia 197
borrowers, rights of 105–6
borrowing 28, 92–106 see also loans
    medium-term 96
    responsible 103
    risks 106
    short-term 95
boycott 164–5
BP 241
brainstorming 200
brand loyalty 259
branded goods 141

branding 259
Brexit 458, 467
Buchheit, Paul 194
budget 21 see also household budget,
    national budget
    balanced 42
    deficit 42–3
    surplus 42
budget comparison statement 58–61
budgeting 32, 41–8
    benefits of 42
building societies 63, 86, 87, 98
business(es)
    documents 294–311, 312, 332
    ethics 444–5
    financial planning 271–86
    ideas 196
    impacts of, and government 445–7
    operating cycle 282–4
    ownership, forms of 199–200
    plan 288–92
    success criteria 242

CAD (computer-aided design) 228
CAM (computer-aided manufacture) 228
Camara Education 191
capital 129, 278, 373
    expenditure 20, 271
    resources 3, 159
capital acquisitions tax (CAT) 130, 406
capital gains tax (CGT) 129, 406
capitalist economy 377
car insurance see motor insurance
carbon
    footprint 165, 177
    tax 128, 402
Card Verification Code (CVC) 77
Card Verification Value (CVV) 77
carriage
    inwards 323
    paid 297
cash book rule 312
cash on delivery (COD) 297, 310
cash flow 27
    forecasts 284–6
    managing 283–4
cash with order (CWO) 297, 310
casual employment 210
caveat emptor 142
celebrity endorsement 269
Celtic Tiger 422, 439
Central Bank of Ireland 98, 406
Central Statistics Office see CSO
centrally planned economy 377
chain store 262
channels of distribution 261
charge card 79
charities 382
cheque 67, 71
child benefit 10, 11
choices, rational 371–2
CIM (computer-integrated manufacturing)
    228
cinema advertising 265
circular flow of income 384–5
clean technology 238
climate change 439
cloud computing 225
CoderDojo 191
Coillte 194
collateral 102, 272, 279, 281
Collison, John and Patrick 183
commercial organisations 235
commission 13

Commission for Communications Regulation
    (ComReg) 153
Commission for Energy Regulation (CER)
    152–3
commodities markets 387
Common Agricultural Policy (CAP) 462–3
Common Fisheries Policy 465
Common Security and Defence Policy (CSDP)
    466
communism 377
Community Employment (CE) programme
    213
Community Enterprise Scheme (CES) 213
compensation 107–8, 112
Competition and Consumer Protection
    Commission (CCPC) 152, 446
compound interest 88–9
comprehensive motor insurance 111
computer hacking 229, 240
computer-aided design (CAD) 228
computer-aided manufacture (CAM) 228
computer-integrated manufacturing (CIM)
    228
concept development 202
consumer(s) 136–43
    behaviour 387
    choices 157–70
    complaints 146–7, 149–55
    ethical 162–71
    informed 163
    protection 144–56
    responsibilities 142–3
    rights 141–2, 464
    wise 137
Consumer Protection Act 2007 144, 147–8,
    445
Consumers' Association of Ireland (CAI) 141
contactless payments 69
contract of employment 209–10
contribution (insurance) 110
converting currencies see exchange rate
cooling-off period 96, 98, 105
Cork Jazz Festival 193
corporate social responsibility (CSR) 165, 444
corporation tax 355, 399, 406
cost 6
    of sales 323
    per unit 140
cost-benefit analysis 430–4
cost-plus pricing 260
credit
    cost of 104
    history 281
    note 146, 305–6
    transfer 67, 70
credit card 77–9, 95, 275
    interest 77–8
    statement 77
credit (Cr) side 50, 312
credit unions 63, 86, 87, 98
creditor 275
creditworthiness 99
critical illness cover 114
crowdfunding 279
CSO (Central Statistics Office) 421
    Household Finance and Consumption
        Survey 78, 95
cultural enterprise 192–3
currency, foreign 450
current
    account 64–76; opening 65–6
    ratio 360–1
customer relationship management (CRM)
    230

customs duty 127, 130, 323, 406
CVC (Card Verification Code) 77
CVV (Card Verification Value) 77

database 179, 225
debenture 279
debit card 67, 69
debit (Dr) side 50, 312
debit note 307–8
debt
    capital 273, 363
    external 354
    national 419–20
    servicing 419
debtors, managing 283
declining principal 104
deductions from pay 14, 132
    statutory 14
    voluntary 14
deferred payment 275
delivery
    costs 297
    note 302–3
    systems 174–5
Dell 240, 444
demand 387–91
    curve 389
    effective 387
    factors affecting 388–91
    schedule 389
demand deposits 86
department store 262
deposit account 64, 76–7, 85–7
    terms and conditions 85
    types 86
depression 422
desk research 251–2
desktop publishing 225
digital technology 224–32
    benefits 227–8, 230–2
    costs 229–32
    opportunities 230
diminishing marginal utility, law of 387
Diners Club 79
direct debit 67, 70
    mandate 70
direct intervention policy 427
direct taxes 130
DIRT (Deposit Interest Retention Tax) 85, 86,
    90, 129, 130
discount
    cash 297
    trade 297
discount retailer 262
discretionary
    expenditure 20
    income 15
disposable income 15
disposal, end-of-life 169
dividend 10, 11, 87, 278, 335
Domino's Pizza 198
double entry bookkeeping 312–21
    double entry rule 315
Doyle, John 239
Dublin Fire Brigade 239
Dyson, James 185, 196

eBay 10
EBS (Educational Building Society) 87
ecological footprint 165
e-commerce 179
economic
    changes 435
    cycle 422
    growth: 236, 421–5; effects of 437–40
    indicators 413–25
    policy see government economic policy
    resources 370
    systems 376–8

economics 370
economies of scale 174, 455
economy 376 see also capitalist economy,
    centrally planned economy, false
    economy, free market economy, mixed
    economy, sectors of the economy
Edison, Thomas 185
education, higher 438
Education and Training Boards Ireland (ETBI)
    213
Electric Picnic 193
electronic point of sale see EPOS
email 177, 225
embargo 454
employee(s)
    legislation protecting 219–22
    qualities of 211
    records 217
    rights and responsibilities 216
employers 215
    rights and responsibilities 217
employment 209–13, 417–18, 437 see
    also casual employment, contract of
    employment, fixed-term employment;
    full-time employment; part-time
    employment; self-employment
Employment Equality Acts 1998–2011 220–1
endowment policy (life assurance) 111
energy efficiency 238
enterprise 182–94, 374 see also cultural
    enterprise, financial enterprise, social
    enterprise
    in the community 193
    in the public service 194
Enterprise Ireland 197, 454
entrepreneurs 183–9, 196–203
    characteristics of 184–5
    financial 190
    skills of 186
Environmental Protection Agency (EPA) 447
E&OE (errors and omissions excepted) 297
EPA (Environmental Protection Agency) 191
Epictetus 28–9
EPOS (electronic point of sale) 225, 228, 251
equity capital 273, 363
Erasmus+ programme 464
estate 31
Ethical Consumer organisation 162
euro area 460–1
European Central Bank 418, 460
European Commission 458–9
European Council 458
European Health Insurance Card (EHIC) 464
European Parliament 459
    Members (MEPs) 459
European Union (EU) 457–67
    aims 458
    budget 465
    Council 460
    Court of Auditors 460
    funds 462
    institutions 458–60
    laws 458–60, 464, 5
    membership of: benefits 462–5;
        challenges 465–6
    origin 457
eurozone 460–1
exchange rate 79–80, 462
excise duty 127, 130, 399, 406
exclusions (insurance) 117
expenditure 19–29
    capital 329
    current 20, 271, 329
    discretionary 20
    irregular 19
    planning 24–6
    prioritising 21
    recording 24, 49–56
    revenue 329

expenses, business 330
exporting 450
exports
    invisible 450
    visible 450

Facebook 236
factor markets 387
factoring debt 275
factors of production 159, 373–4
fair labour certification 166
fair trade 162, 443
Fairtrade 162, 170
Fairtrade Labelling Organisations
    International (FLO) 162
false economy 22, 140
family income supplement 10
feasibility study 203
field research 246–7
final accounts 322, 332
    analysing 353–66
finance, sources of, for business 272–81
    internal and external 273
    long-term 272–3, 278–9
    medium-term 272–3, 277
    short-term 272–5
financial
    abuse 39
    control cycle 58–9
    cost 6–7, 371, 431
    enterprise 190
    institutions 63–4
    life cycle 30–9
    literacy 8
    planning: 30–9; for businesses 271–86
    resources 3, 6, 159
    services 63–81
Financial Services Ombudsman 154
Finnegan, Mairéad 187–8
first party (insurance) 112
fiscal policy 427
fixed
    assets 272
    expenditure 19
fixed-term employment 210
flexitime 210
focus groups 247, 250
food labels 138
FoodCloud 191–2
Foodworks 197
foreign
    direct investment (FDI) 175–6, 432, 462
    exchange 79–80
franchisee 198–9
franchise 198–9, 262
franchisor 198–9
Franklin, Benjamin 124
free market economy 377
free trade 454
fringe benefits see benefits in kind
full-time employment 210

GAA 192
Gandhi, Mahatma 6
Gap 164
GDP (gross domestic product) 420–1
gearing 354, 363–4
    ratios 353
general ledger 313–18
global organisations 235
globalisation 172–9, 455–6
    development of 173
    impacts of 176–7
    reasons for 174
Gmail 194
GNP (gross national product) 420
goods 136
    ethical 164
    inferior 391

goodwill 143
Google 236
go-slow 219
government
    economic policy 426–35; evaluating 428,
        430–4
    expenditure 408–9; capital 408–9;
        current 408
    local 379
    national 380
    revenue: 405–7; capital 406–7;
        current 406
grants 278
green consumerism 165
Green Plan 239
greenfield investment 463
greenhouse gases 165
gross
    margin 356–7
    pay 13, 132
    profit: 323, 328; percentage 356
guarantee 147
guarantor 101

health insurance 114
hire purchase (HP) 96, 277
HiRo Noodles 197
Hogan, Roisin 197
holiday insurance 114
home contents insurance 113
home insurance (buildings cover) 113
household
    borrowing: 92–106; reasons for 93–4
    budget: 41–8; analysing 45–6;
        revising 46
    expenditure 19–29
    income 9–17
    insurance 107–22
    taxes 126–34
house insurance premium, calculating
    117–18
human resources 3, 159

ICT (information and communications
    technology) 177, 224
    and consumer behaviour 177–8
    skills 233
idea generation 202
import(s)
    duty 323
    invisible 449
    substitution 201
    visible 449
importing 448–9
impulse buying 21
income 9–18
    calculation 15
    discretionary 15
    disposable 15
    from employment 11–16
    inequality 439
    irregular 11
    national 420–1
    planning 17
    recording 17, 49–57
    regular 11
    statements 322–6, 328–34
income protection insurance 114
income tax 126, 406
    calculation 133–4
indemnity 109
independent retailer 262
indirect taxes 130
industrial
    action 219
    policy 427
    relations 218
Industrial Relations Act 1990 221
industrial revolution 173

inflation 388, 413–16
    calculation 414
    causes 415
    impact 416
information and communications
    technology see ICT
infrastructure 236, 408, 438
Innocent drinks 196
Insolvency Service of Ireland (ISI) 102
instalment 93
    costs 102–3
insurable interest 108
insurance 32, 94, 107–22
    claim 118
    decisions 121–2
    industry, jobs in 115
    policy: 117; excess 117;
        renewing 120
    premium 107–8
    principles 108–10
    taking out 115–17
    types 111–15
insurance agent 115
insurance broker 115
interest 10, 84, 373
    on borrowing: 93; calculating
        104–5
    compound 88–9
    flat rate 88
    rates 23, 418–19
    on savings: 86; calculating 88–90
    simple 88
international trade 448–54
    benefits of 453
    challenges of 453
    invisible 448
    visible 448
internet 177, 225
    advertising 265
    banking 75–6
Internet of Things (IoT) 232
intrapreneur 194, 200
investing 83–5
    factors 84–5
investments, planning 32
invoice 303–5
invoice discounting 275
inward investment 175
Irish Credit Bureau (ICB) 99–100
irregular expenditure 19

job sharing 210
job production 291
Jobs, Steve 4
jobseeker's benefit 10, 11

Kilkenny 'Cat Laughs' Comedy
    Festival 193
Kyoto Protocol 439

labour 363
    costs 174
    force 417
Labour Court 222
land 373
    pollution 241
    usage 238
Lappé, Anna 168
leasing 96, 277
ledgers 313–18, 332
lenders, to business 354
letter of enquiry 295–6
liabilities 282, 354
life assurance 111
life expectancy 437–8
liquidity 83, 85, 272, 282
    measuring 360–2
    ratios 353
loading (insurance) 112–13, 117

loans 80–1 see also borrowing; finance,
        sources of, for business
    applying for: 98–102; businesses 281
    long-term 97
    medium-term 96
    repaying 102–3
Local Enterprise Offices (LEOs) 194, 197, 211
local
    organisations 235
    services 241
local property tax (LPT) 128, 406
lodgements, to current account 64, 67
loss
    adjuster 115
    leaders 260
    net 328
loyalty card 179

MABS (Money Advice and Budgeting Service)
    102
magazine advertising 265
Mandate 218
manufacturer 261
market research 201, 227–8, 245–53
    analysis 250
    benefits 246
    types 246–52
    uses 253
market segmentation 255–6
marketing 227–8, 255
    global 455
marketing mix 255–69
markets 386–7
Marks & Spencer 164
Martin, Micheál 194
mass production 291, 455
matching principle 94, 272, 273
material fact 109
McCabe, Neil 239
McDonald's 172, 175, 198
m-commerce 225
MEPs (Members of the European Parliament)
    459
Microsoft 176
misleading
    claims 147–8
    practices 148
mixed economy 378, 405
mobile commerce 225
mobile phone(s) 177
    insurance 114
Momentum 213
monetary policy 427
money
    definition of 6
    smart 8
    sources of 7
moneylenders 97–8
mortgage 97, 279
mortgage protection insurance 114
motor insurance 111–13, 116
motor tax 129
multiplier effect 236

Nagle, Peter and James 198
national budget 405, 409–12
    balanced 410
    deficit 411–12
    surplus 410–11
National Gallery of Ireland shop 193
natural resources 3, 159
Nature's Best 197
needs 5, 137, 370–1
Nestlé 445
net
    margin 358
    pay 13, 132
    profit: 323, 328; percentage 356
newspaper advertising 265

niche market 201
Nike 164
no-claims bonus 112
non-commercial organisations 235
not-for-profit organisations 382
notice deposits 86
NTMA (National Treasury Management
    Agency) 87, 419

obesity 438
O'Brien, Aoibheann 191–2
ombudsman 155
Ombudsman, Office of the 154–5
Omidyar, Pierre 10
online
    banking: 75–6; secure 75–6
    booking 178
    stores 262
opening cash 313
opportunity cost 6–7, 23, 93, 371, 431
order 299–300
organisations
    benefits of: 235–39; environmental 238;
        social 237
    negative impacts of 240–1
    types 235
overdraft see bank overdraft
overheads 328
overspending, solutions to 26–8
overtime 11, 12
    ban 219
own-label goods 141, 259

Panama Canal 173
Panama Papers 403
partial loss (insurance) 119–20
partnership 200
part-time employment 210
pay
    gross 13, 132
    net 13, 132
PAYE (Pay As You Earn) 14, 126, 130, 217, 335,
    399
payment protection insurance (PPI) 114
payment terms 297
Paypath 67
payslip 16
penetration pricing 260
pensions 10, 32, 36
perks see benefits in kind
personal accident insurance 114
personal financial life cycle 30–9
piece rate 12
PIN (personal identification number) 68
place (marketing) 261, 456
plastic bag charge 445–6
policy excess 117
pollution 241, 439
    controls 238
PPSN (Personal Public Service Number) 132
premium pricing 260
press release 267
price 260, 388
    global 456
pricing strategies 260
Primark 164
principal 83
private limited company 200
private sector 381
probationary period 210
product 257–60
    branding 259
    design 257–8
    development 202–3

disposal 442
distribution 442
global 455–6
labels 138
launch 203
life cycle 157–8, 168, 258, 441–3
manufacturing 442
placement 269
screening 202
usage 442
production
    factors of 159, 373–4
    processes 291
profit(s) 374
    gross 323, 328
    net 328, 332
    retained 335
profitability 356–60
    ratios 353
profit and loss account 322, 328–34
profit and loss appropriation account 323,
    335
progressive tax 131
promotion 263–9
    global 456
    mix 263
proposal form 115–16
Protection of Young Persons (Employment)
    Act 1996 220
prototype development 203
PRSI (Pay Related Social Insurance) 14, 114,
    217, 335, 406
public
    procurement 462
    relations 267
    sector 379–81
publicity 267
purchases 323
    accounting for 315–16
purchasing, effective 301

questionnaire 246
quick ratio 361–2
quotas 160, 454
    fishing 443
quotation 297–9

radio advertising 264
RainShed 239
ratios
    analysis 353
    calculating 355–6
raw materials 442
receipt 310–11
recession 422
ReCreate 167–8
recycling facilities 238
redress 145–6
reduce, reuse, recycle 167, 169
redundancy 221, 229
refugee crisis 466
refund 146
regressive tax 130
rent 373
rental income 10
repair 146
repatriation of profits 176
replacement 146
report writing 365–6
research 428
research and development (R&D) 200
resources 2–4, 159–60
    capital 3, 159
    economic 370
    financial 3, 6, 159
    human 3, 159
    natural 3, 159
    non-renewable 159
    physical 3

renewable 160
sustainable 167
time 4
responsibilities 215 see also consumer(s),
    corporate social responsibility,
    employee(s), employers, sellers
retailers 261–2
retained profit 278
retirement planning 32
return
    on capital employed 359
    on investment 359
Revenue Commissioners, Office of the 124,
    130, 132, 399
revenue reserves 335
rights 215
Roddick, Anita 167
Roll It pastry 187–8
Rose of Tralee International Festival 193
Ryan, Shíofra 183

Safety, Health and Welfare at Work Act 2005
    445
salary 10, 11
Sale of Goods and Supply of Services Act
    1980 144–7
sale and leaseback 279
sales 323
    accounting for 315–16
    cost of 324
    promotions 267
sampling 248
saving 82–90
    factors 84
    planning 32
    reasons for 84
savings account 64, 86
scarcity 374–5
second party (insurance) 112
sectors of the economy 379–84
self-assessed income tax 126
self-employment 189–90, 211
sell by date 138
sellers, responsibilities of 147
semi-state companies 427
service 136
Shakespeare, William 92
share capital 278
shared sovereignty 458, 465
shareholders 273, 354
shop local 169
shop steward 218
shopping around 26, 65
'Silicon Docks', Dublin 236
simple interest 88–9
single European market 462, 465
SIPTU (Services Industrial Professional and
    Technical Union) 218
Small Claims Procedure 155
SMART goals 288
Smith, Adam 400
smoking ban 194
social enterprise 190–2, 239, 384
Social Entrepreneurs Ireland 191–2
social media 226, 268
SOLAS (An tSeirbhís Oideachais Leanúnaigh
    agus Scileanna) 213
sole trader 199

solvency 354, 362–3
spending
    cutting back 26
    guidelines 20–3
sponsorship 268
spreadsheets 225, 228
stakeholders 225, 237, 354
stamp duty 128, 406
standard of living 437
standard rate cut-off point 132

standing order 67, 70
Starbucks 172, 240
statement of account 308–9
statement of financial position 322, 339–51
state-owned organisations 381
    dividends from 406
stock
    closing 324
    control 301
    managing 283
    opening 323
stockout 301
stress test 102
strike 219
Stripe 183
Student Enterprise Awards 194
subrogation 109–10
subsidiary 172
subsidy 454
Subway 198
Suez Canal 173
sugar tax 429–30, 432–4
Super Bowl 266
Supermac's 198
supermarket 262
suppliers, to business 355
supply 391–8
    curve 392–3
    and demand: 395–8; law of 396
    factors affecting 393–5
    schedule 392
surveys 247–9
sustainability 160
    lifecycle approach 441–3
sustainable
    businesses 169
    consumption 160–1
    development 160, 437–47
    economic growth 440
    products 441–4
    resources 167
    technologies 167
Sustainable Energy Authority of Ireland
        (SEAI) 447
SWOT analysis 289

tablets 226
T-account 50
take-home pay see net pay
TalkTalk 240
target market 256
tariff 454
tax see also capital acquisitions tax, capital
        gains tax, carbon tax, corporation tax,
        household taxes, income tax, local
        property tax, motor tax, self-assessed
        income tax, sugar tax, VAT, vehicle
        registration tax

avoidance 126
credits 132
evasion 126
liability 125
progressive 131
rate 132
regressive 130
types of 130–1
taxation 124–34, 399
    direct 130
    impact of 131
    indirect 130
    levels, in different countries 125
    planning 32
    principles 400
    purposes of 124–5, 401–3
Teagasc 197
technology
    in business 225–33
    impact of 223–33
telephone banking 75–6
television advertising 264
teleworking 210, 229
term deposits 86
term policy (life assurance) 111
terms of sale 295, 297
Tesco 240
test marketing 203
third party (insurance) 112
third party motor insurance 111
third party, fire and theft motor insurance
        111
third sector 382
time, as a resource 4
time rate 12
Toepfer, Klaus 157
token work stoppage 219
totalling an account 52–6
trade see free trade, international trade
trade union(s) 218
    dues 132
trading
    account 322–6, 328
    partners 451
traffic congestion 439
transnational corporations 172, 175–6
transport 174–5
travel insurance 114
trial balance 318, 332
Triodos 81
turf cutting 465
Twitter 236

Ulster Bank 229
underinsurance 119
unemployment 212–13, 417–18
    effects 418
Unfair Dismissals Act 1977–2007

uninsurable risk 122
unit pricing 140
United Nations (UN)
    Millennium Development Goals 166
    Sustainable Development Goals 440
USC (Universal Social Charge) 14, 126, 132,
        217, 406, 431
USP (unique selling point) 202, 260
use by date 138
utmost good faith 109

value for money 140
VAT (value added tax) 125, 127, 130, 297, 355,
        399, 406
    accounting for 315–18
    system 316–17
vehicle registration tax (VRT) 129
venture capital 278
video conferencing 226
voluntary
    organisations 383
    work: 205–9; benefits of 208–9

wage(s) 10, 12–13, 373
    minimum 431
wants 5, 137, 370–1
Ward, Iseult 191–2
warranty 147
water pollution 241
WEEE Ireland 443
whole-life policy (life assurance) 111
wholesaler 261
Wi-Fi 226
will 31
windfall 10
withdrawal slip 67
withdrawals, from current account 64, 67–71
word processing 225
work 205
    benefits of 212
work to rule 219
workers' rights 464
working capital 282
    ratio 360–1
Workplace Relations Act 2015 222
Workplace Relations Commission 222
World Trade Organization (WTO) 174
write-off 109